Jeremy M

Jeremy Musson is a writer and broa...
curator and an architectural historian. He was Architectural Editor
for *Country Life* for ten years. He has written articles on historic
country houses, from Garsington Manor to Knebworth House, and
is the author of four books, including *How to Read a Country House*.
He also co-wrote and presented the popular TV series, *The Curious
House Guest* on BBC2. Jeremy is married with two children.

Praise for *Up and Down Stairs*:

'Architectural historian Musson brings alive the symbiotic
relationship between the houses, their owners and the workers'
Financial Times

'Entertaining saga of the class divide' *Daily Express*

'Intimate and absorbing study' *Sunday Times*

'Musson is excellent on the changing face of service in the 20th
century . . . There are not many servants' voices that have survived,
but where they exist, Musson lets them be heard' *Spectator*

'Entertaining . . . Personal anecdotes bring this well-researched
book to life' *Mail on Sunday*

Also by Jeremy Musson
The English Manor House
100 Period Details: Plasterwork
How to Read a Country House
The Country Houses of Sir John Vanbrugh

Up and Down Stairs

The History of the Country House Servant

JEREMY MUSSON

JOHN MURRAY

First published in Great Britain in 2009 by John Murray (Publishers)
An Hachette UK Company

First published in paperback in 2010

5

© Jeremy Musson 2009

A CIP catalogue record for this title is available from the British Library

ISBN 978-0-7195-9730-5

Typeset in Monotype Bembo by Servis Filmsetting Ltd, Stockport, Chesire

Printed and bound by Clays Ltd, St Ives plc

John Murray policy is to use papers that are natural, renewable and recyclable products and made
from wood grown in sustainable forests. The logging and manufacturing processes are expected to
conform to the environmental regulations of the country of origin.

John Murray (Publishers)
338 Euston Road
London NW1 3BH

www.johnmurray.co.uk

To my amazing mother, Elizabeth (1942–2009)

Contents

Introduction

A SERVANT, ACCORDING to Dr Johnson in his famous *Dictionary* of 1755, was 'one who attends another, and acts at his command – the correlative of master'. It is curious to think that, until the 1950s, the very term was as commonplace as any word relating to housekeeping among the upper and middle classes. Yet by the 1960s and 1970s, the word had virtually disappeared from everyday use.

Johnson's definition is essentially repeated by *The Shorter Oxford English Dictionary* of 1979 but also gives a second meaning – originating from late medieval English – 'One is who is under the obligation to render certain services to, and obey the orders of a person, or body of persons, in return for wages or salary.'[1] The word 'servant' thus traditionally encompassed the status of a trades' apprentice to his master, and was often extended to other labourers in employment. The term domestic servant seems to have emerged to distinguish it from the increasing significance of the 'civil' servant, someone who worked for the government.

For those who love looking around country houses, the servant should be regarded as an indivisible part of the story. Like great machines, these houses combined public and private functions, as places of residence and hospitality, as well as of political and estate administration. They were built not only for the occupation of a landowning family but also had to accommodate a large body of servants to run it, whose duties included not only providing food, heat and light but the maintenance of precious contents and furnishings that needed constant attention. This book will focus on the domestic servant of the larger country house, rather than of the town house or the middle-class household.[2]

The first chapter begins in the 1400s, and after 1600 each century has a chapter to itself. The two that cover the period up to 1700 are naturally more of an overview, fleshing out those who would have worked in a large landowner's household, spelling out those lives and duties which can be deduced from limited available sources. From the seventeenth century, through memoirs and letters such as those of the Verney family, and books by authors such as Hannah Wolley, we start to get a much more vivid sense of connection with the complex life stories and responsibilities of country-house servants.

The chapters on the eighteenth and nineteenth centuries focus closely on the different roles and responsibilities of servants, identified via treatises, wage lists and numerous household regulations, alongside published and unpublished diaries and letters, of both employed and employer. From the twentieth century to the present day, the focus is much more on actual memoirs, including interviews conducted with a sample of current and retired domestic and estate staff, as well as with country-house owners from all over the British Isles. These living memories give us an insight into the way big houses functioned in the past and continue to do so today. These recollections often supply a contact with the interwar years, when the senior servants of the time had received their training in the Edwardian period.

One of the overriding themes is the changing role of the sexes in service. Medieval and Tudor households, for instance, were principally staffed by men – even in the kitchens. From the late seventeenth century, however, female staff began to outnumber the males, and the female housekeeper took on key management duties of overseeing the female staff, as the mistress by proxy. Cleaning duties, the kitchen, the laundry and the dairy became largely the preserve of women, which perhaps, despite the intervention of technology, the two former still remain today.

There is also the distinct issue of both the visible and the invisible household. In medieval and Tudor times, establishments were deeply ingrained with ideals of servants being on display and public hospitality, but in the seventeenth century an increasing desire for privacy led to a separation of lower servants from the public spaces occupied by the landowner's family. This was achieved by means of architectural divisions and household management. It is at this point that separate staircases for servants and separate servants' dining halls come into being and the bells to summon servants begin to appear.

Menservants, especially footmen, were the subject of taxation from 1777 until the 1930s, producing the distinct oddity, found in some country-house archives, of printed licences for 'dogs, menservants and armorial bearings'.[3] But while footmen added a glorious presence in their richly coloured uniforms, known as liveries, and their powdered wigs, their duties were practical too, as bodyguards and attendants on coaches, or as carriers of messages. Their daytime manual duties, such as cleaning silver and fine glass, were overseen by the butler.

The increasing specialisation of domestic service, with certain duties attached to dedicated zones within the house and within the service areas, is a defining feature of the nineteenth and early twentieth centuries, when the management and hospitality of country houses seems to have reached a pitch that was much admired by international visitors. The start of the First World War marked an inevitable decline in numbers of such large household staffs (for economic reasons if no other), and the Second World War was an even more significant watershed.

The apparent evaporation, in the later twentieth century, of the servant-supported, country-house way of life, which had defined the image of the British nation in the previous centuries, is, of course, a subject of fascination in itself. But was it quite so clear cut? Some country houses maintained surprisingly large staffs right up until recent times, at least until the 1960s, and some beyond. The dramatic image of the funeral procession in May 2004 for Andrew Cavendish, the 11th Duke of Devonshire, reminds us that not only are some country houses still well staffed but that they and their owners continue to be served by dedicated and skilled people who take the greatest pride in their roles.[4]

It is important to remember that in the Middle Ages, senior household officers, themselves minor landowners, would not have thought twice about being called a servant to a noble lord. The word had none of the social stigma associated with it in the early and mid twentieth century. Incidentally, until the eighteenth century, the word 'family' was used interchangeably with what we understand as a 'household' to cover *all* the persons who lived under one roof. It thus embraced all live-in domestic servants, although it was used in the legal, Latin sense of meaning everyone who came under the authority of the head of the house – the paterfamilias.[5]

From the late seventeenth century onwards, servants were more likely to seek ways of moving on, either to new and better jobs, or sometimes out of domestic service altogether,[6] although the word 'servant' continued to be applied to men and women of considerable ability and experience, such as stewards, French chefs, butlers and housekeepers. Moreover, the world of domestic service was itself subject to many distinct levels of internal hierarchy, reflected in areas such as address, dress, meals and accommodation. The more senior the servant, the better the status and the related rewards. Positions that offered fringe benefits could be particularly attractive.

In 1825, a footman could earn £24 a year and he also received free accommodation, clothes and much of his food (and might possibly get tips as well). This compares well to the average agricultural wage of around 11 shillings a week, with some upward variation at harvest, out of which workers would have to feed and clothe themselves and their families, as well as pay rent.[7]

In the 1870s, a skilled French chef in a country house could earn as much as £120 a year while an experienced butler could hope to earn around £80. Even a young footman might be paid £28 annually plus food, accommodation, and an allowance for clothing and hair powder. This puts many country-house servants into quite a different league from the worst-paid industrial workers of the time. One survey of labour in Salford in the 1880s suggested that over 60 per cent of industrial workers lived in near poverty, earning less than 4 shillings a week, from which they had to find shelter, clothing and food.[8]

One key theme that emerges across the centuries is the mutual interdependence of the country-house world. Many country-house servants served the same families for most of their working lives, and there are numerous examples of deep attachment, loyalty and mutual respect. A particularly vivid and well-celebrated example of this is illustrated by the series of portraits, commissioned by the Yorke family during the eighteenth century, of their servants at Erddig, near Wrexham (now owned by the National Trust), and the doggerel verses that described and celebrated their roles in the household – they famously commissioned more portraits of their servants than of their own family.[9] Bequests to servants can be traced from the Middle Ages onwards, recognising the trust and loyalty of individuals, and intended to help make secure their old age.

In the post-medieval world, the changing perception of individual liberty led to a continual re-examination of the role and profession of the residential domestic servant, whose regimented lives and dependent positions ensured the existence of the country house. The challenges to landed power, the changes brought by the industrial revolution and a new political idealism all had their impact on the way servants saw their work. By the early nineteenth century, the word itself had begun to take on more negative associations, of subservience to an inflexible class system.

For instance, William Tayler, an experienced footman, wrote in his diary in 1837: 'The life of a gentleman's servant is something like that of a bird shut up in cage. The bird is well housed and well fed, but deprived of liberty, and liberty is the dearest and sweetes[t] object of all Englishmen. Therefore I would rather be like the sparrow or lark, have less of housing and feeding and rather more liberty.'[10] But elsewhere he reflected that he could not understand how tradesmen and mechanics could sneer at the domestic servant, as, by virtue of his exposure to more variety, richer experience and greater mobility, he saw so much more of the world than they did.

Whatever modern observers feel about the idea of domestic service, there is no doubt that it was defining feature of country-house life for centuries, and these pages will reveal something of the extraordinary range of men and women on their staffs, whose contribution should be valued in its own right.

The story of the country-house servant is a very human one, as varied as any other working career in agriculture and industry. However, they are also unusual in that, unlike the vast majority who worked as single-handed, general domestics in middle-class town houses, they had more opportunities for career progression and social life.

Above all, the story of a country-house servant on a landed estate of any size was always one of a community of people with closely inter-related careers and lives, often at the centre of a self-sufficient and insulated environment of an agricultural estate.[11] The statistician W.T. Lanyon noted in 1908 of one country-house environment: 'the premises constituted a settlement as large as a small village: carrying coals, making up fires and attending to a vast number of candles and lamps, necessitated the employment of several footmen.'[12] The lives of the servants were reflected in the physical form and layout of the country house, a theme that is explored throughout this book.

Moreover, domestic servants made up the largest contingent of the *dramatis personae* of the country house, even if they are less well recorded in the history books than those they served. In the late Middle Ages and the Tudor period, noble households might number hundreds of menials, whereas in the eighteenth and nineteenth centuries such households had reduced to between twenty-five and forty indoor servants. Often there would be an even bigger staff for the gardens and the home farm. Even in living memory, until 1939, a landowning family of just six people could be looked after by a substantial resident indoor staff of around twenty.

There are no simple national statistics for people employed in domestic service in country houses alone. Nationally, larger households in the Tudor era would have accounted for several thousand souls, from higher-ranking gentleman attendants down to the boy turning the spit in the kitchen. There were probably around 1,500 great households with staffs of between 100 and 200.[13]

In the late nineteenth and early twentieth centuries, great country houses generally employed in the region of thirty to fifty indoor staff, and if one includes outdoor staff, of gardeners, grooms and gamekeepers, the total might reach many times that figure. The Duke of Westminster employed over 300 servants at Eaton Hall in the 1890s, while the Duke of Bridgewater retained some 500 staff at Ashridge and, indeed, was said never to refuse a request for work from a local man.

At Welbeck Abbey, in Nottinghamshire, where in 1900 the Duke of Portland employed around 320 servants, his rule was recalled as one of 'almost feudal indisputable power'.[14] Moreover, major landowners often had staff spread over two or three estates as well as a London house, although in many cases this would be a skeleton staff only, with the core skilled individuals travelling with their employers from place to place, itself a considerable logistical operation. As a result the staff of the country house was also that of the London house when in use by the landowning family.[15]

However, even when such households were at a peak in the late nineteenth and early twentieth centuries, the numbers of aristocratic and wealthier gentry country-house servants could not have accounted for more than 15 to 20 per cent of the national total of domestic servants.[16] During that period domestic service was one of the major forms of employment. In 1851, for instance, 905,000 women and 134,000 men worked as servants. The total number nationally is thought to have been around 2 million in 1901, out of a total population of 40 million, making domestic service the largest employment for English women, and the second largest employment for all English people, male and female, after agricultural labour.[17] In the census of 1911, domestic servants accounted for 1.3 million, outnumbering the 1.2 million in agriculture, and the 971,000 in coal mining (and, incidentally, the same number of those involved in teaching today).[18]

After the Second World War, the world of the country house changed out of all recognition, and the enclosed, stratified and hierarchical communities of domestic servants evaporated. Houses that must have hummed with activity, at least below stairs and behind the green baize door (invented in the eighteenth century to increase soundproofing), became quieter, emptier places, in a process that had begun back in the 1920s with increased taxation and the effects of the Great Depression.

After 1945, when their wartime use came to an end, many large country houses were not reoccupied because landowners were unable to recruit – and afford – the staff to manage them. As country houses cannot function without help, those that remained in private ownership relied, as some do today, on a loyal and dedicated staff. Whilst there are still butlers, house-managers, housekeepers and cooks, few are resident. The mid-to-late twentieth century became the era of the daily cleaner – with agency staff brought in, often on a regular basis, for larger-scale hospitality and special events.

According to Fiona Reynolds, Director-General of the National Trust, most of us in Britain – where less than a hundred years ago domestic service was still one of the largest employers – will have ancestors who were in service. This prompts our interest in the whole working of the house, its domestic spaces as well as the grand state rooms. Both have – after all – always been entirely interdependent.[19]

Although the country-house servant might be seen as belonging to a separate and elite group, with modest relevance to the rest of the world, they were the same staff who moved back and forth between the country house and the London town house where so much political entertaining went on, thus playing their role in that arena.[20] The servants of aristocracy were the scene shifters and wardrobe mistresses of the pageantry of British politics.

Moreover, country-house servants are ever present in many of the best novels and stories that define our sense of national identity, both in our own eyes and in those from other countries. When I began this project, I asked Professor Cannadine, then the head of the Institute of Historical Research in London, for advice. His first words to me were: 'You must look very carefully at P.G. Wodehouse.' And he was right; Wodehouse has helped to form the image of the servant in the modern imagination. His stories are a study in upper-class life, of course, but, for all their humour, it is the well-observed detail that makes them so effective: in the mixture of formality and intimacy, the potency of the emotional dependence of the upper class on those who worked for them. Jeeves was a manservant – a valet, a 'gentleman's gentleman' – rather than a butler proper, but valets often become butlers and certainly travelled to countless country houses in their roles, as Jeeves does in the stories.[21]

If Jeeves is compared to Wodehouse's other fictional butler character, Beach, the long-suffering attendant to the Earl of Emsworth at Blandings Castle, it is clear that they are cut from the same cloth. But remember, too, the delicious tug of war that goes on between the earl and his head gardener, the tough no-nonsense Scot McAllister. Their subtle battle of wits must have been played out time and time again in the English country house, between the specialist servant and his or her employer.

The artful servant, in the service of a not quite so bright master or mistress, has a long history and was a familiar theme in the drama of classical Rome, where servants or slaves were depicted as either cunning or foolish. The heroic figure of Figaro in Mozart's famous opera is a classic example of a smart servant outwitting his master. Napoleon described the original character as depicted in Beaumarchais' play, on which Mozart based his opera, as 'revolution in action'.[22]

The struggles of servants, their right to be respected as distinct individuals, and their dependent and often vulnerable status, were a particular focus for the eighteenth-century English novelist – even if sometimes viewed as tragicomic. Daniel Defoe's *Moll Flanders* (1722) begins with a pretty young woman taken into service as a companion, prior to her seduction by one of the sons of the house, which leads to her extraordinary and picaresque career.

Samuel Richardson's *Pamela* (1741) describes the efforts of an attractive maid to resist being compromised by her young master after the death of his mother; she holds out for marriage and in the end succeeds. Henry Fielding considered this tale so pious, and its outcome so unlikely, that he wrote a parody, *Shamela*, and the perhaps better known sequel, *The Adventures of Joseph Andrews* (1742), about her fictional and equally virtuous brother.

The hero of Tobias Smollett's *Humphrey Clinker* (1771) is a worthy young man who is taken on as a footman and serves his master faithfully until he finds eventually that he is his employer's long-overlooked natural son. William Makepeace Thackeray's *Vanity Fair* (1847–8) hums with the curious intimacy of the lives of both servants and employers. One of the central figures, the clever but flirtatious governess, Becky Sharp, is contrasted with the more traditional, long-serving, country-house servants of her baronet master, Sir Rawdon Crawley, whose younger son she successfully marries.

Charlotte Brontë's *Jane Eyre* (1847) offers another vivid portrayal of the path of the educated single woman in the role of a governess, this time in a remote country house, working alongside a housekeeper and a staff, often in the absence of their master. The same is true of Henry James's *The Turn of the Screw* (1898), although he can hardly have had the first-hand insight that Charlotte Brontë brought to her novel.

John Galsworthy's *The Country House*, set in 1891 and published in 1907, opens with a description of the coachman, first footman and second groom, the latter two in 'in long livery coats with silver buttons, their appearance slightly relieved by the rakish cock of their top hats', waiting for a train bringing guests for a house party,[23] a defining feature of nineteenth- and early-twentieth-century country-house life.

How realistic were these portrayals? We cannot be sure. In 1894 the novelist George Moore published the fictional – and improbable – account of a maidservant, *Esther Waters*, seduced and made pregnant by another servant. She is disgraced and cast out, but later returns to marry her seducer and even to care for her original, pious mistress who has been financially nearly ruined and is living in a few rooms of her once-opulent country house.

Despite his own upbringing in an Irish country house, making him familiar with being waited on by servants, George Moore is said to have paid his London charlady to fill him in on a maidservant's life while he was writing the book.[24] Vita Sackville-West's *The Edwardians* (1930) paints a brilliant portrait of country-house life, in which the young duke derives considerable emotional security from the servants who have brought him up, is an essential part of his character, based on her own memories of a childhood at a very well-staffed Knole.

It is perhaps the novels of the interwar years that contribute most to our imagined version of a servant-supported lifestyle. Think of Daphne du Maurier's chilling portrayal of a sinister housekeeper, Mrs Danvers, in *Rebecca*, or Evelyn Waugh's mysterious butler Phibrick in *Decline and Fall* (1928), or his depiction of Lord Sebastian Flyte's touching pre-war visit to his nanny in *Brideshead Revisited* (1945). In contrast, whilst Agatha Christie's novels teem with companions, secretaries, maids, cooks, butlers and gardeners, they are rarely more than cut-out characters.

Famously, D.H. Lawrence's *Lady Chatterley's Lover* (1960) focused on the relationship between a gamekeeper and his employer's wife. It is ironic to note that, in the court case prompted by the furore over its graphic descriptions of sex, the charge of obscenity foundered, in part at least, due to the prosecuting barrister's remark: 'Is this a book you would even wish your wife or your servants to read?' This became a *cause célèbre*, illustrating the disconnection between the world of the privileged, servant-employing Establishment, and the essential freedoms of everyone else. The whole case seemed to turn on this remark and the prosecution dwindled into a joke. Penguin won the case and went on to sell 2 million copies. Why, in the late twentieth century, should any adult not choose their own books?[25]

In the 1970s, the popular television series *Upstairs, Downstairs* re-created life in an MP's London home, following the parallel stories of the servants and the employer's family. Although first proposed as a comedy, it was made as a drama series. A more recent example, a fruit of the imagination rather than observation, is Kazuo Ishiguro's novel, *The Remains of the Day* (1989), filmed in 1993. This evocative account of the personal tensions and professional pressures on senior country-house servants in the middle of the twentieth century interweaves their lives with the political events of the day.

The film of *Gosford Park* (2001), directed by Robert Altman, with a screenplay by Julian Fellowes, made a particular virtue of creating the servants'-eye view of the action above stairs. Mr Fellowes told me in a recent conversation: 'What I was trying to express was that in these great houses there were two different worlds all operating within feet of each other.' Fascinated by the complex world of the country house and every detail that a servant would be expected to know, he also warned of the dangers of imagining that every house was the same in all respects: 'We had a great debate about whether menus for the day were sent up to the mistress on a silver tray or not. A number of former servants with memories of the 1930s were advising us, each of whom recalled an entirely different way of doing it.'[26] As for contemporary domestic staff, Mr Fellowes observes: 'Money is always spent on comfort and part of being comfortable is being looked after well. Every generation evolves its own version of what that means, and what we have in our age is often an "impermanent" staff, where cooks are regularly hired for house parties but are not permanent members of staff, bringing something of the fluidity of service as it was known in the eighteenth century.'[27]

Country houses on the bigger estates that are still in private hands have staff to take care of family, house, garden and park. When country houses began opening to the public in the 1970s or 1980s, their staff numbers often swelled, restoring the kind of working community of the pre-war years. Large numbers no longer 'live in', but it is still usual to find at least one member of staff living in a flat, or an attached residence, for reasons of security. Some country-house staff today may be housed on the estate or locally and come in daily. As the Countess of Rosebery observed on a tour of her family's home in 2008: 'We – and they – all have our own private lives now.'[28]

With the reduction in staff has also come a change in dynamics. At Bryngwyn, a compact Georgian house owned by the Marchioness of Linlithgow, the household is looked after by Christine Horton. Twenty-five years ago she had come to be nanny to the marchioness's son; now she is not only PA, cook and housekeeper, but a close friend. She said: 'I suppose that my relationship with the family has lasted a lot longer than many marriages.'[29]

At Chavenage, a manor house in Gloucestershire, the Lowsley-Williams are devoted to their daily, Della Robins, who had also originally arrived over forty-eight years ago to help with the children, and is now their cleaner. Mrs Robins recalled in an interview: 'When I came there was a butler, housekeeper, cook and nanny, and two or three cleaners – and now there's only me.'[30]

At Stradey Castle in South Wales in 2006, Sir David and Lady Mary Mansell-Lewis still lived in traditional style, but with many fewer staff than there had been only a few decades earlier. When I interviewed Sir David (d. 2009) with his former chauffeur, Ken Bardsley, perhaps the most touching moment was when Sir David recalled how he picked him out of a line-up to be his soldier-servant while serving in the Welsh Guards: 'Little did I know I was picking a man who would be a friend for the rest of my life.'[31]

Holkham Hall in Norfolk is a great country house still in private hands and still operating as the heart of a great country estate. Before the First World War the house had fifty indoor staff, while in 2006 the present earl employed just an administrator, a butler, a cook and three cleaners who came in daily, to help look after the family and the house, 'much aided by technology' and with secretarial help from the estate office. There are three full-time gardeners, and the house and estate were also supported by an estate buildings department, a woods department and a farms department.[32]

So much of the vanished pre-war and immediate post-war world of large staffs still survives in living memory. The final chapter draws on the recollections of a number of people who work or have worked in country houses, offering insight into the historic country house, of lives devoted wholly to others.

Landowners who spent their childhoods in pre-war country houses have equally sharp recollections. When I was shown around the complex of back rooms and attics at Dalmeny in Scotland by the Earl and Countess of Rosebery, I found that the service quarters had been used for largely the same purposes from the early nineteenth century right up to the 1960s. The present earl, born in 1929, could remember those rooms being occupied by a traditional staff when he was small, with gardeners still using yokes to carry buckets of coal.

As we walked around, he was able to describe, almost as if commentating on a reel of film, his own vivid memories of the staff who had worked for his father – a son of the great Victorian prime minister; his mother was a Rothschild.[33] Not untypically, the Roseberys themselves now live in a comfortable private apartment on the first floor of the house, while the richly furnished state rooms are opened to the public and used only on occasion.

In the butler's pantry (now a store room), there was once a big basin under the window, a plate warmer and a table, as well as some comfortable chairs. Lord Rosebery recalled: 'The butler had an office elsewhere but spent most of his time here.' In his parents' day there was usually a butler, two footmen and a boy. 'The footman slept in the small room off the pantry, so that he could be beside the room where the silver was locked up.'[34]

Beyond the pantry is a series of offices and the now busy estate office occupies what was once the housekeeper's room. Lord Rosebery says: 'The housekeeper and the odd man were here permanently, but all the other staff really travelled between my parents' other houses with them.' He points out the original still room: 'Here they prepared breakfast and afternoon tea, leaving the kitchen free for the bigger meals.'

The former servants' hall has a spacious area at the end, which was where they used to wash up after the servants' meals: 'No one was allowed into the kitchen except the kitchen staff.' The ground floor of the old kitchen is now a lecture hall; you can still see the roasting oven, but the main range was removed during electrification in the 1930s. 'There was also a room for kindling and a room for the "odd man". This room was shown as the oast house in the original plans, but I can remember it being used to trim and refill oil lamps.'

What staff does he employ today? 'In the 1970s we had around four live-in staff, a cook, a housekeeper, a nanny and a nurserymaid for the children. Now we have two cleaners who clean our flat, as well as the rooms opened to the public and the estate office, but no cook. The cleaners come in nine to five and we don't have any live-in staff.'

As there have been many detailed studies of servants in different periods, this book is an intentionally broad sweep of history, bringing together the world of the medieval page with that of the Edwardian footboy, and the buttery and pantry of the Tudor mansion with the butler's pantry of the nineteenth-century house. The subject has much to teach us about the human condition as well as about the nature, form and atmosphere of country houses. For many servants, their employment might have been just a job; some were hard pressed and discontented; others found their work so rewarding that they spent their whole working lives with the same family, perhaps advancing from menial roles to ones of considerable responsibility.

The below-stairs community, with its inevitable tensions and interactions, seems often to have been one of warmth and colour. Henry Moat, the famous butler at Renishaw Hall, whose role in the life of Osbert Sitwell has brought him his own entry in the new

Oxford Dictionary of National Biography, once wrote to his former employer, Lady Ida Sitwell, looking back fondly on his arrival in service in 1893: 'You were a fine young lady then full of high spirits and fun. I would not have missed the career for the earth . . . I never felt lonely when I think of my past life, the cinema is not in it.'[35]

I

The Visible and Glorious Household

From the later Middle Ages to the end of the Sixteenth Century

BETWEEN 1400 AND 1600, the households of great landowners were many-layered and complex. Records of the lives of the servants responsible for all the manual work and the careful administration of these castles, abbeys and manor houses are varied and patchy, but one or two characters catch our eye. Some are more senior and long-serving, such as those servants kindly remembered with in legacies by Sir Geoffrey Luttrell; or those who moved on to greater things, such as Geoffrey Chaucer, who started life as a young page to the Countess of Ulster; or such figures as John Russell, usher to Duke Humphrey of Gloucester, who wrote a treatise on the duties of servants in the 1460s, or Penne, the butler at Wollaton, cited in the household regulations of the 1570s, required to keep his buttery 'sweet and clear'.

Like supporting characters in a Shakespeare play, these attendants carry verbal messages and money, provide trusted intimacy, receive confidences, act as bodyguards or bear food and wine in ceremony to their lord's table. Among them are henchmen or young gentlemen attendants, puffing up their chests and defending the honour of their respective households, just as in the opening scene of Shakespeare's *Romeo and Juliet*. They are the absent figures for whom Petruchio calls in *The Taming of the Shrew*, Act IV, scene I:

> 'Where be these knaves? What! no man at door
> To hold my stirrup nor to take my horse?
> Where is Nathaniel, Gregory, Philip?'

In this period the whole household, from the top to the bottom, gave attendance, physical help, safety and, most importantly, dignity to their lord and master. Their presence and activity ensured the display that underlined the position and power of their employer. In return they received, food, clothing and wages, security, and often not a little influence and opportunity of their own. In medieval English the term 'servant' was apparently used to describe someone employed to provide labour for a family and given lodging within the household; thus it was their accommodation within the (often peripatetic) household that defined their role.[1]

The households of the great landowners were slickly managed with some sophistication, far from the grungy chaos so beloved of film-makers. From the 1300s it is apparent that today they would be more akin to the running of a smart military regiment or a very grand hotel, with great emphasis laid on etiquette, discipline and carefully kept accounts. The aristocratic household was certainly complex, serving many functions at once.[2]

Lordly magnificence was not created merely by the presence and costliness of rich materials, and the consumption of fine food and drink, but by servants, and the semi-ritual nature of their behaviour and deference: whether keeping their lord company, dressing him, or serving his food and wine. His reputation derived from the quality of their service and the richness of their dress.

The numbers involved in these households right up into the late sixteenth century could be breath-taking – although the household itself could shrink or swell as necessary. The Earl of Warwick travelled to London in the mid-fifteenth century with 600 liveried servants; William Cecil, Baron Burghley, employed 120 in 1587; while at the end of the sixteenth century 144 served the Duke of Norfolk at Framlingham Castle. Royal households, which set the standards, held the largest numbers. The 1318 *Ordinance* lists 363 servants in Edward II's household, with 129 in the stables alone, whereas Henry VII's is thought to have comprised over 800.[3]

In the thirteenth century around ninety great magnates ran what we would describe as 'great households', with roughly another forty-five bishops, abbots and priors living in similar style. And despite our modern view that this was a dangerous and insecure time, the numbers of these households apparently continued to grow, so that by the end of the fifteenth century it is now thought that there were perhaps as many as 1,500 landed individuals maintaining an aristocratic lifestyle.[4]

The Earl of Derby's household in the mid-sixteenth century numbered between 115 and 140, only six of whom were women. The preponderance of males was probably, as suggested above, a reflection of the need for physical security, as the servants of a great household could still in theory be called on to act almost as a private army. In the household of courtier Sir Thomas Lovell in 1522–3, there were still only five female servants out of a total of at least ninety.[5]

The medieval and Tudor aristocrat expected a life of comfort, protection and elegance for himself and his immediate family, provided by tolerably well-mannered, cleanly dressed, deferential and dutiful attendants, who would in turn need trusted, more manual assistants. They, too, needed to be well cared for, to ensure their loyalty, trust and obedience, and in order to carry out their duties effectively. In such a household even the most menial servants would expect a greater degree of comfort and permanence than they would as an agricultural labourer.[6]

The senior servants – the leading household officers – played a particularly critical role in maintaining order and prestige. They would have been responsible for the management of houses and estates, and all that that entailed, overseeing maintenance, heating, cleaning and, above all, sustenance. The feeding of not only the family but a whole multitude of attendants and servants, as well as the hospitality shown to visitors of all ranks, lay at the heart of medieval culture, and was often on a massive scale.

We may be surprised by the survival of words in contemporary life that link us to this distant-seeming world. The word 'waiter' meant originally an attendant who literally waited until needed, for whatever purpose. The word 'menial' literally meant those who worked for the household, from the old French word *mesnie*, derived from the Latin *mansionata*. This survival also extends to some of the distinctly English rituals in such places as City corporations and guilds, or Oxford and Cambridge colleges, such as the habit of having a separate high table for the Masters and Fellows of a college, and for the pudding course to be taken in a different room from the dining hall.[7]

This applies not only to these traditional, rarefied environments, self-evidently rich in historical reference, but to our everyday lives, for even the word 'bar' in an English pub comes from the plain, practical, wooden-plank surfaces of the buttery in the medieval great hall, from which the beer was served. It is a strangely comforting thought, as well as a reminder of the semi-public nature of the early country-house community, however hierarchical in nature.[8]

It cannot be emphasised enough that the life of a great medieval household was profoundly hierarchical. Just as a king was served by a nobleman, the nobleman would be served by a gentleman of his household and so on down the ranks. This tradition is reflected in the titles of senior courtiers in the royal household today, where many of the medieval household titles persist in an honorary form, from Lord High Chamberlain to the Master of the Horse.[9]

Most importantly, the grander households were also essentially mobile institutions, with great lords and their attendants travelling from residence to residence, towing with them the necessary furniture while drawing provisions from associated agricultural estates.[10] In addition, they were effectively the seat of a mini-government from which extensive landholdings and local justice were administered. They took their cues from the central government, such as it was, in the form of the royal court.[11]

Anyone with the mildest interest in the historic houses of the British Isles will have visited at least some of the great halls built by the medieval and Tudor aristocracy. You may have stood, for instance, beneath the vast expanse of roof in the hall at Penshurst Place in Kent, built in the fourteenth century by Sir John de Pulteney, merchant, banker and four times mayor of London, or in the expansive spaces concealed within the massive walls of late-fourteenth-century Bodiam Castle in Sussex, or the surviving sixteenth-century great hall at Rufford Old Hall, Lancashire, which survives from the mansion built by Sir Thomas Hesketh.[12]

The architecture of the great country houses of the aristocracy in this period inevitably reflected the need to accommodate large entourages, with separate lodgings for visitors and senior attendants. The life of the household was centred on the great hall, which was usually entered through a porch at one end. The porch led directly into a 'screens passage', which divided the hall from the three doors leading to the kitchen, buttery (a store for beer and wine, deriving from the same word as butt and bottle) and pantry (for bread and perishables, from *pain*) for bread. The kitchen would itself also be divided into specialist departments: sauceries, confectioneries, sculleries, poultries, larders, a cellar for wine and a chandlery for candles. As well as the lord's wardrobe (a chamber for storing precious metals), there was usually a wardrobe devoted to cloth and spices.[13]

The far end of the great hall was known as the 'high' end, often raised on a dais; in the centre of the room there would be an open fire. From the later fourteenth century, the high end was usually lit by an oriel window or projecting bay. In the early medieval period, the head of the household would dine at the high end, with lesser members of the household dining on trestle tables that could be cleared away; in large households there were often multiple sittings for the main meal of the day. The flavour of these households can still be captured when dining in the historic Cambridge and Oxford colleges.[14]

By the fourteenth century, the head of the household would normally have eaten in a withdrawing apartment, although his food would still be carried in procession through the hall before being served to him there. The sheer scale of surviving kitchens from the late Middle Ages – notably those at Durham Castle, in which all the offices are preserved – make vividly apparent the importance of cooking in aristocratic life.[15]

In the great households of barons and bishops, of the most successful merchants, or highly placed public officials, hundreds of men sustained the power and privilege of this elite – and in ever-increasing numbers. Also servants begat servants, so that the senior servants often had servants of their own – 'a child of the chamber and a horse-keeper' at least.[16]

In the deployment of residential apartments, great hall and kitchen, lodgings and counting houses, the architecture directly reflected the number of people who made up a noble household. Indeed, the scale of both combined would have meant more to the contemporary observer, as today we tend to see these buildings as empty spaces, as redundant as a medieval tithe barn.

Changing attitudes and expectations of living conditions; the competitive consumption of the medieval nobility's lifestyle; changing behaviour and attitudes to personal comfort: all were reflected in the gradual evolution of the physical relationship of different areas: the kitchens and related offices, the great hall, and the development of more private withdrawing rooms or chambers, which would be used for sleeping, dressing, washing, living, eating and receiving privileged visitors.[17] Most houses were entered through service courts.

Servants were always part of the everyday life of the landowner. The famous fifteenth-century Paston letters, written by members of an East Anglian landowning family to one another, are filled with intriguing detail suggestive of the presence and activities of household servants, who might sometimes deliver them (as well as necessary sums of money and other requests) to the addressee. At the end of one letter, Margaret Paston writes to her husband John in 1465: 'Pecock shall tell you by mouth of more things than I may write to you at this time.'[18]

In many ways it is the importance of the safe transit of money that catches our eye; John Paston II wrote to John Paston I (23 August 1461):

I suppose ye understand that the money that I had of you at London may not endure with me till that the King [Edward IV] go into Wales and come again, for I understand it shall be long ere he come again. Wherefore I have sent to London to mine uncle Clement to get 100s. of Christopher Hanson, your servant, and send it to me by my servant, and mine harness with it which I left at London to make clean.[19]

Sometimes the issue is the recruitment of servants; in the same letter John Paston II wrote: 'I send you home Pecock again; he is not for me. God send grace that he may do you good service, that by estimation is not likely. Ye shall have knowledge afterward how he hath demeaned him [self] here with me. I would, saving your displeasure, that ye were delivered of him, for he shall never do you profit nor worship.'[20]

Another typical reference comes in the letter of Margaret Paston to John Paston I, dated 24 December 1459: 'I pray that ye will essay to get some man at Caister to keep your buttery, for the man that ye left with me will not take upon him to breve [account] daily as ye commanded. He saith he hath not used to give a reckoning neither of bread nor ale till at the week's end, and he saith he wot wel that he should not con don it; and therefore I suppose he shall not abide.'[21]

In 1462, one servant, John Russe, admonished John Paston in London on the consequence of his long absence, giving his master in effect a good talking-to on paper: 'Sir, I pray God bring you once [again] to reign among your countrymen in love . . . The longer you continue there the more hurt grows to you. Men say you will neither follow the advice of your own kindred, nor of your own counsel, but continue your own wilfulness, which . . . shall be your destruction.'[22]

Sometimes this closeness could be a danger. There was a considerable furore when Margery Paston married her lover, Richard Calle, who had run the family estates with great efficiency but was still a servant; he was considered of a lower rank, and he owned no land. The couple married secretly in 1469 and for a time were banished.[23]

A steward was usually the most educated and the most powerful individual servant, often identifiable by name. If their literary stereotype is anything to go by, stewards could be a source of anxiety to families who saw their potential for becoming over-powerful, for marrying vulnerable widows or daughters. This betrayal of trust is referred to in the song sung by Ophelia in *Hamlet*: 'It is the false steward that stole his master's daughter.'[24]

As can be seen from the Paston letters, some deeper attachments occurred between senior servants and ladies of the household. Certainly some stewards were highly ambitious and successful, and marriage into a noble family could help advance their interests. One most famous example is John Thynne, the son of a Shropshire farmer, who was steward to Edward Seymour (later Protector Somerset) and later bought land in his own right. He married the heiress of Richard Gresham and eventually built Longleat. Seymour's gentleman usher,

Francis Newdigate, married the dowager duchess Anne and became MP for Wiltshire in 1559.[25]

But many senior late-medieval servants would have been deeply devoted to their masters. One such, John Russell, speaks to us across the centuries via a blank verse treatise that he wrote in the 1460s, titled *The Book of Nurture*. Written in the form of an instructive discourse with an inexperienced but hopeful young man looking for opportunity and advancement through service to a nobleman, it details the duties of servants to a great lord at the time.[26] Russell also wrote another treatise titled *The Book of Courtesy* and both were based on his experience of having spent most of his life in service.

Russell himself says that he learnt all these sciences 'with a royal prince, to whom I was usher and also marshall'. His master was Humphry, Duke of Gloucester, who died in 1447, the younger son of Henry IV. Duke Humphry, whose library forms the core of the famous Bodleian Library in Oxford, built a much admired palace, Bella Court, later known as Placentia in Greenwich, on the site of which was built the Greenwich Naval Hospital.[27]

Despite his scholarly interests, Duke Humphry chose to endure the burning heat of court intrigue and politics. He was for a time the Regent of England, yet had to endure the humiliation of having his second wife imprisoned for witchcraft. Shortly afterwards he himself was arrested for treason, dying in captivity a few days later. A trusted, long-serving, able and literate servant such as John Russell would have provided much of the stability and order of Duke Humphry's life, as well as himself being less subject to the whims of political fortune than any immediate family member.

What sort of man was an usher or a marshal? When the great fourteenth-century poet Geoffrey Chaucer in his *Prologue to the Canterbury Tales* wrote of the innkeeper of the Tabard who comes up with the idea of the story-telling on the pilgrims' journey that is the basis of the *Canterbury Tales*, he describes him as 'full fit to be a marshal in a hall'; he goes on to depict a man of presence and authority.

Mr Russell must have been just such a person, if perhaps more ascetic and clerical – with a slightly bloodless face, as in the famous portrait of Henry VII. He may well have been highly conservative, as his verse treatise has an unmistakably Jeeves-like tone of amiable, but indefatigable, certainty and authority. Mr Russell's treatise – which like all such works may itself have been based in part on earlier writings – is effectively a manual of service, outlining the more responsible roles of the noble household in the late fifteenth century, and probably those of the century before as well.

Intriguingly, it was later published in edited form by the entrepreneur early printer, Wynkyn de Worde, as the *Boke of Keruynge* (1513), which in itself suggests that by the sixteenth century there was a wider market for such manuals of servants' duties, as wealthier Tudor merchants and officials from non-aristocratic and non-courtier backgrounds took an increasing interest in details of etiquette, which were traditionally passed down in on-the-job training. Indeed, another version was published in 1577, by Hugh Rhodes, *The Boke of Nurture or Schoole of Good Manners*.[28]

The upper servants of the day were the men who were on show and who had direct physical contact with the aristocrats they served. But while Mr Russell's account genuinely helps us visualise the roles and activities of great houses, he says little about the lower servants, such as the young boys who would have had the grimmer manual tasks of cleaning and carrying, or turning the spit in the kitchen. They were probably recruited from local peasant families and were paid off when the household moved on to another residence.

The most junior servant was the scullion, derived from the French word *escuille* for a dish. This individual washed cooking utensils and dishes in the kitchen, and was usually also expected to clean and sweep those service rooms and their associated courtyards. In the later centuries this was the task of the humble scullery maid.

Mr Russell does not mention any women. This is because they were few in number in later medieval and Tudor households, aside from the immediate companions and attendants of the lady of the house, any unmarried daughters still at home, or nurses for children. If they appear elsewhere they were usually employed only in the very humblest roles, often as washerwomen. Indeed, many early household manuals advised against employing women, for moral reasons, in monastic tones that imply they would be a distraction to the men.[29]

The great medieval and Tudor kitchens seem to have been staffed principally by men, partly because strength was needed for larger-scale catering. The evidence of bequests suggests that numbers of women servants began to grow from the fifteenth century. By the sixteenth century female servants were certainly more commonplace, especially in the households of gentry, although not in positions of major responsibility.[30]

The earliest mention of a lowly menial female servant in English is thought to be that in a late-fourteenth-century translation of the writings of Bartholomaeus Anglicus, a thirteenth-century English friar who taught at the schools in Paris, translated into English by John Trevisa, chaplain to Lord Berkeley. His references to the 'servaunt-woman' make uncomfortable reading to a modern reader, for she is to be 'put to office and woerke of traveylle, toylinge and slubberynge'. In addition she is fed on 'grosse mete' and 'kept lowe under the yoek of thraldom and of servage'.[31]

Our man, Mr Russell, was at the other end of the household hierarchy, a *maître d'* figure. We do not know much about him outside the description that he gives in his treatise.[32] Like many who spent part of their career in the service of a great household during the late medieval and Tudor periods, he was likely to have come from a minor landowning family, although he may equally have been the son of a senior household officer. Indeed, he could conceivably have worked his way up the ranks from quite humble origins.

Mr Russell's treatise, written in the 1460s, speaks in its very organisation of self-discipline and order: 'All the officers I have mentioned have to obey me, ever to fulfil my commandment when I call, for our office is the chief in spicery and cellar, whether the cook belief or loth.' Mr Russell clearly had to assert himself against the master cook. This almost comical aside hints at inevitable tensions between highly skilled senior officers, another feature echoing through the centuries right up until the present day.[33]

But Mr Russell, diplomatically, celebrates the need for different skills in the great households, writing: 'All these diverse offices may be filled by a single person, but the dignity of a prince requireth each office to have its officer and a servant waiting on him.' Presumably the 'diverse offices' were divided up in different ways, depending on the size and wealth of the household.[34]

The fictional narrator figure of this treatise meets a young man in need of an occupation, and agrees to teach him 'the duties of a butler, a panter, of a chamberlain, and especially, the cunning of a carver', all of which were normally learnt by observing the practitioners in action. A 'henchman', or young man from good background working as an attendant as part of his education or training for life, would begin by looking after the cups at the end of his lord's table and observe in action the panter, butler, waiter, cupbearer, sewer and carver, through whose ranks he himself would rise.[35]

Good manners and good carriage were highly prized in this environment: 'Be fair of answer, ready to serve, and gentle of cheer, and then men will say: "There goes a gentle officer" . . . Be glad of cheer, courteous of knee, soft of speech; have clean hands and nails and be carefully dressed. Do not cough or spit or retch too loud, or put your fingers into the cups to seek bits of dust.'[36]

Mr Russell also goes into other similar delicacies of behaviour that would not go amiss in a modern etiquette manual for restaurant waiters: 'Do not pick your nose or let it drop clear pearls, or sniff, or blow it too loud, lest your lord hear . . . Retch not, nor spit too far, nor laugh or speak too loud. Beware of making faces and scorning; and be no liar with your mouth. Nor yet lick your lips or drivel . . . Good son, do not pick your teeth, or grind, or gnash them, or with puffing and blowing cast foul breath upon your lord.'[37]

He outlines the duties of pantler and butler, starting with the duties of the first. The pantry in the medieval great house or manor house was the room between the kitchen and hall, from which bread and other perishable food was served: 'In the pantry you must always keep three sharp knives, one to chop the loaves, another to pare them, and a third, sharp and keen, to smooth and square the trenchers with.' During this period, the 'trencher' bread acted as a plate from which food would be eaten and after the meal distributed to the poor as alms. Mr Russell continues: 'Always cut your lord's bread, and see that it be new; and all other bread at the table one day old ere you cut it, all household bread three days old, and trencher-bread four days old.'[38]

After bread comes the salt, an expensive commodity, the supply of which was regarded as an indication of status; hence the expression 'below the salt', which means being a person not invited to sit at the top table. Similarly, we speak of a man being 'not worth his salt'. The salt cellar itself was then often an elaborate object of some beauty. The mid-fifteenth-century inventory of Sir John Fastolf's Caister Castle, made after his death, lists two great silver-gilt salts, shaped like towers (one weighing eighty-six ounces).[39]

Then after the preparation of bread and salt comes the care of napkins and tablecloth. 'Good son, look that your napery be sweet and clean, and that your table-cloth, towel and napkin be folded neatly, your table-knives brightly polished and your spoons fair washed.'[40] Next comes the wine: 'Look ye have two wine-augers, a greater and a less, some gutters of boxwood that fit them, also a gimlet to pierce with, a tap and a bung, ready to stop the flow when it is time.'[41]

For the duties of a butler in charge of the buttery – that is to say, the room off the great hall from which beer and wine were served – Russell wrote: 'See that your cups and pots be clean, both within and without. Serve no ale till it is five days old, for new ale is wasteful. And look that all things about you be sweet and clean . . . Beware that ye give no person stale drink, for fear that ye bring many men into disease for many a year.'[42] These instructions remind us that regulations were often inspired by issues of cleanliness and health, just as they are today. Indeed, it is surely the pursuit of hygiene and healthy practices that multiplies the numbers of servants needed in a great household at this date.

Now everything is ready. 'My son, it is now the time of the day to lay the table. First, wipe it with a cloth ere it be spread, than lay on it a cloth called a cowche. You take one end and your mate the other, and draw it straight; and lay a second cloth with its fold on the outer edge of the table. Lift the upper part and let it hang even. And then lay the third cloth with its fold on the inner edge, making a state half a foot wide, with the top.'[43] Thus the table would appear like a long, crisp box of linen.

Side-tables or cupboards were also covered with a cloth and used to display precious cups, ewers (or jugs) and basins, as an indication of status: 'Cover your ewery-cupboard with a diapered towel, and put a towel round your neck, for that is courtesy, and put one end of it mannerly over your left arm; and on the same arm place your lord's napkin, and on it lay eight loaves of bread, with three or four trencher-loaves. Take one end of the towel in your left hand, as the manner is, together with the salt-cellar – look you do this – and take the end of the towel in your right hand with the spoon and knives.'[44]

The setting out of the table reflects the sparse, elegant laying out shown in fifteenth-century illuminated manuscripts and paintings.[45] 'Set the salt on your lord's right hand, and to the left of your salt, one or two trenchers, and to the left again, your knife by itself and plain to see, and the white rolls, and beside them a fair folded napkin. Cover your spoon, napkin, trencher and knife so that they cannot be seen; and at the other end of the table place a salt with two trenchers. Bread could be wrapped in the napkins. When your sovereign's table is dressed in this array, place salts on all other tables, and lay trenchers and cups.' After all this has been completed, 'set out your cupboard with gay silver and silver-gilt, and your ewery board with basins and ewers, and hot and cold water, each to temper the other.'[46]

Even the actual physical movement was considered significant: 'Carry a towel about your neck when serving your lord, bow to him, uncover your bread and set it by the salt. Look that all have knives, spoons and napkins, and always when you pass your lord, see that you bow your knees.'[47]

After that, he has to watch the other servants to make sure the food is distributed correctly and according to precedence. 'Watch the sewer to see how many pottages he covers, and do ye for as many, and serve each according to his degree; and see that none lack bread, ale or wine.'[48]

The carver's duties are also explained, for carving was always done in public: 'Thy knife must be clean and bright: and it beseems thee to have thy fair hands washed. Hold always the knife surely, so as not to hurt thyself, and have not more than two fingers and the thumb on thy keen knife.' Describing different techniques for cutting fish, flesh and fowl, he adds: 'Touch no manner of meat with thy right hand, but with thy left, as is proper. Always with thy left hand grasp the loaf with all thy might . . . You do not right to soil your table, nor to wipe your knives on that, but on your napkin.'[49]

Various meats were carved differently. Brawn was cut on the dish and slices lifted off with the knife; with a fawn, kid or lamb, the kidney was served first, after which the carver had to lift up the shoulder and remove the tendon of the neck. Capon, chicken or teal pies had to be taken out of the crust, the wings minced and then stirred with the gravy so that it could be eaten with a spoon. In a typical menu three such courses would be followed by one of fruit.[50]

The server (or sewer) was expected to 'Take heed when the worshipful head of any household has washed before meat and begins to say grace, then hie you to the kitchen where the servants must attend and take your orders. First ask the panter or officer of the spicery for fruits, such as . . . plums, damsons, grapes and cherries which are served before dinner according to the season to make men merry, and ask if any be served that day.' Then he must confer with the cook about the dishes to be served and have the 'surveyor' carry them to him, which he would then 'convey to the lord'. Men should be standing by 'to prevent any dish being stolen'.[51]

Over and over again, Mr Russell emphasises the hierarchy of the servants, and who was to obey whom, a recurring theme throughout the centuries. A line of command was essential for discipline and smooth management: 'Panter, yeoman of the cellar, butler and ewerer, I will that ye obey the marshal, sewer and carver.'[52]

Mr Russell's treatise also gives us a delicious portrait of a lord being dressed, which was the responsibility of the chamberlain (in charge of the chamber, the more private apartment of the lord). We exchange the public ritual of dining for the somewhat more intimate ritual of the bedchamber that was just as elaborate in its own way.

The duty of a chamberlain is to be 'diligent in office, neatly clad, his clothes not torn, hands and face well washed and head well kempt. He must be ever careful – not negligent – of fire and candle.' Once again, the manner and conduct of the service are stressed. It is always more pleasant to be looked after by men who are in good spirits, although this is not always easy: 'Be courteous, glad of cheer, quick of hearing in every way, and be ever on the lookout for things to do him pleasure; if you will acquire these qualities it may advance you well.'[53]

The very preparation of the master's clothes fell to the chamberlain, to whom a yeoman and a groom of the chamber would report for more manual tasks: 'See that your lord has a clean shirt and hose, a short coat, a doublet, and a long coat, if he wear such, his hose well brushed, his socks at hand, his shoes or slippers as brown as a water leech. In the morning, against your lord shall rise, take care that his linen be clean, and warm it at a clear fire, not smoky, if [it] be cold or freezing.'[54]

This is so practical and obvious that some sections of this treatise could equally have been applied to the Edwardian valet: 'When he rises make ready the foot-sheet, and forget not to place a chair or some other seat with a cushion on it before the fire, with another cushion for the feet. Over the cushion and chair spread this sheet so as to cover them, and see that you have a kerchief and a comb to comb your lord's head before he is fully dressed.'[55]

It is no wonder that, given the scope of medieval heating, the chamberlain would position the lord by his fire before he is dressed:

> Then pray your lord in humble words to come to a good fire and array him thereby, and there to stand or stand pleasantly; and wait with due manners to assist him. First hold out to him his tunic, then his doublet while he puts in his arms, and have his stomacher well aired to keep off harm, as also his vamps [short stockings] and socks, so he shall go warm all day.
>
> Then draw on his socks and his hose by the fire, and lace or buckle his shoes, draw his hosen on well and truss them up to the height that suits him, lace his doublet in every hole, and put round his neck and on his shoulders a kerchief; and then gently comb his head with an ivory comb, and give him water where with to wash his hands and face.

After that the chamberlain was to kneel and ask which robe or gown he wants. 'Before he goes out, brush busily about him, and whether he wear satin, sendal, velvet, scarlet or grain, see that all be clean and nice.'[56]

After the lord has left, the room must be set straight, the bed made 'mannerly' and the fire laid ready. The wardrobe must also be attended to, the clothes kept well, with instructions 'to brush them cleanly' and inspect furs regularly against moths. Later,

> when he has supped and goes to his chamber, spread forth your foot-sheet, as I have already shown you, take off his gown or whatever garment by the license of his estate he wear, and lay it up in such place as ye best know . . .
>
> Put a mantle on his back to keep his body from cold, set him on the foot-sheet made ready as I have directed, and pull of[f] his shoes, socks and hosen, and throw these last over your shoulder, or hold them on your arm. Comb his hair, but first kneel down and put on his kerchief and nightcap wound in seemly fashion.

The bed and candles must be prepared, and, in a very human detail, the dogs and cats chased out of the chamber: 'take no leave of your lord, but bow low to him and retire.'[57]

Every comfort was considered, a theme that lies at the heart of the role of the body-servant down the ages. *The Book of Nurture* gives memorable recipes for a sweet-smelling 'bath or stew so-called' and there is also a medicinal version: 'boil together hollyhock, mallow, wall pellitory and brown fennel, St. John's wort, centuary, ribwort and camomile, hehove, heyriff, herb-benet, brese-wort, smallage, water speedewell, scabious, bugloss, and wild flax which is good for aches − boil with leaves and green oats together with them, and throw them hot into a vessel and put your lord over it.'[58] This was the original herbal bath essence.

Among the other offices that Mr Russell detailed were his own, that of usher and marshal. Above all, the marshal must know the precedence of the nobility, an essential skill for upper servants well into the twentieth century, as well as 'all the estates of the church' and their status.

To show off his part-royal duties, he recites the hierarchy from the top, beginning with emperor, pope, and king, continuing down through the copious ranks of late medieval society. An usher or marshal must be able to seat them all appropriately: 'a bishop, viscount, marquis, goodly earl may sit at two messes [dishes to be shared between four] if they be agreeable thereunto'. The key issue is to 'set all according to their birth, riches and dignity'.[59]

Mr Russell's treatise takes us deep into the minutiae and the mind-set of the senior medieval servant. Although these elaborate rituals might seem alien to a modern reader, many practices would have been recognisable in aristocratic households up until the nineteenth century, when technology first has an impact on the roles of body-servants. Some would be recognisable even today. It is perhaps not surprising that caring for a high-status and wealthy employer should require many services that stay basically the same, despite advances in technology and changes in social values.

Noble households regularly moved between the landholdings of the head of the household, although by the end of the sixteenth century there was a greater emphasis on attendance at court. The house-hold on the move must have been one of the great spectacles of the Middle Ages. It was divided usually into three parties. One went ahead to announce the arrival of a lord and to prepare his apartments; another, the main one, comprised the lord and his immediate house-hold, with appropriate attendants. Then came the baggage train, with the cooks, scullions and pack horses, carrying clothes, linen, furniture and provisions for the journey.[60]

Appreciating the scale of this operation helps us understand the rather formulaic layout of the medieval castle and manor house, which assisted the smooth transition from house to house of the mobile household, as well as being able to absorb a visiting lord, his family and attendants. A medieval householder could call on the attendance of knights and squires, who owed military service in return for their landholdings. They made up the 'fighting' household, but were not on permanent alert, and could swell the numbers for a special procession.[61] Later in the medieval period, a smaller group of individuals, then known as the 'secret household', remained in attendance on the lord, his wife and children when it did not suit him to keep house formally; this often coincided with the annual audit, when all the complex expenditure of a household was closely reviewed.[62]

The most elaborate household of the day, which set the standards of visual magnificence and efficiency, was of course the royal household – or, strictly speaking, households, as queens and princes each had their own, not least to emphasise their individual dignity. There is perhaps no modern equivalent of this, other than perhaps great state occasions. The households of the upper nobility naturally largely followed the pattern set by the monarchy, although on differing scales; indeed, they were mirrored in turn by the households of the gentry. Those of leading bishops and abbots played a role in setting high standards of ritual and devotion that would have been imitated by other great households.

In the larger households, the upper servants, overseen by figures such as John Russell, had the principal duties of looking after the family rooms and the great hall. They were expected to be well trained and well dressed, usually in a designated livery, whose colours were chosen by the head of the household and were usually based on the main pigments in the family's coat of arms. In all other respects, they followed the fashion of the day, unlike liveries from the late seventeenth century that tended to deliberate old-fashionedness.[63]

These upper servants were responsible for carrying out the extraordinarily elaborate ritual already described by Mr Russell, which governed their master's every waking moment – from first light to the ending of the day. Their duties usually began early, as in the household of the Prince of Wales, the young Prince Edward, in the 1470s. The main gates would be opened from five in summer and six in winter. As was usual in great households then, the daily round would start with a chapel service, followed by breakfast for the lord and his family. Dinner for the household was served between nine and eleven in the morning. The evening was demarcated by evensong, supper, and the ceremony of 'all night' or seeing the lord to bed. The main gates were closed by nine or ten.[64]

As Mr Russell's treatise shows, the entertainment of great visitors was central to the life of the noble household. Another late-fifteenth-century treatise sets out the protocol for receiving a guest who has arrived during a mealtime, describing how he should be taken to his chamber, through the great hall, to be greeted courteously by the marshal and ushers. An usher should take his servants to drink at the bar of the buttery and show them their master's sleeping quarters; he should also ensure that bread, beer and wine were taken to his chamber.[65]

All this was not just for protection, but for dignity's sake. Remember the argument in Act II, scene IV, between King Lear and his daughters about his need for retainers, when he is asked to reduce his retinue, eventually to one. When Regan says, 'What need one?' he replies in agony: 'O! reason not the need: our basest beggars/ Are in the poorest thing superfluous.' The actual physical presence of even a few retainers was quite simply the *sine qua non* of aristocratic life at any level. This 'need' is hinted at by Elizabeth Stonor, of Stonor in Oxfordshire, who strikes a plaintive note in a letter to her husband, written in March 1478: 'And I pray you that you will send me some of your servants and mine to wait upon me, for now I am right bare of servants.'[66] It was difficult to emphasise your noble or gentry status without the proper attendants.

The nature of such a household, recounted in detail only fifty years after John Russell's treatise but with many of the practices there described still in vogue, is to be found in the remarkable document known as the Northumberland Household Book. The household regulations of Henry Algernon Percy, 5th Earl of Northumberland, were drawn up in 1511/12 as a process of audit and good management, supplying a rare example of a non-royal list of household members and its arrangements. These regulations relate principally to his two houses, Leaconfield Castle and Wressil Castle, providing an extraordinarily vivid portrait of the great household at its fullest, at the beginning of the century when it started to become unfashionable to retain one on a permanent basis. The list of those in the household is worth inspecting here in some detail.[67]

Leaconfield, or Leconfield, Castle was near Beverley in Yorkshire. It no longer survives but was described by the antiquary John Leland thus: 'Leckinfield is a large house, and stands within a great moat, in one very spacious court; 3 parts of the house, saving the main gate that is made of bricke, [are] all of timber. The 4th parte is fair, made of stone, and some brick . . . the Park thereby is very fair and large.'[68]

In 1541, the earl hosted a visit from Henry VIII there. Wressil Castle, now known as Wressle, also in Yorkshire, was a similarly extensive complex and survives only as a ruin.

The original manuscript is preserved in the archives of the present Duke of Northumberland at Alnwick Castle. It is a remarkable leather-bound document, as heavy as an old bible, and carefully indexed with little sealing-wax knobs on strings, suggesting that it was very much for practical reference, covering every aspect of the finances, feeding, heating and transporting of a large noble household. The text was transcribed, edited and reprinted in the eighteenth century by the bishop and antiquary Thomas Percy, who was struck then by how like a royal household it was. It includes a list of 'those abiding in his household' at Michaelmas in the third year of the reign of Henry VIII.

First comes the earl's blood family and their immediate personal attendants: 'My Lord, My Lady, My Young Lord and his two brothers, and their servants, each having a yeoman and a groom'. There were three servants for the nursery alone, 'viz. 2, rockers and a child to attend in nursery'; the rockers were literally people, presumably women, hired to rock the cradle. Then there were 'three Gentlewomen for my Lady and two Chamberers for my Lady', and 'My Lord's Brothers every [one] of them with their servants'.

Next come the four upper servants (and their servants): 'My Lord's head officers of household', namely the chamberlain (and his servants: a chaplain, a clerk, two yeomen, a child of his chamber and his horse-keeper), and the steward (whose list of servants matched that of the chamberlain). Then the Treasurer and his servants (including his clerk and his horsekeeper); and the controller (and his servants, a clerk and his horsekeeper). In the household of a major landowner these were all powerful men with considerable economic influence and patronage of their own.

Then, as with most noble households until the Reformation, came the numerous clergy who organised the daily services and said masses for the souls of the dead. In the earl's household there was 'the Dean of the Chapel and his servant, the Survisor [a supervisory chaplain] and his servant, two of My Lord's Council each with their servants; the Secretary and his servant; my Lord's Chaplains in household' of whom there were six. They included the almoner who would distribute alms, the 'master of grammar' or schoolmaster to the young in the household, 'a Chaplain to ride with my lord' and three more clergy.

All households had regular services, whilst some held as many as six or seven masses throughout the day. In larger noble households, the clerics, being well educated, might also have served as secretaries, to maintain estate records and accounts.[69] The Reformation of the 1530s brought an end to the huge numbers of priests attached to a single household. Although retained chaplains and daily prayers remained common, this must have changed the atmosphere and habits of many of the great households.

The Dissolution of the Monasteries in 1535 also caused the break-up of the households of great abbots, which until then had set the standard of devotion and ritual practice, and were certainly highly regarded for the education of the young. The closing of such establishments must have had an impact on English culture, even in terms of the numbers of highly trained household servants who must have lost their jobs.[70]

In the Earl of Northumberland's household, the next rank of household officers – made up of gentlemen – are listed: the ushers, carvers, servers (sometimes known as sewers), and the waiters and henchmen. These would largely be drawn from noble or gentry backgrounds and would provide immediate attendance on the earl while simultaneously learning the skills of serving described in John Russell's treatise.

The next rung down are the 'yeomen', skilled individuals working under the gentleman servitors, as well as the choristers of the chapel. Below them come the yet more 'hands on' servants of the day with very specific responsibilities suggested clearly by their titles. The word 'groom' at this date does not have the sole association with the stables that it has in later times, but rather means a dedicated male attendant, and originally a young boy.[71] There would be a groom for every office: the ewery, the pantry, the cellar, the buttery, the kitchen (the larder), and the hall, plus a groom porter, a groom of the stirrup, a groom of the palfreys (saddle horses), and a groom of the supterman (reserve horse), as well as a groom of the chariot (or carriage).

Even the grooms might have their underlings, including ten children for the offices of the household: one for the wardrobe, one for the kitchen, one for the scullery, one for the stable, one for the carriage, one for the bakehouse, one for the arrasmender (who took care of valuable tapestries), one for the butchery, one for the catery (catering department) and one for the armoury. There was also one man whose job it was to 'serve the grooms of the Chamber with Wood' – for the open fires.[72]

Most large medieval and Tudor households employed musicians, who came rather low in the pecking order. Additional entertainers were presumably employed on an ad hoc basis. The Earl of Northumberland's household included three minstrels, playing a tabouret, a lute and a rebec or early form of fiddle. Some households, like that of Sir Thomas More, also kept a fool, a practice that was especially popular at court.[73]

The Northumberland household list records one footman, two falconers, a painter and a joiner (the latter to assemble, or repair, household furniture). There was also a huntsman in charge of deer hunting, including the preservation of game against vermin and poaching. There was a 'Gardener of the place where my lord Lyeth for the time to have meat and drink within', presumably a hunting lodge. (This is believed to be the hunting tower described by Leland where he is thought to have kept his 'secret household' during audits.)

There were ten in the accounts office, including two clerks of the foreign expenses, one clerk of the works, one clerk of the wearing book, and two clerks to write under the clerks of the foreign expenses. The whole number, at the time of this survey in 1511/12, 'of all the said persons in Household is 166'.[74] There is some evidence that the full number was not permanently in attendance, but served in rotation.

Every particular of the house's activity is accounted for in this book, showing how scrupulously a large household had to be run to avoid chaos, or, more importantly perhaps, embezzlement and theft, problems still current today in any large establishment. Considerable economic management was required, so the book sets out in meticulous detail the provision of all meats, fish and hops for brewing. It also covered liveries, which we will look at later in this chapter. There was also stipulation that all bread should be baked on the premises and not bought in, and that beer likewise be brewed by the household itself. To give just one example, the breakfasts allowed for each level in the household were specified down to the exact quantities of bread, fish and beer each was to receive. Beer would be brewed on site and was regarded as a kind of healthy liquid bread rather than an intoxicant.[75]

To modern eyes, these households seem more like tribes or villages than a single entity. They were a complex organism of interrelated activities and duties.[76] In principle, servants were often employed for a year at a time, although even in the greater households many carried on working for the same masters for decades. There are even recorded cases of contracts being dissolved between masters and servants by virtue of the unacceptable behaviour of a master.

However, there were also numerous examples of generous bequests reflecting long and harmonious relationships based on great loyalty and mutual trust and, no doubt, the need to give long-serving retainers some security in their old age. Many great landowners had special relationships with particular hospitals (that is, almshouses), such as the Bishops of Winchester with St Cross, and the Duke of Suffolk with God's House at Ewelme.[77]

Sir Geoffrey Luttrell of Irnham, who died in May 1345, left numerous bequests to his servants. These included 40 marks to his chamberlain; 10 marks and a robe and the apparel of the hall to William the porter; 20 shillings to his chaplain; and 5 marks for clothing to his confessor. One cook, John of Bridgford, received 10 marks and a robe, together with the brass and wooden vessels of the kitchen. His pantler and butler (here a combined post), John of Colne, received 10 marks, a robe and the vessels of the pantry and buttery. There was even a bequest of 5 marks to a maidservant, Alice de Wadnowe.[78]

Luttrell was also notably the commissioning patron of the great Luttrell Psalter with its famous illuminations, now preserved in the

British Library. Those illustrating psalms 113–14 show food being prepared in a kitchen, and then being carried by servants (including the loyal John of Colne) to be served to Sir Geoffrey and his household. The miniatures are considered so distinctive that some of the figures depicted at the table may be actual individuals.[79]

It is possible that some servants provided support and loyalty beyond expectations. A valued friendship between master and servant was later recorded by the 9th Earl of Northumberland: 'And in this I must truly testify for servants out of experience, that in all my fortunes good and bade, I have found them more reasonable than either wyfe, brothers or friends.'[80]

Service in a great household in the late medieval and Tudor periods was looked upon by most of those employed as something of a privilege – and the complex hierarchies of staff would have reflected those of society at large. Even the yeoman servants (who had more everyday work) enjoyed a degree of security and patronage. They could also expect what was then a reasonable standard of living, certainly in terms of subsistence, food and drink, as well as lodging (all of which formed a substantial part of their wages). Not surprisingly, because of the degree of intimacy mentioned, servants might often be drawn from the same families, generation after generation. For instance, the surnames of servants in the accounts of John Howard, 1st Duke of Norfolk, in 1462, are largely the same as those for the 2nd Duke in 1525.[81]

Some servants, like our friend John Russell, might remain in noble service for their whole careers, enjoying impressive promotions. In the fourteenth century, William de Manton was wardrober to Elizabeth de Burgh; by 1340 he had become the clerk of her chamber. Later still he was her executor and after her death he transferred to the household of her son-in-law, the Duke of Clarence. In 1361–5 he had reached the post of keeper of the wardrobe to Edward III.[82] Households would break up on the death of a nobleman, not least because by that time an adult son might well already have a full household of his own.

If, as the Northumberland Household Book makes clear, the household servants were mostly male, they were also predominantly young; indeed, a significant proportion of the young male servants were effectively attached to the house as part of their education, to learn etiquette, discipline and all manner of social polish, as well as to benefit from their proximity to powerful men. It is important that we see this process through medieval rather than modern eyes. For such service was not considered servile; rather it was an expected and necessary part of the life of a young aristocrat.

These young attendants, from noble and gentry backgrounds, would serve for a designated period as if at a finishing school. This weaned them from reliance on their own household servants and prepared them for the duties they would command of others when they were heads of their own establishments. It made them familiar too with protocol on great occasions and taught them personal conduct as well as domestic organisation. It was also intended to give them political connections that could lead to advantageous marriages or positions at court, and certainly to lifelong alliances.

Daniele Barbaro, the sophisticated Venetian ambassador to England in the 1540s, regarded the practice of sending children away at seven or nine, for seven or more years, as somewhat cruel and remarked on their 'want of affection' for their children. He asked English nobles why they did it and they replied: 'in order that their children learn better manners. But I, for my part, believe they do it because they like to enjoy all their comforts themselves, and that they are better served by strangers than they would be by their own children.'[83]

The young Geoffrey Chaucer was famously a page in the household of Elizabeth de Burgh, Countess of Ulster (d.1363), and the wife of Prince Lionel, one of the sons of Edward III. Indeed, the earliest documentary evidence for Chaucer's life are payments in her household account books for clothes and a gift 'for necessaries at Christmas'.[84] In the late fifteenth century, the child Thomas More waited in the household of Cardinal Morton. As William Roper, More's son-in-law, recalled in his biography, *Vita Thomas Mori*: 'In whose witt and towardnesse the Cardinall much delightinge, would often say of him unto the nobles that dyvers tymes came to dyne with him: This child here wayting at the table, whosoever shall live to see it, will prove a marvellous man.'[85]

Well-bred young men would often receive a certain amount of formal education, sometimes with a cleric or later a professional schoolmaster in the nobleman's household. They were often following in the footsteps of their fathers and grandfathers, going to the same households for their education – much as later landowning families had attachments to different public schools and Oxford and Cambridge colleges. This habit was beginning to decline during the sixteenth century, when children might equally be sent to grammar schools, or to university, or to the Inns of Court.[86]

Roger Ascham, who was employed as tutor to Princess Elizabeth, wrote a famous book, published in 1570, when such household-based education was still very current. Its lengthy title was: *The scholemaster, or plaine perfite way of teaching children to understand, write and to speake, the Latin tong, but specially purposed for the private bringing up of youth in Ientlemen and Noblemen's houses.* His book was in part inspired by a conversation concerning the scholars of Eton who were running away as a result of too heavy beatings. Ascham's father had been steward to Lord Scrope, and he himself had been educated not at a school but in the household of Sir Humphry Wingfield.[87]

Most attendants in a medieval and Tudor household were rewarded with 'liveries', literally a living allowance. Originally, this meant more than just clothing (which later became the principal meaning associated with the word) and certainly covered money, food and goods, such as candles and wood. Clothing was usually dispensed as cloth, in a quantity and colour chosen to reflect the status of the recipient. Livery badges were worn in addition, often showing the family crest or coat of arms. Academic gowns in universities still continue this tradition of reflecting hierarchy in differentiated dress, as do the judiciary.[88]

These liveries acted both as a payment and also as a badge of belonging, an expression of being part of a great household, much like an army uniform. This meant that anyone wearing a livery would automatically come under the protection of that lord. Neat uniforms all in the same colours helped underline his prestige. In the household of Sir William Petre, secretary to Henry VIII, ordinary servants were given new clothes in spring and autumn. In the winter they wore grey frieze, a coarse woollen cloth. In the summer this was replaced by grey marble, a parti-coloured worsted cloth that was woven to resemble the flecked veins found in marble.[89]

Most servants would be fed by the household, except grooms and pages of the marshalsea (or stables, derived from the old English word meaning 'seat of the horsekeeper') who were more likely to be paid cash wages in lieu of food. Numbers of portions served are recorded in household checker rolls, in terms of units of four (a mess) in which food was served.[90]

The upper servants who ran the great households must have been men of considerable ability and have identified very closely with their masters. George Cavendish, gentleman usher for the household of Cardinal Wolsey, Archbishop of York and chancellor of England, described in detail his experiences as Wolsey's 'gentleman usher'. He served Wolsey both at the height of his fame and in his final disgrace, 'contynually duryng the terme of all his troble until he died' in 1530. Cavendish's account gives us a glimpse into the most prestigious non-royal household on the eve of the Reformation.[91]

Wolsey was, according to his biographer, served by a great number of 'noble men and worthy gentilmen of great estymacion and possessions wt no small nomber of the tallest yomen [i.e. yeomen] that he Could get in all this Realm'. The physical appearance of the servant was as important a factor in the sixteenth century as it was for footmen in the eighteenth and nineteenth centuries. Mr Cavendish thought it quite right for a nobleman to prefer 'any tall & comly [i.e. handsome] yoman unto his servyce'.[92]

Every day in Wolsey's hall at Hampton Court there would be three tables, each seating three principal officers: a steward, who was always a doctor or a priest, a treasurer, a knight, a controller, and an esquire, all of whom carried at all times their white staffs of office. The description of one of Wolsey's two cooks suggests the prestige of such a post: 'Now in his privy kitchen he had a Master Cook who went daily in Damask, Sattin or velvet with a chain of gold about his neck.' Two particularly tall yeomen were picked to stand at his gate. In addition to the never ending list of servants for every conceivable need, Wolsey maintained a considerable number of clergy and choristers, as appropriate to the household of an archbishop and chancellor of England.

In his own chamber, he had his high chamberlain, his vice-chamberlain, twelve gentleman ushers, and a small army of attendants dedicated to serving him in his private apartments, including the Earl of Derby, who had six attendants of his own. As well as a substantial secretariat, there were four footmen which were dressed 'in riche Runnyng Cootes [coats] when so ever he rode any journey then had he a herald at arms, also a serjeant at arms'. So the list goes on, including an 'instructer of his wards', which was literally a teacher or tutor for the young. According to his checker rolls, Wolsey's household numbered around 500 persons.

Mr Cavendish proudly recorded the household attendants' appearance when he accompanied Wolsey on embassies to the Holy Roman Emperor, Charles V: 'his gentilmen beyng in nomber very many clothed in lyuere cootles of Crymmosyn velvelt [i.e. livery coats of crimson velvet] of the most purest Colour that myght be invented wt chains of gold abought ther nekkes. And all his yomen and other mean officers in Cottes of ffyne skarlett.'

The progress of the embassies is portrayed in some detail, as are the entertainments that Wolsey gives the king at Hampton Court: 'Such pleasures . . . devised for the king's comfort & consolation as might be invented or man's wit imagined the banquets [pudding course] were set forth with masques and mummerys in so gorgeous and costly manner that it was an heaven to behold', along with 'all kind of music and harmony set forth with excellent voices both of men and children'.

These descriptions give some sense of the extraordinary level of organisation in the great households that went into the grandest display at major events, involving astonishing numbers and extravagant cost. The breathless admiration of this contemporary witness illustrates the pride taken by a serving man in his own modest contribution.[93]

After Wolsey's downfall, Hampton Court became a palace for Henry VIII, and it is here that the magnificence of a Tudor kitchen can be truly understood today. This is partly due to the sheer scale of the surviving Great Kitchen, built in 1530. It was not the privy kitchen of the king, but catered for those household officers and members of the court who were entitled to be fed there in the Great Hall, some 600 in number.

The king usually ate privately in his privy chamber, while higher-status courtiers and household officers ate in the Great Watching Chamber. Leftovers from the tables were gathered up to be distributed to the poor by the almoner. Another 230 household servants also received a daily ration, eaten in their own rooms or work stations (their leftovers were delivered to the scullery).

Each meal consisted of two courses served in the Great Hall, in messes (a dish to be shared between four), and served by the senior man at the table. The Historic Royal Palaces Agency, which runs Hampton Court, has recently instituted an impressive programme of demonstrations reproducing the most vivid experience of a sixteenth-century kitchen at work anywhere in the world.[94]

It is less easy to form a clear picture of where most servants slept. For reasons of practicality and security, most personal servants had to remain within calling distance of their masters or mistresses and thus slept close to them, perhaps even sharing their chamber, or lying down in the passage outside.[95] Most senior household servants would have slept on pallet beds that would be taken at night to the rooms where they conducted their business during the day and then stored away again the following morning. Designated rooms might be contained within the courtyard range; for instance, such rooms as are mentioned in the 1522 inventory of Compton Wynyates in Warwickshire, which boasted a porter's lodge, a master receiver's chamber, a steward's chamber, a wardrobe and a yeoman's chamber.[96]

Some servants might still have slept in the great hall (as they certainly would have done in much earlier times, as suggested by the passage in the famous Anglo-Saxon poem *Beowulf*, describing the whole household sleeping in the hall) or in the kitchen, although not in the domestic offices, which would be kept locked. By the sixteenth century there was some attempt to monitor this, at least in the regulations for Henry VIII's household, which forbade scullions to 'lie in the nights and dayes in the kitchens or . . . by the fire-side'.[97]

The inventories of mid-fifteenth-century Caister Castle in Norfolk, built by Sir John Fastolf, shows that by this date senior servants were usually assigned their own chambers. Twenty-eight rooms were occupied by a total of thirty-eight beds, and some twenty-two rooms are identified with individuals or officials of the household. Servants of all ranks were likely to have been expected to share beds at times. John Russell's *Book of Courtesy* makes mention of the etiquette to be used if asked to share a bed. It was, for instance, considered polite to ask which side of the bed the other person wanted to sleep on, and then to lie as far away from them as possible.[98]

The *Book of Courtesy* gives the dimensions of a shared pallet bed:

Grooms shall make litter and stuff pallets out,
Nine foot in length without a doubt,
Seven foot certainly shall it be broad,
Well watered and bound together, craftily trod,
With wisps drawn out at feet and side.

Presumably such a bed would be used by more than one person at one time.[99]

Chambers in the base court accommodated other officials, including the lord's cook, stableman and gardeners, while some servants were given pallet beds and blankets at their places of work, in the bakehouse, stables and gardeners' rooms. At Bishop Waltham Palace in Hampshire, adapted in the fifteenth century, there appears to be a sizeable dormitory over the newly built brewhouse and bakehouse.[100]

Rooms of servants were certainly often shared. The inventory in 1542 of Sutton Place in Surrey shows that all the laundrymaids slept together and, in another room, the 'lads' of the kitchen bedded down alongside the fool.[101] There are a number of areas in the roof spaces within service buildings attached to medieval houses that have windows, which is presumably because they could be used as service or occasional guest accommodation, as at the fourteenth-century Westenhanger Castle in Kent.[102] The 1575 inventory of Lacock Abbey, Wiltshire, shows that the porter there had a bed (at 1s 6d) that was more valuable than that of the gardener (1 shilling) as well as more bedding. Such gradations emphasised the hierarchy of the household.[103]

The valets of the household of Edward III had the right to pallet beds, with canvas bedding stuffed with straw, rushes or even broom.[104] The clergyman William Harrison took a dim view of the straw pallets used by sixteenth-century servants: 'If they had any sheet above them it was well, for seldom had they any under their bodies to keep them from the pricking straws that ran oft through the canvas of the pallet and rased [sic] their hardened hides.'[105]

Habits and customs of great households were always changing, and varied between households, but there was overall a surprising consistency up to the end of the sixteenth century. Some flavour of country-house hospitality as it survived into the Elizabethan period can be gauged from the survival of the Willoughby Household Orders, drawn up by Sir Francis Willoughby, a wealthy member of the gentry, in 1572 for Wollaton, before major rebuilding took place.[106] The senior household officers, recorded in payments, were then Henry Willoughby, steward, George Cam, gentleman of the chamber, Thomas Shaw, controller, and Richard Wrigley, head gardener.

Two men were responsible for the accounts, William Marmion and William Blythe. The household included only a small number of women. Lady Willoughby apparently oversaw the children herself, along with two nurses, and was attended by two gentlewomen, Elizabeth Mering, her lady-in-waiting, Marjory Garner, and three other women (including, unusually, a female fool called Mary).[107]

Ritual and ceremony described in these regulations were still designed to hold a household together, absorbing the all too obvious tensions between the stewards, bailiffs and serving men in their struggle for power and influence; many were the younger sons of local landowning families. These dissensions may have been a major factor in the undoing of larger households in the early seventeenth century, which were becoming more and more difficult to fund, and perhaps also to control.[108]

The gentleman usher was then one Robert Foxe who, according to the regulations, was to 'supply the place of the usher, whose office is first of all to see that the hall be kept clean and that his groom sees no doggs come there at all. He is diligently to have a good regard of every person that comes into the hall, to the end that if they be of the better sort, notice may be given to the master, or to some head officer that they may be entertained accordingly.' People were seated and served according to their rank, as were their servants.

Even if they were not of the highest rank, guests were still to be treated with respect and offered food and drink: 'If of the meaner sort, then [he is] to know the cause of their coming, . . . to the end they may be dispatched and answer'd of their business, provided always that no stranger be suffered to pass without offering him to drink.'

The usher was expected to preserve the standards of behaviour:

> Upon intelligence given from the clerk or the cook that meat is ready to be served, he is with a loud voice to command all gentleman and yeomen to repair to the dresser. At the neither [sic] end of the hall he is to meet the service, saying with a loud voice, 'Give place, my masters,' albeit no man be in the way, and so to goe before the same service until he come to the upper end of the hall.

After the lord has been served in his private dining chamber, '[The usher] is to place in the hall in dinner and supper time all noblemen's men which be fellows together, and all gentlemen according to every of their master's degrees'. He was also to form the clerk of the kitchens how much food was needed. This was done in order that proper hospitality could be offered, reflecting the dignity of his master.[109] Lesser servants could also be called in to serve, if there was a large number of visitors: 'Three or four of the meanest sort of servants, as namely the slaughterman, the carter, and some of the best grooms of the stable, the allowed pages and boys in the house, to attend upon the first dinner, and they to have the remainder thereof'.[110]

The usher was required to keep discipline: 'if there shall be any stubborn persons, he is to expell them out of the hall'; to keep the noise down by saying, 'Speak softly, my masters.' He must not fetch and carry but command the butler and panter to do so.[111]

There were strictures too for the butler, Penne: 'his office is ever to keep clean and sweet his buttery, and likewise his plate and cups, making sure every day to have fresh and clean water.' His duties were also 'to keep the great chamber clean, to make fires there, and to provide for lights in due season, and to cover the boards and cupboards there, having good regard to the cleanness of his linen'.[112]

The butler was responsible too for distributing bread to the servants of the household who did not dine in the great hall: '[he] is to use good discretion in serving forth of the bread and beer to the houses of office', including the kitchen, the bakehouse, and the nursery.[113] These regulations give a vivid illustration of the survival of traditional practices in the later Elizabethan period and the demands of a gentry household of considerable numbers.

But by the very end of the sixteenth century, there was a noticeable gear-change in the old traditions of the household. One anonymous writer, known only as I.M., produced the verse treatise, *A Health to the Gentlemanly profession of Serving-men*, published in 1598. Apart from his initials, its author's identity is unknown but he was probably a higher household servant of some sort. He laments the decline in standards of service, essentially complaining that service in an aristocratic household was no longer a post for a gentleman.[114]

We hear similar laments in every generation. Those who devote their careers to maintaining an elaborate etiquette experience a change in customs and inevitably feel that standards have slipped. They would feel that their world – perhaps the world – was falling apart. In the late sixteenth century large households had to be reduced for the sake of economy. Prestige was sought not through service in a noble household but through the patronage of positions at court and county government.

I.M. bewailed the 'decay of Hospitality and Good House-keeping' that had brought about the decline of the traditional corporate flavour of the aristocratic household in which hospitality was paramount. He outlined the household as it had once been, the better calibre of men formerly called upon to serve: 'First, they were chosen men of witte, discretion, government, and good bringing up' which qualified them for being involved in the serious business, political affairs, and worldly wealth of their lords and masters.[115]

They would also be men of 'valoure and courage, not fearing to fight in the maintenance of their Maister's credite in his just quarell', of 'strength and activitie', to be excellent in the shooting, running, leaping and dancing like those henchmen in the opening scene of *Romeo and Juliet*. Finally, they were 'men of qualitie' to be seen in haulking [hawking], hunting, fyshing and fowling with all such like Gentlemanly pastimes.'[116] These 'were known from the rest by the names of Serving men' and were drawn from a gentlemanly background, as distinct from those in more servile roles.

Although it has to be admitted that the author was probably chiefly concerned with his own loss of status, and evidently thought little of the ordinary working men who came under his command, for him the joy of the service hierarchy was that it inextricably linked all the layers of society:

> Even the Dukes sonne [was] preferred Page to the Prince, the Earles seconde son attendant upon the Duke, the Knight's seconde sonne the Earles servant, the Esquires son to weare the Knyghtes lyverie, and the Gentleman's sonnes the Esquire's [sic] Serving Man. Yea, I know at this day, gentlemen['s] younger brothers that weares their elder brothers Blew coate and Badge, attending him with as revered regard and duetifull obedience, as if he were their Prince or Soveraigne.[117]

Nor did they think this hierarchy 'servile', whilst 'their fare was always of the best, their apparel, fine, neate, handsome and comely'.[118]

It seemed to the author that things had altered beyond redemption: 'The First is, the compounding of this pure and refined mettall (whereof Servingmen were first framed) with untryed dregges and drosse of less esteeme. The seconde is the death and decay of Liberalitie.'[119] Also, younger generations were no longer willing to lay out huge sums on the maintenance of large, unwieldy households, preferring instead to spend extravagantly on luxuries that their parents disdained.

In 'I.M.'s view the upstart new gentry, who were descended from tradesmen, with their preparedness to take on the children of yeomen in place of the better-bred serving men of former times, spelt the beginning of the end:[120] 'The Golden world is past and gone.'[121] It is a pity we do not have any records of the views of the hard-working yeoman's sons, who no doubt considered themselves to be operating much more efficiently and practically than their over-bred predecessors. Whether I.M.'s perception of events was true or not, the nature of the great household was certainly changing. It would rely less and less on large numbers of well-connected attendants, whilst still requiring a degree of comfort, magnificence and hospitality that depended on the skills, labour, and loyalty of others.

2

The Beginning of the Back Stairs and the Servants' Hall

The Seventeenth Century

IN THE SEVENTEENTH century, the households of landowners continued to be complex and hierarchical, but there was a shift from an emphasis on precedence and outward display to one of a more personal, moral and civilised way of life. This was the era of the cultivation of the Renaissance ideal of the gentleman. This adjustment affected the nature of relationships within noble households, which were very different from those of the early and mid-sixteenth century.[1]

The process of change was probably given additional impetus by the economic and social disruptions of the civil war and the Commonwealth in the middle of the century, not least because aristocrats formerly in exile brought home new ideas and patterns of behaviour. The most famous example was the arrival of dining *à la française*, with all the dishes laid out on the table at once, which remained the main form of service until the nineteenth century.[2]

From matters of display, particularly grand dining, to the most minor aspect of country-house life, from estate and household accounting to the removal of slops, households continued to be served by a skilled body of servants whose whole lives might be spent in the service of one family. Somewhat smaller than the medieval community, the seventeenth-century household was still treated in a very hierarchical manner, but as the century progresses there is less emphasis on public service from a gentle-born attendant, and more on developing the specialised roles of the professional domestic servant.

Fynes Moryson, writing in 1617, recorded a proverb that England was the hell of horses, the purgatory of servants and the paradise of women, 'because they ride Horses without measure, and use their

Servants imperiously, and their Women obsequiously' [i.e. with excessive courtesy]. He also noted that households were generally smaller than those of the previous century.[3]

By the end of the seventeenth century, the barrier between employer and servant is drawn more vividly, not least in architectural terms, as from the middle of the century separate 'servants' halls' begin appearing, showing that it was becoming the norm for the servants to dine separately – and out of sight. This custom increased throughout the seventeenth century. More private family dining arrangements are found, and the provision in attics for servants' sleeping garrets is more common, as the aristocratic family wanted less immediate contact with the more menial servants. By this time, we really have moved into the world of upstairs and downstairs.

As historian Mark Girouard described it so memorably in *Life in the English Country House*: 'The gentry walking up the stairs no longer met their last night's faeces coming down them.'[4] However, on a normal day the timing and management of menial servants would probably have been carefully calibrated in the grander houses to avoid such unpleasant encounters.

Aristocratic households continue to be somewhat peripatetic, moving between rural estates or between their country seats and London houses. In the early seventeenth century Sir John Hobart of Blickling Hall in Norfolk used to reduce his staff from twenty-seven to seven when he left his primary seat for a period in London.[5]

There might be as many as 120 staff, as in the Earl of Dorset's household at Knole. Sir Thomas Wentworth of Wentworth Woodhouse (later Earl of Strafford) maintained a staff of sixty-four, including forty-four male servants, six female servants and a chaplain. The household of Sir Edward Carr of Aswarby in Lincolnshire (who in his will made bequests to forty-five servants, thirty-seven of whom were male) incorporated two tutors and a chaplain. A more typical household size for the landed gentry would have been that of Sir John Brownlow of Belton, who at the time of his death in 1679 employed thirty-one servants, twenty-one of them male.[6]

The drive for privacy in the early years of the century was related to emerging ideals of order and economy, as well as to a new sense of cultivation and decorum (even 'taste') that reduced the expectation of the open-house largesse of the late medieval era. One Sir Hugh Cholmley recorded in his memoirs: 'In spring, 1636, I removed from the Gate-house into my house at Whitby, being now finished and fit to receive me; and my dear wife (who was excellent at dressing and making all handsome within doors) had put it into a fine posture, and furnished with many good things, so that I believe, there were few gentlemen in the country, of my rank, exceeded it.' He wrote with pride about his well-ordered life: 'having mastered my debts, I did not only appear at all public meetings in a very gentlemanly equipage, but lived in as handsome and plentiful fashion at home as any gentleman in all the country, of my rank.'

He was pleased too with the number of his staff and their household management:

> I had between thirty and forty in my ordinary family, a chaplain who said prayers every morning at six, and again before dinner and supper, a porter who merely attended the gates, which were ever shut up before dinner, when the bell rang to prayers, and not opened till one o'clock, except for some strangers who came to dinner, which was ever three or four besides my family; without any trouble; and whatever their fare was, they were sure to have a hearty welcome. Twice a week, a certain number of old people, widows and indigent persons, were served at my gates with bread and good pottage of beef.

Sir Hugh compared his own well-ordered housekeeping with that of his grandfather, who always had a crowd of riotous retainers.[7]

The gentleman attendant was still a feature of the early part of the century, but it was rare to find one at its end, except in the role of the steward, who might still be a minor landowner serving a greater lord in his district. Chaplains and secretaries might be well connected and would certainly be well educated. It was common to find a gentlewoman attendant to the lady of a household but this would be increasingly in the role of companion rather than social equal. The governess (also a feature in the sixteenth century) now becomes a familiar component of country-house life, and, as in the nineteenth and twentieth centuries, she was expected to come from a superior background.[8]

The seventeenth century seems to be a critical period in which women assume more and more of the servant roles in a country house, partly because they were cheaper but also because they were able to take on more senior housekeeping duties. Indeed, one could argue, this is the century that established as key characters both housekeeper and governess.

One speaker for the emerging figure of the senior female servant, just as John Russell wrote of the duties of the senior male servants a century and half earlier, is Hannah Wolley. As she was born around 1622 and died in the 1670s, her life spanned the middle years of the century, seeing her through the civil war, the Commonwealth and the Restoration.[9]

Mrs Wolley is a rather modern character, for although she had spent some years in domestic service, she was notably entrepreneurial, using her experience to become an admired – and imitated – author. From the age of seventeen she was in service to a noblewoman, almost certainly Anne, Lady Maynard, who died in 1647. Mrs Wolley continues to have something of a reputation as a writer of recipes today; indeed, she is thought to have been one of the first female British authors to make a reasonable living from her writing, but her reputation rested on her career in service to aristocratic families from the 1630s.[10]

Lady Maynard was the second wife of the 1st Baron Maynard, a gentleman of the Privy Chamber who had been an MP and was lord lieutenant of Cambridgeshire in 1620.[11] He built a house at Easton Lodge, near Bishop's Stortford in Essex, which was given an additional wing and chapel in 1621.[12] The house was completely rebuilt in 1847, but the original can be seen in a 1768 engraving. The site is still discernible in the west wing of Warwick House and a gatehouse on the Stortford Road.

Tantalisingly, an inventory has survived for the house as it was in 1637, entitled 'A Booke of all the householdstuf in Eston Lodge'. It differs from other contemporary inventories in that it does not include clothes and jewels, but is notable for detailing the richness of the furnishings and especially the needlework. It offers a detailed record of the house of Mrs Wolley's youthful service. Lord Maynard died in 1640 'due to a fever brought on by zeal in the King's Service' in putting down an army mutiny.[13]

She presumably left service not long after, as she is next heard of in 1646, when she married Jerome Wolley, master at the free grammar school in Newport, very close to Little Easton. She also helped her husband run a school in Hackney for a time. After he died, she married in 1666 one Francis Challiner, who died before February 1669. She published *The Ladies Directory* in 1661, which was quickly reprinted, following it with *The Cook's Guide* in 1664, *The Queen-Like Closet* in 1670, and *The Ladies Delight* in 1672 – all principally recipe books. Her last authenticated book was *A Supplement to the 'Queen-Like Closet' or A Little of Everything*, which appeared in 1674, with recipes, notes on household management, and instructions for embroidery and letter writing. Her books all show her to be highly educated and able.

Cooks then were still principally men and among her contemporaries her principal rival was fellow author and male master cook Robert May, who had worked for Lord Montague, Lord Lumley, Lord Dormer and Sir Kenelm Digby. His *The Accomplisht Cook* was first published in 1660. In the expanded edition of 1684 he writes of the 'Triumphs and Trophies of cooking' that he created for his earlier patrons, as well as of his alarm at the fashion for French male cooks, who remain much in evidence for the next three centuries.[14]

Mrs Wolley's output is essentially recipe books. *The Ladies Directory*, for instance, sets out a series of recipes for dishes and home remedies, including preserves, jellies and waters with medicinal value. The longer title is 'the ladies directory in choice experiments & curiousities of preserving in jellies, and candying both fruits & flowers: Also, an excellent way of making cakes, comfits, and rich-court perfumes. With rarities of many precious waters; among which . . . excellent water against the plague: with severall consumption drinks, approved by the ablest physicians.'

The Cook's Guide was dedicated to Lady Maynard's daughter, Lady Anne Wroth, and her granddaughter, Mary: 'The Duty I owe to your Ladyship, and the rest of your noble Family, commands more than this book is able to Express; but since ill fate hath made me altogether incapable of any Worthy return of your Love and Bounty, be pleased to accept this as a Signal of what I am obliged to.'

Her second dedication to Mary, the daughter, is a little more revealing, referring explicitly to the importance of the lady of the house being able to direct and educate her own servants in the arts of housekeeping. She writes:

> The sublimity of your Lady Mother's affairs I fear will not permit her very often to view this book; besides her Ladyship needs it not, her acceptation and approbation hereof is my honour only, not her benefit; your practice will be my content, and I doubt not your own. It is a miserable thing for any Woman, though never so great, not to be able to teach her Servants; there is no fear of it in you, since you begin so soon to delight in those Sciences as may and will accomplish you.[15]

Mrs Wolley refers to having prepared a banquet for King Charles I, presumably while in service to the Maynards. She writes of 'very choice Receipts [recipes] . . . from my own Practice, who have had the honour to perform such things for the Entertainment of His late Majesty, as well as for the Nobility'.[16] No painted portrait of Mrs Wolley survives, as far as I am aware, but in her writings we get more than a flavour of a Mrs Beeton-like character and tone of voice.

The Gentlewomans Companion was first published under Wolley's name in 1673, although Wolley herself complained that this was a plagiarised version of her own manuscript brought out by the publisher, Dorman Newman, trying to cash in on her success and popularity.[17] But then it was quickly reprinted in 1675 and still carried her name as author. It contains a biographical note in the beginning, 'A Short account of the life and abilities of Authoress of this Book', in which the assumed author cites her modesty, her previous books and listed her skills, including 'Preserving all kinds of Sweet-meats wet and dry', 'Setting out of Banquets', and 'All manner of Cookery'. It claims that at the age of fifteen she was 'intrusted to keep a little School', and was already in the enviable position of accomplishments in Italian, singing, dancing and instrument playing.

After two years, she was taken on as a governess to 'a Noble Lady in the Kingdom' who 'was infinitely pleas'd' with her learning. During this time she learns the arts of cooking and preserving, and became 'acquainted with the Court, with a deportment suitable thereunto.' After her mistress's death, she moved to employment with another lady whom she serves – first in the role of governess, then of steward-ess (or housekeeper) and finally of secretary – for another seven years, in which she 'kept an exact account of what was spent in the house' and gained knowledge of 'Physick and Chirurgery [i.e. surgery]'.[18]

Although this may not be an entirely accurate picture, much of this biographical material seems to have been adapted from Mrs Wolley's previously published books. Her known works, and those possibly by other hands under her name, all make much of the fact that gentlewomen may have been 'forced to service' on account of being 'impoverished by the late calamities, viz. the late Wars, Plague and Fire', as Mrs Wolley herself observed in her confirmed autograph work, *The Queen-Like Closet*.[19]

The stresses on aristocratic and gentry families in this period might well have driven some widows and daughters into service in other households just to survive. *The Gentlewomans Companion* (1675) encourages parents to 'endeavour the gentile [gentle] education of their Daughters, encouraging them to learn whatever opportunity offers, worthy [of] a good estimation. *For riches hath wings, and will quickly fly away*; or Death comes and removes the Parents, leaving the Children to the tuition of merciless and unconscionable Executors.'

If they are not trained in the arts of housekeeping, parents lay their daughters open to having to accept more humble jobs: 'their Daughters are often exposed to great hardships, many times content-ing themselves to serve as Chamber-maids, because they have not the Accomplishments of a Waiting-woman, or an House-keeper.'[20] The same book records the duties of the governess to the children of the gentlewomen, a feature of country house life long before the nine-teenth century: 'They who undertake the difficult Employ of being an Instructress or Governess of Children should be persons of no mean birth and breeding, civil in deportment, and of extraordinary winning and pleasing conversation.'

A governess is to study 'diligently the nature, disposition, and inclination of those she is to teach'. Aside from books of piety, the author also recommends romances 'which treat of Generosity, Gallantry, and Virtue', including Sir Philip Sidney's *Arcadia*, as well as all 'productions of the needle', plus rock-work, moss-work and cabinet-work, in addition to preserving, conserving and distillation: 'those laudable Sciences which adorn a Compleat Gentlewomen'.[21]

Lady Anne Clifford recalled her governess Mrs Anne Taylour with affection as one of the main influences on her life, along with her tutor. She had plenty of companions to choose from in her adult life too, as illustrated in an extremely rare document at Knole in Kent. Described as '*A catalogue of the Household and Family of the Right Honourable Richard, Earl of Dorset*', it hangs in a frame in the part of the house occupied by the present Lord Sackville and lists all those who made up the household of the Earl and Countess of Dorset (the play-boy grandson of the 1st Earl and his serious-minded wife, Lady Anne) as it was between 1613 and 1624.[22]

The Knole catalogue details where staff would sit for meals, whether in the Great Chamber, the Parlour, the Great Hall, at high and long tables, the Dairy, or the Kitchen and Scullery. It even mentions the handful of permanent staff who stayed in Dorset House in London when the main household went elsewhere.

The size of the household of Lady Anne's second husband, Philip Herbert, Earl of Pembroke, in the mid-seventeenth century was of a similar number, as recalled by John Aubrey in *Brief Lives*:

'Tis certain, the Earles of Pembroke were the most popular Peers in the West of England; but one might boldly say, in the whole Kingdome. The Revenue of this Family was till about 1652, 16,000 pounds per annum. But with his offices and all he had thirty thousand Pounds per annum. And, as the Revenue was great, so the greatnesse of his Retinue, and Hospitality were answerable. One hundred and twenty Family uprising and down lyeing: whereof you may take out six or seven, and all the rest Servants, and Retayners.[23]

The Knole household list illustrates just the same type of 'Family'. The Knole catalogue itself is, unusually, written on vellum, which suggests that it may have been drawn up for a commemorative purpose rather than merely as a record; indeed, it is accompanied by a humble prayer for the health of the household and especially the mistress, signed by Henry Keble, yeoman of the pantry. The presence of the names of all the servants adds a considerable resonance to the document, with surnames that might still be found in Kent today. Vita Sackville-West certainly made use of them in her novel, *The Edwardians*, set in Knole in the early twentieth century, for example calling the butler Vigeon, who on this household list appears as the huntsman.

It may well have been some sort of a memorial of the household who had stood by Lady Anne (she became Countess of Pembroke after the death of the Earl of Dorset) during the period when she was being denied her rightful inheritance (which had been seized by the Earl of Cumberland), the mistress's woes and successes having been shared by the whole household. Being of a famously indomitable spirit, she held out for her inheritance. She later wrote of the castles that Cromwell pulled down: 'Let him destroy my Castles if he will, as often as he levels them I will rebuild them, so long as he leaves me with a shilling in my pocket.'[24]

It seems that the family usually ate in private, upstairs in the Great Chamber, and the senior servants ate in the Parlour (today the private family dining room, and long known as the Poet's Parlour after the portraits that hang there), but on certain days all might still eat with the immediate family and some senior attendants on the raised dais in the Great Hall.[25]

There would have been a degree of ceremony at mealtimes, perhaps similar to that observed in the lodgings of the courtier, the Earl of Carlisle, by Thomas Raymond, a nephew of one of Lord Carlisle's retainers: 'I have often seen his diet carried from his kitchen across the court at Whitehall, 20 or 25 dishes covered, mostly by gentlemen richly habited, with the steward marching before and the clerk of the kitchen bringing up the rear, all bareheaded. This for the first and as many more for the second course.'[26]

At the 'Parlour Table' sat the senior household officers, whose responsibilities, education or birth put their status only just below that of the family. The women are waiting women; notably the men, including the chaplain, steward, and the gentleman of the horse, are given the title Mr, are referred to as gentlemen and are ranked above those who worked with their hands.

At the 'Clerk's Table in the Hall' came the next rung of senior servants, skilled and dependable, including clerks of the kitchen, who were in charge of purchasing kitchen provisions, Henry Keble, a pastryman, three cooks, a slaughterman, a groom of the great chamber, two gardeners, a caterer or provisions purchaser and one Lowry, 'a French Boy'.

The yeoman of the buttery eventually absorbs the roles of the pantry and by the end of the century has become the butler, operating from a room known as the pantry or butler's pantry, whilst the groom of the chamber remains an identifiable post well into the twentieth century, by which time it has responsibility for the condition and presentation of public rooms.[27]

It is notable that the gardeners are here in the senior rank of yeoman servants; given that there are only two of them, they probably had additional labour brought in as necessary.[28] It is worth remembering that this was the age of gardeners such as John Tradescant. The elaborate gardens of the seventeenth century required head gardeners of impressive tradecraft. The Company of Gardeners, incorporated in 1605, specified apprenticeships of seven years and enumerated the skills expected of the professional gardener for 'the trade crafte or misterie of Gardening', which included 'planting grafting Setting sowing . . . covering fencing and removing of Plantes herbes seedes fruites trees Stockes Settes and of contryving the conveyances to the same belonging'.[29]

Tradescant, who in died 1638, is perhaps the most famous of the early-seventeenth-century gardeners associated with a great country house, as he was the principal gardener to Robert Cecil (created Earl of Salisbury), and working at Hatfield by 1610. A contemporary note on expenditure refers to work in the kitchen garden there: 'diging dunging sowing & planting of Earbes Rootes hartichokes . . . & all other Earbes nessicarie [necessary] for the kichen with the keepping Clene of the gardin & geving Attendance for the sarving of the house with thes Nessicaries'. Under the gardeners in that kitchen garden alone were three workmen, two labourers and six women weeders at 6d a day, suggesting the scale of gardening operations in the early seventeenth century.[30]

At Knole, the nursery staff are also mentioned in the household catalogue, but presumably they dined in a chamber dedicated to the nursery. At the 'Long Table in the Hall' were seated various attendants, and, among others, a barber, the groom of 'my Lord's Chamber', the yeoman of the wardrobe, the Master Huntsman, the yeoman of the great chamber, a falconer and an armourer.

The group comprising the stables and coach staff includes various grooms, plus a chief footman with six junior footmen under him. Clearly many more footmen were employed, in contrast to the single individual footman listed in the household of the Earl of Northumberland in 1511. Also footmen were evidently regarded as part of the coaching establishment and ranked separately from those of the chamber and the kitchen, although by the end of the seventeenth century the footmen had become the principal serving attendants in the dining room. Coach travel was more and more important in the seventeenth century, as carriage design improved and they increasingly became an object of display, leading John Evelyn to regret the speed at which everyone travelled and yearn for the more stately progress of former years.[31]

Among the lowest-ranking servants at Knole were the servants of the servants: the steward's man, a multitude of every type of groom, the under farrier or blacksmith, the chaplain's man, two huntsmen including George Vigeon, the bird-catcher, a postilion (who rode on the forward pair of horses to help keep them heading in the right direction), the armourer's man and *his* servant, and two men to carry wood for fires.

At the Laundrymaids' Table, which may not have been in the hall, sat a number of women, including Lady Margaret's maid, 'a Blackamoor', and a porter. Confined to the Kitchen and Scullery were another group, also including 'a Blackamoor'.[32] The two black servants were presumably slaves, and one of the named men or boys may have turned the spit in the kitchen.

Lady Anne Clifford kept a detailed diary, which provides further insight into the challenges posed by her life, as well as the closeness of mistress and household. Her marriage to the Earl of Dorset was notoriously difficult, and the servants played a sensitive role when unwelcome news had to be passed from one spouse to the other. Their relationship was evidently problematic, not least as a result of the complications surrounding her inheritance. She writes in May 1616:

> Upon the 2nd came Mr Legg [the earl's steward] & told divers of the Servants that my Lord would come down & see me once more, which would be the last time that I should see him again.

Lady Anne was then separated from her own child and household servants had to arrange everything.

> Upon the 3rd came Baskett [the earl's gentleman of the horse] down from London & brought me a Letter from my Lord by which I might see it was his pleasure that the Child should go the next day to London, which at first was somewhat grievous to me, but when I considered it would both make my Lord angry with me & be worse for the Child, I resolved to let her go. After I had sent for Mr Legg and talked with him about that and other matters and [I] wept bitterly.

The steward presumably was the only person in whom she could openly confide at the time. It could be risky for servants to take sides in such fallings-out, given their dependent situation.[33]

> Upon the 4th being Saturday, between 10 & 11 the Child went into the Litter to go to London, Mrs Bathurst & her two maids with Mr Legge & a good Company of the Servants going with her . . . [on the 10th] came the Stewards from London whom I expected would have given warning to many of the Servants to go away because the Audits was newly come up. Upon the 11th being Sunday, before Mr Legge went away I talked with him an hour or two about all this Business & matters between me & my Lord, so as I gave him better satisfaction & made him conceive a better opinion of me than ever he did.[34]

In November 1619, she also records losing at gambling to two of the household's senior servants: 'Upon the 2nd I had such ill luck with playing at Glecko [a card game] with Legge & Basket that I said

I would not play again in six months.'[35] Evidently Lady Anne would often spend private social time with senior servants, as almost as if they were members of her family. In her old age she had a portrait painted of herself, in which one panel depicted her as a young girl, with the portraits of her tutor Samuel Daniel and her governess Mrs Anne Taylour – who had helped frame the mind that survived so many vicissitudes – hanging above her.[36]

The fortunes of a whole household could rest very uneasily on the fate of a master or mistress imprisoned for treason in the politically volatile years at the beginning of the century, or caught up in the civil war. This is illustrated by a tearful letter from Lady Arbella Stuart, a cousin of Charles I, to Gilbert Talbot, Earl of Shrewsbury, dated 16 July 1610, shortly after she and her husband, William Seymour, had been arrested after their secret marriage. As both were possible claimants to the English throne, the king's permission was required for their union. In fact she died in 1615 while still in capitivity.

She writes pathetically of her servants and their uncertain future:

> If it please your lordship theare are diverse of my servants with whom I [never] thought to have been parted [from] whilest I lived; and none that I am willing to part with. But since I am taken from them, and know not how to maintain either my selfe or them, being utterly ignorant how it will please his Majesty to deal with me I weare better to put them away [dismiss them] now, than towards winter. Your Lordship knowes the greatnesse of my debts and [my] unablenesse to do for them either now or at Michaelmasse.

Michaelmas was a traditional date from which servants were hired or released from hire. She continues: 'I beseech your Lordship let me know what hope you can give me of his Majestie's favour with out which I and all mine must live in great discomfort.'[37]

The dependent status of household servants was a critical aspect of the loyalty and patronage that they owed to the head of the household, an important nexus of relationships illustrated by the letters and accounts of the richest landed proprietor of the Protestant settlement of Ireland in the early seventeenth century. Richard Boyle, the 1st

Earl of Cork, was a Kent-born adventurer who built up a considerable estate in Munster, centred on Lismore Castle, which has passed by descent to the Duke of Devonshire.

In 1640, Boyle's annual income from these estates was probably around £8,000; during the period 1629–39 he was the lord justice and lord treasurer of Ireland. Whilst an extraordinarily astute politician, he experienced great insecurity, on the one hand being persecuted by the lord deputy Wentworth, and on the other subjected to an armed siege by forces led by the Irish Catholic gentry in 1641. He died in 1643.[38]

Lismore Castle, an ancient bishop's palace, which he adapted rather than rebuilt, has changed out of all recognition from its seventeenth-century form. In Cork's time the house is known to have been richly furnished, with extensive silver. Typically for a late-sixteenth- or seventeenth-century household of status, the quantity of servants was an expression of status in itself, as well as supporting the exercise of power (which took on an extra significance, being part of the Protestant settlement).

Some flavour of the life of this still peripatetic household is given in a manuscript set of brief regulations for the earl's English house, in Dorset, *A Form for the Government of the Earl of Cork's Family at Stalbridge*, which was built in the 1630s. The regulations are signed by Thomas Cross, his steward, and include reference to daily household prayers:

1. First, All the Servants except such as are Officers or are otherwise employed shall meet every morning before Dinner, and every night after Supper, at Prayer.
2. That there be lodgings fitting for all the Earl of Cork's servants to lie in the house.
3. That it shall be lawful for the Steward to examine any Subordinate Servant of the whole Family concerning any Complaint or Misdemeanour committed, and to dismiss and put away any inferior Servant that shall live dissolutely and disorderly either in the House or abroad, without the especial Command of the Earl of Cork to the contrary.

4. That there be a certain number of the Gentlemen appointed to sit at the Steward's Table, and the like at the Waiter's Table, and the rest to sit in the Hall at the Long Table.

5. That there be a Clerk to the Kitchen to take care of such Provision as is brought into the House, and to have an especial eye to the several Tables that are kept either above Stairs, or in the Kitchen and other places.

6. That all the Women Servants under the Degree of Chambermaids be certainly known by their names to the Steward, and not altered or changed upon every Occasion without the consent of the Steward, and no Schorers [vagrants?] to be admitted in the house.

7. That the Officers every Friday night bring in their Bills to the Steward whereby he may collect what hath been spent, and what remains weekly in the House.[39]

The household is still described here as 'family', as in the Latin sense in which it was used in the medieval and Tudor periods, meaning everyone in it. Note the emphasis on moral issues, particularly the separate treatment of women, and how discipline was exercised by senior offices with their lord's consent. Lord Cork took a seemingly inordinate interest in the details of the lives and marriages of his servants, and was evidently proud of the settlements he made on them.[40] For example, in 1628 he recorded: 'My wife's woman Mrs Mary Evesham was contracted to Mr John Ward of Dublin by my cousin Robert Naylor my chaplain, in the nursery of Lismore, in the presence of myself, my wife, my son, and Mr Whalley, and in the presence of them all I gave her £100 in gold which she presently gave her new betrothed husband.'[41] Although he clearly did employ indigenous Irish, his senior servants at Lismore were largely brought over from England.

The Earl of Cork's many bequests to his servants rewarded the long service of trustworthy individuals who created a secure and dignified oasis around him amid the tumult of early-seventeenth-century politics. During this period of upheaval, his sons (including Robert, who later became a famous scientist) were stranded in Europe on their Grand Tour in the care of their tutor Mr Marcombe, who had been recommended to Lord Cork by Sir Henry Wotton, provost of Eton. They had to cool their heels in Marseilles, waiting for money that was held up by the Munster rising before being able to travel on. An employer placed great trust in such a man.

Lord Cork's bequests include one of £20 to William Chettle, who 'waited upon me in my chamber and carried my purse for above 26 year)', plus 'a debt of £195 stirling all other my wearing Linnen and Apparell which I shall have at my Death and is not disposed of in my Last Will + Testament'. Bequests of clothing may have been made for their resale value as well as for everyday use. In his will, he asked his son to continue to employ Chettle in this capacity; indeed, he asked his son to maintain all the servants so mentioned. Old Davy Gibbons, the footman messenger, was rewarded for thirty years' faithful service with a lease of lands, to which Lord Cork added money to stock the farm. There is also evidence of the clothes left to servants, to William Chettle: 'a new cloak that I had never wore of London Russet lined throughout with black velvet', to John Eddow, 'French green satin doublet with points of gold and green' and to John Narron: 'a tawny satin doublet'.[42] Perhaps they were worn, or perhaps more likely sold for their monetary value.

The many examples of household servants being remembered in employers' legacies in the seventeenth century are testimony to the two-way traffic of loyalty and interdependence in the aristocratic and gentry household. Such legacies went principally to the senior servants, such as stewards, cooks and butlers, the more intimate and personal attendants, but not exclusively so. In 1675, William Dutton of Sherborne, Gloucestershire, left annuities amounting to £91 a year to twelve of his servants. In 1684, Sir John Borlase of Bockmer House, in Buckinghamshire, made annuities of £190 shared between ten individuals. Some servants might receive cash legacies: Richard Windwood of Ditton Park, Buckinghamshire, left £20 each to his menservants, and £10 to the women.[43]

Some bequests provide an insight into the love-hate world of country-house service. In a will of 1686, Sir Nicholas Bacon of Shrubland Hall, Suffolk, originally left a bequest of £20 to Edward Inolds, the boy who waited on him, but later cut him out of the will, describing him as 'that ungratefull' rogue. In 1697, Sir Richard Earle of Stragglethorpe in Lincolnshire made a legacy to his servant, Thomas Waller, rather touchingly 'begging of him to be sober'.[44]

The employer's responsibility for the welfare and morals of members of his household, exemplified by such bequests, is reflected in the many seventeenth-century manuals of guidance on household management, which emphasised this strongly. Robert Cleaver's *A Godlie Forme of Householde Governmente* (1603) exhorts masters to look after their servants, 'not onely in providing for them wholesome meat, drink and lodging, and otherwise to help them, comfort them, and relieve and cherish them in health as well in sicknesse as in health.'

Cleaver also advised that the master should rule and correct the menservants, and his wife the maidservants, a recurring theme right up to the early twentieth century, 'for a man's nature scorneth and disdaineth to bee beaten of a woman, and a maides nature is corrupted with the stripes of a man.' Servants, Cleaver wrote, should in their turn be 'so full of curtesie as not a word will be spoken by their masters to them, or by them to their masters, but the knee shall be bowed withall: they can stand hour after hour before their masters, and not once put on their hat'.[45]

A sense of responsibility for the lives of your employees was surely not unreasonable in the circumstances of the time. Some guidance, however, seems alarmingly harsh today. Sir Miles Sandys in 1634 wrote of the importance of the householder addressing the morals of those in their care: 'as neere as you can, to beate down Sinne in them, especially that of Swearing.'[46]

Clearly, physical chastisement of servants was not uncommon. Adam Eyre, another Puritan and a captain in the civil war, recorded in his diary for 9 October 1647: 'This night I whipped Jane for her foolishness as yesterday I did for her slothfulness . . . and hence I am induced to bewail my sinfull life, for my failings in the presence of God Almighty are questionless greater than hers are to me.'[47]

In his tract, *An Exposition of the Domesticall Duties* (1622), William Gouge wrote: 'Some [employers] make no difference betwixt servants; but esteem of bad and good all alike; they think that the best servants do but their duty. . . . But it is a point of wisdom to account a duty as a kindness; especially when good will of heart is joined with outward performance of duty.' Paying good wages was, he thought, just such a matter of duty: 'When masters do altogether detain their servants' wages; this is a crying sin, which entereth into the ears of God.' Employers should value the skills and loyalty of their staff, for 'Masters and Mistresses are flesh and blood as well as servants, and so subject to weakness, sickness, old age, and other distresses, wherein they may stand in great need of servants' help.'[48]

Sir Henry Chauncy eulogised as a model employer Sir Charles Caesar of Bennington (who died in 1624). He was apparently treated with some awe by his servants.

> very regular in his Life, and orderly in his Family [meaning household], which made the Lives of his Servants very easie, and his House very quiet, never reprimanding a Servant oftner than once, and if the Party offended again, he was silently discharged without Noise or Notice of his Displeasure.[49]

Often in the story of a particular house, one servant stands out on whom the head of the household especially relies. Sir Henry Slingsby, 1st Baronet of Red House in Yorkshire, was eventually executed under the Commonwealth for his allegiance to the king. But in 1638, before the civil war overturned his world for ever, he recorded his whole household of thirty, including sixteen male and eight female servants, whom he called good, faithful and diligent. In the middle of describing his house, he paused to observe of one carved-relief portrait:

> There is above ye door that goes into ye inner chamber a head carved in wood like a Roman head, wch I caused to be made for him yt keeps ye chambers & has charge of ye Wardrobe, as a remembrance of him that has so long & faithfully serv'd. This man Francis Oddy was servant to my father many years & since has served me: my father at his death [1634] . . . did recommend this man Francis Oddy to me having good experiences of his fidelity and diligence & even such I find him hitherto. He serves me in ye way of upholsterer wn there is need to furnish ye Lodging rooms and dress ym up: he serves me for a caterer to buy all manner of provisions for the house, & to keep the wine cellar. He is of a very low stature, his head little,

& his hair cut short, his face lean and full or wrinkles, his complec-
tion such that yt shows he has endured all wethers: his disposition
not suitable wth ye rest of his fellow servants which does either by
diligence breed envy, or else through plain dealing Stir up Variance
& having a working head [good intelligence] is in continual
debate.[50]

Sir Henry Slingsby also recorded his trouble keeping cooks:

Last Sunday my Cook George Taylor went to be marry'd to a maid of
Doctor Wickhams at York, & if she be so head strong as they say she
is, he will after find his service here freedom in respect of the bondage
he must undergo. This cook hath been the freest from disorder of five
several cooks w[hi]ch I have had since I became a housekeeper; some
of w[hi]ch hath been w[i]th out all measure disordered [referring to
their drunkenness] and for their curiosity in the art of cookery I do
not much value.[51]

The calamitous downside of country-house service, favouritism, is
all too vividly illustrated by the story of Florence Fitzpatrick, the
young Irish footman who was caught up in the extraordinary downfall of Mervyn Touchet, the 2nd Earl of Castlehaven, when his large
household at Fonthill Gifford, in Wiltshire, imploded with intrigue
and sexual misconduct.[52] The case demonstrates not only how the
intimacy of the country-house community could have its dark side
(some believe that the earl was the victim of a conspiracy more
inspired by property rights than morality) but also how a young man
could prosper as the favourite of a rich peer and landowner.

Another servant, Henry Skipwith, a favourite of Lord Castlehaven's,
became involved in a liaison with the earl's wife, apparently at the
earl's instigation. Whether or not his heir, James, Lord Audley,
objected to this, when the earl gave Skipwith some £12,000, Lord
Audley was so taken aback that he petitioned the king in the 'hope to
find him a father when my own forsakes me'. Lord Audley may well
not have foreseen the drastic outcome of his initial appeal, which led
within a few months to his father's imprisonment, trial and subsequent execution for engaging in sodomy with his footman Florence
Fitzpatrick, and assisting in the rape of his wife by another manservant, Giles Broadway. Both menservants were also executed, perhaps

reflecting the Privy Council's fear of the social subversion that these events represented rather than the issue of criminal sexuality.[53]

On the witness stand, the countess described her husband's involvement with 'prostitutes and serving boys', and claimed that he had encouraged her to have sexual intercourse with his favourites in the household, one of whom was John Anktill. The younger son of a Dorsetshire family who had first arrived as a page to Lord Castlehaven, Anktill worked his way up to become a steward of some of the earl's estates. In 1621, he was elected as an MP to represent the family interest, which was a common enough occurrence. Without the earl's permission, he married Lord Castlehaven's eldest daughter. He was called as a witness in the trial, in the course of which he is described as having been the sexual partner of both the earl and the countess.[54]

Henry Skipwith, Lord Castlehaven's closest servant, who had much prospered in his master's service, was born to a father of no set occupation and a mother who distilled 'hot waters', yet within a few years he was sitting at a lord's table. Skipwith was named in the trial as the lover of not only the earl and the countess, but of the earl's fifteen-year-old daughter-in-law, Lady Audley.

Lord Castlehaven claimed that the charges were a conspiracy and that he had been guilty of nothing more than unusual generosity to his servants; it was certainly unusual to be convicted on the evidence of only your wife and servants: 'It is my estate, my Lords, that does accuse me this day, and nothing else.' He and his two menservants were dispatched together in May 1631.[55]

There may well have been some element of politics involved, as these events took place in the years that led up to the civil war. Although complex in political terms, the conflict did not give birth to a major social revolution of the type that might have set household servants against their employers. In the regions, most of the smaller landowners seem to maintain their traditional allegiances to major local families.[56] Similarily, servants in noble households seem to have largely followed the allegiances of their lord and master.

Certainly, household servants often became involved in military actions, not least in the sieges of houses belonging to Parliamentary and Royalist owners equally, as in the famous Basing House siege in 1645, or in the 1643 siege of Brampton Bryan Castle in Herefordshire. The defender of the latter was Lady Harley, whose unusual first name was Brilliana, and who was the wife of a Member of Parliament who under Cromwell was Master of the Mint. This indomitable woman withstood a sustained Royalist offensive at the head of her household servants, with only one military veteran and a Hereford doctor to advise her. Shortly before it took place, she wrote to her son of how her servants were being harassed by soldiers, and during the hostilities she noted the mortal wounding of a household servant: 'on August 18: our honest cook received a shot through his left arm.'[57] He died a week later. The siege was lifted, but brave Lady Harley soon succumbed to pneumonia, after which the house fell to the Royalists.[58]

In ancient custom, a landowner summoned to bear arms for the king would come at the head of some portion of his household servants, armed for action. An echo of this expectation is suggested by the summons sent by Lord Pembroke and received by Sir Edmund Verney, Knight, of Claydon House, Buckinghamshire on 7 February 1639, which refers directly to the attendance of servants: 'His Majesty's royal pleasure is that all occasions set apart you be in readiness in your own person by the 1st of April next at the city of Yorke, as a cuirassier in russett arms, with gilded studs or nails and befittingly horsed, and your servants which shall wait upon you horst in white arms, after the manner of a hargobusier [mounted rifleman], in good equipage.'[59] Sir William Russell's troop included 'twelve of his servants in scarlet cloaks, well horsed, and armed'. Colonel Edmund Ludlow went to war accompanied by Henry Cole, an old family retainer who had been his father's groom.[60]

Claydon House was never attacked, although Sir Edmund's wife's old family home at Hillesden was besieged, taken and destroyed by fire. Sir Edmund never returned to his own home and died, reputedly still holding the king's standard, at the Battle of Edgehill on 23 October 1642. A servant was sent to find his body and bring it home, but was unable to recover it.[61]

Daniel Defoe's *Memoir of a Cavalier* (1724), now thought to be based on an actual seventeenth-century memoir, includes one account of a household of servants acting in concert like a small private army, commanded by their mistress whose husband was fighting elsewhere, in a similar spirit to that of Brilliana Harley. As he recounted: 'our men had besieged some fortified house about Oxfordshire, towards Thame, and the house being defended by the lady in her husband's absence, she had yielded the house upon her capitulation.' One of the stipulations of her surrender was that she was 'to march out with all her servants, soldiers and goods', but they are intercepted by some drunken troops on the road. 'The lady, who had been more used to the smell of powder than he imagined, called some of her servants to her, and, consulting with them what to do, they all unanimously encouraged her to let them fight.'[62]

Many servants fought at their employers' side, literally standing by men and women to whom they owed loyalty and service, as much as to the cause their masters espoused. There is one particularly moving story recorded in Aubrey's highly anecdotal *Brief Lives*, describing a servant's identification of the corpse of Lucius Cary, 1st Viscount Falkland, killed in 1643 at the Battle of Newbury. The account concludes: 'The next day when they went to bury the dead, they could not find his Lordship's body; it was stript and trod-upon and mangled, so there was one that wayted upon him in his chamber would undertake to know it from all other bodyes, by a certaine Mole his Lordship had in his Neck, and by that marke did find it.' This touching account illustrates more than any other the intimacy of domestic service.[63]

Exile touched many of the landowning families of England, after the wars subsided. Edmund Verney's son Ralph, initially a supporter of the Parliamentary cause, took his family with him to France in voluntary exile, returning in 1653. The large number of private letters among the extensive Verney papers are littered with references to the problem of maintaining servants while in exile. Sir Henry Newton wrote to Ralph Verney: 'I forgott in my last to acquaint you with the parting of my Boy Estienne, Who having of a long time play'd some prankes, made me at last resolve to pay him his arrearages.' He was rude and openly defied his employers.

Drunkenness was also a problem: 'though he knew he was complained of, hee was so sencelesse as for a whole afternoon when my wife and I were abroad with a coach to neglect us and bee debauch'd with another lacquay [who] should have been also following the coach.' The poor feckless child did indeed run away after a beating but he was caught by another servant.[64]

Lady Verney struggled to keep her favourite maid, Lucy (sometimes Luce), whose brother wanted her to leave service with the Verneys. Lucy confided to her mistrees that her brother had promised to settle 'seven or eight pounds a year upon [her] for her life and be good to her' if she agreed to come home, and had threatened that he would disown her if she refused. He was a man of '2 or 3 hundred pound a year and scorns that his sister should serve'. This vividly illustrates the shift in the social status of service in noble and gentry households after the civil war.

This state of affairs was vexatious to Lady Verney because Lucy suited her so well, both for coming from a decent background and for not being wealthy in her own right.[65] Lady Verney wrote to her husband: 'for I know I cannot expect ever to have so good a servant again and for my greater trouble he will have her away before Christmas'. She felt she was unlikely to 'get one that knows how to dress me that will be content to do half the work that she does, for they are all grown so fine that one cannot have any chamber maid that will serve under 4 or 5 pound a year wages at least and besides they will neither wash nor starch'.[66]

Finding English female domestics when in exile in France had also been a challenge: 'I know no English maids will ever be content (or stay a weeke) to faire as these servants faire . . . Noe English maide will be content with our diet and way of liveing: for my part, I have not had one bit of Rost meate to dinner.' Of one possible local maid, Sir Ralph Verney wrote somewhat disparagingly to his wife: 'it is hard to find one here of our Religion . . . [but this one is] a civile wench and plays well of the Lute, and she is well clad and well bredd, but raw to service'[67]

Later, Sir Ralph Verney's bachelor uncle wrote confidentially to advise his nephew that he had engaged a maid who would travel with them into France 'For £3 per annum. Because you writ me word that you were in love with Dirty Sluts, I took great care to fit you with a Joan that may be as good as my Lady in the dark, and I hope

I have fitted you with a pennyworth.' It is not known whether the maid was subject to her master's advances after this lascivious introduction, although the letter goes on to hint that Sir Ralph had already slept with his wife's faithful maid, Luce.[68]

When Lady Verney returned home to Claydon House in Buckinghamshire after four years' absence she learnt what might happen to a dwelling when no longer sufficiently cared for, complaining to her husband: 'the house is most lamentably furnished, all the linen is quite worn out . . . the feather beds that were walled up are much eaten with Ratts', the roasting spits were 'eaten up with rust' and 'Musk-coloured stools . . . spoiled, and the dining-room chairs in rags'.[69]

In January 1653, when his exile came to an end, Sir Ralph Verney wrote from Brussels to a friend, Dr Denton, of his preparations to return to the house at Claydon, reflecting on his new situation and the need for economies against the awareness of status: 'If I must keepe house which I am willing to doe if you advise it, I will keep but one woeman kind, who must wash my small Linnen (bed & board linen shall bee put out) and cleane both house & Vessels which she may doe for I sup not; if she could cook also I should not bee sorry.'

He had views too about the men he might employ: 'for men I intend to keep only a Coachman & 2 footmen; or a Vallet de chambre & one footman; or which I like much better a Page & a Footman, but if persons of my condition keep not pages in England I will not bee singuler, though they are used here and in France, & by reason they ride behind the coach, not in it, are better than any Vallet de chambre.'[70]

He then addressed the matter of the housekeeper, who continued to live at Claydon, asked what other servants were still in place and what new household supplies would be needed. He later sent down a new male cook and asked the steward to encourage the new arrival to use his leisure in learning to read and write, as he was worried that 'Idlenesse may spoil him'; presumably he hoped the new cook could make use of the growing number of printed cookery books. He wrote later to ask whether the housekeeper approved of the newcomer, stressing his views on smoking and drinking: 'I shall suffer no man that's either debauch[ed] or unruly in my house, nor doe I hier [hire] any servant that takes tobacco, for it not only stinks upp my house, but is an ill example to the rest of my Family.'[71]

Sir Ralph wrote to his faithful steward William Coleman, in preparation for a return to the house many years later, after a trip to London on 7 July 1696, and asked that two village men be employed to lie in his bed and air it, as in those days there was a great fear of the consequences of sleeping on damp linen: 'When Hicks and Parrot lie in my bed give them strong beer and keep my coming as private as you can.' Later he wrote to Coleman, asking after his health: 'Pray be careful of a cold and advise the other servants to be so too . . . I had much rather my business be undone, than you should receive any prejudice [harm] by doing it.' Sir Ralph's relationship with his housekeeper in his final years was such that she often chided him when she thought him in the wrong. Between 1692 and 1717, she wrote him at least 106 letters.[72] Sir Ralph also had a trusted secretary, Charles Hodges, who not only wrote his letters and looked after his money but witnessed legal documents. At the end of the century he was one of the three most senior servants at Claydon.[73]

Sir Ralph's son Edmund (known as Mun, who died in 1688) had famously less straightforward relationships with his servants. His chief servant, Nurse Curzon, was described as 'old, crazy and decayed, and hath more need to have one to look to her, than to look after others'. Edmund was made indignant by servants' petty thefts: 'I caused my little boy Thom Warner to be whipped againe this morning for more faults than this sheet will contain, viz picking pockets, opening Boxes that were lockt, picking locks, stealing, lying etc.'[74]

However, Mun himself was not above having affairs with three women in his own household, and sired at least one child by a servant. Indeed, the mother of one of his illegitimate offspring, one 'Mathew Verney', was the wetnurse to his own children. Mun left her a house and income in his will.[75] John Verney, the eventual heir to Sir Ralph, is said in his turn to have fathered a child with a servant while a young man.[76] Those familiar with Samuel Pepys's diary will need no reminding of the vulnerability of maidservants to the repeated attentions of their masters.[77]

Whilst at the end of the seventeenth century many of the servants in the Verney household may have been recruited locally, some migrated to London to improve their opportunities. In 1695, the coachman who worked for John Verney, Sir Ralph's heir, gave notice 'not to get a better place, but . . . to set up a hackney coach and drive it himself'. John added, in a revealing aside that could have been written in 1895, 'His wife is a proud woman and he hath a little of it himself, and they think it below 'em to be a servant.'[78]

Although the civil war and the Commonwealth may not have changed country-house life overnight, during that period political attention was shifted away from the great households and their country seats, to focus instead on Parliament, London and the court. After the Restoration, the London season is born, following the rhythm of the sittings of Parliament and the location of the court; it was then that the landowner would spend time in the capital and, indeed, invest dizzying sums on his social life there.

The account books of the Earl of Bedford, based at Woburn Abbey in Bedfordshire, show that he still maintained a considerable household at the Restoration, and spent money with the intention of reasserting some of the social prestige and courtliness of the aristocracy, which had been suspended under the Commonwealth. Some relate to the earl's presence in the procession attending the king's return after the Commonwealth in appropriate – and highly expensive – glamour, an illustration of the display felt necessary after the years of Commonwealth austerity.[79]

As it began to expand, there is a sense of the household at Woburn Abbey being gently revived in the same hopeful spirit as the procession of 1660. The account books reveal a somewhat traditional hierarchy, with the steward as the senior officer, and a clerk of the kitchen and the house bailiff as his second in commands. The steward, William Baker, was described as a gentleman and was paid £40 per year, twice the wage of the house bailiff. Baker was succeeded in 1668 by Randolph Bingley, who was still there in 1700, an example of the longevity of senior servants. In 1664, the salaries bill for the whole household was £600.

In what was then the established pattern, the steward was in charge of all the household staff, although responsibility for the footmen and pages was shared between the house and the stables, coming under the steward for duties in the house, and the master of the stables for duties relating to coach or horses. A gentleman of the privy purse, with the splendid name of Dixy Taylor, was authorised to make regular small purchases on behalf of his master, such as 'a coffee-pot, a china dish and coffee' for £1 2s 2d in 1670.[80]

There were normally twelve footmen (double the number listed at Knole in the early seventeenth century), paid between £2 and £6 a year. Two or three of them served the family in closer attendance than the others; one Clem Robinson stands out as especially trusted, judging by the payments made to him for journeys he made. The footmen's liveries were supplied by the master of the horse, as were those of the pageboys. There are numerous mentions in the accounts of silk stockings, shirts, haircuts, periwigs 'for my lady's page' and sometimes accomplishments such as studying music: '1663–1664 For teaching the page of the flageolet [a recorder-like instrument], £2 10s.'[81]

There appear to have been only seven or eight women in the household, reporting to the housekeeper, Ann Upton, who certainly came under the steward, but was clearly an important figure. In the sixteenth century her duties would have been the responsibility of men but by the end of the seventeenth century the female housekeeper, almost as a proxy for the lady of the household, is well established pivotal in the administration of a country house. Even so, none of the women under Ann Upton worked in the kitchen.[82]

That was still run by a man, the clerk of the kitchen, who was responsible for the supplies of butcher's meat, game, fruit and vegetables and dairy produce, purchases that were recorded in a kitchen book that was signed weekly by the earl; the steward would be advanced money each week for the following week's purchase. There appears to have been no home farm and the only major source of meat from the earl's own demesne was his deer park, whilst most of the fish consumed came from the Woburn ponds.

What is surprising is that the more frugal earl's household of the early Commonwealth era of the 1650s, which then numbered only about fifty, became larger and more splendid from 1658 onwards, with relatives visiting the abbey for prolonged periods, often with their own retinues of staff, with the result that annual household expenditure in the 1660s averaged £900–£1,000.[83]

Below the clerk of the kitchen came the cook, who was in turn supported by various boy scullions and turnspits. There were also porters and nightwatchmen, paid between £3 and £4 a year; in the records for 1684, 'to John Bradnock, being his lordship's gift yearly to see all candles out every night £2 And to him for killing rats and mice, etc £1.' The porters received livery uniforms, whilst the night-watchmen did not, but, like the women in the household, they seem to have been made gifts of new clothes from time to time.

With certain exceptions, the staff at Woburn Abbey were also the staff for Bedford House in London, and they moved back and forth with the family. In the London house the only permanent employees appear to have been a housekeeper, a nightwatchman and a gardener.[84] The whole household continued to migrate to London once a year, but after 1660 the annual pilgrimage was larger in terms of numbers and lasted for a much longer period.[85]

The wages of servants in gentry houses appear to have increased somewhat after the Restoration, but still varied considerably. An estate steward who had considerable economic responsibilities in managing the estate would earn the most, £40 or more, whilst in the years between 1660 and 1700 a cook could earn between £4 and £25, a butler from £3 to £10, a gardener anything from £4 to £20, and a coachman between £3 and £10. Of female servants, a housekeeper could earn £6 to £10 and a cook-maid £3 to £9.[86] In July 1699, Alexander Popham of Littlecote in Wiltshire was prepared to pay an exorbitant £40 a year for a new cook to come down from London.[87]

It is interesting to note that whilst stewards were powerful figures (sometimes minor landowners or clerics) who effectively had overall control of their masters' property, they might be required to under-take surprisingly menial tasks. Lord Cholmondley's chief steward William Adams received a request in May 1690 to order a housemaid 'to brush my lord's embroidered waistcoat that is in your custody and take care that the worms doth not get into it'.[88]

Servants expected to have their income topped up with tips or 'vails'. Sir John Pelham, in 1658, recorded his tips to servants at the houses he visited. At Burton Hall in Lincolnshire, he gave £3 12s 6d; at Rufford Abbey in Nottinghamshire, £3 10s. In 1697, when Sir Edward Harley stayed with Paul Foley of Stoke Edith in Herefordshire, his servant, William Thomas, made a record of the gratuities given out: 2s 6d each to the butler, coachman, and a chambermaid, 2s 2d to the cook and, to a groom, 3s 6d.[89]

As we have seen, at Knole in the early seventeenth century two black servants worked in the kitchen. The black servant, often a slave, is ubiquitous in seventeenth-century country-house life, although their stories are not well recorded. In grand portraiture, as in Sir Peter Lely's *Countess of Dysart, with a Black Page*, painted in the early 1650s, or in Van Dyck's *Earl of Denbigh*, young, good-looking black servants appear with some regularity, and clearly are seen as indications of wealth, status and of having international connections.[90]

The English had become involved in the slave trade from the 1560s, when Sir John Hawkins acquired 300 slaves from the Guinea coast – previous to that Henry VIII had a black trumpeter. Queen Elizabeth I, who is known to have had black servants, and whose accounts show that a 'lytle Blackmore' was provided with a fine Gascon coat, nevertheless issued hostile proclamations towards them, such as the 1601 decree that the country should be stripped of 'the great number of Negroes and blackamoors [that] are fostered and powered here, to the great annoyance of her own liege people which covet the relief which their people consume'. The decree failed. Like his predecessor, James I employed numerous black servants at court for their 'exotic' value, where they appeared in plays and masques, and served as musicians.[91]

It was then not long before Cromwell acquired through force West Indian colonies such as Jamaica and Barbados, which added to the trade between the former Spanish colonies, with their established slave populations, and England.[92] By the later seventeenth century, black pages and dark-skinned servants remain popular and fashionable. Pepys, for instance, owned African slaves, mentioning in his diaries that on 30 May 1662 he saw 'the little Turk and Negro' acquired by his great patron, Lord Sandwich, to be pages to his family.[93] Some of these unfortunates received a degree of education, for among the Verney papers is a letter written in 1699 by John Verney's black servant from Guinea.[94]

By the later years of the seventeenth century, the black servant, page and footman had become an established feature of the English country house. One unhappy tale of an unnamed boy, who became the focus of an extraordinary story of intrigue in the 1670s, illustrates the vulnerability of these young people. He was a servant to the Yorkshire landowner and MP, Sir John Reresby, who records his fate: 'I had a fine More about sixteen years of age (given me by a gentleman, one Mr Drax, who had brought him out of the Barbadoes) that had lived with me some years, and dyed about this time of an imposthume [abscess] in his head.'[95]

If that sad end were not enough, the story darkened still further. 'I received an account in October (six weeks after he was buried) from London, that it was creditably reported that I had caused him to be gelt [gelded?], and that it had occasioned his death. I laughed at it at first, knowing it to be false, as a ridiculous story, till I was further informed that this came from the Duke of Norfolk and his family, with whom . . . I had some suits and differences.'[96]

Reresby had a coroner and witnesses inspect the body: 'some that laid him out, the rest that saw him naked, severall bycaus of his colour having the curiosity to see him after he was dead gave in their verdict that he dyed ex visitatione Dei (or by the hand of God)'. At least one more exhumation followed. There is no sadder example of the tragedy of these young black men, sold into slavery when often little more than children, and passed around as exotic objects at a distance of many thousands of miles from their own families or cultures.[97]

As we have seen, by the late seventeenth century women had begun to make up a more substantial proportion of the servant numbers. Clear evidence of this is provided by one of the books published under the name of Hannah Wolley, *The Gentlewomans Companion* (1675), and by *The Compleat Servant-Maid* (1685), which includes detailed information about the principal female roles in domestic service at the time.[98] This list includes: waiting woman, housekeeper, chambermaid, cook-maid, under-cook-maid, nurserymaid, dairymaid, laundrymaid, housemaid, and scullerymaid.[99] Mrs Wolley, a remarkable former household servant, became a popular cookery author, and although this book may not in fact be entirely by her hand, nevertheless it built on her fame.

According to *The Gentlewomans Companion*, in the decades immediately after the Restoration it had become the norm for many roles in domestic service to be increasingly undertaken by women. Whether entirely the work of Mrs Wolley or not, this book has its own place in the history of servants and, indeed, in the history of women's education, offering an insight into the opportunities afforded by domestic service and the perceived character of the whole class of female servants, who had seemed almost invisible in the previous century. As well as having enhanced 'housewife skills', the would-be housekeeper, for instance, must be able to manage servants: 'And as I told you before you must Preserve well; so you must have a competent knowledge in Distilling, making Cates [Cakes], all manner of spoon-meats [liquid foods, especially for children], and the like. Be carefull in looking after the Servants, that every one perform their duty in their several places, that they keep good hours in up-rising, and lying down, and that no Goods be either spoil'd, or embezzl'd.'[100]

A housekeeper's behaviour had to be 'grave and solid' to show that she was able 'to govern a Family', which meant to manage a household. The housekeeper was also by now responsible for the demeanour and behaviour of the lower women servants, and here the injunctions to senior servants echo those in John Russell's *Book of Nurture*: 'all Strangers [should] be nobly and civilly used in their Chambers; and that your Master or Lady be not dishonoured through neglect or miscarriage of Servants. To be first up, and last in bed, to prevent junketing.'[101]

Any chambermaid 'to persons of Quality', it is stressed, must be skilled at washing and mending clothes. 'You must make your Ladies bed; . . . lay out her Night-clothes; see that her Chamber be kept clean, and nothing wanting which she desires or requires to be done. Be modest in your deportment, ready at her call, always diligent.'[102]

Some of these skills are associated with the later role of the lady's maid, whilst the cleaning and fires would have fallen to the house-maid. The 'Nursery-Maids in Noble Families' are advised, with some good sense, 'to be naturally inclined to love young children or else you will soon discover your unfitness to manage that charge'.[103]

The female cook of the day was generally known as the cook-maid; her prowess 'will chiefly consist in dressing all sorts of Meat, both Fish, flesh and Fowl, all manner of Baked-meats, all kind of Sawces, and which are most proper for every sort of Dish, and be curious in garnishing your Dishes'. Economy and cleanliness were key: 'Be as saving as you can, and cleanly about every thing; see also that your Kitchen be kept clean, and all thin gs [sic] scoured in due time; your Larders also and Cupboards, that there be no bits of meat or bread lye about them to spoil and stink.'[104]

The author advises against taking perquisites (meaning leftover food that could be sold for personal profit) but it must have been a common practice: 'do not covet to have the Kitchin-stuff for your vails, but rather ask [for] the more wages, for that may make you an ill Huswife of your Masters goods, and of your Masters good, and teach you to be a thief.'[105]

For under-cook-maids: 'it behoves you to be very diligent and willing to do what you are bid to do; and though your employment be greasie and smutty, yet if you please you may keep your self from being nasty.' Under-cook-maids should observe what their superiors do, 'treasure it up in your memory' and then put it into practice; 'this course will advance you from a drudge to be a Cook another day. . . . Everyone must have a beginning.'[106]

'Dairy-Maids in great Houses' were exhorted to scald their vessels well and milk 'your Cattel in due times'. They must also see that 'Hogs have the whey, and that it be not given away to idle or gossip-ing people, who live merely upon what they can get from Servants.' If pigs or chicken are in their care, they must 'look to them that it may be your credit and not your shame when they come to the Table'.[107] Laundrymaids in great houses were advised that their duty 'will be to take care of the Linnen in the house, except Points and Laces; whatever you wash, do it up quickly, that it may not stink and grow yellow, and be forced to the washing again before it be used'.[108]

Housemaids were not left in ignorance of their duty either: 'Your principal Office is to make clean the greatest part of the house; and so that you suffer no room to lie foul; that you look well to all the stuff, and see that they be often brushed, and all the Beds frequently turned.' At this point the housemaid is expected to 'be careful for, and diligent to all Strangers, and see that they lack nothing in their Chambers, which your Mistress or Lady will allow; and that your Close-stools and Chamber-pots be duly emptied and kept clean'. A housemaid might also be expected to assist in the laundry on a washing day and to help the housekeeper or waiting woman 'in their Preserving and Distilling'.[109]

The lowest in the ranks of female servants was the scullery-maid, who had some of the hardest work of all: 'There are several Rooms that you must keep sweet and clean, as the Kitchen, Pantry, Washhouse, &c. That you wash and scowre all the Plates and Dishes which are used in the Kitchen, also Kettles, Pots, Pans, Chamber-pots, with all other Iron, Brass, and Pewter materials that belong to the Chambers or Kitchen; and lastly you must wash your own linnen.' This could still serve as the job description of a scullery-maid until the early twentieth century, when advances in technology could take over some of its most physically demanding aspects.[110]

In *The Gentlewomans Companion* (1675), the emphasis is also laid on good management of servants and the mistress of the house is urged to keep good hours for her repose, 'that your servants may be the better disposed for the next day's labour'. And later she is told: 'rather be silent if you cannot speak good.'[111]

Also, mistresses are exhorted to give 'kind acknowledgment' of servants' loyalty, and to 'Be not too passionate with your servants.' It was the mistress's responsibility to oversee and set the standard for good time-keeping for her servants, and also to be generous with them, but not to a superfluity: 'as that may entertain a sort [set?] of loose Gossips in corners, the very bane and spoil of servants.'[112]

Some men were suspicious of female power in the household, as can be seen from *Advice to His Son*, written by Henry Percy, 9th Earl of Northumberland, and published in 1609: 'Grip into your hands what power soever you will of government, yet will there be certain persons about your wife that you will never reduce – an usher, her tailor, and her women.' According to the earl, they 'will ever talk and ever be unreasonable; all which your [household] officers will rather endeavour to please then [i.e. than] your self . . . In a house thus governed, factions will be rife, as well amongst your own servants as amongst your friends and hers; for her friends will ever be the welcomest and best used, the train of women friends being ever the longest and most troublesome.'[113]

Some adults wanted to separate their children from the influence of servants of either sex. The Duchess of Newcastle (d. 1673) recorded how her parents tried to keep her away from the domestic staff, refusing to allow 'any familiarity with the vulgar servants, or conversation: yet [they] caused us to demean ourselves with a humble civility towards them, as they with a dutiful respect to us.'

On the other hand, she recognised the dangers of children spending too much time in a great house without supervision lest they ran wild, getting 'into every dirty office, where the young master must learn to drink and play at cards with the kitchen-boy, & learn to kiss his mother's dirty maid for a mess of cream. The daughters are danced upon the knee of every clown and serving man, & hear them talk scurrilous to the maids.'[114]

Rather more poignantly, in *Brief Lives* John Aubrey related that Sir John Danvers once told him that the reason that the gentry liked their sons to take the Grand Tour was to 'wean them from the acquaintance and familiarity with the Serving-men: for then parents were so austere and grave that the sonnes must not be company for their Father; and some company man must have.'[115] This shows how long a tradition the distant parent, and the companionable servant, has been in the English aristocracy.

In the seventeenth century the management of a household began to devolve more from the mistress of the house, to whom it might prove onerous. In the 1670s, Mary Evelyn, the wife of the diarist, landowner and gardener John Evelyn, wrote a memorandum on household management for her husband's young friend, Margaret, then newly married to the politician and courtier Sidney Godolphin, which principally consists of long lists of necessary household items, from linen to pewter and glassware. John Evelyn said later that the young Mrs Godolphin 'never was House-keeper before, had lost her Mother long since & being from a Child, bred in Courts, may be thought (with reproch) not much to have busied her head about Oeconomique matters'.[116]

This friendly letter touched in important ways on the management of servants' food: 'What is left at dinner & that may handsomely be spar'd from the Servants (whom I am sure you will not abridge, but this will be the discretion of your woman, who you say shall be your Housekeeper) may [be] reserv'd for their Supper; though in London they have in most places only Bread & Beer. But here in the Country where they work continually and are much abroad, they will require Supper of Flesh, of which something is kept for your Breakfast.'[117]

A key piece of advice was appointing a trusted female to run the household by proxy, as Mrs Godolphin had asked about how best to manage accounts and servants: 'all I can say is, That if you have a faithful Woman or Housemaid, it will cost you little trouble. It were necessary that such a one were a good Market-woman, & whose Eyes must bee from the Garret to the Cellar; nor is it enough they see all things made cleane in the House, but set in ord[e]r also.'[118] A minor aside suggests that a large residential domestic staff at that time could be controlled by mistress and housekeeper in a way that non-resident domestics could not: 'Use as seldom Charewomen and Out-helpers as you can [because] they but make Gossips.'[119]

To sum up, the faithful housekeeper 'should bee the first of Servants stirring and last in bed, & have some authority over the rest, & you must hear her & give her credit, yet not without your owne Examination & inspection . . . It is necessary alsoe she should know how to write and cast up small sums & bring you her Book every Saturday-night, which you may cause to be enter'd into another for your selfe . . . such a servant (I tell you) is a jewel not easily to be found.'[120] This advice clearly bore fruit. When Mrs Godolphin died in 1678, in his biography of her Evelyn mentions her concern, 'care and esteem of those she left behind, even to her domestic servants to the meanest of which she left considerable legacies, as to the poor'.[121]

In 1685, the Evelyns sent a version of this document to Samuel Pepys, who filed it with a similar specification from Lady Rolles for what was needed in a household. This version ends with a list of the qualities required in a housekeeper, including cooking skills, management of female servants, 'to keepe the Storehouse & all the Houshold-Linnen & mend & make it, & help to fold it when she is at leisure, that she may see it well done'. Lady Rolles' list stressed one point in particular: 'But the chief thing I desire [is that she] be an excellent Cooke, a good Housewife & a willing Servant to doe what I thinke belongs to her place.'[122]

The reduction in the numbers of gentlemen-status attendants was reflected in architectural terms. This is the century of the 'back stairs', with the provision of a separate servants' hall at a distance from the 'polite' quarters of the house. This is vividly illustrated by one late-seventeenth-century treatise on architecture, 'On planning a country house', written by Sir Roger North, in which he observes that 'it is an inviolable rule to have the entrata in the midle. But this must not be the common passage for all things, in regard [to] your freinds [sic] and persons of esteem should pass without being annoyed by the sight of foul persons [that is, the servants], and things must and will be moving in some part of a large and well inhabited dwelling.' He argued: 'Therefore, for such occasions there must be a back entrata. . . . The like is to be sayd of stayres. For the chief must not be annoyed with disagreeable objects, but be releived [sic] of them by a back-inferior staircase.'[123]

As for servants' sleeping accommodation, there was a continuation of the pattern created in the late medieval and Tudor period, in that lower servants' bedrooms were usually in garrets, sometimes in the small rooms behind the upper part of a gable or above stables. In the late 1680s, on a visit to the architecturally advanced Coleshill House in Leicestershire, built in the 1650s, Celia Fiennes noted in her diary 'several garret rooms for servants furnished very neat and genteel'.[124] The evidence of wills and inventories does not suggest that many such rooms, except those of the most senior household officers, were particularly well furnished and they were often shared.[125]

Dining in the early part of the seventeenth century still largely took place in the hall but by the end of the century servants and tenants no longer dined alongside the immediate family in the public sphere of the house. The earliest reference to a servants' hall seems to be in 1654, when the inventory was taken at Aston Hall in Warwickshire, which was built in the 1630s; in the later seventeenth century, such halls are also recorded at Charborough in Dorset, at The Vyne and at Belton House, both in Hampshire.[126] In an inventory of 1664, the servants' hall at Aldermaston House in Berkshire is said to contain a large table, a side cupboard, two old Turkey chairs (meaning that they are decorated with knotted embroidery), an elbow chair, two Turkey-work stools and a candlestick.[127]

In his diary for September 1677, John Evelyn expressed his admiration for the newly built Euston Hall in Norfolk, noting the quality (and the separateness) of the servants' accommodation, with 'appartments for my Lord, Lady, and Dutchesse, with kitchins & other offices below, in a lesser volume with lodgings for servants, all distinct . . . The out-offices make two large quadrangles, so as never servants liv'd with more ease & convenience, never Master more Civil.' Later he adds: 'He has built a Lodge in the Park for the Keeper which is neate & sweete dwelling and might become any gentleman of quality.'[128]

However, when gentleman and amateur architect Roger Pratt wrote down his principles for designing a country house in 1660, he was concerned that bedchambers for family and guests be served by a nearby servants' lodging that had access to the back stairs. Each of the chambers, he declared, should 'have a closet, and a servant's lodging with chimney, both of which will easily be made by dividing the breadth of one end of the room into two such parts as shall be convenient'. Nevertheless, he did not recommend servants' garrets above bedchambers that would be used by guests, as the latter would thereby be disturbed. He recommended a basement kitchen. But above all, the house should be 'so contrived . . . that the ordinary servants may never publicly appear in passing to and fro [on] their occasions'.[129]

On the other hand, his contemporary Sir Roger North thought that the back entrance should be used by the master of the house so that he could superintend his servants at work and talk to them privately, out of earshot of any honoured guests:[130] 'It is no unseemly object to an English gentleman to se[e] his servants and business passing at ordinary times.'[131] Pratt recommended a separate servants' hall in 1660, and North did the same. North argued for a separate servants' hall which was not too close to the parlour, because of possible noise, but not too distant: 'that the servants may be in awe'. The upper servants he thought should have a part screened off, 'for quality (forsooth) must be distinguisht.'[132]

We have reached an age when the well-dressed and well-mannered attendant–companion has been passed over in favour of the dedicated domestic servant, and when the privacy of the aristocratic family has taken on a new importance. But we should not forget that many landed families maintained their ancient traditions with some pride, responding to these new attitudes with only modest alterations. One such was Tichborne House in Hampshire, whose whole household is recorded in the 1671 painting by Gillis van Tilborch of the annual dole ceremony there, presided over by Sir Henry Tichborne, 3rd Baronet, lieutenant of the New Forest and the Royal Ordnance.[133] This ritual distribution of bread to the poor continues today.

In an unusual but moving display, which has its origins in the medieval household, the immediate blood family and all the domestic servants are depicted, with many older and trusted figures shown close to the head of the household. Behind Sir Henry stands the family nurse, Constantia Atkins, while behind Lady Tichborne stands Mrs Chitty, her maid, Mrs Robinson, the housekeeper, and his Roman Catholic house chaplain, Father Robert Hill.

The local people and those about to receive the dole are to the right while the full household is shown on the left of the painting, with the lowly women servants, presumably the laundresses and kitchenmaids, back from the main group near the house. Footmen in typically distinctive, seventeenth-century livery carry the baskets of loaves to be given to the poor on Lady Day or 25 March. The menservants here, whose more public role is clearly evident, still outnumber the women servants but the women are better represented than they would have been in the previous century.

The painting is a truly remarkable image of a country house and all who lived and worked in it, as if it was a whole community on parade. It is also an important record of the dress of the seventeenth-century servant, demonstrating the social hierarchies of a wealthy gentry household.

In contrast, the simple human experience of service, and the desire for human companionship in the workplace, are expressed in a rare letter dated 1664 in which a servant, Jane Greethurst, laments the departure of the friend and fellow servant with whom she used to share her bed: 'I have been soe much alone since I lost your good company which have troubled me very much; I have never laught when I was in Bed since you went away ffor I have noe body to spake to, nor was I warme in my Bed till I put on my Stockings.'[134]

3

The Household in the Age of Conspicuous Consumption

The Eighteenth Century

H OW GRAND TO be so grand. When we visit an eighteenth-century country house today, such as Kedleston Hall in Derbyshire, or Holkham Hall in Norfolk, despite their daunting scale and obvious grandeur we cannot help feeling that such places are the product of a more rational age. This is often reflected not only in the grandest elements of design but also in the careful arrangement of the kitchen wings and related offices – the usual term given to the domestic-service rooms and outbuildings.[1]

These areas contribute to the whole, for, after all, what is a palace without its dependencies, and even if the relationships differ from those of earlier centuries, what is a lord without his attendants? In this period, the kitchen offices are divided ever more precisely into numerous separate and supporting spaces for the preparation of food, for cleaning, for the doing of laundry and for providing well-organised stables and coach houses, a process that continues to be refined throughout the eighteenth and nineteenth centuries. The country house is now, more than ever, a machine for living.

The overall sense of order and stateliness expressed in the architecture of these country houses was, of course, entirely self-conscious. Their scale, detail and symmetry were inspired by the buildings of ancient Rome, and were intended to project an image of status and permanence, but it was always as much a projection of an ideal as it was of a convincing reality. Many older country houses were simply adapted modestly to modern needs (often with the addition of new servants' wings and stables). The fortunes of many landed families waxed and waned with the times, some bankrupting themselves on ambitious building projects.

The commercial interests of England were spreading over the globe. Agricultural improvements, and the beginnings of the industrial revolution (accompanied by an unparalleled political security compared to that of the seventeenth century), meant that for a lucky few there was money as never before, allowing large landowners to sustain surprisingly large numbers of servants.

The great wealth of these men prompted a visiting Frenchman, François, the Duc de La Rochefoucauld, to observe in 1784:

> In general, the English have many more servants than we have, but more than half of them are never seen – kitchen-maids, stable-men, maidservants in large numbers – all of them being required in view of the high standard of cleanliness. Every Saturday, for instance, it is customary to wash the whole house from attic to basement, outside and in. The servants constitute the main part of the employers' expenses: they are boarded according to general custom and the food required is immense – they never leave the table and there is a supply of cold meat, tea and punch from morning till night.[2]

As in earlier centuries, the biggest country houses of this period required a huge body of skilled servants for their running and maintenance, as well as to provide the regular demonstrations of display and deference that an aristocrat expected and required to underline his own prestige. Numerous sets of households rules and regulations were produced in this period, partly in an attempt to control these multitudes, but also resulting from the problems to be expected in managing a large body of staff.

As de la Rochefoucauld suggests, some servants in great houses seem to have lived astonishingly comfortable lives. The wealth and conspicuous consumption of the Georgian country house is captured in a probably apocryphal and certainly preposterous anecdote, related by Horace Walpole, of staying with the Duke of Bedford at Woburn. When a fellow guest dropped a silver coin on the floor, he remarked, 'Oh, never mind, let the Groom of the Chambers have it,' to which the duchess replied, 'Let the carpet-sweeper have it: the Groom of the Chambers never takes anything but gold.'[3]

Also, with the increase in opportunity for travel came a parallel increase in the availability of new jobs, leading to a greater turnover of staff and a migration of trained personnel, often towards the capital. The chance that life as a servant in a country house offered – for learning new skills, for getting an education and for acquiring some sort of betterment and security, as well as adventure – is exemplified in a very rare document of its kind, written by John Macdonald (1741–96), footman, valet, and sometime butler and steward.[4]

His vivid memoirs, first printed in 1790, are among the first published accounts of the life of a domestic servant, of which there have never been many – until the twentieth century. Originally entitled *Travels in Various Parts* to reflect the exoticism of his experiences abroad, Macdonald's reminiscences were published in modern times as *Memoirs of an Eighteenth Century Footman* and they have all the ups and downs of a novel by Fielding or Smollett.

These memoirs remind us that however serene and luxurious life in a great household of the period might seem at this distance in time, it was subject to all the tensions, anxieties and turmoils that are the lot of human beings at any point in history. What is most surprising is the number and variety of Macdonald's jobs, and the extent of his travels, during which he passed with ease between aristocratic, mercantile and military employers. He worked for more than twenty-five masters, for varying intervals, relishing his independence and the mobility of his profession – although his initial training was in a country house in the early part of the century.[5]

This is a flesh and blood tale, in which Macdonald displays his vanity, admits his own faults and forgives those of others with admirable equanimity. Servants were not just items in the account books, any more than the aristocracy and gentry that they worked for were as one-dimensional as their posed portraits might suggest, or as vacuous, haughty and thoughtless as characterisations in period drama would have us believe.

Mr Macdonald's memoir begins with a childhood pitched into destitution that segues into a long and relatively rewarding career in domestic service. From the lowly position of postilion and footman, he rose to become valet and manservant to numerous gentlemen, particularly when on their travels. He was clearly talented as a barber and a cook, judging by his ability to secure a place when he needed one. In early adulthood he opted for service in households kept by unmarried gentlemen. Because, he said, of his good looks he was considered too much of a risk around young wives or daughters, or in a household with a large number of women servants.[6]

The 'affliction' of his appearance was a source of both pride and vexation for him (he asked a friend: 'What makes the women take to me so?'), but it became an advantage during his travels to Asia, especially India (these being the real reason for publishing his memoirs), where his bearing and liveried dress often made him admired as a gentleman: 'They think you are a gentleman because you are dressed in scarlet and that fine gold lace hat.'[7] He is thought to have settled finally with a wife and young family near Toledo in Spain, although history does not relate whether there are Macdonalds there still.

It was the country-house service of his youth in which he acquired his skills and adopted the standards that set him on this path. His experiences and observations of that time are a window on the hopes, expectations and perils facing a young boy with few prospects, learning to work with horses and dancing attendance on the gentry and nobility and, by his own account at least, prospering and improving himself by education and travel. It was not unusual for country-house servants to come from equally disadvantaged beginnings, and children left at the famous Foundling Hospital in Bloomsbury, for instance, were usually trained as domestic servants.[8]

Mr Macdonald's father was, he said, a grazier who became a captain in the Jacobite army and was killed at Culloden in 1746. As their mother had died three years earlier, the five children were now left parentless. Macdonald tells a tale of their wanderings that suggests he was lucky to have survived at all. When his sister found work as a servant, this led to his securing a post as a postilion in a livery stable in Edinburgh.[9]

With his next employer, he immediately moved up in the world. John Hamilton (formerly Dalrymple and a connection of the Earl of Stair) was the owner of the Bargeny estate in south Ayrshire, covering 'twenty thousand acres of ground'. In 1750, Hamilton had ordered a new coach from Hume's of Edinburgh. Its delivery required horses from the livery where John worked, so he accompanied them and was promptly engaged as postilion to the family 'for two pounds a year, all my clothes, and a third part of the vails [tips] . . . I was taken into the parlour, to see if Lady Anne liked her new postilion. I was admired in my livery, for my littleness, being only nine years of age.'[10]

In his extreme youth and confusion, he forgot his new job after delivering the horses, and it was a month before he returned to Bargeny to take up the post, by which time another postilion ('a stout lad about sixteen years of age') had been hired. He describes a tumult of interviews, in whose outcome not only the whole family but the entire phalanx of their servants take an interest: 'Amongst the servants there was a division: for me, Mr Maglashan, the butler, Alexander Campbell, Lady Anne's footman, who afterwards kept the Great Inn at Perth, and Mr Macmorlin, the head-gardener; all the rest being low-country people were against me; but all the ladies were for me.'[11]

There were clearly a great many staff: 'The family have eight upper- or lady-maids, four chamber-maids, two laundry-maids, two dairy-maids, a plain-worker, a first and second man-cook, a kitchen-maid, a butler, two footmen, a coachman with positilions and helpers.' Lady Anne's two sisters often stayed, bringing their own maid and footman. In time John was given a scarlet livery jacket, trimmed with silver and made in Edinburgh.[12]

Bargeny estate today (now known as Bargany) remains in the possession of the Dalrymple-Hamiltons, an ancient lowland landowning family, and in the mid eighteenth century the house would have been one of the major such establishments of the region. It survives still, although in separate ownership. The rolling hilly landscape in which it sits, with dense woodland bisected by the river Girvan, offers beautiful views. The house, built in the seventeenth century, is largely as John Macdonald would have known it, although somewhat updated and extended in the nineteenth century. In his lifetime it would have been very remote, the county town of Ayr being twenty miles away.[13]

Shortly after arriving John expressed an interest in learning to read and was encouraged in this, first by the servants, then by Mr Hamilton and his wife, Lady Anne Wemyss, who 'put me to school, as there was not much to do, only when the coach-and-six was wanted or when any of those young ladies [Lady Polly or Lady Nelly, Lady Anne's sisters] went home or a visiting . . . In the course of time I got [learnt] reading, writing and arithmetic.'[14]

As many able and enquiring servants must have done, John observed with interest the details of gentry and aristocratic life, describing entertainments, as well as landscape, agriculture and architecture, with some sophistication. A willing learner, and in exchange for scraps of meat for the pets he kept (foxes, hares, ravens, otters, magpies), John 'assisted them in the kitchen, particularly in the evening, when I had nothing to do in the stables. By this I learned a little of the art of cookery.'[15]

In these remote communities, favouritism could create considerable tensions, and discipline, both fair and unfair, was more likely to come from senior servants than from the employer. Young Macdonald got flogged mercilessly by the coachman, who had become jealous of the young postilion's favoured place. When this was drawn to Hamilton's attention it placed him in a quandary, for the coachman had a family. Somewhat unusually for the period, but perhaps owing to the isolation of the situation, 'When Mr Hamilton got a servant that answered his purpose, he desired him to bring his family; and he gave them houses.'[16]

Country-house staff were expected to be mobile, travelling between the country seat of the family and its town house: in Edinburgh, in Macdonald's case. Although offering the benefit of introducing some novelty and variety into the lives of the servants, it also required arduous preparation. The Christmas of 1756 was spent in Edinburgh, where Macdonald recorded: 'we never went out with Lady Anne, even an airing, with less than six horses, with the two footmen on horseback, with pistols and furniture complete.'[17] When Mr Hamilton rode alone, Macdonald accompanied him: 'sometimes the servants asked me to dine where my master dined, and by that means I had it in my power to save a shilling or two.' This was a common way in which servants might put money aside (a practice that certainly continued into the twentieth century).[18]

Macdonald went on to work for the Earl of Crawford, but this position soured when the countess took a liking to him, remarking at

one point, 'certainly he is . . . some nobleman or gentleman's bastard.'
Even though he had rescued the Crawfords from a fire in 1757, he
still felt he had to move on. In 1760 he returned to Hamilton's service
as a bodyservant but he remarks: 'I did not know the value of luck,
nor of money. Coming into two such plentiful families, I thought the
whole world was the garden of Eden.'

A recurring problem was that he was 'put out of my latitude by
contrary winds – I mean women'.[19] Lady Anne 'turned off [dismissed]
the house-keeper, chambermaid, and her own god-daughter, when
she thought there was any love between them and Jack'. Mr Hamilton
himself began to fear some intrigue, although Macdonald professes
his innocence. Yet some understanding could exist between master
and servant; there is an illuminating moment when he and Hamilton
are riding near Kilburnie, and Hamilton asks him: 'Have you not a
child in this parish?' Macdonald replies: 'Yes, sir, in that village before
you.' Hamilton makes the quiet rejoinder: 'Well, you may go and see
him: I shall ride gently on.'[20] It is difficult to imagine such a conversation even a hundred years later.

Macdonald's life story is instructive on many levels, not least
because this was a key period for the establishment of the footman as
the conspicuous, gorgeously liveried manservant. Although footmen
continued to be a familiar feature of country-house life throughout
the nineteenth and early twentieth centuries, it is in the Georgian era
that they reach their peak as an item of display in entrance halls and
dining rooms – serving at the table where the aristocracy spent such
vast sums on entertaining – as well as ornamenting expensively
appointed family carriages in town.

It is thought that the word 'flunkey' (apparently derived from the
word 'flanker') was first used early in the eighteenth century as a term
for the ostensibly useless and ornately dressed decorative servant,
footmen in particular. More than any other such group, they seem to
have irritated tradesmen and townsfolk who considered them idle
and scornful, possibly because they were (unfairly) seen as superfluous. As we have seen from Macdonald's earthy memoir, the footman's role could be multi-layered, to encompass specialist cleaning
and manual duties, as well as physical attendance. A footman was

chiefly required to attend at table under the supervision of a butler, and to help with the cleaning of glass and silver, but he must also run messages and act as a quasi-bodyguard.[21]

In his perceptive and mordant work *Directions to Servants* (published in 1745, but written somewhat earlier), the cleric and satirist Jonathan Swift summed up the characteristic self-possession of footmen of the period, conscious of their fine appearance and gaudy plumage. However, it also revealed the surprising complexity of their duties, for in laying bare the common faults of all servants, he devotes the greatest space to the footman.[22]

Swift tartly addresses the footman thus: 'Your employment being of a mixed nature, extends to a great variety of business, and you stand in a fair way of being the favourite of your master or mistresses.' Therefore, he says, 'you are the fine gentleman of the family, with whom all the maids are in love'. He pertly notes that footmen learn from observing the lives of the aristocracy at close hand, while other servants were not given such close exposure: 'You wait at table in all companies, and consequently have the opportunity to see and know the world, and to understand men and manners.'[23]

Footmen were genuinely chosen for their height – ideally, all being roughly the same in that regard – their good looks and ability to look good dressed in the family livery. John Macdonald's memoir alone indicates the problems that male beauty could cause. In 1711, Joseph Addison furnished an amusing account in the *Spectator* of a good-looking footman who worked for a captain of the guard and was in the habit of courting women dressed in his master's clothes. As he observed: 'the Fellow had a very good Person, and there are very many women that think no further than the outside of a Gentleman; beside which he was almost as learned a Man as the colonel himself, I say, thus qualified, the Fellow could scrawl Billets doux so well, and furnish a conversation on the common Topicks, that he had, as they call it, a great deal of good Business on His hands.' It was only when the impostor passed his colonel on the stairs of an inn, when each had a lady on their arms, that the game was up.[24]

Addison makes mention in the same publication of menservants who wait on mistresses at their toilette: 'I remember the time when some of our well-bred County Women kept their *Valet de Chambre*, because, forsooth, a man was much more handy about them than one of their own Sex. I myself have seen one of these male Abigails tripping about the Room with a looking glass in his hand, and combing his Lady's Hair a whole morning together.'[25]

How times had changed. From having been among the most insignificant servants in the medieval and Tudor household, employed principally to run ahead of a nobleman and his party to announce their arrival, and to deliver messages, the footman had become an outward sign of status, as well as playing a vital role in the management of a great house, whether in the country or in London. As well as travelling on the back of a coach, footmen would walk before a sedan chair and follow close behind when their master or mistress went out on foot. Some households maintained a special 'running footman' to run ahead of the coach and announce their master's passage.[26]

Being so valued by the rich and so associated in the public imagination with ostentatiousness, footmen were probably the prime target in the tax raised on male servants in 1777, effectively as a luxury, to help raise funds for the war against the American colonists. Even the hair powder they used was subject to an additional tax.[27] The 1780 return for this tax of a 'guinea a head' suggests that it was levied on some 50,000 menservants although many of them would have been London based. The return also shows that, on average, dukes employed twenty-six male servants and barons fifteen. In 1785, to considerable outcry, these taxes were extended to female servants. In response to objections, the tax was amended for families with children although the tax on menservants technically lasted until the 1930s.[28]

Numbers of staff varied; in the 1720s, ninety individuals managed Cannons, seat of the Duke of Chandos. Forty years later, eighty-six were required at Blenheim for the Duke of Marlborough, while the Duke of Leinster (formerly Earl of Kildare), the premier peer in Ireland, could command as many as a hundred at Carton in County Kildare. The typical aristocratic or wealthier gentry household would have been staffed by between thirty and fifty, with, at the bottom, wages at £4 a year for a stable boy to, at the top, £1,000 for the steward at Chatsworth.[29]

The status of servants was reflected by where and with whom they dined. At Cannons, owned by one of the richest noblemen of the day, the arrangements at the beginning of the century were particularly elaborate. The comptroller, Colonel Watkins, dined with the duke, while the chaplains, house steward and librarian would dine in the chaplain's room.

The gentleman of the horse, in charge of the stables, had his own room where he dined in company with the gentleman usher, who looked after the main rooms in the house, the two valets, called the duke's gentlemen, the duchess's two gentlewomen and the pages. Everyone else, from the butler to the stable boys and odd men, but with the exception of the kitchenmaids, ate in the servants' hall. In most households, the main division was usually between those who dined with the family, those who dined in the steward's room or those who ate in the servants' hall.[30]

In many country houses, many household servants would be recruited from the families of tenant farmers and estate workers. In 1790, John Trusler recommended recruiting country dwellers of simple tastes and manners, in order to avoid 'persons who had aspirations to ape the status of their employers.' Another contemporary writer opined: 'I have often thought of the great interest a nobleman, or gentleman of large estate, might always secure by only the proper choice of his *domestics*. Such an one cannot be without a great number of tenants, who might think their children honoured in the *service* of his lord-ship, and whose tenures would be a sort of *security* for the honesty and good behaviour of the servant.'[31]

By the 1730s the large numbers of well-born attendants, whether gentlemen or ladies-in-waiting, who had been such a feature of the aristocratic household in the previous centuries, have dwindled almost to nothing.[32] Despite their disappearance, there still remained a distinctive hierarchy of servants, which reflected the divisions expressed by the seventeenth-century household. This fell into two distinct groups. There were the skilled and responsible upper servants, including stewards, male cooks, butlers, housekeepers, male secretaries, and sometimes chaplains and tutors, all of whom certainly wore their own clothes rather than livery, and there were the lower-ranking servants, who came under their management and control. The indoor menservants usually wore livery, while the women did the cleaning, or worked in the kitchens, looked after the laundry and worked in the dairy.

In this hierarchy, a steward was usually responsible for managing the house, the accounts and the administration. At the beginning of the century the same individual often acted as land steward, with additional responsibility for estate workers, tenants and estate rentals. Many houses also had a bailiff, who managed the home farm that supplied the needs of the house.[33]

Particularly in the larger houses, however, a separate house steward – in essence a house manager – remained an important fixture right up the end of the nineteenth century, reporting either directly to his master or to the land steward. John Mordant, in his *Complete Steward*, published in 1761, memorably described the house steward as 'Domo-fac-totum, or Major Domo'. The house steward (occasionally known as a chamberlain) would have to oversee the complex operation when the family (meaning the whole household, including most of the indoor servants) decamped to London or one of the landowner's other houses.[34] In some households, the job of house steward and butler might be one and the same.

Giles Jacob's *Country Gentleman's Vademecum,* published in 1717, described the steward's or house steward's duty thus:

> to take and state all Accompts, receive and pay all Monies, buy in the Provision for the Family, hire all Livery-men, buy all Liveries, pay all Wages, direct and keep in order all Livery-men (except the Coachman and the Groom) to be at His Master's Elbow during Dinner, and receive all Orders from him relating to Government; to oversee and direct the Bailiff, Gardener, &c., in their Business; and also the Clerk of the Kitchen, Cook, & Butler, &c., to whom he delivers the Provision, Wine, Beer, &c., who give an Account of the spending [of] it.[35]

Some stewards were French, as their knowledge of French customs and manners was thought to give them a certain *cachet*, as well as making them useful if the family travelled on the continent.[36]

Under the steward, the clerk of the kitchens – a traditional role in the household – managed the needs of the kitchen, identifying what provisions were needed and ordering them, as well as drawing up menus, setting times of meals and supervising service. Thus many of the lower servants came under his control. The instructions drawn up by the 2nd Earl of Nottingham, for his clerk of kitchens at Burley on the Hill, indicate that he not only kept the keys for important provisions, but was also the primary timekeeper. He was charged to 'Fail not to have the dinner ready by 12 of the clock and let the bell then be rung and dinner served up, likewise supper at 7.' At Burley he was also expected to be present at service: 'You must wait at the lower end of the Parlour table that you may be in My Lady's eye and be directed when to go for the second course.'[37]

With the arrival of more specialist foreign chefs (especially French ones) and confectioners, over the century the clerk of the kitchen's role diminished, some of his responsibilities passing to the female housekeeper. It was a position that by 1770 seems to have largely disappeared or at least become one with the role of the male cook, as suggested by wages lists such as that for Arundel Castle, with its 'cook & clark to the kitchen'.[38]

Much was expected of such a person. In 1769, Bernard Clermont wrote in *The Professed Cook* that a cook 'should be a man of thorough knowledge in his profession, capable of forming a bill of fare, and dressing it when approved of. He should be well versed in what is a sufficiency for the support of the family which he is to provide for, be they more or less in number.'[39]

French chefs were popular. In the 1720s the Earl of Leicester recruited his cook, Monsieur Norreaux, directly from Paris and paid him 60 guineas per annum, together with a French under-cook, Jean-Baptiste. English male cooks might find opportunities for acquiring continental culinary arts, as did William Verral, who learnt them from the French cook of the Duke of Newcastle early in the eighteenth century. The male cook was often the highest-paid servant after the steward.[40]

The Duc de La Rochefoucauld wrote in the 1780s: 'English cooks are not very clever folk, and even in the best houses one fares very ill. The height of luxury is to have a Frenchman, but few people can afford the expense.'[41] On the other hand, French cooks were thought to have ideas above their station. In the *London Magazine* of 1779,

James Boswell wrote that 'A French cook's notion of his own consequence is prodigious,' and went on to recount the story told him by the British ambassador to Spain, Sir Benjamin Keen. When interviewing French cooks to work for him, Keen asked one whether he had ever cooked any magnificent dishes. The reply came: 'Monsieur, j'ai accommodé un dîner qui faisait trembler toute la France.'[42]

The number of French chefs increased in the final years of the eighteenth century when the French Revolution drove many across the Channel to Britain. Famously Mr Ude, former cook to Louis XVI, was hired by the Earl of Sefton with the huge annual salary of 300 guineas. In his book he argued that a cook of his fame should never be regarded merely as a servant.[43]

By the beginning of the nineteenth century there could well have been between 400 and 500 great families employing a French or foreign chef who would travel back and forth from London to the country alongside the family.[44] It is worth noting that in the course of the eighteenth century, the time of the main meal of the day shifted from lunchtime to the evening. In the early eighteenth century, the essayist Richard Steele wrote: 'In my memory the dinner hour has crept from 12 o'clock to 3.' By 1800, dinner was usually served anywhere between five and seven.[45]

The *valet de chambre* or valet, reporting to the steward, was a key senior male servant whose chief responsibility was the appearance, dress and presentation of his master. As with John Macdonald, a valet would also need to be an accomplished barber. He would be in continual attendance on his master, accompanying him on all his travels, reflecting glory and making himself indispensable. John Moore wrote disparagingly of the Bertie Woosters of his day in 1780 that:

> many of our acquaintances seem absolutely incapable of motion, till they have been wound up by their valets. They have no more use of their hands for any office about their own persons, than if they were paralytic. At night they must wait for their servants, before they can undress themselves, and go to bed: In the morning, if the valet happens to be out of the way, the master must remain helpless and sprawling in bed, like a turtle on its back upon the kitchen table of an alderman.[46]

Not a liveried servant, the valet would normally be dressed in the manner of a gentleman, with appropriate manners and deportment. Anthony Heasel in the *Servants' Book of Knowledge* (1733) observed that 'A valet must be master of every sort of politeness, to which he must take care to accustom himself without stiffness or affectation.' Valets were also usually expected to speak some French.[47]

The butler, who had been a relatively minor figure up until the seventeenth century, becomes a grander fixture in the household of the eighteenth. In the wealthier establishment a butler reported to a steward, managed the footmen and supervised the waiting at table. As well as having control of the wine cellar, the butler usually had the immediate care of the plate (that is, silver) and fine glass, overseeing the cleaning, storage and security of these valuable items in his head-quarters, or butler's pantry. In the *Servants' Book of Knowledge* Anthony Heasel warns butlers: 'As all the plate will be committed to your care, never suffer strangers to come into the place where it is kept; nor let the place be ever left open.'[48]

A butler in a more modest-sized country house must have a wide variety of talents. One advertisement for a post in Suffolk in 1775 sought 'a Butler that can shoot and shave well'.[49] In 1797, Sir William Heathcote of Hursley indicated that his butler 'Must understand Brewing & Management of the Cellar, Clean his own plate, and do all his own work, as no under Butler will be kept.' Also, 'he Must see all the Family [the servants] go to bed before him, & see every door and window Made fast & secure.' He was expected to answer bells at any time during the day.[50]

The regulations of the household at Wimpole Hall in Cambridgeshire, in the same decade, describe the roles of steward and butler combined in one man:

> The House Steward & Butler is ordered to see weighed, & enter in a book every morning all descriptions of provisions that are brought to the house; and all persons whatsoever, bringing meat fowls of all sorts, Game, Fish, eggs for Kitchen use . . . are to make the same known to the House Steward & Butler, that he may make his entries. In like manner, coals, Oils & Wax candles are to duly entered into his book, on the day of their arrival.[51]

There are phrases in Anthony Heasel's book of advice to servants that are direct echoes of the treatise by John Russell, writing of the medieval household: 'Take great care of your wine and other liquors, not only to keep them in good order, but likewise to prevent their being embezzled, or given away to any person besides those who have a right to them according to your instructions.'[52]

In medieval times the groom of the chambers was a young male assistant to the chamberlain. By the eighteenth century this ancient title had come to apply to a senior manservant, who dined with other senior servants such as the head cook and butler but, unlike them, wore livery. His principal duties were apparently to oversee the presentation and cleaning of the main reception rooms. Among other things, he had to ensure that the ornate furniture was returned to its proper place after it had been used by visitors and that tables were in order. He literally dressed the rooms.

The 2nd Earl of Nottingham at Burley had a long list of the duties of his groom of the chambers that began with: 'You must be careful of the furniture, brushing and cleaning every morning that w[hi]ch is [in] constant use, and the rest also once in the week or oftener if need be.' His other duties related to the maintenance of fires, the replacement of candles and closing of windows and shutters, as well as the care and presentation of the chapel.[53]

The groom of the chambers usually had the key role of greeting and announcing visitors, then directing them to their proper rooms, ensuring that they had everything required for their comfort.[54] Some grooms of the chambers were even trained in upholstery.[55] This individual was certainly among the servants who received a share of the fees when paying visitors were shown round a house. This sometimes led to rivalry with the housekeeper, as apparently happened at Cannons, the home of the Duke of Chandos.[56]

Below the footmen, there were clearly often additional men and boys (by the nineteenth century known as 'odd men') who could help with dirtier, more manual jobs, including cleaning drains and gutters, and clearing away slops. One unusually titled junior male servant is worth noting here, although he is one of a kind. 'The Rubber' is referred to in the early-eighteenth-century 'General Instructions' drawn up for the household at Boughton in Northamptonshire. 'He is under the Direction of the Hous[e]keeper to Dry rub the Floors in the House, to fetch and carry Water for the Hous[e]maids for washing the house, to fetch and carry the Ladders and assist upon the Ladders in Washing the Wainscoat and Cornishes when ordered.' He was also responsible for lighting the fire in the steward's hall, waiting at table there, and helping with carrying in the food.[57]

The female indoor staff were by this time very much under the leadership of the housekeeper. This increasingly essential figure managed the linen, the cleaning of rooms and, if there were no clerk of the kitchen or male cook, the kitchen. Below her would be the female cook, followed by a number of chambermaids, housemaids, laundrymaids, and kitchen and scullery maids. Those housekeeping duties that in the late sixteenth and early seventeenth centuries had been managed by the mistresses of the household were by now largely handed over to a trusted housekeeper. Many of them seem to have done long service, as did Mrs Garnett at Kedleston Hall in Derbyshire, who ran the house for over forty years.[58]

One former housekeeper, Elizabeth Raffald, who had worked for Lady Elizabeth Warburton, put together over 800 recipes for pickling, potting, wines, vinegars, 'catchups', and distilling, which were published as *The Experienced English Housewife* in 1769. This entrepreneurial lady also set up an early registry for servants in Manchester, before running an inn, a profession to which many retired senior servants devoted their savings and energies.[59]

At the beginning of the century, in gentry households at least, housekeepers might well be a family relative of some sort. In 1792, Francis Grose, looking back in time, wrote: 'When I was a young man there existed in the families of . . . the rank of gentlemen, a certain antiquated female, either maiden or widow, commonly an aunt or cousin.' He recalled: 'By the side of this good old lady jingled a bunch of keys, securing in different closets and corner cupboards all sorts of cordial waters' as well as: 'washes for the complexion . . . a rich, seed cake, a number of pots of currant jelly and raspberry jam.'[60] As the housekeeper's room became a place where expensive foodstuffs would be stored under lock and key, the individuals themselves were often depicted in paintings with a large bunch of keys at their waists.

They were more likely to have been a senior indoor maid, cook, or nurse. In the mid eighteenth century, one dairymaid, Sarah Staniforth, unusually managed to work her way up the ladder. After joining the staff of Holkham Hall in 1731, she became housemaid in 1741 and housekeeper in 1750. In this post she was paid £20 a year and remained there until her death in 1772. In her will she left over £1,000.[61]

In grander country houses, a female might be an under-cook to a chef, but in many houses the sole and chief cook might be a woman. While (male) French chefs were popular with the aristocracy, there were many, like Hannah Glasse, who thought their worth exaggerated. She observed in *The Art of Cookery Made Plain and Easy* (1747) that 'if gentlemen will have French cooks they must pay for French tricks'. Her book was intended to instruct kitchenmaids in basic cookery, thus reducing the need for the lady of the house to instruct them herself.[62]

Recruiting a cook could obviously be a challenge. Lady Grisell Baillie's household accounts for 1717 show that one cook arrived on 1 February and stayed just two weeks, whilst the next candidate spent only one night in the house. It was not until July that Lady Grisell found a cook who was content with the situation. Anne Griffith was to get '£7 a year' and '£8 if she does well'.[63] Mrs Delaney, looking for a cook for her country house, regretted the one that got away: 'the cook I gave an account of who was a most desirable servant, said she could not live in the country it was so melancholy.'[64]

In *The Housekeeping Book of Susannah Whatman* (1776), the author stresses how important it was for the mistress, or her housekeeper, to lay down the rules of the house and the kitchen to any new cook: 'When a new Cook comes, much attention is necessary till she is got into all the common rules and observances . . . filling the hog pails, washing up the butter dish, salad bowl etc.: giving an eye to the scowering of saucepans by the Dairy-maid, preserving the water in which the meat is boiled for broth: keeping all her places clean: managing her fire and her kitchen linen.'[65]

Mrs Purefoy, a gentry lady running her small country house, wrote to one candidate cook, Betty Hows, offering to train her in the finer points of her duties, which in her house also meant some cleaning and milking: 'If you can roast & boyll & help clean an House, & make up Butter, & milk two or three cows . . . & you help iron & get up ye Cloaths. If you can do these things wee will endeavour to teach you the rest of the Cookery.'[66]

During the course of the eighteenth century, it appears that the roles of the traditional 'waiting gentlewomen' and the chambermaid gradually merged to become the familiar 'lady's maid', a well-presented servant who would be always in attendance on a great lady. In many cases such a personal maid would sleep in the same room, an adjoining room or even in the passage outside, and travel with her mistress from place to place.

In another book, *The Servants Directory, Improved*, published in 1761, Hannah Glasse outlined the duties of the traditional chambermaid, who is encouraged to 'Take great care to know all your mistress's method and time of doing her business; and be very punctual and acute in your attendance . . . and be sure to have all her linen well air'd and when dress'd or undress'd, fold up everything very neat.' She focuses on cleaning the fine textiles of the day, such as silks, satins and damasks, with special instructions for cleaning flowered silks with 'bread and power-blue . . . and if any silver or gold flowers be in it, take a piece of crimson velvet and rub the flowers'.[67]

The housemaid was essentially the cleaner, doing everything from making beds and mending linen to cleaning floors, doors, windows, carpets and furniture, as well as the scrubbing, cleaning and preparation of fireplaces. A housemaid's day was gruelling. In Hannah Glasse's book she is told to:

> Be up very early in a morning, as indeed you are first wanted; lace on your stays, and pin your things very tight about you, or you never can do work well . . .
> Be sure always to have very clean feet, that you may not dirty your rooms, and learn to walk softly, that you may not disturb the family. The first thing, if in winter, is to light your fires, and clean your hearths; if in summer, the stove rubbed and the dirt in your hearth swept out.

These directions continue for over a page, before the housemaid is advised to move on to locks, then carpets, curtains, windows and shutters, dusting the pictures, frames and plasterwork, before sweeping the room out.[68]

Hannah Glasse includes many accepted techniques for cleaning and is clearly a great believer in fresh air:

> For sweeping the stairs a little wet sand is recommended on the top stair, to help keep the dust down. All this you are to get done before your mistress rises. When the family is up, go into every bed chamber, throw open all the windows to air the rooms, and uncovering the beds to sweeten and air them; besides it is good for the health to air the bedding, and sweet to sleep in when the fresh air has had access to them, and a great help against bugs and fleas.[69]

Whilst scouring the house from top to bottom, housemaids were also expected to be properly modest in deportment and dress, and to be subservient, as is made clear by a note in the 1768 household book of the Duchess of Northumberland: 'They are always to keep themselves clean & neat but not to dress above their station.'[70]

By the eighteenth century, the number of women servants in great country houses had swelled, and many had the most humble jobs. The former scullion, now a female scullery-maid, had to clean the kitchen and wash the cooking utensils used in the preparation of the meals – some of the most unforgiving work in the country house – as well as cleaning and preparing various foodstuffs, especially vegetables.

Hannah Glasse's book gives the scullery-maid a messy and labour-intensive recipe for cleaning pewter, tin and copper: 'Take a pail of wood ashes (either from the baker's dyers or hot pressers, the latter is the best) half a pail of unslack'd lime, and four pails of soft water; boil them all in a copper together, stirring them; when they have boiled about half an hour, take it all together out of the copper into a tub, and let it stand cold, then pour off clear and bottle for use.'[71]

The laundrymaids too had a physically demanding job that was carried out in a series of outhouses, such as a washhouse and a dry laundry (with a range suitable to heat irons), often connected to the main service courtyard. They worked with their hands in very hot water, handling wet clothes such as shirts and neckcloths, bedlinen and towels, which then had to be starched, bleached, dried, pressed and ironed.[72]

The proper care of household linen was reckoned one of the most important demonstrations of good housekeeping and there were massive quantities of it. The inventory at Blenheim in 1740 lists 'Damask and Diaper Napkins Sixty Seven Dozen and five, Table Cloths of the best Sort Ninety three, Stewards Table Cloths twenty Fine Sheets Eighteen pair, Servants Sheets Forty Five pair,' and so on.[73] At Shugborough in staffordshire in 1792, the inventory included '85 Damask tablecloths, 92 dozen damask table napkins, Damask breakfast cloths, 23, Damask tea napkins, 29 dozen,' to which should be added seventeen pairs of 'Holland sheets & pillowcases', nineteen pairs of 'second sheets', and eighteen pairs of 'second pillowcases'.[74]

Laundry work was largely done by hand. Sometimes washing was pounded with wooden bats, but it might also need steeping in a liquid such as urine or lye (an alkali cleansing agent made by soaking wood ash in water to extract potassium salts), as well as soap-washing and boiling. Bleaching was a regular event, and up until the early twentieth century most country houses had specially dedicated bleaching or drying grounds, where linen, which could easily yellow, was laid out on long grass to dry and bleach in the sun – preferably a midwinter sun.[75]

The dairymaid separated cream, churned butter and made cheese for consumption in the house. The dairy was usually specially designed to remain cold and was sometimes an ornamental feature of the grounds of a great house. It had to be kept very clean, as the author Thomas Hale observed in the *Compleat Book of Husbandry* (1765): 'First thing, and the most important of all in a Dairy is Cleanliness. Not only the vessels and utensils but the very Floor, walls and ceiling, everything that is in it and everything that is about it, must be thus managed with the utmost nicety of Cleanliness or there will be continual Damage and Losse.'[76]

The country-house nursery was of prime importance as the birth and upbringing of a healthy male heir were central to the aristocratic mindset. Thus great efforts were made to ensure that babies were kept safe at a period when infant mortality was high among all classes; the mortality rate among upper-class children did not improve dramatically until the later eighteenth century.[77]

Hannah Glasse in *The Servants Directory* takes an unusual view of the nurserymaid's duties: 'A child when it comes into the world, is almost a round ball; it is the nurse's part to assist nature, in bringing it to a proper shape.'[78] Nurses often travelled with their charges. Among the Blount family letters is one in 1787 making preparations for a visit by the son and heir with his family. He writes saying that he will be travelling 'with my wife's maid, two nursery maids, & two men. The children may all be in the great Room . . . we will bring a little bed & bedding for the youngest . . . & the two maids may sleep in the large bed.'[79]

Infants would be cared for by a nurse and a nurserymaid, with additional help when required, and would often be breast-fed in their early months by a specially employed wet-nurse. The eighteenth-century beauty, Georgiana, Duchess of Devonshire, famously defied convention and nursed her children herself, dispensing with a wet-nurse, although she did employ a 'rocker', literally a menial who rocked the cradle but was also expected to clean up the baby's mess. The duchess had to dismiss her for drunkenness: 'I perceived that she made the bed stink of wine and strong drink when she came near it . . . This morning I learnt she had been so drunk as to fall down and vomit.'[80]

Later on there would be tutors for the boys and governesses for the girls, who would attempt to provide a rounded education, always assuming that the boys were not sent away to school. It was a commonly held belief that private education by a tutor produced a more virtuous child.[81] Daniel Defoe, in his book *The Compleat English Gentleman* (published around 1725), noted that aristocratic mothers were unwilling to let their boys go to school to be taught by a social inferior.[82]

The daily round of teaching a child was not necessarily unpleasant. In 1705, Lady Grisell Baillie wrote a note to her daughter's governess on how she should spend her day: 'To rise by seven o'clock and goe about her duty of reading, etc. etc., and to be drest to come to Breckfast at nine, to play on the spinnet till eleven, from eleven till twelve to write and read French. At two o'clock sow her seam till four, at four learn arithmetic, after that dance and play on the spinet again till six and play [by] herself til supper and to bed at nine.'[83]

Mary Wollstonecraft spent some time at the end of the eighteenth century as a governess to the children of Viscount and Viscountess Kingsborough at Mitchelstown Castle in Ireland, of which she wrote: 'I am treated like a gentlewoman but I cannot easily forget my inferior station – and this something betwixt and between is rather awkward – it pushes me forward to notice.' Much alone, she was thrown back on her own company and thoughts: 'I commune with my own spirit – and am detached from the world – I have plenty of books.'[84]

Later in the century, Lady Kildare boldly asked the admired philosopher Rousseau (incidentally himself a former footman) to be her children's tutor, and when he declined she appointed one William Ogilvie to teach her many children on Rousseau-esque principles, with plenty of freedom and time outdoors. Ogilvie was a mathematician, a classical scholar and a French speaker; perhaps because of his education Lady Kildare was prepared to treat him as a gentleman (although when he was appointed, there was much discussion about whether he was a gentleman or not and should be given wax or tallow candles). He taught Latin verse and grammar, French language and English history as well as mathematics to her boys as well as her girls, although the latter had additional lessons in deportment, singing and needlework.[85] He was clearly a success in more ways than one. In her widowhood, Lady Kildare married her children's tutor and they retired together to France.

There were one or two other rare marriages between the classes worth mentioning. In 1785, Mary Cole, an eighteen-year-old lady's maid of great beauty, first received the attentions of the 5th Earl of Berkeley and bore him seven children before he married her formally, causing great confusion later over the inheritance, as the title went to the son born after their marriage.[86] However, one of her younger sons recalled that she had managed the house with great competence. He wrote: 'When she found herself mistress of Cranford and Berkeley Castle, with unlimited sway over the domestic establishment, and the command of an entire revenue of the estate, she exhibited extra-ordinary natural talent for management, and unquestionably saved Lord Berkeley a good deal of trouble that he particularly disliked.'[87] Sir Henry Harpur of Calke Abbey in Derbyshire married an accomplished lady's maid in 1792.[88]

Lady Henrietta Wentworth (the sister of Lord Rockingham) married her footman, John William Sturgeon, in 1764, upon which they withdrew not to France but to Ireland. Horace Walpole in his letters remarked on her legal settlement, which gave her husband £100 a year and entailed the remainder on any children of the union. She had, he said, 'mixed a wonderful degree of prudence with her potion'.[89] Marriages between master or mistress and servant were outnumbered by the illegitimate offspring of similar unions.

The outdoor staff of a country house could be just as critical to the prestige of the country house as the regiment indoors. The stables might be managed by a clerk of the stables (the successor to the gentleman of the horse), who organised the coachmen, grooms and footmen when they were accompanying a coach or a horse. In many households his role might be absorbed into the duties of the coachman, another senior liveried servant who not only had to drive the coach but, along with the other footmen, could act as a bodyguard to the family. His responsibilities extended to the continual maintenance of the horses and the carriages.

In the eighteenth century, the display made by a fine coach and horses of quality, together with the attendant coachman and footmen, was exceptionally important. A visiting American, Benjamin Silliman, wrote in 1805 that 'One great point of emulation is to excel all rivals in the number of footmen. Some of the coaches had two, three, or even four footmen, standing up, and holding on behind the carriage, not to mention a supernumerary one on the coachman's box.'[90]

A coachman would usually be given his livery in addition to his wages. Every second year, Ambrose Campion, the coachman in 1776 to Philip Yorke of Erddig, received a pair of plush breeches, another of buckskin, a waistcoat, a frock greatcoat and boots.[91] His work began at 6 a.m., preparing the stables and the horses, and ensuring that the carriage and harness were cleaned and ready for use.[92]

Tam Youall, coachman to Lady Grisell Baillie at Mellerstain in Berwickshire, was employed as a groom in 1706, at an annual wage of £1 10s, plus his clothes. When he became coachman and moved with the family to London, his annual pay rose to £3. He was still in post in 1740, but was later fined for misconduct or carelessness and injuring another servant when drunk.[93]

The stables of many country houses had space for many kinds of horses, not only to draw the carriage and for riding, but also for hunting, an increasingly popular sport in the late eighteenth century. The supporting servants were often depicted in paintings by George Stubbs, such as the Hunt servants of Lord Torrington.[94] Apart from the twenty-plus stable staff at Holkham Hall in Norfolk in the 1720s, there was a hunt staff, including a fox huntsman with an assistant, a hare huntsman, a whipper-in, a dog-boy, a helper and a gamekeeper. Holkham Hall boasted a coachman's stable and a pad-groom's stable for easy-paced horses.[95]

As in any period, handsome grooms could lead to marital problems. Clara Middleton of Stockeld Park, Yorkshire, became infatuated with John Rose, who had been hired as the groom of the hunting stable but had became her favourite companion on rides – shades of the stories of 'Handsome' Macdonald.[96] It ended in tears, with the Middletons' divorce.

Every house had a head gardener responsible both for the pleasure grounds and for the kitchen gardens that supplied produce for the house. The staff under him ranged from unskilled local women, recruited to weed the gardens, to the jobbing labourer. Head gardeners sometimes went on to become independent landscape gardeners such as William Ewes, head gardener to Sir Nathaniel Curzon at Kedleston Hall, Derbyshire, between 1756 and 1760.[97]

Highly literate and able, some became authors in their own right. One such was William Speechly, who had worked at Castle Howard, Yorkshire, then for Sir William St Quintin, and from 1767 was employed by William, 3rd Duke of Portland, at Welbeck Abbey in

Nottinghamshire. He published *Treatise on the Culture of the Pine Apple* in 1779, followed by a *Treatise on the Culture of the Vine* in 1790.[98]

The scope offered to gardeners of the period had been increased by the mastery of better regulated hothouses or 'stoves'. Using hot-beds of tanner's bark, they could create the hot and humid conditions necessary for tropical plants. Thus by the 1730s most noblemen were the proud owners of hothouses, greenhouses and pineries for exotic fruit. This extension of responsibilities clearly put pressure on garden-ers to acquire the necessary skills and experience.

Those at the top of their game were highly valued. Lord Petre, for example, employed a number of gardeners at Thorndon Hall in Essex, two of whom, John Miller and James Huntback, appear in a 1742 list of his servants as the most important in the hierarchy after the chaplain and the estate manager.[99] In his later years Mr Miller fell from grace. First, Lady Petre wrote to the agent complaining of his unreliability in money matters. In April 1744, he was responsible for a failure to keep the hothouses properly supplied with tanner's bark, so that many plants including the large melon died. He had also allowed all the pineapples to fruit so that there would be none the following year.[100]

A gardener was usually expected to be well mannered enough to act as a guide when showing the gardens to prestigious visitors, if required. Anthony Heasel wrote in *Servants' Book of Knowledge* (1733): 'Take every opportunity of entertaining those who come to visit your master, with a particular description of every thing in the garden, and have always some places ready for them to rest them-selves on, while passing from one part to another.'[101]

One great gardener to an aristocratic house, Thomas Mawe, pub-lished *Every Man His Own Gardener* in 1769. A later writer penned a brilliant portrait of the grandeur of such gardeners. In his introduc-tion to the second edition of John Abercrombie's *Abercrombie's Practical Gardener*, published in 1817, James Mean says: 'When intro-duced to Mawe, whom he had never before seen, poor Abercrombie (as he used facetiously to narrate) encountered a gentleman so bepowdered, and so bedaubed with gold lace, that he thought he could be in the presence of no less a personage than the Duke him-self.'[102]

Another head gardener to a noble household who rose to great national (indeed, international) prominence was Capability Brown, the son of a yeoman farmer, who first worked for Sir William Loraine at Kirkharle. He became Head Gardener at Stowe in Buckinghamshire in 1741, which involved him in major landscape excavation and remodelling. In 1751, after Lord Cobham's death, he left Stowe and worked in his own capacity, charging impressive fees. He earned over £10,000 in 1759.[103]

There was a considerable preponderance of Scottish head gardeners in the eighteenth and early nineteenth centuries. Horace Walpole commented to the Countess of Ossory in 1777 on the absurdity of this; our ancestors, he said, 'were not so absurd to import peaches, nectarines, and pine-apples from the south, and highlanders from the Orcades to look after them'.[104]

At the beginning of the century, gamekeepers were primarily concerned with the preservation of deer. Hunting deer, or stag, was a traditionally aristocratic pastime, and it became an important status symbol to consume, or to make gifts of, venison. Edward Bishop, the gamekeeper at Hursley, Sir William Heathcote's estate in Hampshire, in the 1730s, was charged with looking after the deer population as well as the sheep on the park, whilst destroying vermin. He was also expected to kill game for despatch to London, or dispersal as gifts.[105]

With a sharp rise in the value and status of venison in the eighteenth century came innumerable problems with armed poachers, as illustrated by the Black Act of 1723. This specified that any armed men who were caught with blackened or disguised faces in any 'Forest, Chase or Park' where deer were kept could be put to death.[106] Clashes between gamekeepers and poachers were commonplace in the eighteenth and nineteenth centuries.

In fact, an Act of 1671 had restricted shooting small game and birds to qualified people, namely owners of land with £100 a year, or leaseholders of land worth £150 a year. Lords of the manor were allowed to appoint gamekeepers to enforce these regulations and in 1707, new legislation authorised these gamekeepers to shoot game themselves. Those appointed could be either estate servants, or, increasingly, local gentry who enjoyed shooting pheasants and the like as a sport.[107]

As shooting gained in popularity during the eighteenth century, gamekeepers needed to raise the numbers of game birds, which meant protecting them even more rigorously against poachers, especially at night. One gamekeeper complained of his daytime concentration being ruined because he had 'laid ought [out] Many cold Nights in your Woods and Plantations When the Rest of your servants Were a Bed'.[108] Indeed, battles with poachers became a preoccupation of all gamekeepers.

At Longleat their numbers swelled from two keepers in 1750 to seven by 1787. By 1818, their numbers nationally were recorded as 3,336.[109] The relationship between sport-loving landowning employers and their trusted gamekeepers could be close. The portrait of Jack Henshaw, the gamekeeper of Philip Yorke, which hangs at Erddig, carried the celebratory verse:

> A lover true to fur, and feather,
> Who tired not, nor lost his leather:
> Near forty years, through bush and bry'r
> He beated for the elder squire.[110]

Gamekeepers may well have relished their outdoor role, free of many of the constraints of indoor service, as they were not expected to live in the main mansion.

4

Behind the Green Baize Door
The Eighteenth Century

THE EIGHTEENTH-CENTURY COUNTRY house required huge numbers of staff with increasingly specialised duties. The landowner, or his wife and/or the upper servants, had to not only recruit but retain them. So where did they come from, how were they managed and where did they live? As might be expected, they were often found locally or through the recommendation of a third party, such as a family friend. The letters of aristocratic ladies positively hum with information about potential servants, not least in seeking or giving references. Senior servants – especially stewards and housekeepers in larger households – former senior servants and trusted tradesmen might all be given the task of finding suitable people.

There were also agencies, special registries and newspaper adverts but, as John Macdonald's memoir shows, word of mouth was very effective. The open market took the form of the 'Statute Fair', a country fair that was held every autumn in most market towns and was set aside for the hiring of labour of all kinds. Contracts would usually initially be entered into for one year.[1]

On 22 September 1736 one gentry mistress, Elizabeth Purefoy, wrote to a butcher at Brackley: 'Mr King, I want a cook maid. If you should hear of any that are at the Statute Fair today, I shall be there by and by.' In 1743, she petitioned a Mrs Sheppard concerning another servant: 'I hope the maid will do if she can sew well, that is to work fine plain work as mobs and ruffles. If she comes she must bring a character [reference] of her honesty from the person she lived with last. My custom is to give the servants a shilling for the horse hire & they come themselves & I will give her half a crown because she comes so far.'[2]

Letters from landowners to relations and friends are peppered with references to servants looking for posts, or posts vacant. Among the unpublished letters from Nostell Priory in Yorkshire are some from Jane, Countess of Dundonald, to Sabine, Lady Wynn of Nostell, written in 1776, about engaging a Mrs McPhell on her behalf, and enclosing 'a very ample character of the Housekeeper [who] was in Lord Kinnoul's [Kinnoull's] family'. As the reference was 'very satis-factory', she 'ventured to give her earnest as a hir'd servant from this term of Whitsunday being the 15th of this month till the 11th of Nov[ember].'[3] Lady Dundonald did as she was bid but with some hesitation, because she had not yet heard from Lady Wynn as to her requirements and the wages she was offering, but 'if I hadn't hired Mrs McPhell today she was to have been engaged for another family tomorrow'.

Evidently the arrangement does not work out for Lady Dundonald wrote later that year:

> I'm very sorry to find Mrs [Mc]Phell the Housekeeper has behav'ed ill, and quite disappointed the hopes we had cause to entertain from the character Lady Elizabeth Hay gave of her which I transmitted to your Ladyship. Servants nowadays are so inconsistent as to behave well in one place and ill in another. Idleness, Dress and Insolence are their prevailing vices. It gives me much uneasiness that the woman has been so foolish – how happy she might have been otherwise in your service.

One longs to know the housekeeper's side of the story.

Few such responses remain from the eighteenth century, although one servant at Hall House, near Hawkhurst in Kent, wrote bitterly handing in their notice with the following remarks: 'I see there is no such thing as pleasing you . . . and though I cant please you, I dont doubt but I shall please other people very well. I never had the uneasiness anywhere, as I have here.'[4]

Lady Dundonald had also clearly played a role in hiring a French governess: 'Do tell me my dear Lady Winn does Madame Picq please you? I am very desirous to know if she fulfils the important duties of a governess. I wish her being married be no barr to it.' It was very unusual to hire a married governess, but the Frenchwoman seems to have given satisfaction as there is mention of Miss Wynn's making advances in the language: 'I'm rejoic'd that my friend Madame le Picq gives your Ladyship such satisfaction and that Miss Wynn makes surprizing progress in the French.'[5]

One letter early in the century, from Samuel Heathcote to the father of a young footman, sets out typical terms of engagement: 'If your son be at liberty to come from Mr Hurts, and have his masters free Consent: I shall be willing to take him into my service on the following terms & Conditions'. This included: 'that He serve me as a footman, or in any other Business for the term of four years.' Clearly, in this case flexibility was a prime requirement.

The footman, or whatever else he might be, would get a certain amount of clothing from his employer, such as annually a new hat, a coat, a waistcoat, breeches, one pair of stockings and one pair of shoes, but must find the rest himself. If, at the end of the four years, he had 'faithfully & honestly performed his Service, He shall have fifteen pounds, and shall be then free either to leave my Service or continue longer in, as We can then Agree'. The acceptance of terms, which included making up funds if his vails (or tips) fell short, was signed by both father and son.[6]

In contrast to this commonplace example, we should also remember that in the eighteenth century – indeed, from the late seventeenth century – many others were unable to draw on such parental protection. Young boys were brought from the West Indies, Africa or India as slaves, to become pageboys in aristocratic households. Although some were treated well and given some education, their lives must have seemed so alien as to have been utterly bewildering.

Whilst many like them were slaves by origin, sometimes they were paid wages just as if they were free. In fact, there was some confusion over their legal status right up to the point when slavery was finally abolished in Great Britain in 1833. As early as 1706, Chief Justice Holt wrote that 'by common law no man can have a property in another'. This suggested that as soon as a slave came to England he became free, although this notion was soon squashed by Philip Yorke as Attorney-General.[7]

Slavery was outlawed in Scotland as early as 1778, as a result of the case of Knight versus Wedderburn. Joseph Knight had been purchased in Jamaica and brought to Scotland at the age of twelve or thirteen to be a personal servant. Eventually, Knight married and left the service of John Wedderburn, who later had him arrested. When local justices declared that Knight must continue to be a slave, the sheriff of Perthshire ruled that the state of slavery was 'not recognized' by the laws of Scotland, a judgment upheld by the court of session in that year.

Granville Sharp, one of the active abolitionists of the time, intervened in the case of a young slave, James Somerset, who had been shipped over to England from Virginia. He had escaped, been recaptured and put in irons. Sharp had him brought before Lord Mansfield, who ruled (eventually) for Somerset's release, but ruling too that a slave could not be forcibly repatriated against his will.[8]

Curiously, Dido Belle, the child of a black slave woman and Sir John Lindsay, Lord Mansfield's nephew, and lived in his household at Kenwood. She managed the dairy there and became a companion-servant to her cousin. Mansfield not only left her money and an annuity in his will but confirmed her status as a free person.[9]

Numerous young black servants, forgotten to history, can be glimpsed in portraits of the period. One such is thought to be James Cambridge, who appears in the portrait of the Earl and Countess of Burlington, which now hangs at Lismore Castle in Ireland. The fashion for the possession of a black servant may have been begun by Venetian merchants. Certainly they appear in portraits in great country houses almost as a visual foil to the whiteness and delicate complexions of the young women of the family.[10]

The bitter truth is that black servants were sometimes treated as little better than playthings for the aristocracy, their youth used up far away from their families. The Duchess of Kingston had a page called Sambo, whom she brought up from the age of five or six, dressing him in fine style and taking him to the theatre, where he sat in her box. Once he reached the age of eighteen or nineteen, however, she tired of him and sent him back to the West Indies.[11]

We must be grateful for the fact that there were always critics of this practice. As early as 1710, Richard Steele wrote a letter of complaint to *The Tatler* as if he himself were one such child: 'As I am patron of persons who have no other friend to apply to, I cannot suppress the following complaint: Sir – I am a six-year old negro boy, and have, by my lady's order, been christened by the chaplain. The good man has gone further with me, and told me a great deal of news: as I am as good as my lady herself, as I am a Christian, and many other things.' At one point, it was erroneously believed that slaves who converted to Christianity while in England were automatically granted their freedom. The letter continued: 'but for all this, the parrot, who came over with me from our country is as much esteemed by her as I am. Beside this, the shock dog has a collar that cost as much as mine. I desire also to know whether, now I am a Christian, I am obliged to dress like a Turke and wear a turbant. I am, sir, your most obedient servant, Pompey.'[12]

A memorial stone in Henbury, near Bristol, commemorates the death of a black running footman: 'Here Lieth the body of Scipio Africanus, Negro Servant to ye Rt Hon Charles Williams, Earl of Suffolk and Bristol. Who died ye 21 Dec 1720 aged 18 years.'[13] These high-sounding classical names suggest that black slaves were a high-status possession in a civilised society, a strange reflection on the culture that informed so much of the best literature and architecture of the day. The inscribed verse illustrates the paradoxical and confused attitude to young slaves in Britain. It begins:

I who was born a Pagan and a slave
Now Sweetly Sleep a Christian in my Grave
What tho' my hue was dark my Savior's sight
Shall change this darkness into radiant light.

Black pages were thought of as little more than chattels. Early in the century, a duchess wrote to her mother that her husband was unwilling that she should accept the gift of such a child from a friend and offering to pass him on in her turn: 'Dear mama, George Hanger has sent me a Black Boy, eleven years old and very honest, the duke don't like me having a black, and yet I cannot bear the poor wretch being ill-used; if you liked him instead of Michel I will send him; he will be a cheap servant and you will make a Christian of him and a good boy; if you don't like him they say Lady Rockingham wants one.'[14]

One of the more inspiring stories was that of Ignatius Sancho, which begins in the bleak misery of British-sponsored slavery. He was born in 1729 on board a slave ship; his mother died and his father committed suicide. Ignatius was presented as a gift to three sisters in Greenwich who refused to educate him. He himself wrote years later that he had the misfortune to have been placed 'in a family who judged ignorance the best and only security for obedience.'[15] He taught himself how to read and write and attracted the attention of some of the nobility. The Duke of Montagu met him and took him 'frequently home to the Duchess, indulged his turn for reading with presents of books, and strongly recommended to his mistresses the duty of cultivating a genius of such apparent fertility.'[16]

Aged around twenty, Ignatius ran away and threw himself on the mercy of the widowed Duchess of Montagu, who took him in and employed him as a butler, leaving him a legacy when she died in 1751. Ignatius later went into service, probably as a valet to the Earl of Cardigan, and turned out to be a gifted musician. He left service to become a successful grocer and corresponded with the novelist Laurence Sterne. He also married a West Indian woman who bore him six children. In *The Letters of the Late Ignatius Sancho* (1802), he wrote: 'the latter part of my life has been . . . truly fortunate, having spent it in the service of one of the best families in the kingdom.'[17] He was admired for his wit and erudition.

By 1770, 14,000–20,000 blacks were believed to be living in London, principally as a side effect of the lucrative trade between Britain and its sugar-planting and slave-holding islands in the West Indies.[18] Horace Walpole recalled that the sisters of Lord Middleton had a black servant 'who has lived with them a great many years and is remarkably sensible'. On hearing that the British were sending a ship to the Pellew Islands in the Pacific, this servant exclaimed: 'Then there is an end of their happiness.' Walpole remarked rightly: 'What a satire on Europe!'[19]

Young children from India and China were also taken into service. The Indians were often attached to the households of men who were officers of the East India Company; they appear also to have had the status of slaves.[20] In the Crimson Drawing Room at Knole hangs the remarkable portrait by Sir Joshua Reynolds of Wang-y-Tong, a Chinese page employed by the 3rd Duke of Dorset and brought to England by John Bardby Blake, a schoolfellow of the duke's and an official of the East India Company. The duke was enlightened enough to have his page educated at Sevenoaks Grammar School.[21]

Most landowners appear blind to the unfairness of the life of young slaves, but were ready to find fault with their freeborn counterparts. Grumbling about servants became a national pastime in the eighteenth century. In 1711, the *Spectator* printed a satirical exchange of letters, the first asking the journal to consider

> the general corruption of Manners in the servants of Great Britain . . .
> I have contracted a numerous Acquaintance among the best sort of
> people, and have hardly found one of them happy in their servants.
> This is a matter of great Astonishment to Foreigners . . . especially
> since we cannot but observe That there is no Part of the world where
> servants have those Privileges and Advantages as in England: They
> have no where such plentiful Diet, large Wages, and indulgent liberty:
> There is no Place wherein they labour less, and yet where they are so
> little respectful, nor wast[e]ful, more negligent.

The *Spectator* published an arch response, blaming 'the custom of giving Board Wages [or cash wages in lieu of being fed, when the employer was away]: 'This one instance of false Oeconomy, is sufficient to debauch the whole Nation of Servants.'[22]

Dean Jonathan Swift made remorseless fun of serving men and women, as we have already seen from his trenchant views on the footman. His brilliant satire on the faults of servants of a large household was modelled on an English house but was most likely informed by his experiences in both England and Ireland. Although written in the 1730s, *Directions to Servants* was not published until 1745, after his death. [23]

Swift deals with each member of staff in turn: butler, cook, foot-man, coachman, groom, housekeeper, chambermaid, waiting maid, housemaid, children's maid, nurse, laundress, dairymaid, house stew-ard, land steward, porter and tutoress – and thus supplies a titillating portrait of the servants of an aristocratic household. He revels especially in absurd advice:

> When your master or lady call a servant by name, if that servant be not in the way, none of you are to answer, for there will be end to your drudgery, and masters themselves allow, that if a servant comes when he is called that is sufficient. . . . When you are at fault, be always pert and insolent; and behave yourself as if you were the injured person; this will immediately put your master and lady off their mettle . . .[24]
>
> Never submit to stir a Finger in any Business but that for which you were particularly hired. For example, if the groom be drunk or absent, and the butler be ordered to shut the stable door, the Answer is ready, An it please your Honour, I don't understand horses: If a corner of the hanging wants a single nail to fasten it, and the Footman be directed to tack it up, he may say, he doth not understand that sort of work, but his Honour may send for the upholsterer.[25]

Most memorable of all: 'Never come till you have been called three on four times; for none but dogs will come at the first whistle: and when the master calls "Who's there?" no servant is bound to come; for *Who's there* is nobody's name.'[26]

One cannot help wondering about Swift's relationships with his own domestics, which, given his connection with 'Stella' – the daughter of a household servant – when he himself was a mere secre-tary, were probably not as clear cut as one might think. One nine-teenth-century book of stories about Swift and other Irish wits contains some plausible, if anecdotal, accounts of how he treated his own staff:

> Swift's manner of entertaining his guests, and his behaviour at table, were curious. A frequent visitor thus described them: He placed himself at the head of the table, and opposite to a great pier glass, so that he could see whatever his servants did at the great marble side-board behind his chair. He was served entirely in plate, and with great elegance . . .

The beef once being over roasted, he called for the cook-maid to take it down stairs and do it less. The girl very innocently replied that she could not. 'Why what sort of a creature are you,' exclaimed he, 'to commit a fault which cannot be mended?' . . . [and observed to his neighbour] that he hoped 'as the cook was a woman of genius, he should by this manner of arguing, be able, in about a year's time, to convince her she had better send up the meat too little than too much done'.[27]

Swift also famously held a saturnalia modelled on the Roman festival in which slaves would be served by their masters, as a gesture of humility before the Roman gods, but when a manservant sent back the meat just as Swift was apt to do, it caused him to fly into a temper and chase the servants from the room. Swift himself started life in the service of Sir William Temple at Moor Park in Surrey and, according to Temple's nephew, who disliked him, he was not in those days allowed to dine with the family. This throws an interesting light on the psychology behind his satire.[28]

The real-life issues of the day are perhaps reflected more accurately in the letters of Elizabeth Purefoy, the mistress of Shalstone, a moderately sized establishment in Buckinghamshire. They contain numerous references to servants getting into unfortunate scrapes, either petty theft or unwanted pregnancy, such as the one for 3 May 1738: ''Tis not my dairy maid that is with child but my cookmaid, and it is reported our parson's maid is also with kinchen [i.e. child] by the same person who has gone off & showed them a pair of heels for it. If you could help me to a cook maid as I may be delivered from this, it will much oblige.'[29]

The following year she is driven by similar circumstances to write to a Mr Coleman: 'About 6 weeks ago, I hired one Deborah Coleman who tells me you are her father. I am sorry to tell you that she is very forward with child. She denied it and I was forced to have a midwife to search her, upon which she confessed it was so, and by Mr Launder's manservant whom she lived with.'[30] By 1743, Mrs Purefoy had become more circumspect in her hirings: 'am obliged to you for enquiring after a maid, & if her living at home in a public house has not given her too great an assurance to live in a civilised private family, I think there will be a probability of her doing'.[31] Unwanted pregnancies seen to have been a perpetual hazard for young maid-servants, and then for their employers too.

It was the duty of every mistress to manage a happy household, and misery ensued if she could not. Lord Cowper wrote to his troubled wife Mary on 5 June 1720:

> As vexatious as your very naughty servants have been to you, I am glad you could so far forget their ill behaviour, as to omit it in your former letters: you find turning away one, is no example to mend another, or prevent ye like offence, as you imagined it would . . . the only way to govern them, is to make them so content with their places, yt shall fear turning away; otherwise we hav no restraint upo[n] them.

Lord Cowper went on to remind his wife of the negative impact of too-frequent criticism: 'Their places are good, but they are often so sharply reproached for small faults, yt they grow desperate, hate their places, & so become very easy to comit great [ones].' He noted that the servants 'do not, as I observe, use me or anyone so very ill, as they do ye.' However, he concluded it was up to her to 'turn em away & take em at your pleasure, & when you have [th]em use [th]em as you think fit'.[32]

The Grand Tour featured largely in the lives of young aristocrats of the period, principally young men, but also women. Usually, these tours were conducted in the company of a supposedly trusted servant and tutor, which could sometimes leave the noble traveller in a vulnerable position. In 1773, Lady Coke wrote home in despair after finding herself in the hands of a dishonest servant, one Diehans: 'Think of my distress to be at this distance from England and this Man in my service, who I am obliged in some things to trust, as I have nothing but footmen. I have reason to believe he cheats me in everything.'[33]

Lord Byron recorded his dissatisfaction with the English servant who travelled with him on the continent:

> The perpetual lamentations after beef and beer, the stupid, bigoted contempt for everything foreign, an insurmountable incapacity for acquiring even a few words of any language, rendered him, like all other English servants, an encumbrance. I do assure you, the plague of speaking for him, the comforts he required (more than myself by far), the [dishes] he could not eat, the wines which he would not drink, the beds where he could not sleep.[34]

The logistics of feeding servants were a continual source of comment, although the management of households on such massive scales must have been challenging. A good picture of the daily life, and especially diet, of a large establishment is revealed in the papers of the Marquess of Kildare (created 1st Duke of Leinster in 1766). His rules for the government of his household, again still referred to as a 'family' just as in the seventeenth century, survive in a manuscript version at Alnwick Castle in Northumberland.[35] It offers a valuable insight into the richest and grandest household in Ireland of the period – his country house at Carton. It also gives an impression of the busy life of Lady Kildare, at the centre of a whirlwind of demanding people, writing in a letter to her husband: 'Plagued by servants, worried by the children, my dearest Lord Kildare, I have not been able to sit down and write to you till this minute.'[36]

The steward was charged, among other things, 'Not to allow of Cursing and Swearing about the House &c or any riotous Behaviour but everything done in the most quite and regular Manner [and] To see that every Person do their own Business in the proper Manner and times, and if not, to inform Lord or Lady Kildare of it.' In 1769, Lord Kildare penned a note to the steward: 'I will not permit any dancing to be in any part of the house without my leave or the Duchess of Leinster's, which occasions neglect, idleness, drinking.' The duke wrote another to his English butler on the subject of his pantry, saying that 'he must not by any means admit the pantry to be a meeting or a gossiping place for the under servants', which presumably means that it was.[37]

Most interestingly, Kildare's 'rules for the feeding of the Family', in the absence of Lord and Lady Kildare, set out mealtimes and fare. Good provision for servants was not only a statement of the wealth and patronage of the household but a matter of good administration, as underfed servants could hardly be expected to perform well.

The upper servants (steward, housekeeper, clerk of the kitchen, personal maids and valets) dined in the steward's hall at 4 p.m., on 'Mutton and Broth, Mutton Chops, Harrico or Hashed, Roast or boiled Pork with Pease Pudding and Garden things, Stakes, Roast, or boiled Veal with Garden things when veal is killed at Carton'. Once a week there would be mutton or beef pie; on Sunday, roast beef and plum pudding. 'Particular care must be taken that all meat is well and cleanly dressed and good of the kind.'[38]

The servants' hall – meaning the lower servants – dined at one o'clock on 'boiled Beef, Cabbage and Roots, every Sunday to have a Piece of Beef Roasted and Plum Pudding, or any other kind of Pudding'. Thursdays were boiled mutton or pork, with vegetables, and for supper there would be bread and cheese. Salted fish was served once a week, on Friday, possibly in deference to the Catholicism of some of the servants.[39]

Each person who supped in the servants' hall was given a pint of ale, a common practice in country houses all over the British Isles until the end of the nineteenth century. Whilst there were different regulations about the provision of ale, small beer, which was much weaker, was available to all, 'no Person of the Family to be refused . . . as much as they shall drink', between breakfast and 6 p.m. Beer was regarded, as in the medieval and Tudor eras, as a kind of liquid bread, as ordinary water was then unhealthy to drink.[40]

When the Kildares were based at Leinster House, their town house, the smaller number of servants left behind at Carton were on 'board wages', which meant that their salaries were adjusted to reflect the fact that they had to supply their own meals but could have as much garden produce as they wanted. Married servants were not allowed to live in the house, and the steward was instructed that they were not permitted to eat or drink within its walls 'except now and then, [and] they and their Wives may be asked to Dinner on Sunday to live in Harmony with them so far as to carry on their mutual business to Lord Kildare's advantage'.[41]

The mention of the married servants' dining arrangements is intriguing, as household servants were more often unmarried in English houses. The English agriculturalist Arthur Young, who had worked as a land agent at Mitchelstown Castle and whose survey of the improvements in architecture and agriculture was published in 1780 as *A Tour in Ireland*, commented on the high incidence of married Irish servants: 'Marriage is certainly more general in Ireland than in England. I scarce ever found an unmarried farmer or cottier; but it is seen more in other classes, which with us do not marry at all; such as servants. The generality of footmen and maids, in gentleman's families, are married, a circumstance we very rarely see in England.'[42] In England at this time, there seems to have been a widespread prejudice against employing indoor married servants in English country houses, possibly because of anxiety about divided loyalties, but also to avoid multiplying dependants for the house – and the provisioning of such dependants.

Allowances were given for livery uniforms. From 1 January 1767, footmen at Carton were given 20 shillings a year for 'a Pair of black Worsted Shag Breeches, for a fine Felt Hat with a Silver Chain Loop and Button, and a Horse Hair Cockade'. It was a case of take it or leave it: 'Those who do not chuse to accept of it, to let me know that I may discharge them'.[43]

The duchess's sister Louisa ran a famously meticulous household at Castletown and once wrote to her sibling: 'As to servants I think we treat them too much as if they were dependents [sic], whereas I cannot think them so much so, for I am sure they give us a great deal more than we give them, and really if we consider it, 'tis no more than a contract that we make with them.' This was a gentle reminder to the more conservative sister of the changing nature of the family or household in the traditional sense.[44]

The presence of the copy of the Kildare regulations at Alnwick Castle is an intriguing little mystery in itself. The castle was much restored as the principal country seat of the Duke of Northumberland in the 1750s and 1760s, when it had been virtually derelict. During this intensive building activity, there were also major attempts to monitor the activities of the servants, and the duke and duchess apparently requested a copy of all the household regulations drawn up for Lord Kildare. The archives contain a series of notes made from the late 1760s through to the 1790s, leading up to a final, all-encompassing version dated 16 August 1805.[45] This document may have been modelled on the Kildare Household regulations and was perhaps inspired by the Northumberland Household Book of 1511/12, which was edited and published at about this time.

As well as illustrating the complexity of running large establishments, it reveals that the duke and duchess set great store by good household management as a reflection on themselves. It covers the duties of all the servants, the upper servants in particular, down to such obvious minutiae as who tends which fires in the house: 'The fires, in all the Stranger's Bed Chambers, and Dressing Rooms, are to be taken care of by the servants of those who inhabit them.'[46] Guests would usually be travelling with their own servants or have servants assigned to them.

It is clear from the document's conclusion that the duke's household had not always been so well organised:

> If any servant of any Degree whatsoever, shall presume not to pay the proper attention to these Orders, and Regulations, the Duke is to be immediately informed thereof, and he shall be highly offended with the house steward or any other of the Upper Servants, who shall connive at the Disobedience of these Orders, and not immediately report such Persons as shall make any Difficulty about obeying them; the[re] being determined to establish that Regularity which used formerly to subsist in this family, and which, he is ashamed to say, has for these few last years been scandalously neglected, to the Disgrace of everybody who had belonged to the Family.[47]

There is also a transcript of a memorandum to le Moine, his comptroller, relating to the provision of servants' meals, and trying to confine them to either the steward's room or the servants' hall:

> I am very sorry to perceive by the list sent me in today that a Custom is again this y[ea]r renewed of having more tables among my Servts than the Stewards Room & Servts Hall – I gave a positive order last year that this custom should be discontinued & that the young Ladies, maids, & People of the Kitchen should always dine in the Servts Hall as they had invariably done in my Family, but within these last two or three years.
>
> I likewise perceive that the Place & Rank of my Secretary seems to be completely misunderstood – He is not to be looked upon as a menial servant as the Law of the Land places him above the Station of a Servt & does not include him in the Tax upon servants – He is always to be looked upon at the head of My Family, except in this Castle, where the Grieve, or Constable of the Castle, is my immediate Representative.[48]

There is another version in the collection, 'Regulations and Instructions for the Future Management of the Family, Instructions for the Comptroller', dated 1808 and equally stringent, which covers the oversight of the management of the household, the checking of accounts, the paying of bills and keeping records of expenses.[49] 'You are on no account to pay the least regard to what you may be told about <u>custom</u> – if the thing mentioned is proper, it ought to be adopted, whether it is a custom or not in the Family – if it is improper the sooner it is put to an end the better, & its having been a custom makes it the more necessary to abolish it and guard against it in the future.'[50]

Great attention is paid to entrances and exits, to 'who is introduced by whom – or who may remain on a visit; you are to endeavour to prevent any Person being introduced into the Family who should not be so'. As in previous centuries, emphasis is placed on monitoring who is in the house at any one time, and the comptroller is asked to keep a general register 'to include all the Establishments at my different houses with every one's names and duties.'[51]

On recruiting servants, the comptroller 'must specify their age (& Height, if under Servts) – their county – whither married or single. N.B. Single Persons are always to be preferred to married ones for servants.' The duke was particular about uniforms: 'When the new liveries come home from the Tailor, you will make the Servants parade with them on (the Tailor attending) to see that they are well made, agreeably to the proper pattern, & fit well.' They are then to be 'carefully stored & named'. The comptroller is also responsible for servants' behaviour, 'keeping good hours', and is on 'no account to suffer any gambling – Drunkenness, or other irregularity and improper conduct'.[52]

In a 1768 'Household Book' for Alnwick, which includes many of the earlier draft notes towards these regulations, the duchess outlined her preferred management of the servants' hall, which was 'to be open'd every morning at 9 and to continue so till 10 & then the Usher of the Hall is to lock it up and keep it so until the dinner Bell rings when it is to be open'd for 2 hours & then lock'd up again till their supper Bell rings, when it is to be kept open till the Duke &

Dutchess ring to go to Bed and no longer.' Curiously, she adds: 'All Servants are to find their own knives & forks.'[53]

Another series of drafts, dated to the 1770s and possibly in the duchess's own handwriting, set out the rules for behaviour: 'No swearing or cursing or indecent Language is to be suffered at any of the Tables. If in the Serv[a]nts Hall the person for the first fault to be turned out of the Servants Hall & not re-admitted but on promise of better conduct for the future & if the fault is repeated they are to be turn'd away . . . Maid servants are not to sit gossiping in Servants Hall or even to be near there but at Meal Time & to depart as soon as the Table is clear'd.'[54]

In the same book there is a note on 'Rules for Conduct', relating to her own attendance at church and daily prayers, in which she took herself to task: 'Not to be severe with my servants for small thoughts [presumably meaning faults] and frequent chiding lessens authority. To instruct my servants as far as I am able to furnish them good Books suited to their Capacity and see they attend regularly at church.' She further resolved: 'If any of my Servants are vicious it is my duty to reprove them severely & to employ all sorts of means to reclaim them, but if I find no appearance of success I ought to turn them away.'[55]

At Alnwick and elsewhere, most servants – especially the upper and liveried servants – expected tips (or 'vails') to supplement their annual wages, which were usually given by guests when they came to stay, or to dine, or for other considerations. A servant would sometimes be told how much he might expect in tips before he was hired. One coachman's place, for example, was advertised in 1760 at '£10 per annum with £6 in vails'. In the early eighteenth century, the Earl of Leicester disbursed substantial amounts in vails when on visits to the houses of his friends, giving 10 guineas to Lord Hobart's staff, and 10 more to the Duke of Grafton's. On family visits he would hand a lump sum to a senior servant to distribute to the others.[56]

In *Eight Letters to His Grace the Duke of — on the custom of Vails-Giving in England* (1760), Jonas Hanway railed against the custom of tipping. He imagined the horrors of a country parson invited to stay with a bishop, 'obliged by the tyranny of this custom to pay more for one dinner, than will feed his large family for a week!' He recounted the tale of a colonel staying with a duke who asked his host for the names of the servants. When his host asked him the reason, he replied: 'Why, says he, My Lord Duke, in plain truth, I cannot afford to pay for such good dinners as your Grace gives me and at the same time support my equipage without which I cannot come here; I therefore intend to remember these gentlemen in a codicil in my will'.[57] By 'pay', here he meant 'tip'.

The Duke of Newcastle showed Hanway's letters to George III, who tried to set an example to the nation by banning the acceptance of vails in his own household. This move was greeted with suppressed fury by the royal servants and the next time the king visited the theatre he was hissed by members of his own staff from the anonymity of the gallery. However, he is said to have sat through it all 'with the greatest composure'.[58]

On a more modest scale was this piece of fatherly advice on tipping from the owner of Mapledurham in Berkshire to his son. When Michael Blount went to stay with his uncle at Stonor Park in Oxfordshire in 1761, his father (also Michael) wrote to him, offering hints on what clothes he should take and telling him that

> uncle Strickland will tell you the hours and rules of the house, which I dare say you will strictly comply with . . . When you leave Stonor (which will be the following Wednesday or Thursday, when I will order horses and a servant to go again for you) you must give the maid that makes your bed and fires there <u>half a crown</u>, the butler <u>half a crown</u>, the groom <u>two shillings</u> as you get upon your horse, and the man that dresses your hair &c <u>four shillings</u>. This will be handsome and sufficient.[59]

Some houses of the period might be little occupied for much of the year. At the beginning of the eighteenth century, Lord Fitzwilliam was accustomed to leaving his house at Milton, Oxfordshire, in the care of his steward, housekeeper and chaplain for years at a time. Although he planned to visit Milton every year from 1687, he scarcely set foot there until 1709.[60] As intermarriage between landed families often concentrated estates under one name, many of the wealthiest landowners had more than one country seat and like their medieval forebears would pass the seasons travelling from one to another.

Most major landowners also maintained a London house, or at least spent time in the capital. As the century progressed, they might also visit fashionable places such as Bath, or travel abroad, with the result that many country houses remained principally in the sole care of servants for many months together. Horace Walpole's father, Sir Robert Walpole, famously spent only a few weeks a year at Houghton, Norfolk, when he became prime minister. In his absence the household servants would show the visiting public around his famous art collection.[61]

The architects of the great country houses paid increasing attention to the rational planning of the service areas, particularly the kitchens and rooms for the preparation of foodstuffs, ensuring their interconnectedness with the laundry and dairy as well as with the household apartments that they served. Many houses built in the eighteenth century exemplify the symmetrical arrangement of these apartments, with kitchens and stables arranged either side of the main block, perhaps connected by a semi-raised basement level in between.

The Complete Body of Architecture (1758), by the Palladian architect Isaac Ware, sets out the classical ideals of country-house architecture throughout the century.[62] It included a number of options for the classical house, placing the servants' accommodation in wings. It was in such devices, he argued, that the very nature of architecture is expressed, and his concept certainly expressed the well-established hierarchy of the upper servants. Furthermore, in Book III Ware emphasises the architect's flair for making an aesthetic virtue out of a social necessity – indeed, suggesting that it takes a real architect to work out the best way to incorporate the services and offices into the whole ensemble.

'The next [most important] consideration is for offices, and here comes the first principle of elegance and contrivance in the plan. [The architect] is not to put the kitchen under the parlours, or the stables in a corner of a yard: a bricklayer could do that, we are speaking of the business of an architect . . . here shall arise, with little more expence, a centre, its wings and their communication, the whole regular and uniform.'[63]

Having dealt with the plan of the main house, he addresses the issue of the two wings:

> That on the right hand may contain the kitchen, and offices, belong-ing to it, and the other the stables. The front of the right hand wing may be occupied by a kitchen entirely . . . To the left of the stairs may be a servants' hall, sixteen foot square; and behind that a larder, twelve foot ten by fourteen foot six. In the centre of the other wing may be a double coach-house; for which there should be allowed the whole breadth of the wing, with ten foot six inches width in the clear, and on each side of these may be the stables.[64]

Later, he notes that where kitchens and offices are sited in wings, which is 'commonplace in the country, where the ground is gener-ally the property of the person who builds', for practical reasons 'there must be places of waiting nearer the principal apartments, for those servants whose business it is to be about the person of the master and the lady'.[65]

Again Ware saw an opportunity to use architectural placing and divisions as a way of protecting the aristocracy from exposure to the lowest ranks in the staff hierarchy. However, by careful manipulation of the design you could, he argued, keep the senior servants close at hand, for convenience of communication.

> In this [plan] we shall direct [the architect] to lodge a part of the serv-ants at a distance from the house and a part within it. The upper serv-ants are most wanted about the persons of the master and lady, and these we shall place in a basement stor[e]y under the parlour floor; They can be suffered here because they are cleanly and quiet; therefore there is convenience in having them near, and nothing disagreeable. On the other hand the kitchen is hot, the sculleries are offensive and the servants hall is noisy; these therefore we shall place in one of the wings. This is the conduct of reason; the house-keeper, the clerk of the kitchen, and other domesticks of the like rank, will thus be separated from the rabble of the kitchen; they will be at quiet to discharge their several duties, and they will be ready to attend the master or lady.

[The other servants] will be placed where they can perform their several offices also unmolested; and we shall lay them open to the inspection of the upper servants continually, and place them in readiness to attend the family, by means of a short open passage of communication between the wing in which they are lodged and the body of the house.

[For the other wing:] As we shall propose to lodge in one wing the lower class of servants, the other will conveniently hold the stables; as the gentleman in the country frequently is fond of horses, and has pleasure in seeing them well managed, the same kind of passage may be opened from the body of the house to that wing as to the other.[66]

As Ware makes little reference to the actual personal sleeping accommodation of servants, we must assume he imagined these to have been relegated to attic areas, over the main house, or over the kitchen, the stable or other outhouses, as we have already seen. These quarters, often shared, were referred to as 'garrets' or sometimes 'barracks'. Whilst numerous additions were made to houses in the eighteenth century that bore little relationship to Ware's Palladian-inspired ideals, they nevertheless offer an insight into the architectural thinking, as well as the status and working conditions of country-house servants, of the period.

The increasing separation of the employer's immediate family from the activity of servants was also expressed by the provision of tunnels to allow servants to approach the basement quarters out of sight of the main house. Examples of this can be seen at houses such as Newhailes, Scotland, and Calke Abbey in Derbyshire.[67]

Another great signifier of the more emphatically separate zones of the country house as it developed in the 18th century, between that of the employer's family and that of the household servant, was the gradual evolution of the familiar system of fixed bells to summon servants from the service quarters to the main rooms, as needed. The diaries of Samuel Pepys refer to the fixing of a bell to summon servants from an adjoining ante-room, but by the middle of the eighteenth century more elaborate systems evolved for extending the wires attached to bells, along pipes, often installed by plumbers. The standard method involved bells operated by a wire tension system

In this illumination to the Luttrell Psalter, *c.*1340, depicting a New Year's feast
for the family of Sir Geoffrey Luttrell, servants are shown bearing food from the kitchen
to the table

This 1671 portrayal of the ceremony of the Tichborne dole, an annual distribution
of bread to the poor, shows Sir Henry Tichborne, 3rd Bt, his wife and children,
with household servants to the left

Right: In 1646, the formidable Lady Anne Clifford chose to include portraits of her governess, Mrs Anne Taylour, and tutor, Samuel Daniel when commissioning her own portrait

Left: Old and young together, 1686. This painting shows Bridget Holmes, a ninety-six-year-old maid of the royal household, in the typical dress of a working maid, chasing a young, playful page in blue livery

Above: Coachman and postilion (riding on the lead horse) in livery and a porter receiving guests at the gate, in Jan Sibberechts' view of Longleat, Somerset, late seventeenth century

Right: Brought up by the servants. A family intimate, the nurse (far left) has been included in the group portrait of the 3rd Earl of Oxford, his wife and children, by Gawen Hamilton, 1730s

Above: Love below stairs? This 1783 double portrait of a liveried footman and a housemaid was one of a large number of portraits at Knole, Kent, which records the staff in the service of the Duke of Dorset

Left: Among the many paintings of servants at Erdigg, is this touching early eighteenth-century one of a black postilion in scarlet and gold livery. He was one of many young slaves, usually from the West Indies, working in the British Isles

Right: Specialist labours. The ornamental dairy at Berrington Park on the Herefordshire–Shropshire border. A dairy maid would provide freshly churned butter for the household every day

Below: The heart of operations. The high-ceilinged, late eighteenth-century kitchen at Kedleston Hall, Derbyshire

RULES to be Observed in this HALL.

1 WHOEVER is last at Breakfast to clear the Table, and put the Copper, Horns, Salt, Pepper &c. in their proper places, or forfeit ___ 3
2 THE servants hall Cloth laid for Dinner by 1 o'Clock, and not omit laying the Salt, Pepper and Spoons. ___ 3
3 THE Stool-keepers room knives to be Cleand evry day by the Usher of this hall. ___ 3
4 THAT if any Person be heard to Swear, or Use any Indecent language at any time when the Cloth is on the table. He is to forfeit. ___ 3
5 WHOEVER leaves any thing belonging to their Dress or any Wearing-Apparel out of their proper places. ___ 3
6 THAT no one be suffered to Play at Cards in the Hall before six o'Clock in the Evening. ___ 3
7 WHOEVER leaves any Pieces of Bread at Breakfast, Dinner, or Supper. ___ 1
8 THAT if any one shall be observd cleaning livery clothes or leather breeches at any time of Meals, or shall leave any dirt after cleaning them at any time. ___ 3
9 THAT the Usher to have the Hall decently Swept, and the dirt taken away before dinner time. ___ 3
10 THAT no one shall put any kind of provisions in any Cupboard or Drawer in the Hall after the meals but shall return it from whence they had it. ___ 3
11 THAT the Table Cloth shall after all meals be folded up, and put in the drawer for that purpose. ___ 3
12 THAT if any one be observd wiping their Knives in the table cloth at any time. ___ 3
13 THAT if any stable or other servant take any plates to the stable, or be seen to set them for Dogs to eat off ___ 3
14 THAT no wearing apparel to hang in the Hall, but shall be put in the Closets for that Purpose. ___ 3
15 ALL stable and other servants to come to dinner with their Coats on ___ 3

Left: The eighteenth-century painted board setting out regulations and fines in the servants' hall at Clandon Park, Surrey. Household regulations were common features of country-house life

Below: Many hands. 'Winter', a view of housemaids waiting with warming pans, by George Dance, late eighteenth century. Until the early twentieth century many of the comforts of life in a country house had to be provided manually

Above: Mrs Flynn, the
housekeeper at Castle Howard,
Yorkshire, in the familiar guise
of a guide showing visitors to a
great country-house collection,
a perk that could bring a good
additional income through tips.
Painting by Ellen Best, early
nineteenth century

Right: A trusted friend. Joseph
Florance, chef to the young
Duke of Buccleuch at
Drumlanrig Castle in the early
nineteenth century. A
confidant to his master, he
wrote a letter of advice about
the best way to run the
household accounts. Painting
by John Ainslie

Hannah Cullwick, the epitome of the hard working maidservant,
whose early life was spent in country houses in Shropshire and Suffolk.
She wrote a memoir, revealing the hard grind and monotony of the
manual duties of the humblest maidservants

between a distant pulley and the bell itself. They sometimes could sound in attic quarters, but usually in the servants' hall or in the corridor outside (often improved and updated in the 19th century).[68]

A fine example of well-planned service spaces and service accommodation can be seen at Holkham Hall in Norfolk, one of the finest Palladian mansions of the mid eighteenth century, which certainly had a bell-pull system installed in the 1750s. The patron of the house, Thomas Coke, the Earl of Leicester, sent his executant architect, Mathew Brettingham, on a reconnoitring tour of other houses, asking him in a letter of around 1737 to 'Pray take notice of those doors cover'd with green bays [baize] and the hinges that make them shut of themselves.'[69]

Brettingham recorded the original layout of the servants' areas (largely contained within what read architecturally as a rusticated basement but was in fact a ground floor) and, echoing Ware, he argued that there was a 'peculiar conveniency' in 'having the upper servants' offices, to which the basement stor[e]y is appropriated, placed under the principal apartments, consequently nearer to the master and his company'.[70]

The accommodation at Holkham is based on the great state rooms occupying the centre, with four wings housing family, guests, kitchen and chapel. The kitchen, which took up a whole wing, was supported by an extensive and carefully planned kitchen court, with a scullery, a west larder and another larder, having access to the court; in the yard were chicken coops for fattening chicken, a charcoal and ash bin, and a slaughterhouse; the courtyard attached to the chapel wing housed the laundry with a mangle room and a wash-house underneath the chapel.

The kitchen survives as a handsome and model example of its kind from the era of the grand Palladian mansion; the diarist Mrs Lybbe Powys described it in 1756 thus: 'such an amazing large and good kitchen I never saw, everything in it so nice and clever'.[71] In the family wing (to the south-east) were rooms for the maids (who had direct access via a staircase to the room above), as well as others for the valet and the secretary beneath the Long Library, whilst a footman slept in a small room near the staircase.

The butler's suite, pantry, bedroom and plate room lay close to the family wing, at the west end of the south corridor. The pantry included equipment for washing cutlery and glasses. It is also known that chessboards and backgammon tables were kept here for the use of family and guests. Across the corridor, steps led down to the cellar, and beer was piped directly through from the brewery at the other end of the house.[72]

The housekeeper was based at the opposite end of the corridor, from which she recorded acquisitions and administered the dessert room, still room, laundry and dairy. There was a separate breakfast room for senior servants. A bedchamber was recorded on this floor, possibly for one or more laundrymaids. Two large rooms in the chapel wing, each containing three beds, were recorded in 1774 as accommodation for the housemaids and were later converted to nurseries.

The house steward had a bedroom and an office in the north-east corner of the basement floor; close by was the senior servants' dining room, where the steward, the butler, the housekeeper and the senior footmen, as well as visiting servants of the same rank, would take their dinner, waited on by the steward's room boy. The servants' hall lay just inside the kitchen wing and was no doubt usually comfortably warm all year round.[73] The basement was like a small village.

In the mid-eighteenth century there would probably have been between twenty-five and thirty servants at Holkham, presided over by the house porter, although on special occasions quantities of visitors' servants could swell these numbers considerably. Bedrooms for their particular use were above the guest wing (which was still known as the Strangers' Wing) and in the other attic rooms on the east side. Above the kitchen and the servants' hall lay a suite of rooms that were probably occupied by footmen and other male servants, as inventories record only single beds in each, all four-posters with blue-and-white checked hangings.[74]

The inventories of these great houses, recording the furnishings throughout and their value, often taken at the death of the owner, can be illuminating. *Noble Households: Eighteenth-Century Inventories of Great English Houses*, edited by Tessa Murdoch, offers numerous examples of the furnishings of servants' halls and bedrooms, as well as their working quarters, lending colour and detail to these little-investigated lives.

At Boughton in 1709, amid the damask- and tapestry-hung bedrooms, is a 'Closet where the footman lyes', furnished with 'Bedstead [with] Callico furniture compleat feather bed bolster chequer'd quilt cane chair valued four pounds twelve shillings'. The footmen's waiting room contained 'A folding Table six cane chairs two stuft valeur chairs one cloath and one Turkey wrought Chair Two Camp leather Chairs and a wooden chair valued one pound ten shillings'.[75] The steward's hall, where the senior servants dined, had 'Eleven wooden Chairs four cane elbow Sattees large deal oval Table stone table pair large brass Andirons pair doggs tongs bellows wooden Stool Matt under the Table large wattle mat at the Entrance of the Door Another Table valued five pounds.'[76]

At Kiveton in Yorkshire, the Duke of Leeds' house, the steward's hall, and its adjoining closet, were rather better appointed in 1727, containing 'I Large foulding Wainscoat Table, I Deel Side board Table', as well as a number of pictures, including a 'prospective of Portsmouth', another of Constantinople and another of Tangier. There were also, among the necessaries for meals, eighteen chairs with leather seats, five drinking mugs and eighteen glasses.[77] It was quite common to find the adjective 'old' or 'worn' to describe the furnishings of servants' rooms in these inventories, presumably cast-off items from the main family rooms that were being replaced.[78]

At Blenheim Palace in 1740, there are a number of references to the furnishings of servants' rooms adjoining the bedrooms of their employers. For instance, in the 'Appartment over the Dukes Bedchamber', in 'the Servants Room to this Appartment: A Bed and all Conveniences proper for that use' and in the apartment 'that fronts the grand Parterre' in the servants' room 'A Yellow Bed & all things Convenient for a Servant' – the servants' furniture were considered just too humble to list.[79]

While it is possible to re-create the appearance of servants' rooms of two centuries past, inevitably none comes down to us in an entirely unaltered state with all its original contents intact. It is only in these precisely taken lists that we can read the actual evidence of how country-house servants of the period fared, and wonder how much comfort and refuge was actually provided. These inventories illustrate too the extent to which servants' lives were still physically and functionally embedded in the great country house in the eighteenth century, as they were to remain for the next hundred years.

5

The Apogee

The Nineteenth Century

THE WORK OF the country-house servant in the nineteenth century is especially worthy of attention, not least because of the
greater accessibility of records on the subject, but also because it
could be argued that this century – and the latter part of it in particular – was the apogee of the servant-supported, country-house
way of life. By 1900 the households of landowners, industrialists
and bankers, whether they were buying into or marrying into
landed society (or even both), had reached a supreme pitch of
organisation – prefigured in the eighteenth century. As the *Servant's
Practical Guide* of 1880 noted: 'Without the constant co-operation of
well-trained servants, domestic machinery is completely thrown out
of gear, and the best bred of hostesses placed at a disadvantage.'[1]

At its best, this well-oiled machinery was widely admired by visitors from overseas. In the 1840s, American author Nathaniel Parker
Willis wrote appreciatively of the smooth management of English
country houses: 'An arrival in a strange house in England seems to a
foreigner almost magical. The absence of all bustle consequent on the
same event abroad – the silence, respectfulness and self-possession of
the servants – it is like the golden facility of a dream.'[2]

This was echoed in a remarkable passage in the memoirs of the
black American educationalist Booker T. Washington, *Up from
Slavery: An Autobiography* (1901). Having been born in slavery, and
after beginning life as a labourer, Mr Washington managed to receive
a good education and became an important voice in the search for
African-American rights at the turn of the century. In 1899, a holiday
to Europe led to a period in England, of which he wrote:

On various occasions Mrs. Washington and I were guests of Englishmen in their country homes, where I think, one sees the Englishman at his best. The home life of the English seems to me about as perfect as anything can be. Everything moves like clockwork. I was impressed too with the deference that the servants show to their 'masters' and 'mistresses' – terms which I suppose would not be tolerated in America. The English servant expects, as a rule, to be nothing but a servant, and so perfects himself in the art to a degree that no class of servant in America has yet reached. In our country the servant expects to become, in a few years time, a 'master' himself. Which system is preferable? I will not venture an answer.[3]

The nineteenth century was, of course, the great age of industrialisation and the expansion of towns, up until the 1880s at least (when a serious agricultural depression set in, as a result of competition from North and South American imports of grain and beef). This industrial age concentrated considerable new wealth into the world of the country house, partly because so many established landowners had considerable mineral rights at their command and therefore benefited, both directly and indirectly, from the industrial boom. Others owned land that could be profitably developed as towns expanded.[4]

Industrialists, bankers and other entrepreneurs also invested in land, partly for economic reasons, but also to enjoy the obvious pleasures and social amenities that their property could bring. Thus between the 1840s and the 1880s, numerous new country houses were built, both for landed families and for what is sometimes called 'new money'. Both groups used their landed interests to attach themselves to national and local government.

The other defining feature of the century was the vast expansion of domestic servants being employed in professional and middle-class homes, inevitably echoing the household structures of the aristocratic world. This increased the kudos of working for the real thing, a traditional landed and titled family. As the numbers of full-time domestic servants continued to rise, the established and well-trained higher-ranking country-house servant was looked on increasingly as the model, representing the epitome of a growing profession.[5]

This expansion also offered greater opportunities for the junior servant who wanted to change careers or move upwards. The pool for general servants was much larger, although there is evidence to suggest that life in domestic service in smaller urban households was often more gruelling as well as less companionable. At the same time the burgeoning railways and the better roads of the period made travel easier between country houses, leading to an upsurge of entertaining on a huge scale.

The strains of running these enormous households could be hard on senior servants. The housekeeper at Uppark in Sussex from 1880 to 1893 could be seen as a Victorian archetype: well meaning but hard-pressed and ageing. This particular individual was later looked after by, and even later on made famous by, her literary son, H.G Wells, who rather ungallantly considered her probably 'the worst housekeeper who was ever thought of. She had never had the slightest experience in housekeeping. She did not know how to plan work, control servants, buy stores or economize in any way.'[6] Her story, and the impact of her profession on her son, as can be seen from two of his books as well as some of her own diaries, have much to reveal about the world of the country-house servant.[7]

Mrs Wells certainly looks the part as can be seen from her photograph: a dignified, dowager-like lady, dressed in black, her demeanour giving away none of the anxiety that was evidently always there. At Uppark, a large number of staff sustained the life of just one old lady. It was, as many country houses seemed – particularly to the young growing up in their shadow – the centre of its own universe, although not without its trials and crises.

Many years before her appointment, Mrs Wells had been the beloved lady's maid of Miss Fetherstonhaugh, effectively the adopted daughter of the elderly Sussex landowner and baronet, Sir Harry Fetherstonhaugh. In fact Miss Fetherstonhaugh was born Miss Bullock and was the younger sister of Mary Ann Bullock, a particularly good-looking dairymaid, whom Sir Harry took to wife in his old age, in 1825. We shall revisit her story in Chapter 6. By 1880, when Mrs Wells returned to Uppark, Miss Fetherstonhaugh had been given life tenure.

Sarah Neal (as Mrs Wells was before marriage) had first joined the household in 1850, pleased because it was close to her parents. She later wrote: 'this being a convenient distance from home I frequently go in to see d[ea]r Mother and Father.' She left in 1853 to nurse her mother, and her parents both died later that year. She married Joseph Wells, a gardener from Uppark and the son of the head gardener at Penshurst Place in Kent. Tired of gardening, Joseph became a rather unsuccessful cricket coach and shopkeeper. His inability to support the family drove Sarah back into service aged fifty-eight, as a house-keeper to her old friend.

Wells admitted in *Experiments in Autobiography* (1934) that the change in his family's circumstances probably altered his own destiny in some important ways. His mother's deficiencies were obvious to the family's agent, Sir William King, and to the competent head housemaid, Old Ann, 'who gave herself her own orders more and more. The kitchen, the laundry, the pantry, with varying kindliness, apprehended this inefficiency in the housekeeper's room.'[8]

Wells observed:

> She was frightened, perhaps, but resolute and she believed that with prayer and effort anything can be achieved. She knew at least how a housekeeper should look, and assumed a lace cap, lace apron, black silk dress and all the rest of it, and she knew how a housekeeper should drive down to the tradespeople in Petersfield and take a glass of sherry when the account was settled. She marched down to the church every Sunday morning; the whole downstairs streamed down the Warren and Harting Hill to church.[9]

Sarah Wells may have had a good grasp of the outward details, as evidenced by a footman describing a very different housekeeper in his memoirs of service in the late nineteenth century: 'The house-keepers in those days wore a black silk dress, a little silk apron trimmed with beads, a lace collar, a small apology for a cap, made of white lace, and a black velvet bow on top. The under-maids were more afraid of her than they were of her Ladyship.'[10] Sarah Wells, however, commanded no such respect.

As a boy staying with his mother, Wells was allowed to rummage in the attic next door to his bedroom, to look at engravings, an old telescope, and to borrow books from Uppark's library. His days at Uppark provided the narrative for the early chapters of his novel *Tono-Bungay*, first published in 1909, describing a childhood spent at Bladesover House, a barely concealed version of Uppark. This is how a child in such a household might see the world:

> The great house, the church, the village, and the labourers and the servants in their stations and degrees, seemed to me, I say, to be a closed and complete social system. About us were other villages and great estates, and from house to house, interlacing, correlated, the Gentry, the fine Olympians, came and went. The country towns seemed mere collections of shops, marketing places for the tenantry . . . I thought London was only a greater country town where the gentlefolk kept town-houses and did their greater shopping under the magnificent shadow of the greatest of all fine gentlewomen, the Queen. It seemed to be in the divine order . . . There are times when I doubt whether any but a very considerable minority of English people realise how extensively this ostensible order has even now passed away.[11]

In his biography he recounted a vivid detail of the stratified attitudes 'below stairs' life at Uppark: when the house had received a visit from a real prince who had, however, given a modest tip, the butler Rabbits nearly cried with fury and indignation. He showed the coin to his colleague the housekeeper: 'My mother was speechless with horror. That was a sovereign, a mere sovereign, such as you might get from any commoner!'[12]

In *Tono-Bungay*, Wells's narrator recalls of his mother: 'I can see and hear her saying now, "No, Miss Fison, peers of England go in before peers of the United Kingdom, and he is merely a peer of the United Kingdom." She had much exercise in placing people's servants about her tea-table, where etiquette was very strict. I wonder sometimes if the etiquette of housekeepers' rooms is as strict today, and what my mother would have made of a *chauffeur*.'[13]

Beyond the literary parody, the reality was more painful. Sarah Wells's own diary chronicles her miserable struggles, right up to her dismissal at the age of seventy. On 30 January: 'Busy all day – Wrote to Mrs Holmes hoping she will come and suit. What a worry this house is!!' On 29 February: 'Dairy Woman most disagreeable. What a party!' On 6 September: 'Worried with the Cook leaving, how unsettled this house is.' On 27 October: 'No walk how dull in these under ground rooms!' On 6 December: 'Today the Duke of Connaught arrived, Oh such fuss and work. How I wish I was out of it, what ignorant people as a rule servants are!'[14]

The following January she was given a month's notice, apparently having indulged in some indiscreet gossip about her mistress. Fortunately, by then her son had begun to make money from his writing and as a result she lived in comfort until her death in 1905 at the age of eighty-three.[15]

Housekeepers such as Sarah Wells may well have had several household management books on the shelves of their snug, well-furnished sitting rooms (Sarah's was so described by Wells in his autobiography). One can imagine her tremulously flicking through them in an attempt to solve the problem of the day, just as we in moments of crisis reach for the self-help manual. Two stand out, through whose pages can be discerned the carefully drawn portraits of the key roles of a servant of the period, and the compass of their responsibilities and duties. Even if in somewhat idealised form, they are intended as practical guides. One, published in 1825, was *The Complete Servant being a Practical Guide to the Peculiar Duties of all descriptions of servants . . . with Useful Receipts and Tables*, by Sarah and Samuel Adams.[16]

The other is, of course, the world-famous *Book of Household Management* by Isabella Beeton, first published in 1861, which ran into many later editions. It is less well known that its subtitle first read: 'Comprising information for the Mistress, Housekeeper, Cook, Kitchen-Maid, Butler, Footman, Coachman, Valet, Upper and Under House-Maids, Lady's-Maid, Maid-of-all-Work, Nurse and Nurse-maid, Monthly Wet and Sick Nurses, etc etc – also Sanitary, Medical, & Legal Memoranda: with a History of the Origin, Properties, and Uses of all Things Connected with the Home Life and Comfort.'[17] Thus the reader was always the responsible senior servant as much as the mistress of a household. This celebrated volume began life as articles for various publications, especially *The*

Englishwoman's Domestic Magazine, 1859–61. A comparison of the subtle variations between different editions over the next fifty years would be a fascinating study in itself.

Together these two books are a useful guide today to the shape of the larger households over the central decades of the nineteenth century, throwing light on the duties and daily lives of country-house servants as they developed from their counterparts in the previous century – if in a somewhat idealised form.

Clearly, there had come to be an accepted pattern into which servants could fit when moving between houses and jobs, although there would be wide variations depending on the scale and wealth of the household, the age of the principals and the size of the nursery (as well as the character and general behaviour of the employers).

Whilst thick the Adamses' book was small enough to put in your pocket if you were an ambitious young footman who wanted to improve your understanding for future advancement, and had an unobserved moment when on duty. It is immensely thorough in setting out the duties of servants, scales of pay, advice on recipes for cooking or cleaning, and tables for dealing with traders. According to the authors at least, it was the first book which 'addresses itself to the actual personal practice of [servants'] duties', rather than the many works 'on the moral obligations of masters and servants, and many books of religious advice . . . all good in their way'.[18]

The Adamses speak with some authority because they had both worked as servants from an early age. Mr Adams had been 'educated in a foundation school, entered service as a footboy, in 1770, and during fifty years he served successively as groom, footman, valet, butler and house-steward. His Wife began [in] the world as maid of all work, then served as house-maid, laundry-maid, under-cook, housekeeper and lady's maid, and finally, for above twenty years, as housekeeper in a very large establishment.' The authors add that they had also sought the advice of 'a lady of high rank in whose family Mrs Adams resided'.[19] It seems possible that Sarah, the co-author, might be the same Mrs Adams who is mentioned in papers relating to Wilton in Wiltshire, around 1800, and who had an unusual position of trust there.[20]

At the very end of the eighteenth century, the Earl of Pembroke drew up a series of household regulations for the servants at Wilton, which refer to a maître d'hôtel or head servant, working under a Mrs Adams. For the management of the menservants, this individual's attention was drawn to 'a journal in Mrs Adams' possession of house-keeping proceedings in a House very remarkable for being well kept & served with comparatively few hands by the means of a faith-full & excellent housekeeper, who is consequently well hated by a proportion of the servants under her direction'.[21]

A flavour of the size and character of an aristocratic household in the 1820s and 1830s, at the time of the Adamses' work, can be gained from Petworth House in Sussex, which had always been famous for the scale of its entertainments. The aristocratic diarist Charles Greville described a house party given by the 6th Duke in 1829, where forty people sat down to dinner every day and there were about 150 ser-vants in the steward's room and servants' hall: 'All the resources of the house – horses, carriages, keepers, etc., are placed at the disposal of the guests, and everybody does what they like best.'[22]

In 1819 there were fifty-two indoor servants at Petworth, nineteen of them upper servants who dined in the steward's room, with twenty in the servants' hall and thirteen in the parlour. In 1831 this had risen to ninety-seven, with eighteen dedicated especially to the nursery. In 1834 there were seventy-three in the servants' hall and the total staff of the house was calculated to be 135.[23] The Petworth servants were well known for their loyalty and long service.

Thomas Creevey recorded of a visit in 1828 that the servants were 'very numerous, tho' most of them very advanced in years and tot-tered, and comical in their looks'. A member of the family explained to him that there were more servants at Petworth 'of both sexes, and in all departments, than in any house in England, that they were all very good in their way, but they could not stand being put out of it, and were never interfered with, that they were all bred upon the spot, and all related to each other'.[24]

The familiar intimacy of the kind hinted at by Creevey is also reflected in the album of photographs put together in 1860 by Lord Leconfield's daughter-in-law, Mrs Percy Wyndham. It contains thirty photographs of 'the dear Servants at Petworth', annotated with a handwritten commentary. The photographs, carefully posed, show the staff in formal wear, and many of them were advanced in years even then. The best paid of them was the man cook at £120 per annum; the least paid were the housemaids at £8 per annum.[25]

The servants' quarters, which are neatly contained in one free-standing range along with the kitchens and associated offices, were built in the mid eighteenth century and were used fully throughout the nineteenth and the first half of the twentieth. They are presented to the public by the National Trust, which now owns the house, as they were at the beginning of the twentieth century.[26]

While it can be misleading to compare monetary values over the centuries, it is interesting to dwell on the sample of a more mid-sized country-house household in the early nineteenth century as given in the table of wages in *The Complete Servant*. The budget recorded by Samuel Adams for the 'Household establishment of a respectable country gentleman with a young family', with a net income £16,000 to £18,000, and 'whose expenses do not exceed £7,000', sets out the wages for twenty-seven servants in guineas ranging from the French cook, paid 80 guineas, and the butler, paid 50 guineas, down to the assistant gardener, who received only 12 shillings a week.[27] This last sum was probably a good indication of the average agricultural labourer's wage at the time, in a job that did not include the accommodation or food provided to a domestic servant in a country house.[28]

Not surprisingly, the housekeeper is held up in the Adamses' book of 1825, and in Mrs Beeton's 1861 successor, as the key to a well-run household, after the mistress herself. The Adamses saw her as having 'the control and direction of the servants, particularly of the female servants'. As well as having the care of the furniture and linen, the housekeeper has also inherited at least part of the role previously held by the clerk of the kitchen, namely of 'the grocery – dried and other fruits, spices, condiments, soap, candles, and stores of all kinds, for culinary and other domestic uses. She makes all the pickles, preserves, and sometimes the best pastry – She generally distils and prepares the compound and simple waters, and spirits, essential and other oils, perfumery, cosmetics, and similar articles that are prepared at home, for domestic purposes.'

A housekeeper always oversaw the china closet and the still room, which according to the Adamses was used for preserving fruits and making distilled waters, jam and home-made wines, as well as for the preparation of breakfast and afternoon tea.[29] These duties remained remarkably consistent over the centuries until the later twentieth century and reflect the varied use that could be made of the resources of an agricultural estate.

An idea of the country-house housekeepers of the period can be gleaned from well-known novels, ranging from the kindly ones, such as Mrs Fairfax at Thornfield who receives Charlotte Brontë's Jane Eyre, to such fierce dragons as Mrs Medlock in Frances Hodgson Burnett's The Secret Garden. In real life, as sometimes in fiction, many housekeepers stayed with individual families for many years, becoming almost part of the family, and were certainly often treated as close confidantes.[30] Susan Clarke was housekeeper to the Benyons at Englefield House in Berkshire for over twenty years from 1854.[31] A housekeeper might even be buried beside her employer's family, as was Mary Carryll, the woman who served the ladies of Llangollen.[32] In the churchyard at Highclere Castle in Hampshire, there is a headstone to Anne Goymore, who died in 1831 having served twenty-six years as housekeeper to the Earl of Carnavon.[33]

At Erddig, near Wrexham, Mary Webster, formerly the cook, was promoted to housekeeper and stayed with the family for thirty years until her death in 1875. A ditty written by Philip Yorke about Mary is worth quoting because it stresses storekeeping as a central duty:

> Upon the portly frame we look
> Of one who was our former Cook.
> No better keeper of our Store,
> Did ever enter at our door.
> She knew and pandered to our taste,
> Allowed no want and yet no waste;
> And for some thirty years and more
> The cares of Office here she bore.

Mary did indeed prove to be very frugal; she was found to have left over £1,300 in her will. She was replaced by Harriet Rogers, a former lady's maid and daughter of the family's trusted estate carpenter.[34]

Another long-term housekeeper was shown consideration by the 6th Duke of Devonshire, according to his privately printed *Handbook of Chatsworth and Hardwick* (1845): 'From unwillingness to disturb Hannah Gregory, the house-keeper who dwelt here for a half a century, there had been no attempt made to alter the distribution of these the most agreeable rooms at Chatsworth.' He later converted them into a Grotto Room.[35]

Whilst some housekeepers were married and others were widowed, many seem to have been unmarried but were given the title of 'Mrs' as a mark of respect.[36] They characteristically carried large bunches of keys on a ring attached to their waists (known as a 'chatelaine'), as everything from the linen to the spices had to be kept locked up.[37] By long tradition, no doubt to reinforce a sense of hierarchy below stairs, in some households the upper servants took their meals, or at least the pudding course, in the housekeeper's room, which the junior servants often dubbed 'the Pug's Parlour', whilst in larger country houses this was the function of the house steward's room.[38] Why upper servants were known as 'pugs' is uncertain; it is possible that it referred to the haughty upturned nose and downturned mouth of an upper servant of caricature being compared to those of the pug dog.

As in the eighteenth century, housekeepers were generally delegated the task of conducting passing visitors around the house, usually when the family were away – but not always, as fans of Jane Austen's *Pride and Prejudice* will remember from Lizzie Bennet's unexpected encounter with Mr Darcy whilst paying a tourist's visit to his country seat Pemberley. There is a portrait of Mrs Garnett, the housekeeper at Kedleston, painted by Thomas Barber around 1800, showing her with the catalogue of the Kedleston pictures in her hand. She impressed Dr Johnson with her knowledge, and another visitor recorded that, of all the housekeepers of a noblemen's houses, 'this was the most obliging and intelligent . . . she seem'd to take a delight in her business'. Senior servants were expected to be enthusiastic in their knowledge of family history and their oral transmission of the stories of both house and family.[39]

In 1832, the artist Mary Ellen Best, renowned for her precise interior scenes, visited Castle Howard in Yorkshire and painted the famous Orleans Room (later the Turquoise Drawing Room). Her exact watercolour depicts the ample and dignified figure of the housekeeper in her bonnet, with her bunch of keys, much as she must have seemed when accompanying visitors. This individual was Mrs Flynn, whose conduct came under scrutiny in the winter of 1826–7 when it was noticed that the consumption of tea among the servants was excessive. John Henderson, the resident agent, and James Loch, superintendent of Lord Carlisle's estates, enquired into the matter in minute detail to see whether any theft had occurred, calculating the rate of tea consumption per person and the price of 'Servant's Tea' (a cheaper brand than that served to family and guests).

Today it seems incredible that such a senior management figure would concern themselves with such a trivial matter, but a tea allowance was considered a valuable commodity (tea itself being an expensive, imported item) and was often a separate part of the wages. Mrs Flynn was acquitted of any wrongdoing, and it is now thought that suspicion fell on her as a result of her feud with the cook, Samuel Damant.[40] Housekeepers were required to keep exact accounts of provisions and this incident illustrates the emphasis placed on the accounting and management of those valuable supplies, especially if bought in.

Throughout the nineteenth century, the housekeeper, along with the steward and butler, would be key in the preparation of the house for the reception of important guests, not least because she commanded the linen and supervised the housemaids who would clean and maintain bedrooms. Famously, when preparing for a visit from Queen Victoria, the Duke of Wellington found it hard to persuade his housekeeper that his home was up to scratch. He wrote to a friend: 'I thought that she would have burst out crying while I was talking to Her of the Honour intended and the preparations to be made. She said to me, very nearly in the Words which I had used two nights before to Her Majesty, "My Lord, Your House is a very comfortable Residence for yourself, your Family and your friends; But it is not fit for the Reception of the Sovereign and her Court."' Apart from anything else, she felt that the housekeeper's room was much too small for the Queen's dressers and the steward's room too cramped for the principal attendants to dine in. Improvements were put in hand.[41]

A housekeeper ought, the Adamses wrote, to be 'a steady middle-aged woman, of great experience in her profession, and a tolerable knowledge of the world'. The prudent housekeeper 'will carefully avoid all approaches to familiarity; as that destroys subordination, and ultimately induces contempt.'[42] Mrs Beeton, echoing the writings of Hannah Wolley and Mary Evelyn in the seventeenth century, as well as Elizabeth Raffald in the eighteenth, thought that the housekeeper 'must consider herself as the immediate representative of her mistress, and bring, to the management of the household, all those qualities of honesty, industry, and vigilance, in the same degree as if she were at the head of *her own* family.'[43]

The housekeeper's role was therefore almost that of a mistress by proxy, and many junior female servants would have certainly looked to the housekeeper as their boss. Mrs Beeton asked housekeepers to be 'Constantly on the watch to detect any wrong-doing on the part of any of the domestics, she will overlook all that goes on in the house, and will see that every department is thoroughly attended to, and that the servants are comfortable, at the same time that their various duties are properly performed.'[44]

In most houses there was also a still-room maid, who worked under the housekeeper and in whose steps she might well hope to tread. This maid would usually help look after the china kept in the housekeeper's room, lay out the breakfast for the upper staff in the housekeeper's room and prepare the trays for early-morning tea in the bedrooms as well as afternoon tea in the drawing room, thus relieving the pressure on the main kitchen. Scones, sandwiches and cakes were made in the still room, not in the main kitchen, and the still-room maid might also help with the preparation of meals in the servants' hall.[45]

In households with children, especially with the dramatic decrease in infant mortality rates over the century, several members of staff might be devoted solely to the care of the family's children. It would be headed by a nurse for the younger ones, a role that had turned into that of 'nanny' by the end of the nineteenth century; although the origins of the word are obscure, it can be traced back to the eighteenth.[46] The nurse, or nanny, had a nurserymaid to assist her in serving meals and looking after the infants, whilst the older children would have a governess to give them lessons at home, and sometimes a male tutor, although boys would probably go away to school after a certain age.

Clearly the correct nursing of children was critical in landowning families where inheritance was so crucial an issue. As Samuel and Sarah Adams wrote in 1825, 'as the hopes of families, and the comfort and happiness of parents are confided to the charge of females who superintend nurseries of children, no duties are more important, and none require more incessant and unremitting care and anxiety.' Personality had to be taken into consideration: 'This important Servant ought to be of a lively and cheerful disposition, perfectly good tempered and clean and neat in her habits.'[47]

Mrs Beeton had her own contribution to make: 'The responsible duties of the upper nursemaid commence with the weaning of the child: it must now be separated from the mother or wet-nurse, at least for a time, and the cares of the nursemaid . . . are now to be entirely devoted to the infant.' The nurse 'washes, dresses, and feeds it; walks out with it, and regulates all its little wants'. She had further views on character and attributes: 'Patience and good temper are indispensable qualities . . . She ought also to be acquainted with the art of ironing and trimming little caps, and be handy with her needle.' Below her would be an under nursemaid to clean, dust, make beds, bring up and remove meals, although sometimes a nursery footman or a nurserymaid would help with some of these tasks.[48]

Whilst some nurses might be marvels of forbearance and selflessness on rare occasions they could be monsters. The great politician Lord Curzon left a chilling remembrance of his nanny, a Miss

Paraman: 'She persecuted and beat us in the most cruel way and established over us a system of terrorism so complete that not one of us ever mustered up the courage to walk upstairs and tell our father or mother.' More alarmingly: 'She spanked us with the sole of her slipper on the bare back, beat us with her brushes, tied us for long hours to chairs in uncomfortable positions with our hands holding a pole or blackboard behind our back.'[49] The torture could take yet stranger forms: 'She made me write a letter to the butler asking him to make a birch for me with which I was to be punished for lying, and requesting him to read it out in the servants' hall.'[50] This was the man later given the responsibility of running India as Viceroy.

Stories of the devotion and kindness of nurses and nannies were perhaps more common, with one of the most famous of the period deserving a mention here. Mrs Everest, the beloved nanny of Sir Winston Churchill, joined the family in 1874 within six weeks of his birth and remained with them, eventually becoming housekeeper, until her death in 1895, when Winston was twenty. For this lonely boy this calm, warm, loving character became his closest confidante and emotional ally.[51] Until he was eight he slept in her room, and was fed, washed and changed by her. It was due to her devoted care that he survived pneumonia at the age of twelve. He was distraught when his parents abruptly 'retired' her without pay in 1893, writing to them in protest, and he later paid her doctor's bills himself when he was at Sandhurst. In *My Early Life*, he described how, when he visited her when she was mortally ill with peritonitis, her chief concern was that he has wearing a wet jacket: 'She had lived such an innocent and loving life of service to others and held such a simple faith that she had no fears at all, and did not seem to mind very much. She had been my dearest most intimate friend during the whole of the twenty years that I had lived.'[52]

This degree of affection is sometimes demonstrated in memorials. In the Cecil graveyard at Hatfield in Hertfordshire, there are only three monuments to people who were not direct members of the family. Two were sisters who were nurse and wetnurse at Hatfield for thirty-six and twenty-nine years respectively; the other was Caroline Hodges, the children's nurse, whose tombstone tells that she 'lived in their house for 43 years, a loved and trusted friend'.[53]

A similar series of monuments to beloved, long-serving servants can be found at Highclere in Hampshire. One individual is poignantly remembered on a wall plaque and on a headstone in the churchyard: 'Dedicated to the memory of Mary Morton who died on the 10th of April, 1869, in the Garden Lodge of Highclere Castle, having nearly completed her 96th year. 37 years of that time were spent in the Carnarvon family. This Memorial Tablet is erected by Henrietta Countess of Carnarvon and Lady Gwendolen Herbert, her first friend in the family and her last, to whom she was nurse.'[54]

In January 1820, the Irish novelist Maria Edgworth, who had so celebrated the roles of faithful steward and nurse in her fiction, recorded in her diary the death of the family nurse: 'Poor Kitty Billamore breathed her last this morning at one o'clock. A more faithful, warm-hearted excellent creature never existed. How many successions of children of this family she has nursed, and how many she has attended in illness and death, regardless of health! Lovell intends that she should be buried in the family vault, as she deserves, for she was more a friend than a servant.'[55]

The governess, another female figure associated with the nursery, especially for the education of girls, was made familiar by nineteenth-century writers. Jane Austen is sympathetic to the plight of the governess in *Emma*, whilst Charlotte Brontë created the plucky but sensitive figure of Jane Eyre in her eponymous novel. (Jane's unexpected legacy and subsequent marriage with her former employer would in real life have been a very great rarity.) The governess was in a delicate position, as well as an awkward one, being expected to come from a 'genteel' background yet to be in need of a paid job in a stranger's family. As the Adamses wrote in 1825 – in what reads like a job description for Jane Eyre's fictional post at Thornfield Hall – 'there is a constant demand for females of genteel manners, and finished education, at salaries which vary according to qualifications and duties between 25 and 120 pounds *per annum*.'[56] As they observed:

Teachers in seminaries, half-boarders, educated for the purpose, and the unsettled daughters of respectable families of moderate fortune, who have received a finished education are usually selected for this important duty . . . Good temper, and good manners, with a genteel exterior, are indispensable: for more is learnt by example than precept. Besides the governess who desires to be on a footing with the family, ought to be able to conduct herself in such manner, as never to render an apology necessary for her presence at family parties.

Governesses would be required to teach English, French and Italian, arithemetic, geography and the popular sciences.[57]

Their situation was often made worse by the remoteness of many country houses. Mrs Smith, an archly aristocratic Scot, recalled in *Memoirs of a Highland Lady* her disdain for her own governess, Miss Elphick, in the early nineteenth century: 'I was pert enough, I daresay, for the education we had received had given us an extreme contempt for such ignorance, but what girl of fifteen, brought up as I had been, could be expected to show respect for an illiterate woman of very ungovernable temper, whose ideas had been gathered from a class lower than we could have possible been acquainted with, and whose habits were those of a servant.'[58]

Charlotte Brontë wrote bitingly of a profession she loathed: 'A private governess has no existence, is not considered as a living rational being, except as connected with the wearisome duties she has to fulfil,' a sentiment that must have been shared by countless other servants of all ranks over the ages. Her own experiences had disillusioned her: 'I used to think I should like to be in the stir of grand folks' society; but I have had enough of it – it is dreary work to look on and listen.'[59]

However, there were many aristocrats who looked back on those who taught them with affection and gratitude. Lady Dorothy Nevill recalled her governess, Elizabeth Redgrave, the sister of the famous painter Richard Redgrave, as having 'great cultivation, besides being possessed of a certain distinction of mind . . . Her tender care and companionship – in childhood a preceptress, in after-life a much-loved friend – I have always felt to have been an inestimable boon, for thus was implanted in my mind the love of the artistic and the beautiful which during my life has proved a certain and ever-present source of delight.'[60]

Male tutors might be resident or brought in as required. The Hon. Grantley Berkeley in his *Life and Recollections* (1865) reflected on his patchy education, and that of his siblings:

> The arrangements made for our education did not promise much – a very gentleman like young man, a Mr Benson, came to us from a school near Brentford three times a week to hear us boys repeat our lessons; and an absurd, fat old fellow, named Second, possessing as little pretension to agility as to grace, arrived once a week to teach us dancing . . . the man who taught us most was a man engaged . . . to look after the game. His lessons were readily acquired partly because we were not expected to learn them. [By this he meant, of course, fishing, shooting and hunting, under the guidance of a footman named Reece.][61]

After the housekeeper, one of the most senior and trusted household figures was the cook. It is the female cook that will be considered here, together with the other female servants, whilst the male cook, or chef, will be addressed later in the chapter, in conjunction with the menservants.

Mr and Mrs Adams's advice to the female cook is: 'On her first going into a family [she] will do well to inform herself of the rules and regulations of the house – the customs of the kitchen – the peculiarities of her master and mistress – and above all, she must study, most sedulously, to acquire a perfect knowledge of their taste.'[62]

After breakfast, she would receive orders from the mistress for that day's meals. Her chief duties were the cooking of the evening dinner where, Mrs Beeton observes, 'she must take upon herself all the dressing and serving of principal dishes, which her skill and ingenuity have mostly prepared'.[63] Her morning would be occupied by the pastry, jellies, creams and entrées required for that evening's dinner, and only then would she prepare the luncheon, which would be served after she herself had eaten at midday. A dinner party or house party would be especially demanding, and in the Victorian era would mean many frantic hours of work.

Country-house cooks were often considered rather daunting figures, as the *Servants' Practical Guide* (1880) observed: 'Some ladies stand very much in awe of their cooks, knowing that those who consider themselves to be thoroughly experienced will not brook fault-finding, or interference with their manner of cooking, and give notice to leave on the smallest pretext. Thus when ladies obtain a really good cook, they deal with serving the dinner.'[64] Cooks usually expected certain perquisites, such as leftover dripping, rabbit skins or old tea leaves which they could sell for profit.

The cooks usually managed a kitchenmaid or two, who in turn might rise to the position of cook.[65] Their responsibility, according to the Adamses, was usually 'to take nearly the whole management for roasting and boiling, and otherwise dressing plain joints and dishes, and all the fish and vegetables.' As the cleanliness of the kitchen was one of her foremost duties, the kitchenmaid's first task was to scour the dressers, shelves and kitchen tables with soap, sand and hot water. Then she was to clean up the kitchen and prepare the breakfast to be served 'in the house-keeper's room, and the servants'-hall'. For the rest of the day the kitchenmaid would be 'preparing for the servants' dinner, the dinner in the nursery . . . and the lunch in the parlour', the family dinner and the servants' supper.[66]

Because kitchenmaids often did slightly more skilled jobs such as making sauces, baking bread and preparing vegetables, they were frequently paid considerably more than the unskilled scullery-maid, or scullion. According to the Adamses, her unenviable duties might include lighting 'fires in the kitchen range and under the coppers or boilers, and stew holes', and then to 'wash up all the plates and dishes, sauce-pans, stew-pans, kettles, pots and all kitchen utensils'.[67] She would also assist the kitchenmaid in the messier food preparation, such as 'picking, trimming, washing and boiling the vegetables, cleaning the kitchen and offices, the servants'-hall, housekeeper's room, and stewards' room . . . and otherwise assist in all the laborious part of the kitchen business'. The scullery-maid, often little older than thirteen or fourteen, would be kept up until the early hours, cleaning and washing up after a major event.[68]

No Victorian mistress of any consequence could function without her lady's maid, who ranked under the housekeeper and was usually found only in the wealthier households. Her role seems to have merged those of a waiting woman and a chambermaid. She would be a close confidante of the lady of the house (which might lead to her becoming housekeeper), and would have the added dignity of the title 'Miss', unlike the junior maids who were often called just by their surnames. Lady's maids might have a background in dressmaking or millinery, and sometimes came from more middle-class families than female domestics further down the hierarchy. Those from France or Switzerland were popular, with the French being considered more chic, and the Swiss and German the most practical.[69]

The Adamses, perhaps prejudiced by having worked their way up from the bottom, wrote slightly sniffily: 'The business of the lady's-maid is extremely simple, and but little varied. She is generally to be near the person of her lady . . . In her temper she should be cheerful and submissive, studying her lady's disposition'. Her principal duties are 'to *dress*, *re-dress*, and *undress* her lady', to care for her finer clothes, to attend her in the morning, and to dress and comb her hair.[70]

On the other hand, Mrs Beeton thought the work of a lady's maid more onerous than that of the valet, who was not expected to do the work of the tailor or the hatter, whereas 'the lady's maid has to originate many parts of the mistress's dress herself: she should, indeed, be a tolerably expert milliner and dressmaker, a good hairdresser, and possess some chemical knowledge of the cosmetics with which the toilet-table is supplied in order to use them with safety and effect'. As well as dressing her lady, arranging her hair, and having responsibility for maintaining all her clothes, hats and boots, including mending and cleaning the finer elements, according to Mrs Beeton a lady's maid 'will study the fashion-books with attention, so as to be able to aid her mistress's judgement in dressing, according to the prevailing fashion'.[71]

These paragons were also expected to be smartly dressed, often in the cast-off clothes of their mistress, which habitually set them apart from the other domestic servants, who were generally suspicious of them. Because they would have to stay up late with their mistresses and, indeed, travel with them, packing expertly, they also tended to be younger, in their twenties, and to hope for a post such as that of a housekeeper when they got older.[72]

A list of instructions given to the daughter of Thomas Coke of Holkham Hall, Norfolk, in 1822, setting out the 'essentials for a lady's maid', reads almost as a parody:

> She *must not* have a will of her own in anything, & be always good-humoured & approve of everything her mistress likes. She *must not* have a gr[ea]t appetite or be the least of a *gourmand*, or care when or how she dines, how often disturbed, or even if she has no dinner at all. She had better not drink anything but water. She must *run quick* the instant she is *called*, whatever she is about. Morning, noon and night she must not mind going without *sleep* if her mistress requires her attendance.[73]

Many a maid must have been tempted to make free with her mistress's extensive wardrobe. Lady Dorothy Nevill dismissed her German lady's maid when she discovered that her 'love of the stage' had led to her to take parts at a low theatre 'or penny gaff'. One particular vexed her exceedingly: 'The worst part of the business was that being cast for the part of Marie Stuart, this Teutonic Thespian annexed a very handsome black velvet dress of mine in which to impersonate Scotland's ill-fated Queen.'[74]

The backbone of the household staff, reporting to the housekeeper, was the housemaid – essentially the cleaner. According to the Adamses, the upper housemaid had the care of 'all the household linen, bed and table linen, napkins, towels, &c. which she also makes and keeps in repair, and besides cleaning the house and furniture, and making the beds . . . she [usually] washes her own clothes and has sometimes to assist the laundry-maid in getting up the fine linen, washing silk stockings &c.'[75]

In larger households there would be a head housemaid, and perhaps several other housemaids, between four and seven, who would divide the duties between them.[76] A typical day for the servant with the most hands-on, even 'front-line' role in cleaning and warming the principal rooms would, as their outline makes clear, start early. The housemaid would rise around five o'clock, open the shutters of the usual family sitting rooms, and clear away 'all the superfluous articles that may have been left there'. She would then clean out and re-lay the fires, as well as brush, black and polish the fireplaces. 'By this time the footman will have done all his work in the pantry, and have rubbed all the tables, chairs, cellerets, and other mahogany furniture, and cleaned the brass and other ornaments, the mirrors, looking glasses, &c., in these rooms.' The housemaid would then clean the carpets (strewing them weekly with damp tea leaves to remove dust). Once the reception rooms were done, she should move on to the dining room 'till all is made quite clean, and the rooms are fit for the reception of the family'.[77]

Then, according to the Adamses, 'she repairs to the dressing-rooms of the master and mistresses, and others in use, empties the slops, replenishes the ewers and water-carofts [carafes] with fresh spring and soft water, and fills the kettles for warm water, cleans up the fire-places, lights the fire and cleans the rooms', and then makes way for the lady's maid or the valet to make their arrangements previous to the rising of their superiors. Emptying the slops did not involve carrying chamberpots long distances; instead they would be emptied into pails and cleaned on the spot, or nearby, with fresh water.[78]

After completing this essential task, 'she sweeps down the principal stair-case and goes down to her breakfast.' Then she returns to the bedrooms, airs the rooms, cleans fireplaces and relays the fires, changes her apron and with the under housemaid, makes the beds. In the afternoon, the dressing rooms had to be prepared again for the ladies and gentlemen to dress for dinner. Finally, 'while the family is at dinner, the dressing-rooms must be again prepared; and in the evening the shutters of the bed-rooms and dressing-rooms must be fastened – the curtains let down – the beds turned down – the fires lighted, and the rooms put into proper condition for the night.'[79] As if all this were not enough, senior housemaids might be called on to attend visiting ladies staying at the house without having brought their own lady's maid with them.[80]

In 1838, Thomas Creevey recorded with pleasure his stay at Holkham Hall: 'I live mostly in my charming bedroom on the ground floor . . . A maid lights my fire at seven punctually, and my water is in my room at eight.' The maid called again almost hourly to check that his fire was well stoked.[81]

In some households, housemaids were under instructions to remain completely out of sight of family and guests. In *Memories of Ninety Years* (1924), Mrs Edward Ward, the artist, recollected her stay with the 3rd Lord Crewe, during which she never saw a housemaid except in chapel, 'when a great number would muster, only to disappear mysteriously directly the service was ended'. One morning when needing help from a housemaid, she glimpsed one in the corridor and gave chase, but to no avail. She mentioned this to the housekeeper, who told her that Lord Crewe had given specific orders: 'None of the servants are allowed to be seen by visitors; if they break the rules they are dismissed. Lord Crewe hates women and thinks all his guests must detest them too.'[82]

Housemaids were often subjected to strict conditions of employment. The Countess of Fingall's lady's maid, Miss Devereux, recalled that the housemaids at Mount Stewart, the Marquess of Londonderry's house, were 'kept somewhat like novices in a convent! They were not allowed to go out alone, and every Sunday evening they must put on their bonnets and go to Service in the Chapel.'[83]

In his memoirs, William Lanceley, a servant in the nineteenth and early twentieth centuries, wrote appreciatively of a housemaid colleague: 'Another old servant was the head housemaid, who had been in the family for thirty years. She was always proud to relate that for twenty-five years she had been in charge of the best dinner service and nothing had been broken or chipped. She would allow nobody to handle the plates and dishes, but washed and wiped them herself and she alone would carry them to the dining-room door and wait there to bring them back to the housemaid's pantry where they were washed.'[84]

Two junior levels of female staff were the laundrymaid and dairymaid. The former, who washed 'all the household and other linen belonging to her employers', certainly had one of the most unrelentingly hard jobs in country-house life.[85] The housekeeper of Goodwood in Sussex, Mrs Sanders, recognised this, as is clear from the letter she wrote to the Duke of Richmond's secretary, Dr Hair, in June 1857:

'I thought it right for me to write to Munro Daughter to Acquaint her with her duties that she would be required to do as the place is a very hard one . . . I heard from her this Morning saying it is such a hard place she must decline it as she would not be strong enough.' The same month she reports that one Louisa Carey, the under laundrymaid, was 'very poorly' and adds: 'I am very sorry to think I frightened Munro Daughter with what little I said.'[86]

Mrs Beeton described in some detail a laundrymaid's typical week, including the areas required for her many tasks: a washing house with a mangle, an ironing room and a drying closet. In the wash-house should be 'a range of tubs, either round or oblong, opposite to, and sloping towards the light, narrower at the bottom than the top, for convenience in stooping over'.[87]

The laundrymaid had to sort the washing, putting white linens and colours, sheets and body linen into one pile, fine muslins into another, coloured cotton and linen fabrics into a third, woollens into a fourth, and coarser kitchen cloths into a fifth. Everything had to be recorded and examined for particular stains, for which they would be left to soak overnight. Then the coppers and boilers had to be filled, and fires laid ready to light under them in the early hours of the morning.

The following day, once the water had heated, linen items were rubbed with soap and then boiled, rinsed and hung out to dry or spread out flat in the sun to bleach. All the other fabrics would be washed according to principles that would still be recognised today in the age of the washing machine.[88] When the washing was done, the process was always 'concluded by rinsing the tubs, cleaning the coppers, scrubbing the floors of the washing-house, and restoring everything to order and cleanliness'.[89] And all this without the benefit of rubber gloves.

Washing day was not the end of it either. As Mrs Beeton observed: 'Thursday and Friday, in a laundry in full employ, are usually devoted to mangling, starching and ironing,' all according to the different textiles concerned. 'Linen, cotton, and other fabrics, after being washed and dried, are made smooth and glossy by mangling and ironing. The mangling process, which is simply passing them between rollers subject to a very considerable pressure, produced by weight, is confined to sheets, towels and table-linen, and similar articles, which are without folds or plaits. Ironing is necessary to smooth body-linen, and made-up articles of delicate texture or gathered into folds.'[90] There is no need to look any further for evidence of the hard work that scared off the poor girl at Goodwood.

Female servants in the household were sometimes responsible for washing their own clothes and menservants usually had to make their own arrangements. Many of the bigger laundries at country houses such as Chatsworth in Derbyshire and Powis Castle in Wales catered for the laundry needs of all the other houses owned by the family, including their London town house.[91]

The dairymaid or maids came under the supervision of the house-keeper but worked outside. She did the churning, so that freshly made butter could appear on the table every morning, organised milk and cream supplies for the kitchen and often made cheese as well. She might look after the poultry and collect the eggs for the household.[92] In some households the dairymaid also had some baking duties.[93] The cows themselves were more usually milked by the cowmen from the home farm.

Naturally, Mrs Beeton stressed the key importance of hygiene and cleanliness in this process. The dairy, which, as in the previous century, was often ornamental because it was visited by the mistress and her guests, had to be sited to remain cool, requiring shelter and shade. Its walls should be thick and covered in glazed tiles, and deep slate shelves should be fitted for the milk dishes.

For the essential butter-making process, milk was first strained through a hair sieve (usually made of horsehair and designed to remove any cow hairs). This was left for a day, maybe more, then skimmed with a 'slicer' and poured into earthenware jars for churning, which was usually done two or three times a week, preferably in the morning: 'the dairy maid will find it advantageous in being at work on churning mornings by five o'clock'.

Butter was produced by literally turning the jars for at least twenty to thirty minutes, although this took much longer in winter. When the butter formed, it was put into a wooden bowl with clean spring water and then washed and kneaded, and any excess liquid poured off. At the end of the process, the dairymaid must 'scald with boiling water and scrub out every utensil she has used; brush out the churn, clean out the cream-jars, which will probably require the use of a little common soda to purify; wipe all dry, and place them in a position where the sun can catch them for a short time to sweeten them'.[94]

The male side of the nineteenth-century household was equally stratified and calibrated. As in the eighteenth century, at the head of the male staff of the grandest establishments was the house steward who, according to the Adamses, was the 'most important officer' although he featured only in the households of 'noblemen or gentlemen of great fortunes'. Elsewhere, the most senior staff member would be the housekeeper.[95] A land steward, or agent, would manage the estates, probably with a bailiff to run the home farm.

The house steward's chief duties were 'to hire, manage and direct, and discharge every servant of every denomination'. He must also manage the household accounts, paying all the bills and all the servants' wages. When the household was on the move, he was further responsible for planning and arranging the packing up of the house, especially the valuables, and for transporting goods and people between houses, or between the country house and the London house.[96] The steward (or the butler if there was no steward) was usually charged with overall security, such as locking up windows at night.

He usually had a junior servant reporting to him, known as 'the steward's room boy'. (This individual might also be known as the steward's room footman, hall boy or foot boy, although sometimes all these titles were used.) He would run messages; wait at table in the steward's room; maintain the below stairs' lamps; and clean the servants' boots and shoes.[97]

The steward's job must have been the goal of all ambitious menservants; indeed, they were trained to look upon it as such. As Mrs Beeton observed, 'they are initiated step by step into the mysteries of the household, with the prospect of rising in the service, if it is a house admitting of promotion – to the respectable position of butler or house-steward'.[98]

The steward often acted as something of a companion to the family and head of household.[99] One steward cum secretary seems to have been partly recruited to his role at Burton Constable Hall in Yorkshire on the strength of his musical abilities. Stephen Octavius Jay was a gifted musician and had trained at the Royal Academy of Music. He was described in the will of his master, Sir Thomas Aston Clifford, as 'my friend and secretary'. In a codicil to his will, added in 1870, he left Jay not only an additional year's salary but 'also my violin that is marked with the name of Sir Charles Wolseley'.[100]

One of the major features found in all accounts of life in a great country house was the emphatic hierarchy between the upper and the lower servants. The upper servants – usually the house steward, housekeeper, wine butler, under butler, groom of the chambers, valet, head housemaid and lady's maid – were generally known as 'the Upper Ten'.[101] The lower servants were known as the Lower Five, although in many cases there were more than five. The Upper Ten ate in the steward's room, where they were served by a specially designated steward's room footman or boy (or, if there was no steward, in the housekeeper's room). The Lower Five (a term that encompassed all the other junior indoor servants) ate in the servants' hall.

Under the steward came the butler. Like the steward, he was not a liveried servant but wore clothes similar to those worn by a gentleman, if of an old-fashioned cut or with some distinguishing element, such as a tie unlike that expected of a gentleman, so that in theory he would not be mistaken for one.[102] William Lanceley witnesses the embarrassment caused in the late nineteenth century when the elderly Lord Redesdale, who had rigidly stuck to an outmoded style of evening dress, was famously mistaken at one house for a butler.[103]

A butler's first duty was, according to the Adamses, to see that breakfast was duly laid; either the butler or the under butler would wait on the family during the meal. With breakfast over, the butler was free to take his own breakfast with the housekeeper. He must then be prepared to receive visitors at the front door. At luncheon, the butler arranged the table and brought in the drinks. 'If wine is wanted for the luncheon, it is his duty to fetch it from the cellar; and if ale, to draw or bring it up when wanted.' The butler usually kept the keys of the wine and ale cellar, and maintained the stock book.[104] The care and provision of wine and ale figured largely in the butler's traditional role. As Mrs Beeton observed:

> The office of butler is thus one of very great trust in a household. Here, as elsewhere, honesty is the best policy: the butler should make it his business to understand the proper treatment of the different wines under his charge, which he can easily do from the wine-merchant; his own reputation will soon compensate for the absence of bribes from unprincipled wine-merchants, if he serves a generous and hospitable master. Nothing spreads more rapidly in society than the reputation of a good wine cellar, and all that is required is wines well chosen and well cared for.[105]

At dinnertime

> the under butler or footman lays the cloth, and carries up the articles wanted, under the direction of the Butler, who gives out the necessary plate, kept by him under lock, and generally in an iron chest. [The butler] sets and displays the dinner on the table, carrying in the first dish, waits at the side-board, hands wine round or when called for; removes every course, and sets and arranges every fresh course on the table according to his bill of fare, which is placed at the sideboard for reference; and does not leave the room till the dessert and wine have been placed on the table by him.[106]

The servants were waited on by junior servants who were by this method trained in the discipline of serving at table and clearing away.

Until the early nineteenth century, meals in the grander houses were served à la française, where all the dishes making up a course were laid out together on the table simultaneously. When this was replaced by service à la Russe, the food was served individually to each guest by footmen, with the carving carried out at the sideboard. It took several decades to be fully absorbed into English dining, and inevitably there were frequent compromises of the two styles. The advantages of dining à la Russe were that food arrived hot and there was less extravagant waste. Also servants could control the flow and had to be on hand to serve. At the same time dining became more formal and structured, with greater quantities of dishes and cutlery needed for a larger number of courses.[107]

The menservants in the ranks below steward, butler and valet generally wore liveries. At the very end of the eighteenth century, the Earl of Pembroke's butler at Wilton was responsible for distributing these. The 1790s Wilton household refers to how 'the livery servants are allowed two suits of Frock Clothing, two hats, and one working dress annually, and one Gt: coat every two years, as is the Coach Man.'[108] At Arundel Castle, a series of names have been found inside the lining of a later nineteenth-century state livery coat (which was used only for state occasions), showing how, certainly at that time, they were worn by a succession of footmen.[109]

In large country houses the most senior liveried manservant under the butler was still the groom of the chambers – a rather forgotten figure now, but standard in grander households of the nineteenth century. He ensured that the reception rooms were always in order, the silver properly polished, and the desks and writing tables stocked with appropriate stationery, ink and quills.[110] In large houses at periods of heavy use during a major house party or family entertainment, this could be more arduous than it sounds. A groom of the chambers was sometimes trained in upholstery and made responsible for cleaning valuable objects such as pictures.[111] He also made sure that the state rooms were in presentable order to be shown to the well-heeled tourist, and sometimes acted as a guide.

As well as serving at mealtimes, the groom of the chambers in the more formal country houses had a primary role in the grander moments of ceremony, being on duty in the front hall to announce guests and to receive cards, to open the doors to libraries and drawing rooms, and also to show guests to their bedrooms.[112] In the later nineteenth century his role was often combined with that of a valet.[113] In smaller country-house establishments his duties were carried out by the butler or first footman.

The next senior male figure was usually the valet, although Mr and Mrs Adams considered the duties 'of this servant are not so various nor so important as those of the footman, indeed they are very frequently, and particularly in small families, a part of the business of the footman'.

As the lady's maid does for the lady, so the valet does for the master. He 'waits on him when dressing and undressing, has the care of his wardrobe, brushes and keeps his clothes in good order and ready to put on when wanted'. Preparation was the key: 'every garment or other article of wearing apparel, should be carefully examined, cleaned or brushed on the first opportunity that offers, and then put away in its proper place.'

The valet starts the day polishing his master's shoes and boots, checks that the housemaid has prepared the dressing room, and himself prepares the washing stand: 'fill the ewer with clean soft water, and the caroft [carafe] with fresh spring water – The basins and towels, the hair nail, and tooth-brushes clean, and in their proper places; hot water, and all the necessary apparatus for shaving, quite ready; his dressing gown and slippers airing before the fire.' The valet should then set out his master's clothes for the day, 'with a clean linen or brown Holland wrapper thrown over them, to save them from dust.'[114]

Next, the valet assists with shaving his master and combing his hair. Then when the master has gone down to breakfast, he will 'set the room in order', look over his things, put away his night clothes, wash his brushes and combs, and clean the dressing stand. He had to be on hand for a change of clothes after a ride or a journey, and was responsible for packing sufficient and correct clothes, as well as shaving kit, when his master stayed at an inn or another house, where the valet should set out his clothes as if at home.

A valet was often given his master's cast-off clothes as a perquisite and deliberately cultivated good manners to match.[115] Prince Pückler-Muskau, an early-nineteenth-century traveller to England, remarked that a visitor there might easily mistake a valet for a lord, if he thought courtesy and good breeding were the attributes of the nobility.[116] On the other hand the Duke of Wellington remarked grumpily to Lord Strangford 'that I shave myself and brush my own clothes; I regret that I cannot clean my own boots; for menservants bore me and the presence of a crowd of idle fellows annoys me more than I can tell you'.[117]

However, he was said to have had a good relationship with his own faithful valet, Kendall, who was famously protective of his master.[118]

Lady Violet Greville, who denounced the superfluity of the footman, wrote in *The National Review* in 1892 that the well-trained valet was a most invaluable servant: 'He never forgets a single portmanteau or bag or hat-box; he reads Bradshaw [the railway timetable] excellently, he takes tickets, and tipping the guard efficiently, secures a reserved railway compartment; he brings his master tea, or brandy and soda, at the stations; he engages the only fly [a horse-drawn taxi] at their destination . . . He has the soul of a perfect army commissariat.'[119]

The great country houses continued to employ the male cook or chef, who was 'now a requisite member in the establishment of a man of fashion' and was 'generally a foreigner'. He 'has the entire superintendance of the kitchen while his several female assistants are employed in roasting, boiling, and all the ordinary manual operations of the kitchen'.[120] The exacting nature of his work, 'with the superior skill requisite for excellence in his art, procures him a liberal salary, frequently twice or thrice the sum given to the most experienced female English Cook'. Male cooks were often the highest-paid servant in a household after the steward. The Dukes of Sutherland paid their French chefs £108 annually in 1818, and £200 in the 1870s – the value of the latter in modern-day money would be around £114,000 p.a.[121]

In England, the Adamses observed that 'men cooks are kept only in about 3 or 400 great and wealthy families, and in about 40 or 50 London hotels. But it is usual in smaller establishments to engage a man cook for a day or two before an entertainment.'[122] The grandest houses often had their own dedicated pastry chefs and confectioners. There is a delicious, if somewhat unbelievable, anecdote concerning one Duke of Buckingham who was being forced by circumstances to scale down his spending. When it was suggested that, as he already had a French chef and an English roasting cook, he might dispense with his confectioner, he is said to have replied: 'Good Gad, mayn't a man have a biscuit with his glass of sherry?'[123]

At the beginning of the nineteenth century, the famous French chef, Joseph Florance, worked for three Dukes of Buccleuch for whom he became not just a servant but a confidant and family friend.

He was also admired by the novelist Sir Walter Scott. On one occasion when the celebrated author dined at Drumlanrig Castle, the chef created a dish called *Potage à la Meg Merrilies*, after the character in *Guy Mannering*. His excellent portrait, painted in 1817 by John Ainslie, survives, showing an upright, elegant figure pointing to an elaborate menu, his cook's knife tucked in his belt.[124]

Florance travelled to Lisbon with the 4th Duke, and in July 1827 wrote a letter to the 5th Duke of Buccleuch, significantly advising him on the wise management of his household:

> It must be gratifying to a Nobleman to know how he stands with the world, with his income, and with his expences. To facilitate this, the greatest regularity must be established and your Grace must set the example of enforcing your commands, your Orders will always be given with moderation and reflection . . .
>
> My plan is simple & will be gratifying to all honest men. The expenses of your household must be laid before your Grace once a week without the exception of a farthing. For the day I should recommend tuesday, on monday the steward will gather the bills, and your secretary will arrange them so you may see the whole at one view.

By this means, he argued, all errors or 'false dealing' will be identified. 'All will depend upon yourself to make your Household a happy one, if you have a bad servant part with him, a diseased sheep spoils a whole flock.'[125]

Employers took pride in the skills and training of their chefs. The 6th Duke of Devonshire recalled in his *Handbook of Chatsworth and Hardwick* (1845):

> My cook, Mr. Howard, ought to be the best in the world; for thirty years ago, when at Paris, I modestly requested Louis XVIII, to place him in his kitchen, to which his Majesty immediately consented for some months: and it was kind of the lately restored Monarch, at a moment when many thought him in constant danger of poison; but he was gracious to me, and always said 'Duc, c'est l'air natal que vous respirez.' Mr Howard studied also at Robert's and Very's.[126]

Among the principal outdoor servants attached to the house, the head coachman was often a figure of some magnificence in his imposing livery, according to the Adamses: 'Every genuine Coachman has his characteristic costume. His flaxen curls or wig, his low cocked hat, his plush breeches, and his benjamin surtout, his clothes being also well brushed, and the lace and buttons in a state of high polish.'[127] The fineness of coachmen's appearance was not always matched by their care for their passengers – or other vehicles. Prince Pückler-Muskau criticised some coachmen that he encountered in London: 'As soon as these heroic chariot drivers espy the least opening they whip their horses in, as if horses were an iron wedge; the preservation of either seems totally disregarded.'[128]

The coachman's duties were not confined to driving the horses out on the road, but included overseeing the maintenance of the coach and the care of the animals themselves. 'If not fatigued by late hours on the preceding night, he rises to take care of his horses, at the same hour as the other men,' meaning the head groom and the other grooms. The coachman also oversaw the 'necessary morning business', mucking out and cleaning the stalls. After breakfast, he prepared the stables against the possibility of a visit from the master. He then inspected and cleaned the harness and ornaments, blacking the leather, which was followed by cleaning the coach, down to polishing the glass and trimming the lamps.[129]

Under him came the grooms, who attended to the horses, cleaned the stables, exercised the horses when required, took them to where they needed to be, and so on. As grooms often lived over the stables, this created a separate community within the wider household. In larger establishments there might be as many as sixty horses, as well as several under-coachmen and postilions (the latter rode the lead horse to ensure the good running of the team).[130]

A coachman might even be expected to help in the organisation of moving family and staff from one estate to another, or from the country house to the London house. In 1822, the 6th Earl of Stamford transferred his household from Enville Hall in Shropshire to London for the season. The head coachman, one David Seammen, kept the accounts when eleven of the family's servants used the family's private carriages for the journey, setting off early in the morning and stopping overnight in Coventry and St Albans.[131] The other servants travelled by post-horse (which meant changing horses at regular intervals) and had only one overnight stop, while the earl and his valet, Samuel Church, followed later, also by the post-horse system.

The footman, made familiar to us in the eighteenth century, served the house, under the butler or steward, and attended the coach in livery on journeys. And, as in the eighteenth century, the footman's duties were according to the Adamses 'multifarious and incessant', so he was not merely the liveried flunkey of fiction.[132] For his household duties, he must rise early to get the dirtiest part of his work done first: cleaning shoes, boots, knives and forks; brushing and cleaning clothes; cleaning and dusting the furniture; cleaning all brass, looking glasses, frames and pictures. Next he cleaned the lamps in the family rooms, for which 'his working dress should be generally a pair of overalls, a waistcoat and fustian jacket, and a leather apron, with a white apron to put on occasionally'. Good families 'generally allow the footman a proper dress of this sort, exclusive of his liveries'.[133]

After his early cleaning duties, 'the attendance of the footman will now be required in the breakfast parlour, for which purpose, he must prepare by washing himself, and throwing off his working dress'. Wearing his livery, he set out the table, waited at breakfast and tidied up afterwards. 'The footman now carries such messages and cards as he is charged to deliver.' He was responsible for laying the cloth for dinner, and placing the knives, forks and glasses, while the butler arranged the silver plate and saw that the whole was done correctly.[134]

The Adamses described the service current in the 1820s (*à la Russe*), in which the roles of footman and butler must blend seamlessly: 'when the butler takes the first dish, and [he] is followed by the under butler and footman with the remainder of the fish and soups, which the butler places on the table, and removing the covers, gives them to the footman and under butler, who convey them out of the room.' The servants 'then take their respective stations, the butler at the side-board, to serve the wines or beer when called for; the footman at the back of his master's chair, and the lady's footman, if any, behind his lady.'[135]

After the soup and fish have been consumed, the next course, generally 'solid joints of meat', was served, the plates and dishes of the previous courses being removed by the butler and carried away by the footmen. After the meat had been removed, a third course (usually pastry, pies, tarts with cheese and salads) followed. The groom of the chambers or the footmen then prepared the drawing room, ensuring 'that lamps and candles are lighted, and the card tables set out' and that the chairs and sofas are 'properly arranged'. The butler and footmen finally repaired to the butler's pantry where the footmen washed and wiped the glasses, with the under butler cleaning the plate. The footman would also carry the coffee into the drawing room, plus additional trays of toast and muffins.[136]

When with the coach, 'the footman should be dressed in his best livery, his shoes and stockings being very clean, and his hat, great coat, &c. being well brushed'. He would assist the family to enter or descend from the carriage. He was also required to accompany the ladies of the family on their walks, when 'he should preserve a modest demeanour, and protect [them], if necessary, from intrusion or insult'.[137]

Footmen often travelled with their employers to house parties, which added no small amount of extra luggage to the party. One nineteenth-century footman from Castle Howard in Yorkshire recalled travelling to Welbeck Abbey in Nottinghamshire with two five-foot steel cases to take his suits of full- and half-livery, two leather portmanteaus for smaller liveries, and six hatboxes.[138] At Welbeck and at Longleat special rooms were set aside as footmen's powder rooms, fitted with long looking glasses and washbasins.[139]

Mrs Beeton suggested that the footman 'while attentive to all . . . should be obtrusive to none: he should give nothing but on a waiter [tray], and always hand it with the left hand and on the left side of the person he serves, and hold it so the guest may take it with ease . . . After each meal, the footman's place is in his pantry: here perfect order should prevail – a place for everything and everything in its place.'[140]

In his diary account of his tour of England made in the 1820s, Prince Pückler-Muskau was not entirely impressed by the arrangements of some country houses: 'England is the true land of contrasts – "du haut et de bas" – at every step. Thus, even in elegant houses in the country, coachmen and grooms wait at dinner, and are not always free from the odour of the stable.'[141]

The senior outdoor figure – after the land steward, or estates bailiff, who looked after estate administration – was the head gardener, of whom, according to the Adamses, much was expected:

> to understand his business well, and to be capable of undertaking the management of a gentlemen's garden and grounds, he should not only be perfect in the ordinary business, and the regular routine of digging, cropping, and managing a kitchen garden, but should be also well versed in the nature of soils, manures, and composts, the best methods of propagating plants, shrubs, and trees, the management of the hothouse, green-house, conservatory, hot-beds; and the culture, not only of indigenous, but also of foreign and exotic productions.[142]

The nineteenth-century head gardener usually wielded considerable authority. One such was Sir Joseph Paxton, made famous by designing Crystal Palace. He was born in 1803, the son of a farm labourer, and at the age of fourteen was working with his brother at Battlesden in Bedfordshire, the estate of Sir Gregory Page Turner, and later at the Woodhall estate in Hertfordshire. It was while working for the Royal Horticultural Society at Chiswick that he happened to meet the 6th Duke of Devonshire, who was the ground landlord.[143]

Paxton's good manners, in speaking clearly and carefully to the deaf duke, so impressed the latter that in 1806 he offered Paxton a job at Chatsworth with an annual salary of £70. Besides marrying Sarah Bown, the niece of Chatsworth's housekeeper, Hannah Gregory, Paxton transformed the gardens there and travelled with the Duke on horticultural tours to Europe.

He made Chatsworth's gardens the most famous in England, creating a pinetum and an arboretum, and designing greenhouses and hothouses. There included the largest conservatory ever built, a huge glass construction with a double-curved framework of laminated wood. His assistant gardeners were sent to America and India to collect plants. Paxton eventually became the steward or agent of the Chatsworth estates, a trusted senior servant whom the duke consulted on every matter of importance. As well as designing Crystal Palace, he also rebuilt Lismore Castle in Ireland in the popular picturesque style and served as an MP, receiving a knighthood. In the duke's words: 'The creations of his talent are remarkable and conspicuous whichever way you turn. . . . [He was] the most zealous, and the least obtrusive of servants.'[144]

Although Paxton was perhaps exceptional, the elite head gardeners of the great country houses were generally influential, often innovators or experts with national reputations. They also edited and contributed to gardening journals, serving on the committees of the Royal Horticultural Society, founded in 1804.[145]

In 1886, there were twenty-two gardeners at Hatfield House, plus two women and nine boys who looked after the pleasure grounds and kitchen garden. There were also nine keepers and watchers, assisted by two boys. The stables were staffed by six men and a boy. In addition to the seventeen woodmen, nine parkmen and three boy helpers, Hatfield supported many other estate workers and farmworkers.[146] In the late nineteenth century, at Eaton Hall in Cheshire, the Duke of Westminster employed a head gardener and forty undergardeners. In the 1850s the Benyons at Englefield House in Berkshire employed between fifteen and twenty gardeners.[147]

In addition to their regular staff, country estates could also call on the services of a large group of retired farm labourers, retained on a small wage as 'the gang' to sweep leaves and paths and weed the gardens. This practice explains why, in photographs of late Victorian and Edwardian gardens, everything looks so extraordinarily immaculate – with not a twig out of place: it is an effect that can only be achieved by many hands.[148]

In examining the relationship between servants and their employers, it is interesting to note that it was often said that the quality of the former reflected immediately on the reputation of the latter. The Countess of Fingal recalled Lord Coventry saying: 'I always judge a house and the people who own it by the servants,' to which she added her own view that 'Countries get the governments, and people the servants they deserve.'[149] Good management and good working conditions, combined with a degree of humane discipline, usually meant a more loyal and efficient staff.

Mrs Beeton warned strongly against habitually complaining of servants' deficiencies:

It is the custom of 'Society' to abuse its servants, – a *façon de parler*, such as leads their lords and masters to talk of the weather, and, when rurally inclined, of the crops, – leads matronly ladies, and ladies just entering on their probation in that honoured and honourable state, to talk of servants, and, as we are told, wax eloquent over the greatest plague in life while taking a quiet cup of tea. Young men at their clubs, also, we are told, like to abuse their 'fellows', perhaps not without a certain pride and pleasure at the opportunity of intimating that they enjoy such appendages to their state. It is another conviction of 'Society' that the race of good servants had died out, at least in England.[150]

In a delightful piece of well-observed and well-aimed social critique she wrote: 'When the lady of fashion chooses her footman without any other consideration than his height, shape, and *tournure* of his calf, it is not surprising that she find a domestic who has no attachment for the family, who considers the figure he cuts behind her carriage, and the late hours he is compelled to keep, a full compensation for the wages he exacts . . . and for the perquisites he can lay his hands on.'[151]

Her next point could apply equally to other servants: 'Nor should the fast young man, who chooses his groom for his knowingness in the ways of the turf and in the tricks of low horse-dealers, be surprised if he is sometimes the victim of these learned ways. But these are the exceptional cases, which prove the existence of a better state of things.'[152]

Just as Hannah Wolley's treatises did in the seventeenth century, she took the view that it was mere common sense to treat servants generously and well.

The sensible master and the kind mistress know, that if servants depend on them for their means of living, in their turn they are dependent on their servants for very many of the comforts of life; and that, with a proper amount of care in choosing servants, and treating them like reasonable beings, and making slight excuses for the shortcomings of human nature, they will, save in some exceptional cases be tolerably well served, and, in most instances, surround themselves with attached domestics.[153]

Mrs Beeton emphasised the importance of the role of the mistress in the household: 'As with the commander of an army, or the leader of any enterprise, so it is with the mistress of a house. Her spirit will be seen through the whole establishment; and just in proportion as she performs her duties intelligently and thoroughly, so her domestics will follow in her path.'[154]

Engaging domestics was a duty which required good judgement on behalf of the mistress: 'There are some respectable registry-offices, where good servants may sometimes be hired; but the plan rather to be recommended is, for the mistress to make inquiry amongst her circle of friends and acquaintances, and her tradespeople.'[155] In their turn, servants would look out for potential recruits among their own families and acquaintances. Individuals were recruited young with the intention of training them for life, and whilst junior servants might stay in post with ambitions of moving up, others might have to leave altogether if they wanted to get married.[156]

Great landowners seem to have had a longstanding presumption against employing married servants (especially married indoor servants) or allowing servants, and especially indoor servants, to marry while in post. This does seem to have varied between houses, but was probably based on a presumption of their employer's convenience and a fear of divided loyalty. A servant's hours were long, and seen therefore as incompatible with running another household, their own, and a married servant with dependent children was considered a liability in terms of additional accommodation and divided loyalty. Whatever the reasons for it, it certainly encouraged an expectation that most junior servants would work for a short time, and the senior skilled servants spend a long time in their posts.[157]

While outdoor servants such as head gardeners were sometimes given better accommodation on getting married, indoor servants were in most cases expected to leave to marry. One Yorkshire landowner, Sir Clifford Constable, wrote huffily when one servant resigned to marry: 'You must be aware that you marrying is inconvenient to me besides being a bad precedent to the rest.'[158] Another butler recalled how one butler of his acquaintance asked permission to marry and stay in post and received permission only to be give notice shortly afterwards. His employer argued that he 'wanted his butler always within call; but that since he had got married he was often out, as he went to see his wife.'[159]

However, this presumption could have its positive side for the younger female servants used their early years in service to save a little money, as the board and food was usually covered, and get a training in household skills before marrying. They would often contribute monies home to the parents, especially if there were younger siblings to provide for. Menservants who married, however, often found themselves living separately from wives and children.[160]

6

Moving Up or Moving On
The nineteenth century

WITH SUCH HEAVING numbers of young men and women
required to staff a great country house, it is impossible for a
modern observer not to wonder about the permeability of the class
barriers that divided master and servant. Friendship of a kind may have
been common, but what about love? The incidence was almost certainly more frequent than records allow. Whilst acknowledged
romances were clearly rare, some – such as the one between
Sir Harry Fetherstonhaugh, Bt, and Mary Anne Bullock, his dairymaid
– are the stuff of legend.[1]

A Sussex landowner, Sir Harry in his youth had been a famous
rake, a close friend of the Prince Regent and a lover of Lady Emma
Hamilton. In his later years he overheard a girl singing on his estate
at Uppark, which had been designed for him by Humphrey Repton.
His housekeeper, when asked about the singer, told him it was one
of the dairymaid's helpers. When the old dairymaid retired she was
replaced by Mary Ann Bullock, supervising his delightful ornamental
dairy. With the object of his romantic notions and desire installed in
this pretty, temple-like structure, Sir Harry, unable to contain himself
any more, proposed marriage, saying to the shocked girl: 'Don't
answer me now, but if you will have me, cut a slice out of the leg of
Mutton that is coming up for my dinner today.' The mutton arrived
with a slice cut out, much to the irritation of the cook but to the
delight of the baronet.[2]

Once she had accepted, Mary Ann was bundled off to Paris for an
education, where she learnt to read, write and embroider. They married in the Saloon at Uppark on 12 September 1825; he was seventy-
one, she exactly fifty years his junior. Despite the social disparity, not

to mention the scorn of some local landowners and, indeed, some of Uppark's own servants, the marriage was apparently happy. Sir Harry is said to have remarked to his gamekeeper, 'I've made a fool of myself,' but Mary Ann cared for him until his death in 1846 at the age of ninety-two, on which he left her all his possessions. She lived on at Uppark until her death in 1875, after which it remained the home of her younger sister, whom Sir Harry had adopted. It was she who appointed Sarah Wells as her housekeeper, as described in the previous chapter.[3]

There are other, less well-known stories of genuine affection springing up between employer and servant, such as that of the Earl St Maur, heir to the 12th Duke of Somerset, who had two children, Harold and Ruth, by his kitchenmaid mistress, Rosina Swan. In 1869 he admitted the relationship to his parents, asking his mother on his deathbed to care for his family. The duke provided the children with a house and three servants, and eventually both moved in with their grandparents. Harold was left a property, while Ruth inherited £80,000 and married a member of the Cavendish-Bentinck family.[4]

Another little-known example occurred at the end of the century. John Chaworth Musters of Annesley Park, Nottinghamshire, who was born in 1860 and had been educated at Eton and Christchurch, fell in love with Mary-Anne Sharp or 'Polly', the nursery housemaid in his father's household and the daughter of a Nottingham miner. They went to live in Norway, where his parents had a fishing lodge and where she bore him three sons. They married when they realised they had to return to England for John to take up his inheritance on his father's unexpected death in 1887. Four more sons were born to them. A relation later wrote: 'Close relatives back in England who were aware of the situation were surprised to see how she, the one time nursery house-maid would cope with it all. To their surprise she did so extremely well . . . a truly remarkable woman. Her dress sense and accomplishments were impeccable, and her relatively humble origins were never guessed by many who came to know and love her.' She lost six of her seven sons in the First World War.[5]

Perhaps to avoid such romances or, at any rate, any illegitimate children, many houses operated systems to keep staff and family apart for much of the time. This separation could be taken to extremes. One man's smooth-running household might epitomise his wife's lonely existence. Testimony to this can be found in an interesting account of life in a Regency country house, as seen through the eyes of a young English bride, Catherine Osborne, arriving at her older husband's family home, Newtown Anner in County Tipperary. Her letters home were transcribed and published in *Memorials of Lady Osborne*.[6]

Given the age difference between husband and wife, it is a fair assumption that the management style of the household represented the values of the previous generation: 'The moment we arrived, which was early in the morning, Sir Thomas took me to look at the kitchen garden, which is very extensive, and kept in beautiful order. The gardener attended us. The moment he saw me he took off his hat and said, with all the Irish warmth of manner: "Welcome to your home my Lady."'[7] At first she was not even sure how many servants there were, writing in a letter: 'My maid tells me that they sat down six-and-twenty to dinner in the servants' hall yesterday, and some of the people were out. It is the fashion in Ireland for the upper servants to dine with the rest, with the exception of the kitchen-maid, groom and whipper-in, who attend them and dine afterwards.'[8]

Lady Osborne admitted in the same letter that she used to ask her maid Johnstone to keep her company in her dressing room. 'I make her sit there that I sometimes see a female face – hear a human voice. I never saw a house so still and solitary as this. It is so very much apart from the servants; no door of communication upstairs with their apartments. My maid and I walk along the long corridor, from room to room, without more fear of interruption from a single being than if we were in the deserts of Arabia.' How easily might a maid become the close friend and confidante of a chatelaine in a remote country house.[9]

She also refers to Sir Thomas's secret of good household management: 'He says that a lady should delegate all her authority over the female part of the establishment to the housekeeper and her own maid, and the gentleman to the butler. She should never give any orders to the inferior servants, because that would create confusion.' Lady Osborne observed humbly: 'I am sure his method must be the best, for I never saw a house managed with so much order and regularity in my life; every servant understands his particular business so well, that everything goes by clockwork.' Her mother-in-law may have been casting a long shadow: 'Sir Thomas thinks that a lady should never show herself in the kitchen, because his mother never was in hers.'[10]

To the children who had grown up in them, some remoter country households might have seemed like extended families. Elizabeth Smith (née Grant) put down her *Memoirs of a Highland Lady* in old age, recalling memories of Doune, her family home in the early nineteenth century, and its large but by all accounts somewhat unruly household of 1812. It is a vivid vignette of an isolated rural estate, where the staff were a mixture of local families and recruits from England, and a way of life that she felt had changed out of all recognition by the end of the century:

> Our family then consisted of my father and mother, we three girls and our governess, and our young French companion, Caroline Favrin, William during the summer holidays, Johnnie and a maid between him and my mother, poor Peggy Davidson. Besides her there were the following servants: Mrs Bird, the coachman's wife, an Englishwoman, as upper housemaid and plain needlewoman, under her Betty Ross, the gardener's youngest daughter; Grace Grant, the beauty of the country . . . our schoolroom maid; old Belle Macpherson, a soldier's widow . . . was the laundry maid.[11]

The picture she creates, perhaps partly romanticised because of the distance in time, is of a highly interconnected and intertwined microcosm of society.

> The cook and housekeeper was an Englishwoman Mrs Carr from Cumberland, an excellent manager; a plain cook under her from Inverness; and old Christie as kitchen maid. The men were Simon Ross, the gardener's eldest son, as butler, and an impudent English

footman, Richard, with a bottle-nose, who yet turned all the women's heads; William Bird, the coachman, and George Ross, another son of the gardener's as groom . . . Old John Mackintosh brought in all the wood and peats for the fires, pumped the water, turned the mangle, lighted the oven, brewed the beer, bottled the whisky, kept the yard tidy, and stood enraptured listening to us playing on the harp, 'like Daavid'!

At the farm were the grieve [farm bailiff], and as many lads as he required for the work of the farm under him, who all slept in a loft over the stables and ate in the farm kitchen. [There was also George Ross,] turner, joiner, butcher, weaver, lint-dresser, wool-comber, dyer and what not; his old wife was the henwife. [Old Jenny Cameron] . . . was supreme in the farm kitchen; she managed cows, calves, milk, stores, and the spinning, with another girl who also helped in the laundry in which abode of mirth and fun [or so it must have seemed to a bored young girl in the big house] the under housemaid spent her afternoons.[12]

In addition to a smith, John Fyffe, who came twice a week, there was a 'bowman' who looked after the cattle and who, 'like almost all the rest of them, lived with us till he died'. This is a riveting portrait of a little self-contained world in a remote area, an almost self-sufficient community, which she looks back on with nostalgia, not least perhaps because it located her – the daughter of a landowner who later lost his lands – near its apex.[13]

To contrast this somewhat romanticised view with one of more gritty reality, a number of first-hand narratives of service offer an insight into the experiences of working servants, even at the most manual level. The most remarkable nineteenth-century memoir of a maidservant was written by one Hannah Cullwick, who was born in 1833 and died in 1909.[14] Her recollections of her early life and her diaries provide a window on to what life was like for maids, who bore most of the hardest jobs of country- and town-house life.

Hannah left school at eight years old and entered service shortly afterwards, working in various country houses in fairly junior positions. When she moved to London and became the maid of all work in town houses in London and elsewhere, by her own account it was because she preferred to be largely her own boss rather than have servants over her or, indeed, below her.[15]

Hannah was certainly not afraid of hard work, expressing some pride in her strength and achievements. That her diary was written at all makes a curious tale in itself. She had a long and highly clandestine relationship with Arthur Munby, a barrister who worked for the Ecclesiastical Commissioners, a very Victorian figure. His papers, which are now in Trinity College, Cambridge, include Hannah's remarkable diaries.

They came about because he had asked her to keep a record, describing her life for him in detail. He cherished a special fascination for images of Hannah in her work clothes, with her arms dirty or raw (I leave readers to judge for themselves the weirdness of this). Although they later married in secret, it was not a success, apparently because he succumbed to the temptation of trying to gentrify her. She resisted this and stuck to her guns, begging him in June 1876, 'please let me live as your servant and don't bother me to be any thing else.'[16]

The account that she wrote of her life in the 1840s and 1850s reveals an industrious and independent-minded woman, forced through circumstance to work for her living from an early age, and yet, as is often surprisingly true of domestic servants, able to move quite easily from job to job.

Hannah worked as a nurserymaid at Ryton in Shropshire:

> I stopp'd here through the winter & had a deal of hard work to do, for there was eight children. I'd all their boots to clean & the large nurseries on my hands and knees, & a long passage & stairs, all their meals to get & our own – the nurse only dress'd the baby & look'd over me. I'd all the water to carry up and down for their baths & coal for the fire, put all the children to bed & wash and dress of a morning by eight, & I wasnt in bed after 5.[17]

All this when she was little more than a child herself, perhaps ten or eleven at most.

She found the work uncongenial and managed to find another post with a family with only five children. In 1849, she worked for a clergyman's family in Lincolnshire, where they were kind to her but 'very particular & the young gentleman (Master Scotsman) used to correct me often in talk. I learned a good deal from them and was with them 15 months.' They felt she was too young and when she left in 1850 then gave her a good character for a post at Aqualate Hall, Shropshire, to work for Lady Boughy. By then she was seventeen.

Here life was relatively happy but, in a clear illustration of how fragile some servants' positions were, she was dismissed essentially for larking about while working: 'I got on very well as under housemaid for eight months, but Lady Boughy saw me and another playing as we was cleaning our kettles (we had about 16 to clean, they belong'd to the bedrooms) & she gave us both warning.'[18] Hannah found another job but regretted having to go: 'I was dreadfully sorry to leave that splendid park at Aqualate. I was got used to the servants & I felt happy for I had a friend or two, & John the postillion was such a good-looking fellow & used to take me for a walk in the park with Mary Hart, a nice girl and kind to me. So I was vex'd to leave. I ax'd Lady Boughy if she would please forgive me & let me stop. But she said, "NO", very loudly.'[19]

Nevertheless she gave Hannah a good character, and she went to work at Woodcote in Shropshire as a scullery-maid for Lady Louisa Coates, a daughter of the 3rd Earl of Liverpool. She remarked bitterly on the contrast between her work as a housemaid and the confined conditions of a scullion: 'It was a very different work, & a very different place to me after being used to running along the splendid halls & gallery & rooms at Aqualate as a housemaid. And I had learnt to make beds & to do the rooms for company & all, so that I couldn't help crying when I came to clean the stew pans & great spits & dripping pan, & live only in a rough outhouse next to the kitchen . . . But I got used to it.'[20]

When the family went to Rhyl for a holiday she had less work, although she still had to get the servants' dinner ready. Her master the cook 'said I'd enough dirty hard work to do when the family was at home, & I was [to] go out for walks, if I'd any spare time, so I did.' During this period the solitude grated on her and she missed her sweetheart and the liveliness and companionship she had known:

'I felt lonely . . . But the time soon went by & the family came back, company came to stop, & then the winter with all business as there *is* in a big family, & I forgot I was lonely.'[21]

In 1851, the family took her to London, together with the cook, who said she was a 'good 'un to work & he'd rather have me nor [rather than] Emma the kitchen-maid'. Hannah enjoyed London, but was back after two months with the family, 'to Pitchford again & from there to Woodcote for the two grand balls at Shrewsbury. The company stay'd at Pitchford for them, so we was both very gay & hard-work'd too, for I seem'd as pleas'd to peep through the bushes to see the ladies & gentlemen start as if I was one of them.'[22] She made the acquaintance of a Mr Munby, whom she later nicknamed 'Massa' and who would play a prominent role in her life.

Hannah moved to Henham Hall in Suffolk, the home of the Earl of Stradbroke (whom she calls Shadbroke in her diary). It was a long journey from London to the lodge gates 'where the laundrymaid met me with a man & a cart for my box. The housekeeper star'd at me but didn't speak for ever so long & then said to the char-woman, "She looks young," & then to me, "You can go in the laundry for some tea & then come in to get His Lordship's dinner up."'[23]

Because of the housekeeper's unfriendliness, Hannah's 'heart began to fail me, but the servants was nice in the laundry & I made haste, & put my cotton frock & cap & apron on to be in the kitchen by 6. Mrs Smith the housekeeper was most unkind to me . . . & I was ready to say I'd go back in the morning.' The friendly groom told her: 'Never mind her, she's drunk & doesn't know what she's about – you stop & you'll get on all right.'[24]

When the elderly Countess of Stradbroke, the earl's mother, 'wish'd [the servants] a kind goodbye', she gave the under servants a new cotton frock and half a sovereign each. 'The lady gave me good advice. I wasn't to mind the housekeeper's temper but learn all I could of her, for she says, "She's an excellent cook & baker & whatever you see her do you may be sure it's right."' After showing Hannah some watercolours, the countess 'took my rough hand in her very delicate one, & said goodbye. It *was* the first & last time too that ever a lady like her touch'd my hand.'[25]

By this time Hannah's sister Ellen was living with her at Henham Hall as a scullion. However, Hannah left her position there to be closer to her lover, Munby, in London. Over the next forty years, Hannah took a long series of jobs in private town houses and lodging houses in London and elsewhere, in which she was determined

> to go where only one was kept in the kitchen. And so this was the beginning & the end of me trying to be an upper servant. I had cleaner hands & face, & wore cleaner frocks & aprons & had a kitchenmaid to do the dirty work for me & all that, but I dislike the thought of being over anybody & ordering things, not only 'cause I'd rather do the work myself but for fear anyone shd think me set up or *proud*. No, I've long resolved in my own mind & felt that, for freedom & true lowliness, there's nothing like being a maid of all work.[26]

The entry for Monday, 16 July 1860 was fairly typical of her days after she left country-house service:

> Lighted the fire. Swept the birdroom & dusted the other rooms. Clean'd 3 pairs of boots. Got breakfast up & made the beds & emptied the slops. Clean'd & wash'd up. Put the linen for the wash. Cleaned the brass rods & the bedroom windows & the sills. Put up clean curtains. Clean'd the knives & got the dinner ready; laid the hearth & took it up. Clean'd away & then went upstairs & clean'd the bedrooms on my knees. Got tea. Clean'd away & wash'd up in the scullery. Went on errands & got supper ready. . . . I took a note to Mr Brewer for the Missis & then had supper. Clean'd away & wash'd up to bed at 11.[27]

Yet even this gruelling routine gave her more independence in her own eyes than country-house service. She found the jobs principally through registry offices, or London's famous Soho Bazaar, a servants' recruiting fair.

Even so, Hannah was able to save money. For all its undoubted toughness and insecurity, for many from poorer backgrounds domestic service was a chance to work, make money and acquire training – even an education. In the context of mid- to late-nineteenth-century Britain this was already difficult enough, the alternatives being manual jobs in agriculture, which from the 1880s was in a state of economic depression, or industry.

William Lanceley, a successful butler and steward who served a royal duke among others, started out as a footboy in the local squire's house in 1870: 'My wages were to be £8 per year, with plenty of good food besides; clothes found except underclothing and boots, which I had to provide from my wages. I was then told in a confidential way that if I looked well after the visiting ladies'-maids, cleaned their boots nicely and got the luggage up quickly (which was my job with the aid of the odd man) I should pick up a nice little bit in tips, which proved correct.'[28]

As accommodation, clothing and food were largely supplied by his employer, and tips, he was able to save all £8 during his first year and took it home,

> handing it over with pride to my mother. She had been left a widow with nine children, the eldest 18 years of age, and to make matters worse my father had died in debt. I can still see her face when she took it and then, giving me £2 back, said 'I cannot take it all, lad.' [He left the £2] quietly on the cottage table where I knew she would find it. Next year my wages were raised to £12, and I felt myself a millionaire and saved the whole of it, again disposing of it in the same way.[29]

His duties, which started at six o'clock,

> were as follows: first light the servants' hall fire, clean the young ladies' boots, the butler's, house-keeper's, cook's, and ladies'-maids', often twenty pairs altogether, trim the lamps (I had thirty-five to look after, there being no gas or electric light in the district in those days), and all this had to be got through by 7.30; then lay up the hall breakfast, get it in, and clear up afterwards.
>
> [After the servants' breakfast] My day's work followed on with cleaning knives, house-keeper's room, silver, windows, and mirrors.

He would have to lay up the servants' hall supper and dinner and clear everything and wash up, as well as help to carry meals up to the dining room. After washing up the servants' hall supper, 'this brought bedtime after a day's work of sixteen hours; yet I seldom felt tired as the work was so varied and the food of the best, and we generally got a little leisure in the afternoons.'[30]

In another aside he revealed how country-house service could mean detachment from the values and experiences of home. After four years' service in his second position, 'I was offered a holiday as the family were paying a round of visits lasting six weeks and those servants who cared to take a holiday did so. Very few did in those days and no servant would dream of asking for one unless the family were away from home . . . My first holiday was three days, quite enough at that time. Our cottage homes and food were no comparison to what we left behind.'[31]

Lanceley's saving his entire wage may seem extraordinary but domestic servants had also to bear in mind the prospect of illness, old age and retirement. In the relatively confined world of the country-house servant, where much could be provided in the way of food, accommodation and clothing, there was potential for making substantial savings. The long-standing gardener at Erddig, James Phillips, saved some £4,000, while a laundrymaid at Shugborough was even able to save around £400.[32]

On the larger estates, annuities and legacies often placed retiring domestic servants in a better position than many other kinds of workers of the same era. Lord Northwick left annuities of £5 for his butler, under butler, groom, nurse and coachman (to be forfeited if invested in a public house), with £10 to their widows, and £5 to those of his gardeners and labourers. He added a codicil that paid £100 to everyone who had been in service to him for a full year leading up to the time of his death.[33] At Trentham, annuities to servants included £50 a year to a housekeeper, while many others were entitled to accommodation of some sort on the estate.[34]

Some elderly servants on the larger estates could expect accommodation, perhaps being put into gate lodges and given the lesser duties of gatekeeper, for example. There is a painting at Carnfield Hall in Derbyshire that shows just such a gatekeeper: a retired housekeeper or housemaid by the name of Mrs Mumford, painted in 1890 when she was a hundred.[35] In 1890, the Duke of Portland, who owned racehouses, built a substantial set of almshouses on his estate at Welbeck Abbey called 'The Winnings' because they had been paid for by prize money from a horse race. They provided housing for servants obliged to retire while in service to the duke on account of either ill heath or old age.[36]

Many servants, or former domestic servants, of course, were not so lucky, particularly those whose later years of service were spent in towns. Joseph Chamberlain, in his evidence before the Royal Commission on the Aged Poor in 1893, remarked that people were often reluctant to employ servants over the age of fifty 'and accordingly almost by the necessity of the case, they will have to go [to] the workhouse'. He asserted that in the Birmingham Workhouse then, of the 438 female inmates one in every three had been connected with domestic service in some way.[37] Fear of the workhouse persisted among elderly servants well into the twentieth century.

Servants who had passed their whole lives working for one family were certainly better looked after. One of the most interesting (and as yet unpublished) personal memoirs of a domestic servant in an important country house is that written by Thomas Kilgallon, longterm manservant and valet to Sir Henry Gore-Booth. His diaries, which survive in a typescript version in the Belfast Public Record Office of Northern Ireland, not only give a deeply personal picture of life in service, but delineate the roles, experiences and duties of the whole household as he remembered it.[38]

Kilgallon spent his entire life with Gore-Booth, moving up from a very junior position to become his valet and, ultimately, the butler at Lissadell in Country Sligo, a position from which he retired around 1920. As his memoirs show, he sank his whole life and energies into looking after his employer and his family. Penned in the early years of the twentieth century, they cover the period from the 1860s to the 1890s. Throughout, he continually uses the phrase 'we' when speaking of the experiences of himself and Sir Henry and Lady Gore-Booth, rather than himself and his fellow servants.

A portrait of Mr Kilgallon by Count Casimir Markiewicz was painted directly on to the wall of the dining room at Lissadell beside the sideboard where he would have presided over so many meals. In 1900, Markiewicz had married Sir Henry's eldest daughter, Constance, who became an Irish Nationalist, fought in the Easter Rising in 1916 and was celebrated in verse by W.B. Yeats. What a key presence in her life this strong-minded individual must have seemed, not least as Kilgallon was the first Irish Roman Catholic to be the household's senior servant, an issue that seems to have been little explored in biographies of the countess.[39]

It was in fact very unusual for a Roman Catholic to become a butler in a Protestant-owned country house, even then, and it is testimony to the close relationship that Kilgallon had with the family. In 1911, 68 per cent of servants in Irish country houses were Protestant, and 44 per cent were born in England or Wales. Ninety per cent of butlers and footmen and 75 per cent of cooks in Irish country-house employment were Protestant.[40] As Kilgallon notes, in the 1860s–70s, 'all the heads of department, both inside and out, were either Scotch or English, also those [who] were second in command'.[41]

Kilgallon's career began at the age of ten in 1864 when he was first employed by Sir Henry's brother-in-law, Captain Charles Wynne, as 'cook and cabin boy' on his sailing boat, Kilgallon's father being the skipper of Sir Robert Gore-Booth's yacht. Mr Kilgallon had to 'clean all the brass work, keep the cabin clean, help with the sails and do all the messages ashore'. That season his father died in a tragic accident.

Sir Robert's heir, Henry, took the boy on for the winter, no doubt feeling that the family had some responsibility for him, at first just to look after his boat. 'A short time after Mr Gore engaged me he wished me to be in his room at all the dressing hours for meals and to call him in the mornings, bring his hot water and learn to valet him. I had £8 a year, [and] one suit of clothes.' He adds laconically: 'Wages was small then but most things were cheap. I slept at the stables [in] what is now the outer office. The coachman and his wife and child slept in what is now the inner office. Quite comfortable rooms. Batchelor [sic] gentleman also slept in rooms at the stables. They were equal if not better than many of the rooms in the house.'[42]

Sir Robert was the MP for Sligo, so the family spent considerable time in London, when typically most of the servants went with them. 'The housekeeper did not go there as there was a housekeeper for the London house, a Mrs Tigwell. They [took] the first and second housemaids, house steward, groom [of the] chambers, under butler and first and second housemaids, first and second footman and steward's room boy. All the other servants were put on board wages till they returned . . . [and] allowed milk and vegetables.'[43] These were exactly the arrangements in place at the Earl of Kildare's household at Carton a century earlier.

Henry Gore-Booth became interested in Kilgallon's education, sending him briefly to a private school and later teaching him himself: 'All days we were not sailing I assisted the under butler and footman with their work. It was a happy time. I had no master but Mr Gore. When he was away, I had to write to him, telling him what I was doing with reference to my work and nothing else. He always kept my letters and when he returned he showed me my errors.'[44]

Although senior servants tended to be recruited from the wider world, Mr Kilgallon's memoir illustrates how many of the servants in the house and on the estate were related, either by being married to other servants, or through the marriages of their children. For instance, Mrs Carter, Henry's old nurse, who is described as giving him a 'great hugging' on the announcement of his engagement, was married to the coachman, and her daughter was married to the head gamekeeper. One daughter of Mr Ball, the house steward, was married to Holmes, the huntsman, and his second son, the estate carpenter, was married to Miss Burchell, maid to Sir Robert's wife.[45]

> Gentlemen's houses of this period, and kept in the style as Lissadell was kept had a house steward. Mr Ball was house steward when I came. He paid all expenses in connection with the house, both inside and out that is such as repairs [to] buildings inside or out. He engaged all the servants in the house and stables, paid their wages, and dismissed them when necessary, ordered and paid for all wines. He waited at dinner, but not at other meals. He just handed around the wines.[46]

Kilgallon evoked the service of meals with a neat brevity, almost a shorthand, that is suggestive of a close attention to detail:

> The groom [of the] chamber carved, and with the footmen waited at all meals, dispatched the post, opened all newspapers and ironed them, placed them in the rooms. Attend at the door at the coming and leaving of guests. Attend at the door when carriages leaving. With the help of one or two of the footmen seen to the polishing of all the furniture in the drawing room or reception rooms. Seen to all the writing tables, both reception and bedroom.[47]

Of the footmen, he recalled that there were three:

> first second and third. The under butler he was of course also foot-
> man. Only he had more special duties. He was responsible for keeping
> all dinner silver in order, laying the dinner table. See that all plates, hot
> and cold were ready for use . . . When there was big dinner on,
> Mr Ball, the groom [of the] chamber, three footmen and under butler,
> John Kerins and I waited. I was the only one not in full dress. The full
> dress livery had dark blue coat, red vest, red plush breeches, white
> stockings, shoes with buckles. The footmen wore white thick cotton
> gloves at all times for dinner.[48]

With a sense of awe, Mr Kilgallon summoned up the vision of a
grand party at the house that took place years earlier: 'Lissadell
house on the night of a ball, when fully lit up; to me it looked like
what a fairyland would be like in my imagination at the time, with
all the different coloured dresses of the ladies flitting about [and]
the great number of footmen in their red plush breeches and
vest.'[49]

His recollection of the maids in his early days suggests a certain
sympathy. 'There were three housemaids and help. Their work was
hard. They had to be up at 4 am. There was no hot or cold water laid
on. They had to carry all upstairs. Heavy work emptying baths.
A great many fires in bedrooms.'[50]

The kitchen staff was, as you would expect, 'cook, pastry cook,
kitchen maid scullery maid and help when required. Kitchen boys
whose duties were to light all fires, clean out ashes, scour all coppers,
all cooking was done in coppers. Look after two boilers one in the
top scullery and one in the bottom scullery. From these boilers
[came] all hot water for baths, washing up etc.'[51]

Typically for a larger country house in the nineteenth century,
there was a foreign male chef. 'The cook was a Frenchman called
Friburg. He was fond of whiskey, and engaged George Griggs's horse
and cart to take him to Sligo one or two days a week . . . they sat in
a public house in Sligo till it was time for Friburg to think about
dinner. There was such a great number of servants in the house and
stables and guests and callers, it took a great quantity of meat to
supply all. It was more like a hotel.'[52]

Typically, the ritual of aristocratic life was reflected in the hier-archical arrangements below stairs, particularly for servants' own dining arrangements, which were even more archaic than the fash-ions in gentry dining at the time. 'All the servants did not sit together for all their meals, only for the principal meal, dinner.' As often hap-pened, the house steward took the head of the table, the under butler the other end,

> as there was always two joints, one at each end . . . All the women sat
> on one side of the table. The men the other. The housekeeper sat on
> the left of the steward. The maids according to their rank next to
> her . . . The house steward said grace and when all room servants had
> finished their meat, the others laid down their knives and forks, and
> the steward said grace. The housekeeper rising, the lady's maid
> following, the steward taking up the rear, went to the steward's room
> for the next course, the under servants did not always get a second
> course . . . Steward room servants had the same food that was served
> in the dining room.[53]

They were served at table by the steward's room boy, dressed in livery.

As suggested by many other accounts, most discipline was meted out by the higher servants: 'If you did not carry out the rules, your time would not be a pleasant one, steward and housekeeper would make it very uncomfortable for you.' But there could be compensa-tions: 'At night there was whiskey and wines served. Usually, there was a small dance in the servants' hall once or twice a week for three or four hours. They were allowed beer and a bottle of whiskey for punch. There was an old fiddler gave them music.'[54]

Looking back to the 1860s from the early twentieth century, Mr Kilgallon wrote: 'I often wonder where all the servants slept. I know there were three or four beds in a room. Many of the men had folding or press beds here and there in the pantry and the hall,'[55] – echoes of the sleeping arrangements of the sixteenth-century household.

Former footman and later butler, Eric Horne, left a splendidly rum-bustious kind of memoir reminiscent of that of John Macdonald in the eighteenth century, but which tactfully – but sadly for us – leaves out all the names of the houses and his employers: *What the Butler Winked at* (1923). Despite this anonymity, the stories ring true. His account is much more openly critical than Kilgallon's, starting with his first job as a footman in a country house: 'It is useless trying to describe the thousand and one things that comprise a footman's duties, which in every place he goes to, is different . . . in those days footmen in good families had to be not less than six feet, and taller if possible, to show off the family liveries, and look important.'[56] This frustrated Mr Horne, who was only five foot nine.

His first employer, in the 1870s, was a man of property, title and a miserable-sounding temperament. Indeed, Horne described him as 'the surliest, [most] bad-tempered man I ever met'. The house was a 'very large, an old Elizabethan mansion, partly modernised inside, but in the rooms upstairs Moderator colza oil lamps were used, and wax candles; gas was used in the basement, made on the estate; the passages were so wide a horse and cart could easily go up them. These passages all met in a large stone flagged square, so that it took some time to find the way about.' The household consisted of twenty-five indoor servants. 'We [footmen] had to powder [our hair], and wear breeches and white stockings. The livery was green, covered with yellow and black braiding, the family crest being worked in braid.'[57]

Showing how much distance there could be between butler and footmen, Horne recalled: 'The butler was a pompous sort of man, though a very good sort. He had previously served the Rothschilds. As long as we did our work properly he would not trouble us, in fact he very seldom spoke to us liverymen.'[58] Mr Horne had to valet for the baron, who liked to have his hair parted in the middle. This was never easy as 'he [kept] moving his head about' so it was difficult to get the requisite straight line. The baron used 'some very flowery language. But I was full of life as an egg and free from care. The Baron's bad language was like water on a duck's back.'[59]

Mr Horne had good memories of the companionship of the servants' hall. 'There was a goodly company of us in the servant's hall at night, as the grooms and the under gardeners would come in and wash up all the silver and glass in the pantries; more for company than anything else, for there was nowhere for them to go for miles, in the evenings.'[60] Looking back from the 1920s, he wrote nostalgically of 'the usual old-fashioned usages observed in the servants' hall, such as drinking the "Health" every day, etc., also a certain amount of Esprit de Corps among us all, which at the present day is entirely absent'.[61]

Most country-house establishments held daily prayers, and church attendance was compulsory:

> the pews for servants were opposite to those of the gentry, so that we were under observation all the time. One Sunday the Bold Bad baron sent for the butler and asked him if we had been drinking too much beer as he noticed several of the men were asleep during the sermon. The parson was brother to the Baron; the living was in his gift, so of course he preached a sermon to please him; generally about the lower orders being submissive to their betters . . . No wonder we went to sleep.[62]

Typically for the period, and clearly in part for moral reasons, the sleeping arrangements of men and women were strictly separated: 'All the men slept in the basement.' Equally typically, for security reasons 'the under butler [laid] his bed down in the pantry, across the front of the plate room door, so as to guard the plate at night. To get at it, burglars would have to move his bed: if that did not waken him nothing would.'[63] One member of staff was subjected to a memorable prank: 'One night we arranged to have a game with the under butler, so we got a reel of cotton, put it on top of his let-down bed, taking the end of the cotton down the passage round the next corner with us. When we saw him put out his light we gently began to pull the cotton. We heard him get out of bed, strike a light to see what it was rattling on the top of his bed. Then we thought it prudent to disappear to our own rooms in stockinged feet.'[64] Mr Horne felt: 'All this fun helped to neutralise the bullyings and jawings I got from the Bold Bad Baron when valeting him . . . all his money and power did not make him happy.'[65] Later Horne described being caught in a pillow fight by the baron, as a result of which the first footman was dismissed.[66]

The hierarchy and the segregation by gender were also manifested in the dining arrangements:

> The maidservants only came into the servants' hall for dinner and supper, their other meals they got in their own appartments [sic], the

kitchen maids never came, except when a dance was on. The laundry maids in the laundry, the housemaids in housemaid's room; the dairy maid would feed with the stillroom maids; nursemaids in their nursery; butler, valets, groom of chambers, housekeeper, lady's-maids in the steward's room. So that there is a lot of one servant waiting on another, the under ones of each department doing it, they in turn being waited on, when promoted.[67]

Thus even the meals were like minor military operations, but also seen as a way of training junior staff.

The baron liked to impress but had a frugal side: 'In cases when visitors were staying in the house we wore our dress liveries, with a lot more yellow and black braid plastered up the back and across the front. The butler wore black cloth breeches and black silk stockings. Our silver shoe buckles were on the plate list, and had to be given up when leaving the situation.'[68]

London visits amused some servants more than others:

As the London season came round, we packed up, and went to town. On going out to dinner, or other functions, the Baron always had two footmen standing up behind his C spring carriage, and the coachman with his curly wig on. The Baron was a big bug at his seat in the country, but when he got to London, among the other big bugs, he was not a big bug after all. A London season is very tiring to servants. There is not only the day work, but the night work as well. They would keep us out regularly till one, two, or three o'clock, but we had to start work at the same time as the other servants. Often during the London season we were kept so short of our hours of sleep that I used to go to sleep on the carriage . . . We were all glad to get back to the country house again after the London season with its dinner parties, tea parties, evening parties and night work.[69]

At significant moments, Mr Horne felt hemmed in and desperate to leave service, but in the end he stayed the course:

I felt that I was gradually going into a net, and losing all liberty in life: the constraint became almost unbearable, but what could I do? I had no trade in my hands. I knew nothing but gentleman's service wherewith to get a living. I suppose some men does not feel it, men with no further

ambition than to fritter their lives away from day to day in such a calling; a sort of man-woman existance [sic], at the mercy of the gentry's
whims and fancies; cooped up day and night with out variation.[70]

The pay too was sometimes barely adequate: 'All this time I had been
away in service I always sent the greater part of my wages home, but
in those days a second footman only got £28 a year, and had to pay
his own laundry bill out of that. We were allowed £2 per year for
hair powder, but always used flour.'[71]

Horne found a more congenial berth in the service of an employer
better tempered than the baron:

> It was not long before I met with an under-butler's place to a Noble
> Earl, who had a house in London, in the country, and one in Scotland.
> It requires great strength to polish silver, also great care and endur-
> ance . . . Here our livery was very smart. Scarlet breeches and waist-
> coat, blue coat with scarlet collar and cuffs, trimmed with inch wide
> silver lace, and one epaulet on the left shoulder, white stockings, and
> buckles.[72]

The earl's household was substantial: 'There were twenty-five
indoor servants at this place, besides housemaids at the other houses.
The butler did no manual work, he only superintended the men, the
work was all done for him. All he had to do was to walk into the
dining room, the boy carrying his wine basket, at the last minute, cast
his eye over the table, when all was ready to begin.'[73]

Mr Horne had more respect for this employer than he did for
many of his later ones:

> This place was the best regulated situation that I have ever been in . . .
> When the bell rang to clear breakfast, the butler would answer it. Her
> Ladyship was the sister of a Duke. She would remain in the breakfast
> room, give the butler his orders for the day, how many visitors (if any)
> and which rooms they would occupy, the number that would be at
> meals, also orders for the carriages.
> Then he would come out, and the housekeeper would go in and
> get her orders, she would come out and the cook would go in. Then
> the butler would ring the bell twice for the footman to clear away the
> breakfast. All this took only a few minutes to do. The butler would

come to the pantry and give us our orders. Perhaps he would say to me, Eighteen, or twenty, for dinner, use the silver, or the gilt service, as the case may be . . .

The housekeeper would give her orders to the head housemaid, and stillroom maids. The cook would do the same to her kitchen and scullery maids. Everything went like clockwork, no confusion, no jealousies, no treading on each other's toes; no occasion for saying I didn't know this or that; for each department got their orders, and acted up to them.[74]

Mr Horne was touched, as many servants seemed to have been, by the history, tradition and atmosphere of the house in which he lived and worked:

The Castle was a fine old place, with a wide moat . . . Often I sat up all night with 'Old Daddy' as we used to call him. He had brewed the beer for the Castle for over fifty years, and listen to his tales of olden times, of what they used to do in previous lords times. Still, a great many of the old customs were kept up; we still ate our food off pewter plates and dishes, each with the coronet and crest engraved on them, we also drank our beer out of horns. We had the choice of small beer or tea for breakfast (as tea on its first introduction into England was only drunk by the gentry). [Whether these customs were genuinely old or revived, there is no way of telling.]

Also, no conversation was allowed until after the cloth had been removed, and the health drank. The under butler stands up at the bottom of the table, holds a horn of old ale up in his hands, taps the table twice, and says: 'My Lord and Lady' [and] the others reply, 'With all my heart'. This old custom was observed every day.[75]

In such a well-run and well-cared for house, the turnover of staff might be slower than in many others:

Servants seldom wanted to leave that place, unless they had been there some time and wanted promotion. I think what kept them together to a great extent was [that] we were allowed a dance on the first Tuesday in every month. The mason who worked on the estate, played the 'cello, his son played second fiddle, the tailor played first violin. I played sometimes as well . . . Our programme consisted of lancers, quadrilles, waltzes, schottisches, polkas, Valse of Vienna, Polka, Mazurka, and country dances . . . I think this sort of thing keeps servants together, makes them just one big happy family.[76]

Mr Horne enjoyed working here, but as with many junior men-servants he had to move on to find a more senior position. It was during this time that he became more and more disillusioned with his treatment by the upper classes and their unreasonable demands. There was one baronet and MP whom he described memorably as having 'the brains of a rabbit'. However, he recalled the earl and the castle with unmixed affection.

After going through the daily routine with this Noble family for several years as under butler I thought I would blossom out into a full-blown valet. As I could clean and load a gun, clean a scarlet coat, top boots and leather breeches with the best of them: also I knew about fishing, and what to do on a salmon fishing expedition. Drying the lines, and clothes, etc., ready for the next morning, and dry all the flies that had been used. I felt I wanted to see a bit more of the world before I settled down to the humdrum life of a butler.[77]

The latter part of his story belongs to another chapter.

Horne's many-layered career, moving between multiple employ-ers, reminds us of the mobility of the nineteenth-century servant. Whilst staff would usually be recruited by the house steward, or by the housekeeper where there was no steward, the landowner and his wife usually interviewed any prospective personal attendant.[78] References or 'characters' were all important, but even when the appointment had been made, all might not go to plan.

In the 1840s, Lavinia Jane Watson, the daughter of Lord George Quin, married Richard Watson of Rockingham Castle. Her diaries for the 1840s record just such a case in point. On 1 January 1844, her trusted lady's maid, Lloyd, was ill, apparently suffering from nerves at having to hand in her notice. 'Champion [the housekeeper] broke the ice about Lloyd, who wishes to marry Mr Lloyd; and as it incurred her leaving me, she was in low spirits. Had an interview with the bride and comforted her.'[79]

However, immediately after these affectionate remarks, she expressed her dismay at the character of Lloyd's replacement, writing on 17 February: 'My new maid Stephenson arrived on Wednesday, a short old fashioned, mincing body – won't do.' By 21 February: 'Stephenson going.' On the 23rd: 'Children well. I with bad cough. Took leave of Stephenson and her humble resigned manner on the occasion almost made me feel a lump, and yet I am sure I have never felt less fascinated by anyone. Champion very good about it altogether.' This scenario must have been a familiar contest of sensitivity and self-interest.[80]

Mrs Watson was a close friend of Charles Dickens, who visited Rockingham Castle on several occasions. Old Champion, the housekeeper, is thought by some to have been the model for Mrs Rouncewell, housekeeper in his novel, *Bleak House*, to Sir Leicester Dedlock at his home of Chesney Wold. She is described in Chapter 7 as 'a fine old lady, handsome, stately, wonderfully neat . . . It is the next difficult thing to an impossibility to imagine Chesney Wold without Mrs Rouncewell, but she has only been here fifty years.' Famously, she gives a tour of the house to the visiting Mr Guppy and his friend Walt, with a young gardener opening and closing the shutters, while the visitors are overwhelmed by the size and gloom of the house.

As in the eighteenth century, the recruitment of domestic servants is often mentioned in letters between landowning families. On 3 May 1804, Lady Blount wrote to Francis Fortescue Turvile at Bosworth Hall, Northamptonshire, to say that 'if she is not yet provided with a House & Laundry maid there is a very good one to be had who was bred up by Lady Clifford . . . & when she went to Igbrooke took [her] with her as under nursery maid where she lived within these two years'. The maid in question had also worked at two other houses where the servants had been discharged when the household was broken up but 'had given great satisfaction'.[81]

Goodwood's house steward, Robert Smith, wrote on 19 May 1858 to Archibald Hair, secretary to the 5th Duke of Richmond, of his problems in finding a new recruit for the still room, using personal recommendations and, presumably, servants' registries: 'I have not left a thing undone that I could do about getting a Still Room Maid both Publick and Private but I can find nothing Likely to suit at all – Mrs Sanders would like her to be 30 years of Age and to know Something of cooking and Wages [10 shillings] [but] every body tells me there is nothing of the kind to be had in London.'[82]

Sometimes, as literacy became more widespread, servants themselves would write in pursuit of a position. One young man, who had had the care of five horses, wrote to offer his services to Sir Henry FitzHerbert: 'I understand that you are or will be shortly in want of a Groom . . . I have this morning been to Tissington and Johnson the Keeper (who knows me very well) said that I might in all probability get the situation if you were not already suited.'[83]

References could be less than flattering, as illustrated by this letter from a rector's wife to Lady Alice Packe, dated 18 April 1887: 'Dear Lady Alice, I am afraid I cannot answer all your questions quite satisfactorily about Mary Anne Millington. She was certainly very dirty but perhaps with a strict servant over her she might improve. She was only here six months as a kitchen maid & it was her first place. She was good tempered & I believe her to be honest & steady . . . [but she] wanted a proper training.'[84]

The habit of writing over-positive references for servants whom employers wanted to see move on was a subject of lively debate in the letters page of *The Times* in August 1879: 'too many ladies give unwarrantable characters to servants whom they wish to get clear of'.[85] Nevertheless a character reference was clearly essential for any future positions. As one butler tartly observed in a letter to the same publication in the same year: 'At the whim of the master, the servant starves or he lives.'[86]

The papers of Henry, 4th Earl of Carnarvon, from the 1870s at Highclere include several notes relating to the recruitment of a valet, who might possibly also undertake the role of groom of the chambers.[87] They make moving documents, capturing the life of a manservant in a few lines. They illustrate too how mobile servants' lives were, for even in houses that were comfortable and well run, usually only senior servants would serve for long periods, while younger servants had to move on to get promotion.[88]

One candidate was an Italian, Bernardo Giannienetti, who was forty, and single; valets were unlikely to be married, given the burdens of the job. He had worked not only for General Fox for eight years, describing the general as a 'good friend', but also for the general's uncle, Lord Lilford, for whom he had been valet and groom of the chambers. He was, however, 'not accustomed to hunting clothes', although he did speak five languages, a useful attribute in a valet who accompained his masters on their travels.

Another candidate was George Copsey, aged thirty, who for nine years had been valet to a Mr Stephen Tower of 70 Grosvenor Street and, according to the notes, had worked as a footman but not as a groom of the chambers. He spoke French and a little German, and his last post had been in a commercial situation, for the notes record that he 'left because not comfortable at hotel'. A last note in red pencil states rather bluntly, in a phrase that echoes down the centuries, 'Won't do.'

More promising was William Pratt, who had been a valet and groom of the chambers to the Duke of Montrose, for six years a footman to the Earl of Mount Edgecumbe, and for three years a valet and butler to Lord March (heir to the Duke of Richmond). Although less of a linguist, he could 'get anything in French but not converse'. He was, however, 'used to Hunting and Shooting clothes', which frequently needed brushing and cleaning overnight. Pratt came from Northamptonshire and was thirty-one. Additional notes remark that he was 'steady with horses'. A reference or 'character' was supplied by Lord March, written direct to Lord Carnavon and dated 11 May 1873: 'Dear Lord Carnavon, Pratt left me last July since which time he has been living with a lady in Brighton [in service as a footman] and left her to go to Germany but for some reason or other has not gone and came to ask me if I would give him another character. I believe him to be honest, sober and steady, a very good valet and attentive to his master's needs.'[89]

The Benyons of Englefield House in Berkshire kept a detailed servants' book, where every detail of interest was recorded about their recruitment and training. In a parallel to the Carnarvon papers, it includes a list of questions to be put to applicants. For the butler:

'Where did you live last, and for how long? Why did you leave, and when? What was the establishment, and what were you? This is a regular Family – prayers each morning – punctual – the Plate is under your charge, and you will help clean it – You will lay the Breakfast things, & answer the Drawing Room Bell before 12 o'clock.'[90] The master here was unusually involved in the detail of administering the cellar, for he wrote somewhat peremptorily: 'I keep the key of my own Cellar, & give you out Wine as it is wanted, of w[hi]ch. you keep an account. I order everything, and pay for everything – you order nothing except by my direction. Can you brew? You give out the Ale yourself in a fixed allowance. Can you read and write? Are you married? A Protestant – Healthy – no Apothecaries' Bills [for bought medicines] no perquisites – how old are you? You will valet me.'[91]

Many valets had genuinely interesting experiences as valets and travelling companions. William Henry Clifton, who joined the 13th Duke of Norfolk's service at the age of sixteen in 1851, had become the porter by 1885, and by 1890 was the personal valet to the 15th Duke, whom he accompanied to the Holy Land. His wage, at £80 per annum, was second only to that of the butler. He kept a diary account of his travels in the Middle East with his employer sharing an experience that would have been very unusual for a working-class man in the nineteenth century.

'We saw the house of Nicodemus it is part now of the monastery. A building was pointed out to us as the house of Tabitha . . . April 20 . . . We stopped at Sarris where we found some tents and lunch all ready laid out on the ground. Some chicken, some mutton and two hard boiled eggs on each plate and some bread and an orange. The place was pointed out where the Ark remained for some 20 years'.[92] He also left a memoir of a visit to Spa in eastern Belgium, which includes a reference to his purchase of a French grammar so that he could learn French.[93]

Great households required careful management, for the very practical reason that security was paramount where expensive commodities and valuable objects were concerned. In a community dedicated to the comfort of the landowning family, it was not unreasonable to regulate the noise generated by comings and goings. Myriad examples can be found in country houses of household regulations, often printed, which read like school or college rules. Perhaps the rule existed because the system was regularly abused, illustrating normal rather than proscribed behaviour.

One example of a typically structured set of household regulations in the nineteenth century can be found at Holkham Hall in Norfolk, giving duties, times of meals, rules about access and entertaining in the servants' hall:

> The porter is always to be in livery, and never to be called away to discharge other duties than those which strictly belong to his office. Outer doors are to be kept constantly fastened, and their bells to be answered by the Porter only, except when he is otherwise indispensably engaged, when the Assistant by his authority shall take his place.
>
> Every servant is expected to be punctually in his/her place at the time of meals. Breakfast: 8 a.m. Dinner 12.45. Tea 5 p.m. Supper 9 p.m. No Servant is to take any knives or forks or other article, nor on any account to remove any provisions, nor ale or beer out of the Hall. No Gambling of any description, nor Oaths, nor abusive language are on any account to be allowed.
>
> No Servant is to receive any Visitor, Friend or Relative into the house except by written order from the Housekeeper, which must be dated, and will be preserved by the Porter and shown with his monthly accounts; nor to introduce any person into the Servants' Hall, without the consent of the Porter. No Tradesmen, nor any other persons having business in the house, are to be admitted except between the hours of 9 am and 3 pm, and in all cases the Porter must be satisfied that the person he admits has business there. The Hall door is to be finally closed at Half past Ten o'clock every night, after which time no person will be admitted into the house except those on special leave . . .[94]

This focus on regulation of servants' lives was also expressed in architecture, with some landowners continually updating their service quaters. The servants' hall was central to the working areas and staff accommodation at the back of the house, all of which continued throughout the century to be subject to adjustments of architectural thinking. One typical example of early-nineteenth-century planning is Dalmeny in Scotland, designed in 1819 by William Wilkins in a neo-Tudor style, and resembling the famous Norfolk manor house at East Barsham. According to J.P. Neale in *Views of Seats of Noblemen and Gentlemen* (1825), this comfortable, picturesque house was 'calculated more for comfort and convenience than show'.

Dalmeny is divided into essentially three ranges, with the private family apartments at one end; the main reception rooms, library, drawing room and dining room in the main portion; and the service rooms and double-height kitchen in the corresponding wing. The pivot of the service wing is the butler's pantry and plate store with the butler's bedroom beside it, a common security measure. After that came the steward's office, a small sitting room for female servants and the housekeeper's room, leading to the still room and kitchen, with sleeping accommodation, possibly in dormitories, above. Beyond that were further household offices and the laundry with its own walled drying yard.[95]

For ease of access, the countess's lady's maid had sleeping quarters in the family wing – so she could be on call – while the nursery wing was always above the butler's pantry. In one large bedroom in the tower, which is thought to have been used for visiting ladies' maids because it gave easy access to the bedrooms just below it on the first floor, there is evidence that it was once separated into private areas by hanging curtains, as in a modern hospital.[96]

Even in country houses on a grander scale, it was common in the nineteenth century to add or remodel sizeable areas of service accommodation. When the 6th Duke of Devonshire (1790–1858), the only son of the famous Georgiana, inherited Chatsworth in 1811, he employed Sir Jeffry Wyatville to extend the house to the north with an extensive new wing, incorporating a grand dining room. At the same time Wyatville substantially remodelled the servants' accommodation.

Unusually, the duke himself wrote what was effectively a guidebook, *Handbook of Chatsworth and Hardwick*, privately printed in 1845, telling the story of the house in his own words. Under 'The Offices', he remarked that the East Lobby 'used to be the servants' hall, and a very bad one: it is now used chiefly as a passage in which you must be skilful to avoid falling over all those trunks'.[97]

On the left hand were

the Housekeepers' private apartments, consisting of three rooms that were the tea-room and the footmen's rooms. The sitting-room is very good, though not quite so much so as a friend thought, when he said to me, 'You know your mother had not such a room as this.' It is, however, convenient and light, and overlooks all arrivals; . . . Next to these, towards the North, comes the servants' hall, a beautiful example of Sir Jeffry's stone-work, arched, as the Offices chiefly are, with great solidity and strength.'[98]

He was also clearly proud of the new kitchen although he had reservations about some of the other service areas:

The kitchen itself is handsome and spacious, and contains steam-cupboards, and a hot steam-table; and wood is the sole fuel employed in the high grate as well as coke for the steam contrivances, which, diminishing the quantity of blacks [smuts], must add greatly to the cleanliness of the place . . . The pastry [cook's preparation room] convenient, the scullery awful, and the larder atrocious; for, although it may be airy, and highly convenient for salting, it looks into the abysses of a dusty coal-yard. . . . I spare you bakehouse, washhouse, and laundry: neither will we boast of the poultry-yard; but the dairy, of good architecture, is not bad. You pass under a building that contains the Clerk of works' office and lodging-rooms, and by a gun-room [count] to the Porter's lodge.[99]

Given the ever more complex arrangement of rooms, it is not surprising that the technology of bells continued to develop throughout the nineteenth century, during which period many late-eighteenth-century wire-systems were updated wires. Many early-nineteenth century systems are still visible, if now unused, in the staff corridors of country houses. But the constant ringing of bells could be the source of some contention with staff, some servants walking great distances to find out what was required, before covering the same distance twice to return with the required object. Such strains, indeed, lay at the core of one of the most famous murder trials, when in 1840, a Swiss valet, François Courvoisier, murdered Lord William Russell, uncle of the Duke of Bedford. He was said to have been discovered as a thief and murdered his elderly master, and hanged. But in his defence, he said his master was always finding fault with him.[100] At midnight on the dreadful day, his master rang the bell for attention and Courvoisier went up holding a warming pan to be at the ready. Lord William was furious that his servant should had seen fit to prejudge his request and sent him down. He rang the bell a little later and when the valet arrived asked him to fetch a warming pan. Later he came down, found his valet in the dining room and sacked him; shortly after this, the valet claimed he snapped and killed his master in a fury.[101]

No doubt to avoid such possible irritations some houses installed speaking tubes from the 1840s, although they were also thought to be a risk to privacy (by both parties) and, at the end of the century, internal telephone systems, sometimes routed through the butler's pantry. Better systems were continually being explored, including pneumatic systems and eventually electrical systems, with the little flags in the windows of a glass box that moved to show which room had called.[102]

One of the great bones of contention about servants' accommodation was the potential dampness of subterranean bedrooms, an issue highlighted by a comparison of two great Irish country houses: Lissadell, where Thomas Kilgallon worked, which was constructed in the 1830s and little changed thereafter; and Humewood, built some three decades later.

Lissadell, with its neoclassical style and characterful, late-Georgian design, enjoys a dramatic position near the coast in County Sligo. The English architect, Francis Goodwin, published his designs for the house in *Rural Architecture* (1835), explaining in detail why the service quarters had to be placed below ground: 'The offices, together with the sleeping rooms for the servants, are in the basement, yet, as may be seen by the view of the house, partly above ground. One advantage, if no other, gained by this system is that it raises the floor above them, and therefore contributes to the cheerfulness of the principal rooms, which thus being a little elevated, enjoy a better prospect.'[103]

Goodwin acknowledged that 'many, we are aware, object to offices being at all sunk below the house in a country residence where there is generally ample space for building them above ground, either as wings to the house itself or otherwise.' This was a customary solution in Palladian country houses, including the rebuilt Carton in County Kildare, but Goodwin listed the pitfalls of siting servants' wings above ground: 'If erected as wings, unless consistent with the architecture of the rest of the design, they will rather impair than improve the general effect.' Moreover, it was undoubtedly more expensive, because the architectural quality of the exterior appearance of the servants' wing would have to match that of the central range. Goodwin was adamant, in what was probably a topic of hot debate among architects and landlords at the time, that if 'thus situated, the offices in one wing are at an inconvenient distance from those in the other. Besides which they must more or less interrupt the view from the apartments of the main building.'[104]

His solution was that 'the offices [service rooms] be all placed together; attached to the house, yet still so situated as to be easily screened from sight, and consequently to be erected without any pretension to architecture'. If the establishment is large, he argued, 'this mode is therefore too much like building two separate houses to have the accommodation of one.'[105] Above all, if servants' quarters were placed in the basement, direct access could be arranged upwards to the main rooms of the house. An added advantage was that the principal rooms would thereby have an unimpeded view from any aspect and the pleasure gardens allowed to encircle the whole building.

Nearly thirty years later, exactly the same issues arose at Humewood, designed by William White. White began work in all optimism, presenting a paper on it to the Royal Institute of British Architects that was published in their 1868/9 proceedings.[106] Humewood was commissioned for the gloriously named Mr Wentworth Hume Dick who, like Sir Robert Gore-Booth, was an MP. His house was to be in the High Victorian castellar style, of which Mr White wrote:

'I have endeavoured to incorporate the idea of a Scotch baronial hall with certain Irish peculiarities in the battlemented details – exhibiting the fusion of the good old Scotch and Irish families.' It was, he noted, designed more for the summer recess and the shooting season than as a permanent residence. White repeated the same arguments put forward by Goodwin, in one part using language so close that he was possibly quoting from the text quoted above. He, too, was adamant that siting the servants' quarters underground was the best solution for the servicing of the principal apartments. They must, he said, be vaulted in brick or stone in order to prevent the communication of noise and smells from the basement to the main rooms (an obsession of Victorian architects).

White also argued that the subterranean route was better for the overall design, although this was possibly a method of expressing status by siting the service quarters in relation to the main house in such a way as to raise the floors of the principal rooms used by the family. As White put it: 'In the present instance however, it was of the greatest consequence to elevate the "living" part of the house above the cold and damps of the country, as well as to give a greater command of the magnificent prospects of the neighbourhood, and also to give greater importance to the exterior effect in a wild and mountainous district.'[107]

In the public debate after the paper was read, another architect, Professor Robert Kerr, was recorded as taking issue about the placing of the service quarters, because it was obvious 'at a glance that the lawn must be overlooked from the servants hall and other such offices . . . Mr White's clients we presume do not object to this, but many would object to it very much.' He also noted the absence of a dinner lift: '[Mr White] prefers the use of a dinner stair, to which I make no objection, except that the servants might possibly think otherwise.'[108]

White replied, rather coldly to modern ears, that as it was necessary to have a large basement to protect the principal living rooms from damp, you might as well use the space to accommodate the servants. He conceded that he had to use rough plate glass at some points, carried up to above eye level in the servants' windows.[109]

The plan for Humewood shows the footman's room convenient to the hall, the butler's pantry and the plate room near there too, and the servants' hall close to the kitchen. The laundry is at one extremity, and the stables stand separately. The servants' bedrooms were principally above the kitchen, thus effectively on the first floor and therefore not too damp, with the nurse and nurserymaid sleeping in the nursery wing. Further accommodation was provided in the stable block.[110] However ingenious White's architecture, his defence of the basement solution seems very backward-looking.

There was clearly an obsessive interest on the part of both architects and patrons in the accommodation of servants and the supporting kitchen offices, stables and yards. Careful design and layout were essential to facilitate the multiplicity of duties expected of domestic servants in a nineteenth-century house.

In his *Encyclopedia of Cottage, Farm and Villa Architecture* (1833), J.C. Loudon described the ordered arrangements of rationally planned domestic services, even for a modest country villa: 'The [butler's] pantry is near the dining-room and commands the porch. The servants' hall is beyond the door leading to the yard, and has the effect of being detached from the house, though really within it.'[111] This separation was necessary for both efficiency and cleanliness:

The kitchen is arranged with the same advantages; the door opposite the pantry is only in use for the service of dinner. The scullery is wholly removed from the house. The laundry and wash-house are yet more retired, and immediately under the inspection of the housekeeper . . . The knife and shoe room adjoins the servants' hall.[112]

The Gentleman's House, or How to Plan English Residences from the Parsonage to the Palace (1864) by Professor Robert Kerr offers a good understanding of the evolving approaches to the design of servants' halls and sleeping quarters in the mid to late Victorian period. Kerr outlined the history of the English country house and advised on designing the ideal dwelling, dividing it into 'the first division: the family apartments', the second division or state rooms, and the third division: the domestic offices.[113]

He considered privacy to be of prime importance in the country house:

> whether in a small house or a large one, let the family have free passage-way without encountering the servants unexpectedly; and let the servants have access to all their duties without coming unexpectedly upon the family or visitors. On both sides this privacy is highly valued. It is a matter also for the architect's care that the outdoor work of the domestics shall not be visible from the house or grounds, or the windows of their Offices overlooked.
>
> At the same time it is equally important that the walks of the family shall not be open to view from the Servants' Department. The Sleeping-rooms of the domestics, also, have to be separated both internally and externally from those of the family, and indeed separately approached.[114]

This separation is in contrast to earlier notions of the household as a family or community in itself, however alien that might seem today. 'The idea which underlies all is simply this. The family constitute one community: the servants another. Whatever may be their mutual regard and confidence as dwellers under the same roof, each class is entitled to shut its doors upon the other and be alone.' He observed of the eighteenth-century model, considered in the last chapter: 'In the Classic model privacy is certainly less,' whereas, perhaps oddly, he took the view that 'in the Medieval model, privacy is never difficult of accomplishment.'[115] Kerr clearly regarded the planning of the service quarters as a matter of the utmost importance, with efficiency the primary issue: 'the Family Apartments have to be contrived for occupation; but the Offices for work. Agreeable residence on the one hand and efficient service on other, are different questions.'[116]

The moral standards of the Victorian age were reflected in his attitude to planning: 'the working rooms of the men ought to form one division, and those of the women another. In all good plans this distinction is very clearly to be seen; the Servants'-Hall being properly the point of meeting, with the domain of the butler on one side and that of the housekeeper on the other, and as little necessity as possible on either side to pass the boundary. Separate Passages and Stairs also lead to the private rooms of each Sex.'[117] This division of the sexes is met in many houses at this date.

Addressing the decoration of servants' sitting rooms and bedrooms, Kerr believed that 'all private rooms to be equal to those of a similar class of persons in their own homes – perhaps a little better, but not too much so'.[118] He added a remark that suggested that in the minds of some architects or patrons, servants could be considered as inseparable from the technology of the house: 'every servant, every operation, every utensil, every fixture, should have a right place and no right place but one.'[119] Nevertheless, servants' quarters should be well designed and decorated: 'Cheerfulness . . . will still be desirable; and in the private apartments of the servants, there is no reason why so cheap a luxury should be forgotten. Elegance, Importance, and Ornament would be quite out of place.'[120]

Memorably, Kerr wrote that the kitchen, that most important of country-house offices, had attained 'at last in our own day the character of a complicated laboratory, surrounded by numerous accessories specially contrived, in respect of disposition, arrangement, and fittings, for the administration of the culinary art in all its professional details'.[121] Ranges in country houses were generally coal-fired until the early twentieth century; gas was introduced originally as a supplementary and was available as early as the 1830s.[122]

Although the surprising aspect of Victorian kitchens is their distance from the dining room, this was because Victorians had a horror of cooking smells. Kerr was emphatic: 'It must also be remembered that various household incidents, such as cooking, cleaning, washing, storage of provisions and other goods, and so on, positively engender offensive vapours.'[123] It may seem today that the Victorians were being absurdly sensitive about smells, but a country-house kitchen was coping with conditions more like those of a top modern hotel than a private house, and without the benefit of modern extractors.[124]

Yet, paradoxically, the distance between the kitchen and the dining room was a constant source of concern, for obvious reasons of the logistics of service and hotness of food. Whilst this distance shrank over the century, some was always expected. One change was that the aristocratic family became less tolerant of the sight of liveried servants actually carrying trays of food through the main part of the house. In the 1840s, the Marquess of Westminster at Eaton Hall in Cheshire did not care to see his dinner being borne across the main hall and had the architect, William Burn, insert a new serving stair, directly linking the serving room and the dining room.[125]

Echoing a debate that can be traced from the seventeenth century, Kerr had strictures on the upper servants' offices: 'A position ought to be chosen for the Butler's-Pantry which shall answer for several relations. It must be as near as possible, indeed close, to the Dining-room, for convenience of service. It ought to be removed from general traffic, and especially from the Back-door, for the safety of the plate. The communication with the Wine and Beer Cellars must be ready, and in a manner private.'[126]

Because the butler's pantry was, as we have seen, a practical room where silver and glasses were carefully washed up, it needed to be well lit with a really good sink, often underneath the window, so that items could be minutely inspected. The plate store and the butler's bedroom often formed a part of this suite, and certainly it was commonplace for a butler or footman to sleep across the door of the plate safe. The butler's pantry was often, but not always, one of the nearest service areas to the principal rooms of the house, primarily because the butler and footmen were expected to be on call, whether for serving meals, responding to bells or, indeed, answering the front door.[127]

The housekeeper's room was also key, as we have seen, for the administration of the house, as well as the upper servants' sitting and dining room (where there was not a steward's room). J.C. Loudon decreed in 1833 that it should be 'a spacious comfortable apartment, furnished as a respectable parlour, and situated so that the other offices are easily overlooked [with] all that is necessary for use and comfort in a rather plain way'. Some, such as that recorded in a watercolour at Aynhoe in Oxfordshire, seem very comfortable.[128]

Kerr was specific about minute aspects: 'The Fittings, besides the ordinary furniture of a plain Sitting-room, will consist of spacious cupboards or presses, from 18 to 24 inches, filled with drawers and shelving, for the accommodation of preserves, pickles, fancy groceries of all kinds, cakes, china, glass, linen, and so forth.'[129]

Related to the housekeeper's room was the still room, where tea and coffee were prepared, and preserves, cakes and biscuits made. J.C. Loudon described his ideal still room in some detail, suggesting its importance:

> It should be furnished as a better kind of kitchen, containing a fireplace, with a boiler, a small oven, a range of charcoal-stoves, with a cover; a small shut-up sink, with a water-pipe for a supply of water . . . [There should also be] A range of small closets for the maids, to keep their tea things, tea and sugar, and things used at the housekeeper's table . . . a small looking glass might promote tidiness of person and a piece of common carpet would add to the comfort of the room. The chairs and stools should be neat and substantial, and a small case of well-chosen books should hang against the wall.[130]

In the very grandest houses, Kerr wrote: 'a house-steward is employed as the chief officer of all, assisted perhaps by a kitchen-clerk.' This individual would have an office and a steward's room, which was usually 'a Dining-room for the upper servants, and incidentally a common room for them during the day, and a sitting-room for them in the evening' – effectively an upper servants' hall. He added, 'an incidental purpose of the Steward's-room is to receive visitors of the rank of the upper servants, and superior tradesman-people and others coming on business.'[131] Furthermore, 'there ought to be a comfortable fireside, and a prospect which shall be at least not disagreeable; the outlook however ought not to be towards the walks of the family.'[132]

Often overlooked today, the housemaid's closet was the principal store for the brooms, dusters, pails and brushes used to clean the house. J.C. Loudon wrote in 1846 that it should be

> light and roomy with a plaster floor, with an inner closet for the bed-room night lights, or rush light cases etc, with drawers underneath for

cloths and dusters. There should be pegs and shelves, on which to put anything out of the way . . .

As warm water is very much used by the housemaid, their closet, in a large house, should contain a small copper, for heating water, and, if possible, it should be supplied with water by a leaden pipe, [which] . . . would also be great convenience. In large establishments, the labour of carrying up and down the stairs clean and dirty water is very great, so that a pipe supplying soft water and a sink for [emptying] the slops is necessary in a place of this kind, which should also contain a large box in one corner, for a supply of coals to be used in the upper part of the house.'[133]

A brushing room, for the wet- and dry-brushing of hunting clothes, was frequently encountered in Victorian country-house plans. In the eighteenth century, brushing was often done in the servants' hall. Early brushing rooms seem to have opened off the hall, but later were usually separate. Westonbirt House in Gloucestershire had two brushing rooms, one for the household and the other to be used by visiting valets.[134]

In the early nineteenth century, lamp rooms were common, as the cleaning and refuelling of lamps required considerably more space than replacing candles in candlesticks. However, after the 1890s, the lamp room was gradually superseded by a switch room or generating room providing electricity, with Cragside in Northumberland being one of the first to have electric light throughout. Before the 1870s, new houses always had their own brewhouse, although after this point they were rarer.[135]

Servants' sleeping quarters naturally varied depending on the age and scale of the house. During the nineteenth century, there was an increasing emphasis on separating them from those of the family, whereas up until the eighteenth century close personal servants often slept close to their employers, to be on call. From the mid nineteenth century, the pattern was to remove servants as far as possible from the principal bedroom floor.

For largely moral reasons, as well as practical – in order to avoid unwanted pregnancies – the separation of menservants and female servants was taken increasingly seriously. In the nineteenth century the maids often lived in attics, often accessed only by walking past the housekeeper's bedroom, while the men occupied basement rooms or rooms over the other offices.[136]

Up until the 1840s, menservants often slept in dormitory accommodation, sometimes called the 'barracks'. Later on, senior menservants usually had a single room each, whilst their juniors shared. Housemaids and kitchenmaids would also be expected to share, in twos or fours, while the housekeeper, cook and lady's maid would expect a room of their own, as would the head housemaid and head kitchenmaid.[137]

Some of the best-preserved service quarters laid out in the last half of the century can be found at Lanhydrock in Cornwall. After a fire, it was rebuilt for Lord Robartes by Richard Coad, who had worked on an earlier remodelling of the house. The attention given to the service areas and accommodation reflects the preoccupations dis-cussed in Kerr's book, adapted to the needs of an older house.

The plans illustrate perfectly the multiplicity of service rooms that exemplified the High Victorian country house. In the centre of the south range on the ground floor were the butler's sitting room, bed-room and pantry with a strong room, which had a safe for the plate (silver) and the pantry boy by the door for security. The housekeep-er's quarters were near by, on the other side of the pantry court, with the maids' sitting room adjoining. As usual, the still room was beside the housekeeper's room and the substantial servants' hall completed the courtyard.[138]

Beyond the servants' hall, to the west, were the lamp room and gun room, wine and beer cellars. The huge kitchen 'was built like a college hall with great wooden roof trusses supporting a high roof over.[139] It lay close, but not adjacent, to the dining room. A series of associated rooms were close at hand, with a large scullery to one side, plus a bakehouse, dry larder, fish larder, meat larder, dairy scullery and dairy, which had its own external access. Between the kitchen and the dining hall were a servery and a china closet. The male and female servants' bedrooms were approached via different staircases. The nursery accommodation for the Robarteses' large family was arranged above the servants' hall, still room and housekeeper's rooms.[140]

These areas survived remarkably unaltered and are much cherished. Today they are presented convincingly by the National Trust, which was given the house by the 7th Lord Clifden, who continued to live there until 1966. He would little have imagined the interest that the service quarters would ignite in modern visitors.

Not all nineteenth-century architects revelled in the excessive elaboration of service quarters. In 1880, the architect J.J. Stevenson wrote in *House Architecture* of the need to simplify the intricacies that had become the norm: 'Keeping pace with our more complicated ways of living, we have not only increased the number of rooms, in ordinary houses, but have assigned to each a special use. Instead of the hall and single chamber of the middle ages, with which even kings were content, every ordinary house must have a number of separate bedrooms, at least three public rooms, and a complicated arrangement of servants' offices.' Stevenson sensibly went on to point out how this complexity itself demanded extra labour: 'All these places, with the interminable passages connecting them, have to be kept in order; and, if they increase the facility of doing the work, they increase the labour of the house, and necessitate a greater number of servants.'[141]

As the century drew to a close, there was a growing awareness of the social disparities between master and servant as a matter of political principle. In some households, more thought was given to the continuing welfare and education of servants, although, bizarre as it may seem, a serious concern of this kind could rebound on the reputation of the employer, and not always in a positive way.

But you cannot always please everyone and giving servants too comfortable quarters alarmed some social observers. The diarist Augustus Hare famously always used the word 'luxurious' to describe the houses of the newly rich in a tone of disapproval, and could hardly credit the comfort of the servants at Worth Park, in Sussex, the home of the Montefiore family: 'I went to Worth, the ultra-luxurious house of the Montefiores, where the servants have their own billiard tables, ballroom, theatre and pianofortes, and are arrogant and presumptious in proportion.'[142]

And not only comfortable rooms were criticised, general benevolence could be a problem, too. In the last years of the century, the

Countess of Aberdeen was somewhat taken aback to find herself notorious for her supposedly radical views; indeed, such was the credibility given to the idea that she used to dine once a week with her servants, while Lord Aberdeen was serving as Governor, that Queen Victoria asked Lord Rosebery to look into it: 'we gave our good friend Lord Rosebery the necessary information as to the strictly orthodox character of our household arrangements.'[143] The same rumour reached Edward VII shortly after he ascended to the throne: '[it was] only very recently that an intimate friend of ours, who was staying at an Alpine resort, was solemnly told by another guest at the hotel when visitors came to Viceregal lodge [that] they were liable to be taken to dinner [i.e. on the arm of] by the butler or the housekeeper.'[144]

In their affectionate, co-written memoir, 'We Twa': Reminiscences of Lord and Lady Aberdeen (Vol. II, 1925), Lady Aberdeen mentioned a newspaper article, warning the people of Canada that

> they would have to put up with a lady with a bee in her bonnet with regard to the servant question, one who would never allow her servants to wear caps, and who was in the habit of playing hide-and-seek and other such games with the housemaids and footmen, at all sorts of odd hours of the day. Moreover, it was stated as a fact that Lord Aberdeen and I dined habitually in the servants' hall on certain days of the week.[145]

The real origin of these stories was that Lady Aberdeen had founded 'The Onward and Upward Association' for the benefit of farm servant girls working on Lord Aberdeen's estates, as well as a Household Club for their immediate staff. The first association was intended to give the girls 'an occupation and recreation outside their daily work, and assistance with keeping up their education'. There were also social occasions intended to encourage a common purpose between girls and their mistresses.

The Household Club was 'really the outcome of an uneasy feeling on our part that whilst sharing in various philanthropic movements . . . we were doing nothing in the same direction for the members of our own household . . . nothing to bring all into human relations with each other and ourselves, beyond our daily gathering in the Haddo House Chapel for family worship day by day, and on Sunday evenings' – daily prayers were commonplace in country houses throughout the nine-teenth century.[146] The committee, formed in 1889, was elected annu-ally from the heads of department, both indoor and outdoor. 'Before a fortnight had passed we had a singing class of twenty members . . . and a carving class of twelve members, led by our governess; a drawing class of thirteen members, led by our butler, who attained no mean proficiency as an artist; a sewing class, led by our nurse' and so on. There were social evenings with entertainment provided 'by home talent'.[147]

Lady Aberdeen wrote: 'there is no doubt but that the classes and social gatherings drew all the household very closely together', noting with pleasure that a 'branch of our club was formed, with our butler as secretary', when Lord and Lady Aberdeen were in Government House in Ottawa. She felt that she depended on her servants for everything they did in terms of hospitality and entertain-ment and that the Household Club introduced 'the element of deep, mutual regard and understanding and sympathy for one another's lives, and a basis on which to build a common fellowship for all true and noble purposes, which should surely be the aim and desire of every thoughtful householder'.[148]

Lord Aberdeen even included a letter from J.M. Barrie, refuting the widely circulated rumour that the Aberdeens' relationship with their servants had inspired his 1902 play, *The Admirable Crichton*, about an aristocratic family who are shipwrecked with their butler. It is Crichton's physical dexterity, intelligence and ingenuity that save them and which lead to his becoming effectively their chief. When they are all eventually rescued, he returns without batting an eye to his former subservient role.

It was rather the servants' skills and intelligence, observed by Barrie in the great houses of the aristocracy, that had prompted his teasing allegory, rather than the socially minded projects of a well-meaning countess. Even then, however, the world was already shift-ing. The glory days of the Edwardian country house, the subject of the next chapter, marked a definitive turning point. The structured world of the country-house servant that had seemed, as H.G. Wells suggested in his autobiography, such an assured and confident feature of British achievement and of British life would change out of all recognition in the twentieth century, even if it did not quite disappear altogether.[149]

7

In Retreat from a Golden Age
The first half of the Twentieth Century

W E HAVE NOW traced the story of the country-house servant from the 1300s to the beginning of the twentieth century, a time that is only just out of reach of living memory and is often looked on as the Indian summer of the country-house world. While the great rural households of the time might have seemed foreign to the sixteenth-century servant, used to a more public form of service, they would have been recognisable in daily routine to an eighteenth-century time traveller. In 1900, most major landed estates continued to support large regiments of staff but their days were numbered.

As so often in history, change came in waves. After the great earthquake of the First World War, nothing was ever quite the same. Although many houses continued to employ staff in the same numbers as before (nationally more than 1.4 million people were still employed in domestic service[1]), gradually these numbers were eroded, with new shocks following taxation, inflation and the effects of the Great Depression of the 1920s. After the massive upheaval of the Second World War, the landscape was unimaginably different, as will be shown in the final chapter.

To remain for the moment in the early twentieth century, among these shocks were changing social attitudes and expectations. After the 1870s there was more widespread state education and more widespread literacy. People had access to the popular press, and then to radio and cinema. Those who had had little choice in their professions were presented with immeasurably wider horizons than the previous generation, and young girls became more reluctant to go into service, when they could work in shops, factories and offices.[2]

The deference of traditional service was possibly becoming more difficult to bear in an era of febrile political activity, as the country moved slowly towards universal suffrage. The two significant dates are 1918 and 1928; before the first, no male or female domestic servant, however responsible, had the vote; after 1918, the only women who could vote had to be over thirty; it was not until 1928 that all female servants were enfranchised. Various attempts to set up a trades union for domestic service were unsuccessful, compared to those of industrial labour movements. Until the passage of the National Insurance Act in 1911, there was actually no legislation that legally protected the servant in sickness or old age.[3]

The constant refinement of technology during the nineteenth century meant that light and heat no longer needed so much manual labour. Even the carrying of messages by trusted hands was made obsolete by the successive invention of the telegraph in the 1830s and the telephone in the 1870s. Most significantly perhaps, increased taxation had an immense impact on the economy of the country house. Large staffs began to shrink in the 1930s – some houses dispensing entirely with senior menservants and opting instead for parlourmaids who were paid less. After the seismic shifts of the Second World War, few establishments could return to the complex and stratified staff hierarchies that until then had been so much a part of the cultural prestige and demography of the British country house.

But up until that point, and especially between 1900 and 1914, most of the great country houses of the early twentieth century remained lavishly staffed and complex organisations. The principal jobs were much the same as in the previous century, although with subtle variations reflecting new technologies, such as technicians for private electricity generators, and chauffeurs for cars. (Some services such as laundry were also beginning to be put out to private companies.) However, in the early 1900s the demarcations, refined over a century or more, were drawn more carefully yet than in the preceding hundred years.

This peak of specialisation was underlined by the slow process of training country-house domestic servants from their youth, with upper servants coaching the younger ones in the strict disciplines of their duties, giving them the necessary experience to move on eventually to the more responsible roles of steward, butler, valet, housekeeper, lady's maid and so on. As Ernest King recalled when he started as a hall boy early in the century: 'I suppose I first learnt to be a servant by being a servant to the servants: the table in the servants' hall to lay, the staff cutlery to clean and staff meals to put on the table.'[4]

That these complete and seemingly self-contained communities still existed is clear from so many personal histories, one of the most vivid of the Edwardian period being Frederick Gorst's memoir of life as a footman to the Duke of Portland. The duke's large estate in Nottinghamshire, as well as his other coal mining interests, brought him in 'many millions a year'. He also had a court appointment, as he was Master of the Horse to King Edward VII. At that time, 'the estate of Welbeck Abbey was more like a principality than anything else . . . It was, in a sense, like working for the reigning prince of a small state within a kingdom.'[5]

He was one of the four 'Royal footmen' who worked at Welbeck Abbey, unless they were required for ceremonial duties in the Royal Household in London. Mr Gorst recalled arriving at the former along a private tunnel, 'electrically lighted and wide enough to accommodate a horse and carriage or one motor car'. He was shown to the steward's office by a pageboy who also carried his luggage to his room on the top floor of the abbey, which he would share with another footman.

Although they sound like some of the most comfortable servants' rooms of the day, they were nevertheless shared, a custom that continued until the interwar period: 'I was delighted to see we had an open fireplace, which would be cosy in the winter. The rooms were kept spotlessly clean by a housemaid assigned to the footman's quarters,' a comment that reminds us that in a great household a number of servants were still employed essentially to look after other servants. 'There was a large bathroom which we all shared. Because we powdered our hair before the wide mirror and shelves, it was called the Powder Room.' That evening he explored the house and played in the menservants' billiards hall, in one of the many underground rooms below the lawn.[6]

As well as serving at meals (breakfast, lunch, tea and dinner, in rotation, with every fourth day off duty), Mr Gorst had to 'attend' the duke: 'I sat in a comfortable leather chair behind a twelve foot screen which blocked off a corner of the room. I could not see the Duke nor could he see me.' Despite bells being a part of domestic technology at least since the eighteenth century, 'his Grace disliked ringing a bell for a footman when he wanted something, so the man on duty always sat ready within earshot to answer his "hello," which was his way of summoning us.'[7]

Poor Mr Gorst found this pretty dull, but a touch of humanity enters the story at this point: 'I must say I thought this was a boring assignment, but suddenly the Duchess appeared from behind the screen and handed me several newspapers and magazines. "Gorst," she said, "move a lamp over to the chair and read if you like. There is no reason not be at ease. However, be sure not to fall asleep in case his Grace needs you."' The duchess was clearly considerate to her footmen, not least because at Welbeck they were rather well fed and she wanted them to keep in trim. To this end, as well as giving them each a bicycle and a bag of golf clubs, she decided that all four had to be instructed in 'callisthenetics in the gymnasium at the specified hours and she engaged a Japanese ju-jitsu expert to train us.'[8]

Mr Gorst wore the royal livery, rather than the Portland livery of the footmen who served only at the house and not at royal functions. Breakfast and luncheon were served in an ordinary or off-duty livery: black trousers, a waistcoat of livery cut, knee-length boots, a white shirt and a white bow tie. For tea and dinner, they wore the small scarlet livery and powdered hair; 'This consisted of a short scarlet coat, a scarlet waistcoat, purple knee breeches, white stockings, black pumps with bows, and a square, white bow tie.'[9]

Typically, liveries were matched to specific grades of occasion: 'We wore formal luncheon and dinner liveries only when there were guests, and the full-state uniform was used only for state occasions.' Unsurprisingly, 'I soon found that I spent a good part of my time dressing, and undressing, and changing my uniforms,' as many footmen serving in great aristocratic houses must have found.[10]

During a shooting-party, lunch was taken in the dining room: 'We footmen served them from our stations at the sideboard which held roast game in season, leg of lamb, game pie, roast chicken, and roast ham. There were always platters of eggs Rochambeau, fish, a garnished entrée of chicken en gelee, and salad. The sweet was often rice pudding.' In the evening, at seven-thirty the dressing gong sounded, and at eight-fifteen the guests assembled for dinner. No cocktails or sherry were offered because the duke thought they dulled the palate.[11]

For Mr Gorst, the perfection and attention to detail that characterised the great Edwardian country house were summed up in the menu card: 'on the table before each place was a silver holder with a menu card of the dinner bearing the crest of the Duke of Portland. When the chef, Monsieur David, had made up the menus, Mr Spedding had them written out in old fashioned script. Then they were placed on the table by the groom of the chambers.' Mr Gorst remembered these holders and menu cards with nostalgia, 'because they, more than any other . . . represented the perfect detail dispensed at Welbeck. I am sure there are few houses today which are still run as Welbeck was then. Time has altered many things: most of the great homes have changed hands, and in this restless world of ours there is neither the wealth nor the patience for such exquisite details.'[12]

He vividly evokes the strict social division below stairs, which had increased in intensity in the nineteenth century:

> Position and rank also took precedence in the hierarchy of the servants. They were divided into the 'upper servants' – also called the 'Upper Ten', and the 'lower servants – referred to as the 'Lower Five'. [The royal footmen] belonged to the Lower Five. The two groups did not mix socially, the lines were drawn more strictly perhaps than those whom we served. Moreover, we ate separately. The Upper Ten took their meals in the steward's dining room and they were waited upon by two steward's room footmen.[13]

The Upper Ten had white wine, claret, and beer for lunch and dinner. He added proudly: 'The china, silver, and glass which was used to serve them, and which was taken care of exclusively by the steward's room footmen, was much finer than the gentry had in some of the smaller houses in England.'[14]

Servant hierarchies had their own dress code:

> Mr Spedding [the steward], the wine butler, the under butler, the groom of the chambers, the Duke's valet, the housekeeper, head housemaid, and ladies' maids – and any visiting ladies' maids and valets – were designated the Upper Ten. At Welbeck, visiting ladies' maids were expected to wear a dress blouse for dinner, and the visiting valets were required to wear smoking jackets for late supper.[15]

For Gorst, looking on the scene from a junior position, the social divide could clearly be quite galling: 'The Upper Ten came to the table similarly dressed and full of their own importance. Their evening meal was in the nature of an intimate dinner party except when there were visiting maids and valets, often as many as forty at one time.' It was a different story for the others:

> We, the Lower Five, ate our meals in the Servants' Hall, the old refectory of the Abbey. We Royal footmen ate at the same time with the housemaids and stillroom maids. The two footmen on duty always carved and the hall porter and the hall boys served the meals. We had two or three fresh vegetables served with the meat and potatoes – all good, solid food which came to the table piping hot and nicely served. We had delicious bread that came directly from the bakery and freshly churned, country butter.[16]

The ritual echoes of the table, observed in Welbeck's servants' hall, still had echoes of the medieval and Tudor worlds: 'After the main course, the maidservants left the table. The sweet was served to the menservants and maidservants separately. The maids had theirs in their own departments, in the stillroom or the housemaid's sitting room, where they had a table laid in readiness. Traditionally the men and woman servants were always separated before the end of the meal.'[17]

Snobbery was rife: 'At Welbeck the upper servants adopted an arrogant attitude towards the under servants. Mr Clancy, the wine butler, was the haughtiest and most pompous of all.'[18] On the other hand, Mr Gorst recognised the greater responsibilities and the hard work put in by those he served under, the chief steward Mr Spedding and others. He expressed particular admiration for the under butler, Mr Owens, who was in charge of all the silver and gold service. He alone was in control of the plate closet, which contained enough silver to serve hundreds of people. 'There was also a complete gold service to serve fifty people; in which every conceivable utensil was included.'[19]

Work even left time for romance, and Mr Gorst fell in love with one of the still-room maids, walking and cycling with her away from the house. She lived in the maids' corridor, which was referred to by the servants as the 'Virgin's Wing', while the prim head housemaid, who was in charge, was known as the 'Head Virgin'.

Mr Gorst professed genuine interest in the great house he served, still occupied today by descendants of the duke; describing it as 'a castle of unparalleled magnificence and solidity'. Among the extraordinary additions made by the eccentric 5th Duke of Portland in the nineteenth century were many tunnels and underground rooms, including the vast ballroom, 160 feet long and 63 feet wide.

> The principal tunnel, connecting the kitchen wing to the main portion of the house, was laid with trolley lines so that large wagons, all fitted with rubber wheels, could move noiselessly along the tracks and carry the food as quickly as possible to the main dining room. The wagons were fitted with plates heated by hot water on one side to keep the dishes hot, and on the other there were cold steel plates for chilled food.[20]

The pinnacle of staff entertainment at Welbeck was the annual servants' ball, held in the underground ballroom and adjoining reception rooms, which 'were beautifully decorated just as though the Duke and Duchess were giving a ball for themselves'. Staff and estate tenants were invited and no expense was spared: 'An orchestra from London had been engaged and a swarm of fifty waiters.' Mr Gorst attended in livery, feeling free when the duke and duchess left to change into his own dress clothes. Seeing the staff out of uniform had a profound impact on him:

> It was quite a revelation to see all of the members of the staff in ball dress. Even the prim head housemaid looked quite chic in a velvet gown, and the head housekeeper, who wore a low cut blue satin gown, was almost unrecognizable without her stiff, black dress and her belt of jingling keys . . . [it seemed that] we had acquired a new kind of indi viduality and gaiety for the evening, and, stranger still, that we were seeing each other from a new aspect – as people not as servants.[21]

After the sudden death of his sister at a young age, Mr Gorst decided to seek adventure in America, closing his final pages with the Edwardian country house still at its height. The First World War followed hard behind, blowing a chill through every aspect of British life, hard-fought victory though it may have been, and changing the world of the country house for ever. (One side effect was the rapid decline in the use of London town houses, once occupied by many families for only a few months every year and most of which were given up in the 1920s and 1930s.)

The household at Welbeck was so extensive that it is worth describing the servants' roles in some detail, department by department. Over sixty were employed in the house, with two hundred more in the stables, gardens, home and laundry. Welbeck was a 'principality' indeed, with a large estate beyond the house and its immediate dependencies. The indoor staff mostly lived in the house, while top servants such as the duke's secretary were accommodated in separate houses; farmers, gardeners, stablemen and garage men mostly had their own cottages.[22]

The kitchen and the service of meals were the domain of the steward, the wine butler, the under butler, the groom of the chamber, the four royal footmen, two steward's room footmen, two pageboys, the head chef, the second chef, the head baker and the second baker. There was also a head kitchenmaid, two under kitchenmaids, a vegetable maid, three scullery-maids, a head still-room maid with three still-room maids under her, a hall porter, two helpers (both boys), a kitchen porter and six 'odd men'. (These were literally odd-job men, whose wide variety of duties included attending to drains and roofs; they tended not to graduate into footman-butler roles.)

For the household and personal 'body' service, there was the head housekeeper, the duke's valet, the duchess's personal maid, their daughter Lady Victoria's personal maid, as well as a head nursery governess, a tutor, a French governess, a schoolroom footman and a nursery footman. A phalanx of fourteen housemaids were the cleaners of rooms, the preparers of fires and the makers of beds.

As with many new country houses built in the early twentieth century, as well as those owned by richer or more enthusiastically forward-looking individuals, there was a dedicated electrical plant. This was staffed by six engineers (for the house and the plant itself) and four firemen (who worked on the electrical plant and the steam-heating plant). There was also a telephone clerk and assistant, a telegrapher, and three nightwatchmen. In the early 1900s, the horse and car continued to co-exist uneasily. There was still a head coachman, a second coachman and ten grooms (including an assistant coachman) as well as twenty strappers and helpers. The garage had a head chauffeur, fifteen ordinary chauffeurs, two washers and, remarkably, fifteen footmen (two of whom were to be on the box at all times).

The estate management fell to an estate manager and the duke's secretary. Spiritual and cultural concerns were the province of a resident chaplain and organist, a librarian (for the famous Titchfield library), a library clerk, and dedicated housemaids just for dusting the books. In the racing stable, the stud groom could command fifteen assistants. Six 'house' gardeners looked after the indoor plants, whilst the gardens were cared for by between thirty and forty gardeners, plus forty to fifty roadmen. The home farm was supervised by a head farmer, assisted by between fifteen and twenty men. This was not the end of it: Welbeck had its own fire station, staffed by a chief and six helpers; a gymnasium with a Japanese trainer; a golf course with a head greensman and ten helpers; a laundry, managed by a head laundress and twelve laundresses, plus a staff of three window cleaners.[23] The massive size of the household gives some credence to the story that a guest who once arrived at Welbeck Abbey was picked up in a

Mr Dine, former butler at Petworth. He had previously been the groom of the chambers, a senior footman responsible for the presentation of reception rooms

Mrs Bragg, lady's maid to Lady Leconfield at Petworth House. The photograph is taken from an album made for Lady Leconfield by her daughter-in-law, Mrs Percy Wyndham

The senior menservants at Petworth House, Sussex, c.1870.
The steward (far right, standing) wears formal but 'civilian' dress,
the footmen are in livery and the lodge keepers in top hats; the stately chef
sits in the centre of the picture

Above: The servants' hall at Chirk Castle, near Wrexham, adapted for such use in the eighteenth century. Servants' halls are recorded from the mid seventeenth century, and were where most servants ate, though senior staff such as stewards and housekeepers dined separately

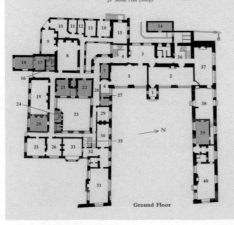

Ground Floor

Left: The plan of Lanhydrock in Cornwall. Originally a Jacobean house, it was extensively rebuilt after a fire in the 1880s. The well-preserved service areas exemplify the high Victorian specialisations below stairs, and the carefully segregated male and female zones

The barracks bedroom at Mamhead, Somerset. Shared bedrooms were the norm for most servants from the middle ages until the interwar period; shared beds were still common until the nineteenth century

The great double-height kitchen at Lanhydrock was the central point of a series of supporting sculleries, pantries and larders, and had kitchen ranges with specialist ovens

The footmen's livery room at Lanhydrock, with livery coats hanging in the cupboards; these were worn by footmen of the Tregonig family at Landue. The room was also used for brushing the livery clean

In gorgeous finery: the Egerton family's coachman (Mr Parker) and footmen (Mr Way and Mr Durham) standing outside their London home, dressed in state livery for the coronation of George V in 1911

Thomas Kilgallon, valet and butler to Sir Henry Gore-Booth MP. Mr Kilgallon left a detailed memoir of his life there between the 1860s and 1900

Elaborate gardens such as that at Waddesdon Manor in Buckinghamshire, home of the Rothschilds, required a large team of gardeners. George Johnson, the valued head gardener, sits officer-like in the centre of the front row, c.1910

The great British nanny: Nanny Messenger with the young James Dugdale (now 2nd Lord Crathorne) in the 1940s. She lived and worked at Crathorne Hall, Yorkshire, from 1939 until her death in 1976, presiding over a daily nursery tea shared by all family and visitors

Michael Kenneally, who joined the staff at Sledmere Park, Yorkshire, in 1952, as a pantry boy, aged eighteen. He became footman and then butler in 1959, working for the family over forty years. Christopher Simon Sykes, said that 'he turned buttling into an art form'

THE MAID WHO WAS BUT HUMAN.

Changing times: H.M. Bateman's 1922 *Punch* cartoon 'The Maid who was only Human' illustrates a new attitude to the traditional deference servants were expected to show to their employers

Long service: a party given by the 11th Duke of Devonshire for the staff at Chatsworth House, Derbyshire, in 1963. Among those present were 123 people who had worked for the estate for over twenty-five years, and fifty-two who had worked there for over forty years

Above: A modern household: the indoor staff at Holkham Hall, Norfolk, painted recently by Andrew Festing for the Earl of Leicester, including archivists, the butler and cleaners

Left: The great British daily: Della Robins has worked as a cleaner for forty-eight years at Chavenage House near Tetbury, Gloucestershire

taxi, rather than a staff car, which he thought rather strange. Later, however, it was explained that he had arrived on the day when the chauffeurs' XI played the footmen's XI.[24]

Former servant Gordon Grimmett catalogued another great household of similar dimensions, at Longleat in Wiltshire, as it was staffed in 1915. There was, he recalled, a steward, an under butler, a groom of the chambers, a valet, three footmen, two odd men, a pantry boy, a steward's room boy, a hall boy, a lamp boy, a housekeeper, two lady's maids, eight housemaids, two sewing maids, two still-room maids, six laundrymaids, a cook, two kitchenmaids, a vegetable maid, a scullery-maid, a dairy woman, chauffeurs and grooms (groups who were 'sworn enemies'), a steel boy (who polished metal) and a 'tiger' (a small boy who rode on the coach in livery). The outdoor staff comprised forty gardeners, a home farm staff of around twenty, and a maintenance team including carpenter, bricklayer and painter.[25]

In 1902, the Earl Fitzwilliam at Wentworth Woodhouse in Yorkshire employed sixty-three indoor servants, and for his funeral that same year twenty-two lady's maids and valets, accompanying visiting mourners, also stayed in the house. The garden, stables, park, and home farm were cared for by more than three hundred staff. The house, which had not been much modernised by that date, had five miles of corridors, along which fuel for light and heating had to be carried by hand.[26]

Of the great country houses operating at this level, Waddesdon Manor in Buckinghamshire is memorable especially for the large numbers of gardeners in the early twentieth century, working on what was already one of the greatest and best-staffed gardens of the time. In 1898, after the death of Baron Ferdinand de Rothschild, Waddesdon was inherited by his sister, Alice de Rothschild. She set herself the task of preserving the house, collections and standards of hospitality set by her brother, although her contribution is seen principally in the garden. In this she had a trusted right-hand man, whose career and qualities are typical of the great Edwardian country-house gardener.

George Frederick Johnson, who took over as head gardener in 1904 and remained until 1952,[27] first arrived at the age of seventeen, the son of an under gardener working at Swakeleys, in Middlesex. For the next five years he was trained, as was usual, in all the different departments. He learnt German and went to work in Austria for Ferdinand's brother, moving on to the garden that Alice owned at Grasse. When the post of head gardener at Waddesdon became vacant, in 1904, Alice offered it to him: 'Johnson, my head gardener here has given me notice that he does not wish to stay on; he is a very good man and [the] place and plants are in excellent order – I do not like changes and I know you well. I offer you the place of head gardener here.' She said he could rely on advice from the bailiff 'until you thoroughly understand the place' and, indeed, expected him to take counsel from the retired head gardener, Jacques, and from Gibbs, who was gardener at the family's other house at Eythrope. The job came with 'a furnished house, coal, milk, potatoes, vegetables, – a horse and cart at your disposal; the doctor and medicine gratis for you and your household'. Not only that but the salary was generous: 'To begin with I shall give you £100 a year. If you stay with me and give entire satisfaction, you will gradually be augmented up to 130 pounds a year.'[28]

A handful of letters survive from Alice to Johnson, written when she was regularly away in France, while her other private papers have been destroyed. 'Quality is the one thing you must study in all your work at Waddesdon, economy too as long as you can effect it by good organisation, but not by lowering the quality of the fruit, vegetable and flowers.'[29] As in previous centuries, country-house gardens usually supplied not only flowers to decorate the house, but also a considerable amount of the fruit and vegetables consumed by the household.

Johnson could command around fifty-three staff, with fourteen being employed directly in the greenhouses. The gardeners were divided into different teams, each with its own foreman: the kitchen garden; those tending fruit; those tending specialist plants grown for exhibition or competitions; those supplying bedding plants; those supplying flowers for arrangements in the house. Younger gardeners (many of whom joined in their teens and were usually single) lived together in a bothy, a house that had its own housekeeper and maid who cooked and cleaned for the men; there was also a reading room so that, when they had the time, they could study books and horticultural journals, although their working hours were long: from 6.30 a.m. to 5 p.m.[30]

Alice's letters buzz with the minutiae of garden matters, illustrating her competitiveness and showing how she expected confidentiality from her gardeners. One gardener, Marcel Gaucher, working at Waddesdon in the early 1920s, described her as 'extremely demanding'. His father 'had the feeling of having to continually pass an examination when working for her, and [remembered] how she always said: "You must never give out the exact name of the plants to my friends, even my closest ones." '[31]

During the First World War, some of her letters to Johnson refer poignantly to the deaths of young estate gardeners, as well as those of her own nephews. One is dated 4 April 1917: 'I am sorry to hear of the death of another Waddesdon man at the front. I should like you to express my most heartfelt sympathy to his mother and to his widow – This war is indeed a very cruel war.' Another is dated 20 November 1917: 'thank you for your letter of sympathy. I am profoundly grieved by the untimely death of my two young kinsmen, so brave, so bright.'[32]

Johnson's story is not dissimilar to that of John Macleod, the head gardener at Monteviot in the Borders, working for the Marquess and Marchioness of Lothian, appointed to his post in 1903 and remaining there until his death in 1944. He was first apprenticed as a gardener in Strathmore and in 1900 became foreman gardener for the Duke of Wellington. In 1902 he returned to Scotland before taking up his appointment at Monteviot, with more than twenty gardeners under him, at an annual salary of £65.[33] According to his grandson, fuel was paid for by the estate, as were the fees for his children to attend grammar school. His terms of appointment included mention of fifty-five tons of coal annually, of which six were for the head gardener, five for the garden bothy, with the balance for the hothouses and glasshouses. In 1915, when he was offered the role of assistant superintendent of parks for the city of Glasgow, his reference was exemplary: 'he is very good with the men and gets a large amount of work out of them, and in a very quiet way.' When Lady Lothian heard of the offer, however, she doubled his salary to persuade him to stay.[34]

Gardeners and other outdoor servants were paid in cash wages and given cottage accommodation; they were not expected to live in the house nor to eat in it. Many head gardeners, such as the two examples above, were much respected and valued by their employers; the gardens of a country house contributed to its setting and were still intended to impress visitors. Loelia, Duchess of Westminster, recorded how her own love of gardening was engendered by her head gardener, Mr Barnes, the 'marvellous and creative' being who managed thirty-five gardeners, with eighteen in the glasshouses, and 'fulfilled my extravagant plans'. She was honest enough to add: 'Of course, I never actually did anything myself; I never dug a hole with a trowel or put a bulb in or anything like that.'[35]

If gardens added to the prestige of a country house in the early years of the twentieth century, so too did the great shooting parties of the period. These legendary social events, which usually took place over a matter of weeks rather than weekends, would need intricate and careful planning. The steward, housekeeper, cook and the entire indoor staff were involved in preparing ahead for a full house, as well as when the whole event was in full sail.

The gamekeepers – rearing birds and protecting them from depredations by poachers or vermin – would have to ensure that numbers would be sufficient, and at the turn of the century the bags could be in the thousands. One famous gamekeeper, Tommy Taylor, keeper at Elveden for a half a century, confirms in his memoir that by 1914 some 20,000 pheasants were bred annually for the sport, cared for by complex system of underkeepers.[36]

As well as the rearing of game birds, the shoots themselves would require an almost military-style management of underkeepers, loaders, cartridge boys and beaters, who by walking up from a given point would drive the birds towards the guns. This system provided a great deal of sport to the crack shots of the early twentieth century, while in more recent years wild-bird shooting, using dogs rather than beaters, is increasingly favoured.

The great Edwardian shooting parties – whether at shooting lodges in Scotland, or on the great shooting estates such as Blenheim, Chatsworth and Elveden Hall in Suffolk (bought in the 1890s by the

Earl of Iveagh), not to mention Sandringham – define our image of country-house life. Yet they became increasingly elaborate only in the later nineteenth century, especially after the Prince of Wales, later Edward VII, became an enthusiast. Lord de Grey, who was present at one great Edwardian shooting party, contrasted its excesses unfavourably with the past: 'When I am sitting in a tent taking part in a lengthy luncheon of many courses, served by a host of retainers, my memory takes me back to a time many years ago when we worked harder for our sport, and when seated under a hedge, our midday meal consisted of a sandwich . . . I am inclined to think those were better and worthier days.'[37]

Shooting parties on a lavish scale declined with the First World War, as did the taste for the very large 'bags', but many great estates kept up shoots of considerable style. Loelia, Duchess of Westminster, recalled her first shoot in the 1920s at the home of her future husband at Eaton Hall, Cheshire: 'The clothes were so interesting. All the keepers were dressed in green velvet tailcoats and black top hats trimmed with gold braid, so that you could spot a keeper whenever you wanted to . . . The beaters came through the wood just like a Breughel picture, and they wore white smocks . . . and large red felt hats with wide brims.' This was for safety as much as for spectacle, as it also meant that the head keeper could readily command their movements.[38]

Lady Phyllis Macrae, daughter of the 4th Marquess of Bristol, had similar memories of interwar shooting parties, with guns coming to stay with their wives, valets and lady's maids, 'and very often a chauffeur and a loader, and they all expected to be put up. The loader was quite often the gentlemen's gentleman [valet] – he was perhaps the first footman who had been taught to load. A few of them did teach the chauffeurs to load.'[39]

Behind the scenes of these social events with all their luxury and finery were the servants of the house, inhabitants of a partly invisible world behind the green baize door, explored in the last chapter. Their accommodation in the newer country houses of the early twentieth century was given particular attention by Herman Muthesius, German cultural attaché, whose admiring account was published in 1904–5.

Deeply impressed by English country-house life, he remarked that its 'most genuine and decisively valuable feature' was 'its absolute practicality' over 'the superficially decorative side'. It seemed to him that centuries of domestic life in such establishments had refined many elements into their best and most practical version, although he recognised that they were still predicated on a large servant body.

Amusingly, it was the very multiplicity of rooms with dedicated purposes (which only fifty years later would seem so completely superfluous when there were not the working hands to fill them) that for him represented the 'high level of culture' in the English country house. He wrote: 'the continental observer may find that the residential quarters are not so very different from what he is used to, but the domestic quarters come as a total surprise.'[40]

According to Muthesius, everything took place in a continental kitchen, from cooking to cleaning – including the servants' social life. He contrasted this with the English country house, in which 'the management of the household is broken down into a dozen different operations, for each of which a room is provided'. These arrangements, in his view, had reached an 'exemplary level', being placed in recently built country houses in side courts, rather than in basements. This solved three problems: service was made easier; there were no stairs to climb; and it reduced the transmission of cooking smells. It also made the living conditions of servants much healthier.[41]

He noted the provision of the various spaces that had been a feature of the eighteenth- and nineteenth-century house: a large kitchen, a scullery,

> a second kitchen known as a still-room, larders for dry stores, meat, game, milk and butter, store-rooms for wood, coal for the house and for the kitchen, cleaning rooms and store rooms for lamps, boots (Motcombe [Dorset] even has one [a brushing room] for riding breeches), a pantry and bedroom for the butler, with adjoining plate room, a housekeeper's room with adjacent laundry room and a communal dining room for servants.[42]

Muthesius examined every aspect of country-house design in his book, noting especially the provision of a servants' hall, which by the early twentieth century had become more comfortable than in the previous one:

> besides the domestic room already mentioned, all larger and even medium sized houses in England have a servants' dining-room known as the servants' hall. It is a large, long room; it must be as near to the kitchen as possible but at the same time the butler and the house-keeper must be able to keep an eye on it from their rooms. It is not only used as a dining-room but also as a communal sitting-room for the lower servants during their free time.[43]

Its position seemed to him to be dictated by protocol and practicality:

> It is never situated that it can overlook the front door to the house, to prevent visitors feeling that the servants' eyes are upon them as they arrive. It must however be in closest proximity to the tradesmen's entrance, since it also serves as a waiting-room and visitor's room for all visitors of the rank of the lower servants (the housekeeper's or steward's rooms fulfil the same function for the upper servants).[44]

Staff bedrooms continued to be strictly segregated by gender, senior servants having dedicated bedrooms and junior servants sharing dormitories. The introduction of electricity at the end of the nine-teenth century might well have ushered in a more radical approach to country-house technology – indeed, it had been installed in some country houses since the late 1880s and 1890s. However, the innate conservatism of the landowning class, and the availability of cheap labour, meant that, as Clive Aslet observed in *The Last Country Houses*, there was little motive for change: 'only when it became apparent that the supply of willing labour could not be increased did owners begin to look seriously into the alternative possibilities' of the labour-saving new technology.[45]

Novelties such as centralised vacuuming systems appeared in new houses built in the early years of the twentieth century, as well as other useful and functional inventions, such as the internal telephone system at Waddesdon Manor in Buckinghamshire, with handsome handsets for the aristocracy and less glamorous earpieces in the servants' quarters.[46] The butler's pantry at Castle Drogo in Devon, a picturesque castle designed by Lutyens for Julius Drewe, and completed only in the 1920s, boasts a memorable internal telephone exchange as part of an unusually handsome sequence of service rooms.[47] In older houses, house telephones seem to have been popular, using the old wiring tubes of the bell system, but the public telephone network soon had an even greater impact on country-house life, allowing all sorts of communication that had in the past required the services of a trusted domestic.[48] Although at first it only added to the duties and responsibilities of the principal menservants expected to answer the telephone and take messages.

In contrast, the new technology might itself quickly be made obsolete. In 1913, new motor-driven laundries were installed at houses such as Sledmere in Yorkshire and Carberry Tower in Scotland, but during the interwar period, as attempts were made to reduce domestic expenditure, many country-house laundries were closed and laundry sent out to an independent contractor.[49]

Modernisation took place at different rates in different houses, so assumptions cannot be made that innovations in new-built country houses in this period would typically be found in older ones. The conservatism of country-house owners made many slow to modernise their historic houses, certainly before the First World War.

This is illustrated in Lady Diana Cooper's memoir, *The Rainbow Comes and Goes* (1958), recording vivid childhood memories of Belvoir Castle in Rutland, where her grandfather, the 7th Duke of Rutland, led an almost fendal life, dying in 1906. Born in 1892, she remembered the many additional hands thronging the long corridors of the house, such as the gong man, 'an old retainer, one of those numberless ranks of domestic servants which have completely disappeared and today seem fabulous. He was admittedly very old. He wore a white beard to his waist.'[50] Even more evocative were the water men who, before Belvoir was replumbed at the beginning of the twentieth century, still carried water by hand around the house:

> The Water-men are difficult to believe in today . . . They were the biggest people I had ever seen, much bigger than the men of the

family, who were remarkable for their height. They had stubby beards and a general Bill Sykes appearance. They wore brown clothes, no collars and thick green baize aprons from chin to knee and on their shoulders they carried a wooden yoke from which hung two gigantic cans of water.[51]

The point is even more clearly illustrated at Longleat, where the young Gordon Grimmett was responsible for refilling hundreds of oil lamps:

by 1915 electricity was no new invention, and some big houses by that time were either on the mains or if too remote, had their own generators. Others had compromised by using gas.

Not so the Marquis of Bath, who felt that to install either would disfigure the house. The rooms had been designed for oil lamps or candle light, and if he were to change to electricity not only might it mutilate the ceilings and walls but the character of the rooms would change. He had the same feelings about central heating. Many of the gentry agreed over this, mainly I think because it was considered unhealthy, if not downright effete.[52]

Henry Bennett, a footman at Chatsworth in Derbyshire in the late 1920s and early 1930s, came up against similar attitudes:

when we moved to Bolton Abbey [in Yorkshire] or Hardwick [in Derbyshire] there was no electric light; oil lamps and candles were the order. A man was kept to see that the lamps contained oil, wicks trimmed and lamp glasses cleaned. It was the footman's duty to put the lamps around the house. His Grace invariably liked candles, so quite a number of lighted candles adorned his study. When the ladies retired at night, the footmen had to extinguish the lamps and place electric torches, silver candlesticks and matches outside the Drawing-Room for guests to pick up and light themselves to their room.[53]

Lady Fingall's recollections of the plumbing and lighting at her husband's family home, Killeen in Ireland, were scarcely any different: 'all the bedrooms were lit by candlelight. Nothing, of course, could be more becoming than that lamplight and candlelight.

Fourteen candles were an average to light a large bedroom . . . Then every drop of bath water was carried, and we all had our baths in front of the fire.' They had no bathroom at Killeen until after the First World War.[54]

As these testimonies suggest, large household staffs, close in character to those of the pre-First World War household, generally continued into the 1920s and 1930s. However, there can be no doubt that the demands of wartime dramatically changed the attitude of the generation who might normally have been expected to go into service, not least because so many of the younger servants themselves enlisted. Nationally, four hundred thousand domestic servants left their work, whether for war service in the army for the men, or work in the munitions factories for the women.[55]

Calls for volunteers were answered by all classes, and employers of menservants found themselves the target of additional appeals. At the beginning of the war, landowners were encouraged, in a leader in *The Times* dated 12 August 1914, to release any staff they could do without: 'There are large numbers of footmen, valets, butlers, gardeners, grooms, and gamekeepers, whose services are more or less superfluous and can either be dispensed with or replaced by women without seriously hurting or incommoding anyone.'[56]

In January 1915, *Country Life* magazine ran a series of questions, beginning: 'Have you a Butler, Groom, Chauffeur, Gardener, or Gamekeeper serving you who, at this moment should be serving your King and Country?' followed by 'Have you a man preserving your Game who should be helping to preserve your Country?' The Earl of Ancaster guaranteed an income to the wives and families of volunteers, giving £5 to every man who enlisted.[57] John Whittle, a hall boy at Sudeley in Gloucestershire, recalled meeting one servant in 1930 whose employer had summoned him in 1914 'and suggested that he "do his duty". He said that he [would] be joining today, if possible. He joined the Guards and later, in the front line used to pray that he would be injured. In due course he was, and survived to be a chauffeur.'[58]

Among the thousands of men from all walks of life who died in the trenches and on the battlefields were landowners and their heirs, adding to the insecurity of the country-house way of life, already beset by economic uncertainty, inflation, and rising taxation. Understandably, many men who had been in domestic service before the war did not choose to return to it. New and unfamiliar experiences began to broaden society's understanding of servants' lives. Violet Firth, a middle-class woman who had undertaken a gardener's work, was shocked by the treatment of servants, having become one herself: 'It offends the innate self-respect of a man or woman to be treated as an automaton.'[59]

The real crisis in the servant-supported country-house way of life was an economic one. This was quite simply the result of a reduced return from land rentals at the same time as an increase in taxation and a rise in wage levels. A vivid illustration of this can be found in the diaries of Colonel James Stevenson of Braidwood in Lanarkshire. In 1915, on 6 November, he wrote: 'The lower orders have a great deal of money – more than they ever they had before. The landowners are those who suffer as their rents remain the same – taxes enormously increased & very much higher wages have to be paid to servants on account of competition of public bodies, county councils, parish councils &c who are most extravagant in the wages they give – not having to pay them themselves'.[60]

The economic equation for a landowner could be compared in his mind, a wage bill for one employee equating to the value of one farm rental. In 1917, on 2 June, he is beside himself as an employee had asked for a pay increase from 25 shillings to 34 a week: 'but as I can't lay my hand on another man I had to give it . . . Lapsley's wage comes to within a few pounds of the rent at Bushilhead farm [a farm on his estate he rented out]. The lower orders are having the time of their lives just now.'[61]

In 1924 he made a furious entry in his diary on 6 March, on the subject of the departure of a cook; 'the woman in the kitchen has made up her mind to leave tomorrow at only a week's notice – quite illegal but I will let her go. The lower orders are beginning to think that they are not bound by any law. I don't much regret her, as she is stupid, fat & no great cook – but it is difficult to put anyone in her place at a moment's notice.'[62]

Some shrewd individuals were quick to recognise the impact the war would have on the whole world of service. In 1920, the architect Randal Phillips observed in *The Servantless House*: 'girls who formerly accepted the shackles of what was little better than domestic drudgery came into a new liberty. They got good wages for what they did and they got far more time of their own than they ever had before in domestic service.'[63] On the other hand, some of the households that had been run by women during the war found they could dispense with the services of men. It was in this period that the parlourmaid began to feature on the staffs of smaller country establishments and London houses, although less so in the great country houses.[64]

William Lanceley, a house steward in the 1920s, commented in his memoir *From Hall-Boy to House-Steward* (1925):

> The Great War undoubtedly upset service and this is not to be wondered at by those who know the servant question. The war called for hands to help, and many servants responded to the call. The work they were asked to do was a novelty to them, the pay was big and they had short hours, hundreds being spoilt for service through it. It made those who returned to service unsettled. They had money to spend and time to spend it when on war work, and to come back to [having liberty on] one or two evenings a week was to them a hardship.[65]

By the 1920s, 'Service had no attraction for the fairly educated young man or woman. It is looked down upon – they want to do something better, and often school friendships are broken through sheer snobbishness.' He illustrated this with the example of a young person saying, 'I like Lettie better than any girl, but you know I cannot introduce her to my new friends as she is a servant.'[66]

Lanceley himself felt that there were still great attractions to life in service, especially in the big house, with good food, opportunities to move up the ladder, the variety of being in a rural situation with an annual period in London. In his view, no servant was really overworked, and the differences in servility between domestic staff and office workers were exaggerated: 'the head of a firm, the manager and foreman are held in far greater awe than my Lord or Lady.' Perhaps he was influenced here by the fact that, owing to his experience and seniority, he was by then not in awe of his employers, but their close confidant.[67]

Eric Horne, a former footman, valet and butler, whose racy memoirs were published in 1923, turned a more cynical eye on the life of the aristocracy, but could not disguise a certain dismay at the decline of the world in which he had spent so much of his working life, which he attributed to the immediate post-war years: 'Now that England is cracking up as far as the Nobility is concerned, who are selling their estates, castles, and large houses . . . it seems a pity that the old usages and traditions of gentleman's service should die with the old places.' The new rich, in his opinion, made fat by the profits of war, were a poor substitute: 'You cannot make a silk purse out of a souced [sic] mackerel.'[68]

Horne's affection and respect for some of his employers is evident, just as he is driven by others to despair and fury. He wrote that he had 'lived in the service of a noble family who were ruined by the war; they were such nice people to their servants that, could I have afforded to do it, I would have worked for them for nothing'. These enlightened aristocrats had to reduce their indoor servants from twenty-five to just three. The bleak economic climate brought about the collapse of the social whirl that had once centred on the London house. In leaner times, Horne missed the pageantry of pre-war Belgravia, with 'pairs of horses and carriages, with footmen powdered and breeched, silk stockings, and a lot of pomp and show'. In contrast to these happier experiences, he had worked in some places where it required 'the temper of an angel to take some of the insults of the gentry'.[69]

He certainly felt that the deep social gulf between the classes could not be sustained indefinitely and recalled with irritation how servants were treated like chattels and loaned between employers for big events, 'in the same way the poor borrow a frying pan, or a rub of soap'.[70] His bitterness at the behaviour of some of his employers, although by no means all, was sharpened by the death of his wife in the 1919 flu epidemic. He had been obliged to live separately from her for much of his working life by the accepted conditions of service that compelled many domestic staff to be (or behave as if they were) single and live separately from their families.[71]

In the period directly after the First World War, the struggle to recruit new servants prompted the Ministry of Reconstruction to set up a government commission that revealed, if nothing else, what people already in service disliked at the time.[72] This turned out to be not so much the work but the social stratification and deference demanded of them, as well as the lack of personal freedom. Despite much contrary assertion in the letters pages of newspapers, domestic servants were not being tempted away from service by the newly established 'dole', as they were not included in the scheme until 1946.[73]

Ironically unemployment created by the Great Depression forced many women back into domestic service in the late 1920s, when it is estimated that there were 1.1 million of them in service. By the late 1930s this figure had risen to nearly 1.5 million, although a greater proportion were non-residential or day workers.[74] However, this did not necessarily mean that the numbers of those in country-house service increased, since at that time rising taxes, combined with falling land values and rentals, forced many aristocrats and gentry to reduce their households, while selling off their secondary estates and London houses to concentrate their resources on their principal seats.[75] As this led to the traditional hierarchies being thrown open to greater challenges, it also increased resentment among some in domestic service.[76]

Gordon Grimmett, in his memoir published in *Gentlemen's Gentlemen* and edited by Rosina Harrison, evokes one of the humblest jobs in a country house. He joined the staff at Longleat in Wiltshire at the age of fifteen as a lamp boy, going on to become a footman and working for the Astors at Cliveden before leaving service. Lamp boys were common in country-house service until the 1920s. He slept in a dormitory with six beds, which he shared with the two under footmen, one of the odd men, the pantry boy and the steward's boy: 'there was also a dressing-table and about four rickety chairs: that was the sum total of the furniture.'[77]

He would get up at six, collect sixty shoes for cleaning and distribute hot-water jugs. At eight o'clock he would have breakfast, after which he cleaned knives in a special machine. At 8.45 he would light the 140 candles in the chapel for the morning service attended by all the staff, during which he would be on organ duty. After chapel he would be responsible for gathering up all 400 of the lamps at Longleat, which, as we have seen, was still lit by oil lamps and candles because the marquess was loth to disfigure the old house with electricity. Each one had to be cleaned, trimmed and refilled. He had some help from the odd men and other boys, and many lamps were delivered to him by other housemaids and footmen although 'collecting and replacing them itself meant a few miles walk every day'. He would trim the wicks and then 'fill the lamps from the large oil tanks, paraffin for the corridor and staff lamps, and colsa oil for the house.' Then he polished the funnels, globes and stands. 'The sheer monotony of the job took some beating.'

Mr Grimmett would tackle twenty at a time, which would be collected and replaced by others. He would also replace all the candles. After tea, he would light all the lamps in the corridors, basement and cellars, while the footmen lit those in the main rooms, also helping him to put the shutters up. Despite the dullness of this drudgery, he thought his job easier than the housemaids'.[78]

In the early afternoon, he would have to move outside the day bed of the young Viscount Weymouth, who had a weak lung for which a daily dose of fresh air was recommended; often the two boys would walk the dogs together afterwards. 'I learnt a lot from him and I think perhaps he did from me. I didn't envy him, nor have I ever been jealous of my employers.' After a year, Mr Grimmett became third footman, perhaps because the older men had gone to war.

His colleague Rosina Harrison remembered him as 'an excellent footman. He was like an actor; he'd be playing the fool in the wings but from the moment he went on stage he was straight into his part. It was the theatre of service which appealed to him, the dressing up in livery with almost period movement and big gestures that fitted the Louis Quinze dining-room at Cliveden.'[79]

Charles Smith, born in 1908, served Lord Louis Mountbatten for fifty years. He too went into service at the age of fifteen after a serious illness prevented him continuing to work in a coal mine. The idea of an alternative occupation came to him while he recuperated on an uncle's farm: 'Four miles away, commanding the horizon and always the focal point of my eyes, was the seventeenth-century grey-stoned Welbeck Abbey, the home of the Duke and Duchess of Portland. It held considerable fascination for me, and one morning I put on my jacket and breeches – hand-me-downs from the village Squire's son – and cycled to the Abbey.'[80]

He rang the front door bell, which was answered by a liveried footman who sent him round to the tradesman's entrance:

A reassuring glimmer appeared in his eye as he closed the door on me and by the time I got to the rear he had alerted the steward of the house whose task it was to employ the servants . . . [He was engaged as hall boy for £25 a year.] As hall boy I had very little contact with the Duke and Duchess; I attended to the whims and needs of the fifty senior servants.

[He was later promoted to steward's room footman literally the footman who attended to the upper servants' meals, the yearly increment for which was £10.] There were also peripheral benefits, including two free suits of clothing a year, special allowances for laundry and beer, the provision of meals, and a comfortable room of my own in the house.'[81]

He moved on to work as a 'schoolroom footman' for the Earl and Countess of Derby, attending to their orphaned grandchildren. Most colourfully, he assisted at the Derby House ball, given the day after the Epsom Derby, dressed in full footman's livery of a gold and silver embroidered red tail cut-away coat and a stiff-fronted wing-collared shirt and white bow tie; blue velvet knickerbockers; pink silk stockings; and silver-buckled black pumps. 'My hair was waved and powdered white.'[82] In 1930, he was recruited as a travelling footman to Lady Louis Mountbatten, from which he progressed to being valet to Lord Louis, then butler, as described with great gusto in his book, *Fifty Years with Mountbatten* (1980).

In the great landowners' houses, the staff numbers in the early years of the century stayed at a similar, or only slightly reduced, level between the wars. In the interwar period, Chatsworth in Derbsyhire employed a comptroller, who ran all the Cavendish houses, whilst the staff of Chatsworth itself comprised a butler, the duke's valet, an under butler, a groom of the chambers, two footmen, a steward's room footman, a housekeeper, the duchess's maid, a head house-maid, two second housemaids, two third housemaids, two sewing women, a cook, a first kitchenmaid, a second kitchenmaid, a vege-table maid, two to three scullery-maids, two still-room maids, a dairymaid, six laundrymaids and the duchess's secretary, all of whom lived in the house.

The Chatsworth footmen still powdered their hair until the 1920s, and until 1938 always wore livery if there were more than six for dinner. Some staff, many living in estate cottages, came in daily, including the odd man, an upholsterer, a scullery man, two scrubbing women, a laundry porter, a steam boiler man, a coal man, two porter's lodge attendants, two night firemen, a night porter and two window cleaners.[83]

In the 1920s and 30s, when all the families of the children of the 9th Duke came to stay for Christmas, they each bought with them a nanny, a nursery maid, a lady's maid, a valet and sometimes a chauffeur and a groom. This swelled the numbers of resident ser-vants over the festive period, so on Christmas Day itself 'there were about a hundred and fifty people to feed – thirty to forty in the dining-room, twenty in the nursery, up to thirty in the steward's room, up to fifty in the servants' hall, and some meals in the house-maids' room.'[84]

In 1928, Cliveden, whilst smaller in scale as a whole, was certainly run on the model of a great country house, and required a small army of servants. The indoor staff comprised the steward, Edwin Lee, the valet, Arthur Bushell, the under butler, three footmen, a hall boy, two oddmen, a house carpenter, the chef, Monsieur Gilbert, three kitchenmaids, a scullery-maid, a dairymaid, a housekeeper, Mrs Moore, a still-room maid, a head housemaid, three under house-maids, and two daily maids. Lady Astor's maid, Rosina Harrison, wrote a remarkable memoir of her life in service, from which this list is taken. There was also a maid for the Hon. Phyllis Astor, a head laundress, Emma Gardener, three laundrymaids, a telephonist and a nightwatchman. A nanny, Miss Gibbons, two nursemaids and a governess made up the nursery staff.

The gardens were in the care of the head gardener, W. Camm, an outside foreman and eight gardeners, looked after by a bothy house-keeper. The greenhouse had its own foreman, six gardeners, and one 'decorator', responsible for the flower arrangements. The total out-door staff for the estates, stables, stud farm and dairy farm totalled fifty-two. They included a gamekeeper, Ben Cooper, assistant game-keeper, a head groom and three assistants for the stables, a boatman, a head chauffeur, Charlie Hopkins, a stud groom, three foresters, an estate foreman, Ben Emmett, six painters, two carpenters, two gen-eral workers, a bricklayer, a plumber and mate, three electricians, and a part-time clockwinder. There was also a home farm.

The London house at no. 4, St James's Square, had a full-time staff of a housekeeper, a head housemaid, two under housemaids, an odd man, a carpenter and an electrician. Also based there were a controller, Miss Kindersley, who looked after all the Astors' households, three accountants, and a number of secretaries, as many as seven during Lady Astor's period as MP. Even though Cliveden was not at the centre of a great agricultural estate, the size of its household as a whole is on a par with the great lists of the Earl of Northumberland in 1511, or the Earl of Dorset in 1613.[85]

Whilst the Astors' footman, young Gordon Grimmett, thought the housemaids' work much harder than his own as a young lamp boy, it was junior maids in the scullery and kitchen who, like their counterparts in the nineteenth century, had the most physically demanding jobs. Rosina Harrison recalls the grand steward at Cliveden, Mr Lee, saying of the young scullery-maids: 'Poor little devils, washing up and scrubbing away at dozens of pots, pans, sauce-pans and plates up to their elbows in suds and grease, their hands red raw with the soda which was the only form of detergent in those days. I've seen them crying with exhaustion and pain, the degrada-tion too, I shouldn't wonder.'[86]

That life was tough is borne out in many other memoirs, although some among them had pleasant memories of the houses where they had been employed, describing as their 'happiest days' time spent working in the company of a large body of servants. As the century progressed they were also permitted more freedoms than had been the lot of their predecessors, although younger servants were still obliged to leave to marry until the 1930s.

In 1971, the present Lord Crathorne recorded an interview with his family's cook, Mrs Davidson, who had worked at Crathorne Hall in Yorkshire from the 1920s, and who had first arrived there in 1910, aged fourteen, through Hunt's Registry in London. A lot of young people went into domestic service, she recalled, 'because there was nothing else for us to do'. She was first employed as a scullery-maid, one of twenty-six indoor servants on the staff of one of the great Edwardian country houses, completed only in 1906.

> I had to get up at four o'clock. We had to get ready for all the staff and we had to get the kitchen ready for Mrs Dugdale coming down, floor scrubbed and silver sand put down, the table with a cloth and all the knives put neatly on the table. And then she would come in and go through the kitchen and scullery and out into the larder, the game larder, back in and into the inside larder and then came down and sat at the table to look at the menus which were all in a book.
>
> We had breakfast in the kitchen and the housemaids in the Hall and the Housekeeper and valets and butler in the housekeeper's room. We had ours at 8 o'clock. After breakfast we did more cleaning, and there would be about twenty copper pans we had to clean . . . There were four of us in the kitchen and we did the vegetables. I just did the vegetables and cooked them.

Although they did not get to bed until eleven, the staff 'used to have fun amongst ourselves' and there was always 'good food' for the servants.[87]

From the scullery Mrs Davidson was promoted to still-room maid, 'where you make the cakes and bread, and biscuits, and do the dining room washing up and dessert dishes, and all the morning trays. That was one step up. I was [there] four years.'[88] Gradually, she moved up in the hierarchy.

Sometimes, experience might be gained in unorthodox ways. In one place where she was kitchenmaid, 'the cook used to get drunk, and I used to have it all to do'. She worked at Bramham Hall near

Wetherby, before returning, just after the First World War, to Crathorne Hall, at the request of the housekeeper, to be the principal cook there. There were four in the Dugdale family plus twenty-six servants, whose feeding was her responsibility. On shooting parties there could be seventy to cater for because the beaters were given hot food as well. In 1927, Mrs Davidson married a groom, Albert, who also worked at Crathorne, and left service to devote herself to him, but she soon went back at her employer's request and with her husband's blessing, remaining the family cook for the next thirty years.[89] Initially, meals were served by a butler and first and second footman, in a pink and fawn livery, but footmen and formality dwindled away after the Second World War.

Mrs Davidson's observations on the catering responsibilities for a large household of staff as well as family are echoed in many memoirs, as is the pattern of staff meals being served in different rooms, reflecting their stratification, which seems so extraordinary today. Anne, Countess of Rosse, was very conscious of these fine distinctions: 'There were still when I went to Birr, for each day, six different lunches in six different rooms. The staff could on occasion meet and talk together – Nanny could gossip with the housekeeper in the housekeeper's room, or Miss Martin the governess could gossip with Nanny either in the schoolroom or the nursery. But eating together – NO.'[90]

Mrs Jean Hibbert, who worked at Gordon Castle and then Goodwood House in the interwar years, from the late 1920s until her marriage in 1932, harked back to her time as a housemaid in her detailed, amusing but unpublished memoirs. Her first post was at Gordon Castle in Moray, after which she wanted to move on elsewhere to become a second housemaid. When she sought a reference from the duchess, so that she could take up a post at Wilton House,[91] to her surprise the duchess responded with a telegram: 'You are not to leave my employment. If you want a change come to Goodwood.' Mrs Hibbert wrote to one gardener she had met to ask his advice about accepting this offer and he encouraged her to do so – they later married. An added incentive was that the first housemaid from Gordon Castle, Annie Cowie, had already moved to Goodwood. So she travelled from Rothes in Scotland, via London, to Sussex.[92]

'There were seven housemaids and our rooms were in one of the towers of the great house. We were all Scots as the Duchess liked us best, but we did not like the head housemaid who was from Glasgow . . . The maids had a sitting room with a fire on the ground floor but no fires in the bedrooms.'[93] Typically the staff ate together in the servants' hall, except for the butler, the lady's maid, the house-keeper and the butter cook (a specialist chef), who all ate in the steward's quarters.

The maids rose at 5.30 every day to get the public rooms ready before the family came down, yet Mrs Hibbert retained great affec-tion for these apartments and took pride in her work:

> Now that I was second housemaid my duties were largely cleaning in the main part of the house which was much older and more beauti-fully furnished than Gordon Castle. I particularly loved the fine paintings . . . Goodwood is famous for its Canalettos which I could see every day. When you think of it, people pay to visit such places now but I had those lovely rooms to myself every day in return for some hard work. Dusting, cleaning floors, polishing, laying fires and using the newly-fangled, heavy Hoover sweeping machines were my jobs but the worst part was cleaning steel grates until they shone.[94]

She also polished the dining-room table before breakfast at 7.30. When the family were up their bedrooms were cleaned and their beds made. After the maids had had their own lunch, they had to be on hand to help carry food between kitchen and dining room.[95] They were given two hours off after lunch, and one afternoon off every week. Also (she thought as a result of economies), Mrs Hibbert had the duties of lady's maid to Lady March, the duchess's daughter-in-law.

She heard some local gossip about the West Dean estate, where 'the morals of the guests were supposed to be so loose that the garden boy had to ring a bell fixed to the corner of the house wall at 6 a.m. called "the change beds bell", so that housemaids would find the right husbands and wives together in bed when they delivered their morning tea at 7!' Even Mrs Hibbert thought that this was probably quite apocryphal but it has echoes of the bed-hopping life of the aris-tocracy in Vita Sackville-West's *The Edwardians*.[96]

At Goodwood in the 1920s, staff numbers were still high. There were twenty-seven indoor staff: the steward, who looked after the accounts; the butler; the housekeeper; the cook; the duke's valet; the duchess's maid; the porter who sat in a cubbyhole by the main door and took in messages and post; five footmen, seven housemaids, two pantry boys, three kitchenmaids, three still-room maids and two scullery-maids. Then there was staff for the laundry, the stables, with both horses and cars, and the garden, where fourteen gardeners worked under the head gardener, his deputy and his foreman, seven of them under Mrs Hibbert's future husband, Spencer Hibbert. An additional team of gardeners looked after the pleasure grounds and cricket green, not to mention the gamekeepers and woodsmen.[97]

Mrs Hibbert looked on the then Duchess of Richmond as 'an excellent employer' who threw a good Christmas party and sometimes treated the maids to an afternoon at the theatre with tea at the Grosvenor Hotel. When she and Spencer Hibbert became engaged to be married, they handed in their notice as was usual. However, the duchess, 'knowing my family was far away and very poor . . . offered to organise and pay for the wedding from Goodwood House'. She even gave Mrs Hibbert furniture for their new home. The wedding breakfast was 'a magnificent spread and lovely wine which the Duke gave us as his present and a fine three layered wedding cake . . . the kitchens had been working hard and in secret because I knew nothing about it.'[98]

Some young women, unable to pursue an expensive higher education during the Great Depression, found careers in service the only option. Lavinia Swainbank began work in 1922, which was 'not an easy time to be starting out on one's career. For those were the days of depression on the Tyne.' Although Miss Swainbank had passed the eleven-plus, a shortage of money hampered all her attempts to go further: 'Thus at sixteen I entered into a career of drudgery, where long hours and very often inadequate food were accepted standards of a life that was thrust on one out of sheer necessity.' She was taken on in a hotel as a 'tweeny' (or between-stairs maid), then became second housemaid: 'ultimately I reached my peak as third housemaid in one of the stately homes of England'.[99]

When she was a second housemaid in 'gentleman's service' for an elderly lady and two spinster daughters, her daily timetable had echoes of service in a country house during the previous four centuries:

6.30 Rise. Clean grate [and] lay fire in Dining Room. Sweep carpet and dust. Clean grate and lay fire in Library. Sweep and dust. Clean grate and lay fire in billiard room. Sweep and dust. Polish staircase. Clean grate and lay fire in Drawing Room. Polish floor. Clean grate and lay fire in Morning Room. Sweep and Dust vestibule. Sweep and dust Blue Staircase.

All that before the 8 am. Breakfast in the Servants' Hall. 9 am. Start bedrooms. Help with Bedmaking and slops and fill ewers and carafes. Clean grates and lay fires. Fill up coal boxes and wood baskets. Sweep and dust bedrooms. Clean bathrooms. Change into afternoon uniform. 1 pm Lunch in Servants' Hall. Afternoons, clean silver, brass, water cans, trim lamps. 4 pm Tea in the Servants' Hall, 5 pm light fires in bedrooms, 6 pm cans of hot water to bedrooms, 7.30 pm, Turn down beds, make up fires, and empty slops. Fill up coal and wood containers. Leave morning trays set in housemaid's pantry.[100]

Some of her other duties were more pleasurable: 'Early mornings, three times a week, I opened the massive front door, to admit the head and under gardener who used to arrive with masses of fresh blooms and proceed to make exquisite floral arrangements in the hall and public rooms. Later they brought fresh vegetables to the cook.'[101] Despite the grind, 'Time passed pleasantly enough here. The other servants were kind, the food was excellent' and she even had a bike to get into town.

Her next position was more enjoyable even if the accommodation was modest: 'here for the first time I really learned the meaning of gentlemen's service. For the first time I was treated as a human being by people with heart and consideration for all their staff. We were even granted the then unknown privilege of two hours free in the afternoon, either to rest or sit in the lovely gardens.' She read books from the library and became interested in the history of the place and the duke's family, whose 'ancestors became real characters to me'.[102]

She had happy memories of the servants' ball, when the family waited on their staff. There were frequent house parties when the family returned from London: 'although this meant more work, to me it was exciting to witness how the other half lived and there was no bitterness in this. I used to love to watch over the banisters the young people in their wonderful dresses.'[103]

There was a lot of fun to be had in the servants' hall too: 'a gramophone and stacks of up to date records, where the gardeners, grooms and under chauffeur joined the indoor staff of maids and footmen for dances after the day's duties had ended. We had dart board, cards, and the ever popular Ludo and snakes-and-ladders, in fact everything to make a contented staff.' Curiously enough, Miss Swainbank observed: 'I found here that class distinction began and ended in the Servants' Hall.'[104]

Another Scottish maidservant, Jean Rennie, born in 1914, had won a scholarship to university but was unable to take up her place because her father was unemployed. Having lost her own job in a mill, she got another as a housemaid: 'My greatest horror was the knowledge that I would have to submit to the badge of servitude – a cap and apron.' One compensation was the beauty of the castle and the gleaming kitchen, but she was appalled by seeing leftover butter and jam at tea in the servants' hall: 'I could remember so many hungry children – and here was good food being contemptuously pushed aside.'

She was quickly initiated into 'the mysteries of being a house-maid during the day. The beds, the "slops", the carpet-sweeping, the dusting. I gradually learnt whose job was which, and that one must not do anyone else's job. Not even to help them. So nobody helped me.' Her initial impressions of the cook were of 'a vast mountain of a woman in spotless white. When I came to know her afterwards she was a gem of goodness, honesty and generosity. But first, at work, she was rather frightening.'[105] This was no doubt the case with many senior servants and new juniors.

Of the more senior women in the English country-house household, the lady's maid retained a primary importance up until the Second World War, and perhaps a little beyond. Rosina Harrison was lady's maid to one of the liveliest hostesses of the era, the American Lady Astor. Born in 1899, the daughter of a stonemason on the Marquess of Ripon's estate in Yorkshire, from the first Rosina was determined to travel. Her mother advised her to train in dress-making and to learn French. She started as a 'Young Lady's Maid' to the young daughters of Lady Irene Tufton, in their house in Mayfair and at Appleby Castle, Cumberland, then worked for Lady Cranborne, daughter-in-law to the Marquess of Salisbury, with whom she first got her proper taste of travel in France and Italy.[106]

She arrived at Cliveden in 1928 to be a lady's maid to Phyllis Astor, Lady Astor's daughter, at a salary of £60 a year, nearly three times what she had been earning with Lady Cranborne. She was briefed on the Astor family by the famous steward, Mr Edwin Lee, who had been a sergeant major in the First World War. Her working conditions were good: 'My room at Cliveden was large, well decorated and comfortably furnished with bed, two easy chairs, a couch and two big wardrobes.'[107]

Rosina helped Phyllis Astor dress, maintained her clothes and accompanied her on visits: 'We went together to a few country house parties in Leicestershire, Rutland and Northamptonshire . . . and to the Duke of Buccleuch's palace in Scotland, Drumlanrig Castle. I was of course responsible for looking after riding habits and these weren't easy to cope with. Some evenings she'd come in soak-ing wet and spattered with mud, yet the next morning she would have to appear looking spotless.'[108] In 1928, Rosina travelled to the United States, after which she became Lady Astor's personal lady's maid.

At first she was overwhelmed by her employer's fiery temper and exacting demands but a turning point came when she stood up to her: 'My lady, from now on I intend to speak as I'm spoken to. Common people say please and thank you, ordinary people do not reprimand servants in front of others and ladies are supposed to be an example to all, and that is that.'[109] Lady Astor later apologised. In an aside that offers us an insight into how these relationships worked, Rosina Harrison observed: 'Now all this sounds very trivial, but if you want to know how it was possible for two people to live closely for thirty odd years it is important . . . as the years passed our relation-ship mellowed and the rows became more like verbal skirmishes.'[110]

In many accounts, the relationship of the family children of a country house to the servants attains a surprising pitch of intimacy and trust. It is notable that many people from aristocratic backgrounds growing up in the 1920s to the 1950s are inclined to say today that they 'were brought up by the servants'. For many twentieth-century biographers of the English country house, the most interesting aspect is the dynamic between children and domestic servants. One of the most memorable butlers of the late Victorian and Edwardian era is Henry Moat, who joined the household of Sir George Sitwell at Renishaw Hall in Derbyshire in 1893, first as footman and then butler-valet, where he took on a primary importance in the lives of the Sitwell children.

Mr Moat's profile in Sir Osbert's famous biography, which was written in such detail because of his conviction that his world was vanishing for ever, gives him a special place in English literature. Indeed, it gives him a substantial entry in the new *Oxford Dictionary of National Biography*. Sir Osbert's nephew, Sir Reresby, had vivid memories of this remarkable man, whose bedroom at Renishaw Hall had its own staircase to the butler's pantry, and from which a rod of iron was inserted through the plate-room door, thus securing the house's silver.

Mr Moat, together with the beloved nurse Davis 'who lived for children and their love', were for Sir George's three children, Edith, Osbert and Sacheverell, the mainstays of their emotional life during their early years. All three became famous writers. In *Cruel Month*, the first volume of his famous autobiography, *Left Hand! Right Hand!*, Sir Osbert examined this bond: 'Parents were aware that the child would be a nuisance, and a whole hedge of servants, in addition to the complex guardianship of nursery and schoolroom, was necessary, not so much to aid the infant as to screen him off from his father and mother.'[111] Thus, he argued, in a subtle way 'children and servants often found themselves in league against grown-ups, and employers. The female child sought shelter with the nurse and housekeeper and cook, the male in the [butler's] pantry. Certainly, I learnt more, far more, from talking to Henry and Pare in the pantry from their instinctive wisdom and humour, than from more academic sources.'[112]

Henry Moat, whose wonderfully irascible yet devoted relationship with Sir George is detailed in the same book, noted later that
Sir Osbert's *Who's Who* entry read: 'Educated during holidays from
Eton'. He was quick to retort: 'Well, Sir, I make bold to claim some
of that, because whether you were at Scarboro', Renishaw or
abroad, if you or Master Sachie wanted to know anything about
things on earth, the sea, under the earth or in the air above, you
generally came to me, even when you had a tutor, and often the
tutor came too.' This gently bantering relationship between employer
and employed, and their long-standing interdependence, are typical
of early-twentieth-century memoirs, illustrating that a butler might
be looked on as a friend by more than one generation of a family at
the same time.[113]

In this context it is interesting to note that the great
P.G. Wodehouse, inventor of that ultimate symbol of the skilful and
dedicated English manservant, Jeeves, grew up – typically for many
upper- and upper-middle-class children of his generation – in
England while his parents worked abroad. Wodehouse's biographer
Robert McCrum makes clear that this often meant staying with
aunts, clergyman and nautical uncles. As they lived on what
Wodehouse himself called 'the fringe of the butler belt', he observed
wryly: 'There always came a moment when my hostess, smiling one
of those smiles, suggested that it would be nice for [me] to go and
have tea in the servants' hall.' He learnt to laugh there, in the company of footmen and housemaids. 'I forgot to be shy and kidded
back and forth with the best of them.'[114] What psychological forces
were at work when, while in an internment camp in Germany
during the Second World War, he wrote a story in which a peer
returns to the stately home he has leased out, disguised as the
butler?[115] His first story about Blandings Castle has two people disguised as lady's-maid and valet manoeuvring their way through the
complex etiquette of the servants' hall.

Lavinia Smiley, one of the daughters of the Hon. Clive Pearson
who restored Parham Park in West Sussex, wrote a particularly
evocative account of a 1920s country-house childhood, titled *A Nice
Clean Plate*. As with so many memoirs of the early years of the

aristocracy, her recollections are interwoven with affectionate memories of servants, from maids to footmen:

The indoor staff at Parham (until 1939) consisted, with slight variations, of: Mr Cridland, the butler, Mr Hill, the valet, three footmen and the odd man, a hall boy and a night watchman. There was a housekeeper, Mrs Evans, her mother's lady's maid, Miss Metcalfe, the head housemaid (Jane), and three other housemaids, Mrs Dawson the cook, her two kitchen maids, a scullery-maid, and a still-room maid, as well as (a succession of) nannies and a nursery maid. Outside there was a stable staff, headed by Mr Lancaster and a team of gardeners, as well as a house carpenter called Mr Gee, and an electrician called Mr Greenfield. There was another housekeeper, and three maids, who stayed in their London house.[116]

Lady Smiley recalled her parents' staff with affection: 'we found life there [tea in the housekeeper's room with the senior staff for company] less of a strain than it often was "through the front".' She could recall the family ritual of children descending to the drawing room for 'Children's Hour', when they spent time with their parents, 'During "Children's Hour" one of the footmen would come in and put coal on the fire, and possibly dear Mr Cridland the butler would come creaking in with a message for my mother on a silver salver . . . [her father] had a very happy relationship with Mr Cridland, who had been sent to Cambridge with him as a young valet. They had been together ever since . . . My father was much cast down when Cridland died; they were very fond of each other.'

Some relationships were more strained: 'The first nanny I can remember was a horror. She was ugly and a bully and was eventually dispatched, taking with her a great deal of our gloom. She beat us with a hairbrush, and threatened to put sticking plaster on our mouths if we committed the unspeakable crime of Answering Back. And burnt our hands on the tea pot.'

Typically for memoirs of an interwar, country-house life, 'Nanny was permanently at war with the cook and would send insulting messages inside the vegetable dishes: "The children cannot be expected to eat this."'[117]

Mrs Richard Cavendish, looking back on her childhood at

Compton Beauchamp, Oxfordshire, recollected that her parents would never be there during the week: 'Nanny Abbott took charge of us and during the week we did exactly what Nanny said. We had walks, and then we rode our ponies . . . we messed about and had a few lessons.' She had warm memories of one family retainer: 'the butler, Frederick, was the nicest fellow that ever walked. When my parents were away, we were allowed to fish from his pantry window into the moat.' Not unusually in those days, their governesses 'never stayed, because we were so nasty to them.'[118]

In 2008, Sir John ('Jack') Leslie, Baronet, explained the make-up of the household of Castle Leslie, County Monaghan, in the 1920s and 1930s. At the time of writing, he lives there still and has recently celebrated his ninetieth birthday, although the house is now run in part as a hotel by his niece, Sammy Leslie.

> Mr Wells, our last butler, who was English, was here through the war, and for a while afterwards we had Mr Murray, although he was more like a senior footman. The butler in the early part of the century was Mr Adams, with two footmen under him; at that time maids slept in rooms accessible only by passing through the housekeeper's room. I think most of our junior servants tended to come from the estate or local village. My grandmother lived here until she died in 1944, and [between the 1920s and 1930s] she certainly gave the orders for the meals for the day to our cook, then Annie Simpson.
>
> My father was a bit of a revolutionary and a Roman Catholic convert, more interested in forestry and writing, and I think he just took the servants and the smooth running of the house as a natural part of life.

His father was, in his youth, very influenced by the Castle Leslie forester, Mr Vogan, who, according to his sister, was described by their grandmother as the boys' 'real governess', even though they had two, one French and one German.

> My grandmother also had a German personal maid, called Winter. In the kitchen there was a cook, kitchenmaid and scullery-maid, and the housekeeper, Rose Mead, who looked after all the female staff and was level with the butler. There were three housemaids and the junior

one looked after the nursery. There was a butler and a footman (sometimes two), the odd man, who looked after the boiler and the fuel, and the coachman-chauffeur. I think there was a pantry boy. The under servants always ate in the servants' hall, which was under the dining room, and the upper servants in the butler's room, which was under the drawing room.

I had governesses in the late 1920s and early 1930s, a whole string of them, all from England, and then I had tutors, a Mr Marks, recommended by the headmaster of Downside, and a Mr Ireland. They would eat with us in the dining room, and dress for dinner every evening. He slept in a room near mine and I can remember him calling out, telling me to switch off my light and stop reading in bed.[119]

The Hon. Mary Birkbeck, daughter of the 2nd Lord Somerleyton, was born in 1926 and grew up at Somerleyton Hall, Norfolk. She has vivid memories of life there in the 1930s. Between 1928 and 1935, the family shared the house with her father's parents who owing to ill health were unable to cope with managing the estate:

During the intervening seven years we were all together – parents living in the north wing, grandparents in the large rooms behind baize doors and us children in the nurseries on the top floor. The other top floor rooms were bedrooms for the house and kitchenmaids. Male servants, footmen and so on, slept in the lower tower rooms or on the ground floor near the pantries.

Mrs Birkbeck recalls being aware of the early start made by the maids and how they would not be seen in the front of the house after the family had risen.

There were eighteen indoor staff before the war including Nanny, the nurserymaid, and two ladies' maids who cared personally for my mother and grandmother. Mr Cole the butler lived with his family in the village and came in every day on a bicycle.

We children lived more or less in the nursery, supervised by Nanny and waited on by a series of nurserymaids. The favourite of these was Violet – known affectionately as 'Oddy'. She later married William Beechner, the head footman, known by us as 'Willikins'. The latter often accompanied us, plus Nanny, for happy picnics by the lake where he taught us how to swim – on the end of a rope.

There is no criticism of my parents but it is hard in modern times to realise how little we children saw of them – it was simply not the fashion. Our parents probably saw more of us than most landowning families, in that we were routinely dressed up by Nanny and taken down after tea for a 'children's hour' when we played cards and listened to the gramophone. In the summer they used to take us for picnics. There were always wonderful small ponies led by Jack, my father's ex-soldier groom who taught us to ride.

For Mrs Birkbeck as a child:

The stables and gardens were full of lovely people – always so nice and kind to the children and inclined to take our sides in the event of misbehaviour behind our parents' backs. My childhood by any standards was privileged, but it had some disadvantages compared to a modern childhood; for instance, because of the class structure it was incredibly lonely. I was not allowed to go to the village school and we seldom saw other children unless they were brought in chauffeur-driven cars 'to play' from other equally privileged establishments.

When war was declared in 1939, 'Everything changed. Everyone fit to do so was called up for some form of service and Somerleyton Hall itself became an advanced Dressing Station.' Looking back on those pre-war days, Mrs Birkbeck feels that in many ways she was 'brought up by the servants' and stresses her personal view of them: 'they were wonderful people – my grateful memories of their friendship, loyalty and love know no bounds.'[120]

Sir Peregrine Worsthorne, former editor of the *Telegraph*, recalled in his recent memoirs the butler who served his mother and his grandmother, James Burton: 'James embodied job satisfaction long before it was invented . . . Having him as a member of our family brought us many advantages over and above the advantages of what he did as a butler so well. If we broadened his horizons, he certainly broadened ours.'[121]

Sir Peregrine also recalled how James, a First World War veteran of the trenches, became as butler: 'an expert on the care and mainten-ance of beautiful furniture, pictures silver, objets d'art as well as wines – notably champagnes.' He was also a walking encyclopaedia on 'the minutiae of good manners', famously out-staring Winston Churchill who had tried to grab a bottle of champagne out of his hands at the dinner table.'[122]

These affectionate accounts of what seems now a different world remind us that such households persisted solidly up to the eve of the Second World War. These communities, and those who grew up and trained in them, are alive in the memories of thousands of people who were in service in the second half of the century, during which country-house staffs have metamorphosed into something rich and new.

8

Staying On: A Changing World
The later Twentieth Century

T HE SECOND WORLD War was clearly a major watershed in the style, character and condition of the servant body employed in country houses. Nothing would ever be the same. Although some owners of large establishments reassembled their sometimes extensive staffs immediately after the war, many more found it simply too difficult. The diaries of James Lees-Milne attest to the struggles of aristocratic ladies suddenly trying to run such houses without enough help.[1]

This scarcity of personnel had a huge impact on the practicality, even desirability, of maintaining a large historic house. Many were given up, either taken into care by the National Trust, leased, or sold for institutional uses, such as schools or hotels. A critical factor was the inability to recruit new servants, not merely to look after the landowner's family personally, but also to maintain the contents and fabric of the house. The loss of the 'odd man' who had once swept the gutters and cleared the drains was in many ways as significant as the loss of a steward or a butler.[2]

Those estate owners who had survived the trials of the immediate post-war years, keeping together their houses and collections in the teeth of every adverse circumstance, continued to call on the services of certain key individuals, supplemented by daily cleaners. On the bigger estates they could often draw on support from the estate works department for some of the essential care and maintenance that in earlier times had fallen to the indoor staff.

Indeed, in certain country houses those who had trained up in service returned to their pre-war employment and worked on into retirement in the 1960s and 1970s. For some observers, this is when the final watershed came: when the whole generation trained before the war finally retired.[3] The remarkable story of Harvey Lane, the butler of Leigh Manor in Shropshire, is symbolic of this. He trained as a house-boy and then as a footman to William Bridgeman, later 1st Viscount Bridgeman, becoming butler in 1920 and remaining with the family until his death in 1989. He served both the 2nd Viscount Bridgeman and his grandson and heir, David Stacey, many years his junior.[4]

When demobbed from the armed forces, Mr Lane returned to his former post as butler in 1945, but with little additional help. Mr Stacey observed with wry amusement the silent tussle between man and master:

> at every opportunity [Harvey] would bring out the silver and the white linen tablecloth and make sure that the dining room was used in the style which he expected from a lord. My grandfather, a man of great humility and no pretension at all, hated this kind of behaviour – he would have been much happier eating in the kitchen – but Harvey would always get his way and would appear in a white jacket and insist on serving at the table.

Mr Lane continued to work, despite being confined to a wheelchair, right up until the 1980s, becoming a close friend to his employer, who was young enough to be his grandson.[5]

The size of post-war staffs generally depended on the age and income of the employer. The older generations often tried to stick to the way of life they had been brought up to, but were usually forced to reduce staff numbers over the decades in the face of higher taxes, inflation, and a wholly modern desire for increased privacy.[6] By the 1970s, the advantages of new technologies, which had promised so much in the interwar years whilst not actually delivering very much, had begun to make a noticeable difference. This was especially true of central heating and modern vacuum cleaners. By the 1980s and 1990s, the younger generation of country-house owners were accus-tomed to doing much more of their own day-to-day cooking.

Where staff were still employed, they were also expected to be adaptable and flexible. This meant that while some traditional titles survived, individuals often took on much wider duties than had ever been demanded of them before. Mr Lane at Leigh Manor found himself doing the job of butler, footman, houseboy and gardener all rolled into one. As David Stacey points out, 'but for the fact he couldn't drive he would have become the chauffeur as well.'[7]

By the end of the twentieth century and the early years of the twenty-first, there is such diversity in domestic service and it has been so little researched that it is impossible to discuss entirely representative patterns of staffing. Equally, although the word servant is no longer used, most country-house owners continue to employ some staff to make living in their houses feasible. Very often, without staff it is impossible to make opening their houses and gardens to the public viable and profitable. A by-product of this has been an increase in the colleagueship and camaraderie among staff that had so declined in country houses in the immediate post-war years.[8]

Certain themes seem to be representative, so this chapter will examine a sequence of individual stories, based on interviews, to illustrate some of those key themes; such as the continuance of practical support, the link between members of staff employed on a large estate, the prevalence of long service, long-standing associations with the estate, and personal loyalty. Many domestic and estate staff on the point of retirement today began working in the late 1950s and 1960s, often having just left school at the age of fifteen. They can remember working alongside senior staff who had been trained in the 1920s and 1930s, in a world more intimately connected with the late Victorian and Edwardian apogee than might seem apparent.

First, it is important to understand the dramatic impact of the Second World War. Between 1939 and 1945 most major country houses were turned over to wartime uses, whether for military occupation, to provide a home to evacuated schoolchildren, or to house government departments relocated far from the hazards of the Blitz. As for their staff, young men in domestic service often went into the armed forces while women either joined the auxiliaries, or helped the war effort by working in munitions factories, much as they had in the First World War.[9]

At the end of the war things were never going to 'return to normal' (not least because change had first begun in the 1920s). The economic and physical strains of worldwide conflict were followed by the Labour landslide victory of the 1945 election, leading to a massive increase in taxation, especially death duties. All of this seemed to herald a new age in which the communities of the old country-house world could hardly expect to return to pre-war practices.

Many country houses simply did not revert to private domestic occupation. A sad number of important historic buildings were abandoned, sold off and ultimately demolished. These losses to our culture were catalogued by the Victoria and Albert Museum's 1973 exhibition, *The Destruction of the Country House*, which showed how the trend, which had begun in the 1920s and 1930s, only intensified with the economic and political situation after the war.[10]

In her illuminating account of a life of service, first as maid, then as cook, in town houses in Hove and in London, titled *Below Stairs* (1970), Margaret Powell described returning to domestic work during the Second World War, having left it some years earlier: 'Large houses that were once opulently furnished and had had a large staff were now reduced to no staff at all; just someone coming in for a few hours daily. Much of their lovely stuff had gone; they had had to sell it to pay their income tax.' She worked mostly for elderly ladies, who 'accepted their change in status with fortitude'. One told her wistfully, as she polished a silver tray, of the silver service that had once stood on it: 'when the butler carried it into the drawing room, it used to look a picture of safety and security. We never thought our way of life would change.'[11]

When the collapse of the country-house world was recognised in the immediate post-war era, leading civil servant Sir Ernest Gowers was commissioned by the government to write a report, eventually published in 1950, on these threats to the national heritage as they occurred.

> In past times, the great houses of this country and their grounds were maintained by their owners mainly from the rent of their estates. The estate and mansion formed a single economic whole; the former provided not only income and produce but also servants to run the house and craftsmen for the upkeep of its fabric. Now owing to economic

and social changes, we are faced with a disaster comparable only to that which the country suffered with the Dissolution of the Monasteries in the sixteenth century.[12]

Whilst he could see that taxation, meaning estate duty and increased income tax, was primarily responsible for this 'impending catastrophe', Gowers thought that problems in recruiting staff could prove almost as decisive:

A secondary factor is the growing difficulty of getting, and the expense of paying, the necessary staff, both indoor and outdoor. In the heyday of these houses wages were low and service at the big house, around which the whole social life of the neighbourhood revolved, was much sought after. Those conditions have disappeared. There is not now the labour available for domestic service; there is not the desire to do it; and there is not the money to pay for it.[13]

For those who did return to service, there were both disadvantages and advantages. The disadvantages were almost always that the senior posts survived but without the support of the traditional young trainees, learning their skills by serving the servants, and essentially doing the heavier and messier work. In an interview given in 1971, Mrs Davidson, cook at Crathorne Hall, Yorkshire, remembered the impact of the Second World War on the life of the house: 'the men had to go to war, then we had parlour maids . . . After the war there weren't nearly so many servants. It was the same as it is now, me and Nanny and Mr Jeffreys [the butler], a housemaid, a kitchenmaid and someone else to help.' The family shut down a part of the house and created a new kitchen nearer the dining room. 'We worked harder after the war; you just had to fill in all sorts.'[14]

The advantages were often the relaxation of the rigid class distinctions that had persisted up until the Second World War. Those skilled servants who returned to service were increasingly highly valued and, despite their extended workloads, were also likely to be treated with greater consideration and given greater independence than they had experienced before the war. Mrs Davidson approved of the removal of social barriers: 'the young people coming now [as guests], compared with those earlier in the century, are nicer. We were servants, I mean we looked to them [the earlier generation] as if they were superhuman beings, and they weren't . . . The changes that have taken place are for the better, in the old days you worked hard for people and you never saw them.' Her employer's grandson, Lord Crathorne, remembers with gratitude the contribution made by the whole household in Mrs Davidson's day to his family's life: 'They took tremendous pride in their work. I recall Mrs Davidson writing a letter about how hard the work was, and then on the next page she said that they were the "happiest days of my life".'[15]

Some domestic servants had remained in service throughout the war and were perhaps in a unique position to consider its impact on their world. When the Second World War broke out, Rosina Harrison, Lady Astor's lady's maid, was still a senior figure, if in a much reduced but busy crew: 'some of the men were called up, others enlisted, and some women went into the Services or industry.' More time was spent in Plymouth, for which Lady Astor was MP, whilst Lord Astor opened a hospital in the gardens of Cliveden, with a wing given over to nurses and doctors.[16]

During the war, the house was still managed well by the steward, housekeeper and a skeleton staff, most of them dailies, but Rosina felt that 'the old order had changed' before her eyes. It seemed to her a 'period of stagnation for town and country houses. It was also a time of enlightenment, too, for in many places where for years scant attention had been paid to kitchens and the servants' quarters below stairs, mistresses were now paying the penalty.' Before the war they had hardly visited such rooms, but now, 'They were having to work down there themselves and, suddenly, with the bombing, the basement rooms became the most important in the house – and the most lived in. Yet many of them were damp, dark, poorly heated and their cooking and cleaning facilities were old fashioned.'[17]

There were other, fundamental changes: 'no longer did the distinction of servant and master apply. We were family. We'd soldiered together, looked death in the face and suffered the loss of many friends. We'd been shown qualities which no other circumstances would have demonstrated to us, and had shared emotions that would otherwise have remained hidden.'[18]

The appalled discovery by Miss Harrison's mistress of how inadequate and uncomfortable kitchens could be was echoed in the charming memoir, *The Private Life of a Country House, 1912–39* (1980), by Lesley Lewis, recalling her country-house childhood in Essex: 'A scullery opened out of the kitchen, its two wide shallow sinks under the window having wooden plate racks on one side. It was not until I washed up here myself, in the 1939 war, that I realised how inconvenient the equipment was. Possibly the sinks had not been too low in the days when most people were shorter, but the width across them to the taps was singularly ill-adapted to any human frame.'[19]

Some domestic servants found being in the armed forces almost easy by comparison to the discipline and long hours of domestic service. Arthur Inch, the son of a butler and later a butler himself, was first a footman to the Marquess of Londonderry. He served in the RAF during the Second World War, which seemed to him almost a liberation: 'In fact, the comparatively shorter hours in the forces was a revelation to me. I'd never had so much free time plus all the free passes when going on leave.'[20] After the war, he did not return to work in service until the 1950s, after which he became butler to the Kleinworts, remaining with the family for twenty years. One of his co-footmen from Londonderry House, who also went into the RAF, became a civilian pilot after the war rather than re-enter domestic service.[21] When he retired, Arthur Inch was adviser both to the National Trust and to the makers of the film *Gosford Park*.

The plunge in the customary level of household staff must have hit some country-house owners hard. When asked when he thought the fundamental change occurred, Sir John Leslie replied: 'In most big houses the staffs stayed the same until the 1950s. The Wingfields, Lord and Lady Powerscourt, certainly had footmen in livery at Powerscourt until the early 1950s, and there was a gatekeeper with a top hat and a cockade. Here at Castle Leslie, there were about ten servants in the house before the war, then it fell to five, then one, and finally only people coming in from the village. It happened gradually, and you just acclimatised to the change. However, we probably took them too much for granted.'[22]

Barbara Cartland, born in 1901, was familiar with the comfort and security represented by the well-staffed country house. A small section on managing staff in her *Etiquette Handbook: A Guide to Good Behaviour from the Boudoir to the Boardroom* (1962) is testament to how different that world had become: 'only a few people today are fortunate enough to have living-in servants, who are no longer called servants but "the staff". . . . It should be obvious that to retain the services and remain in the good graces of these invaluable people the old-fashioned autocratic attitude is as dead as Victorian bustles.' Above all, she said, 'it is no longer good manners to keep people "in their place".'[23]

Her advice on giving dinner parties in an increasingly servant-less age is interspersed with comments on how to manage 'Without staff'. At first, she considers the case with staff: 'For a dinner party of eight or ten I have four courses: Fish or soup/Meat or game/An exciting pudding/Savoury/Dessert/Coffee/ *Without staff: Three courses will be plenty for your party.*'[24] Some aspects of her advice, however, have a curious echo of manuals of housekeeping going back to the seventeenth century: 'Female servants should always receive orders only from the wife; males from the husband. If occasion arises for one or the other to pass on an order then it should be "Mr Brown wants you to . . ." or "Mrs Brown asked me to tell you that . . ." These days it is rarely possible to say "your master" or "your mistress".'[25]

She took the view that some rules still persisted when addressing staff, especially if you were fortunate enough to employ any of these fast-vanishing people: 'Housekeeper (almost an extinct race) is called Mrs by her employers and the staff whether she is married or not. Cook-Housekeeper is called Mrs by her employers and staff whether she is married or not . . . *Butler* (more usually a manservant these days) is called by his surname only by his employers and "Mr" by the staff.'[26]

During the 1950s and 1960s, to supply the gaps left in houses, in both town and country, there was a sharp rise in domestic servants brought in from overseas. Mrs Cartland cautiously advised: '*Foreign Staff.* Most people these days employ one or two foreigners in place of the aforementioned staff. These are usually called by whichever name is the more easily pronounced.'[27] In the same period, it became more difficult to recruit native domestic staff. Many who entered domestic service, not only from all over Europe but from places as remote as St Helena and Jamaica, were unlikely to have been trained in the traditional country-house system, yet eager to find employment in a difficult economic climate.[28]

At Chatsworth, the then duchess was unable to recruit new servants prior to opening the house to the public for the first time in 1948. The present Dowager Duchess observes: 'I imagine because people had been so badly paid in service before the war.' Her mother-in-law's path crossed with that of the Hungarian sisters Ilona and Elizabeth Solymossy, cook and housemaid respectively to Kathleen, Marchioness of Hartington, the Devonshires' widowed daughter-in-law, who had died young earlier that same year. The Devonshires invited them to recruit a team of nine of their compatriots to help prepare and clean the house for opening. As the duchess recalls in her book, they 'immediately made their presence felt by setting about the rooms methodically and thoroughly, dressed like Tabitha Twitchit in cotton kerchiefs against the dust, while delicious smells of goulash in the kitchen passage reminded one that the Hungarian takeover was on'. In their capable hands, the house was made ready for its public opening in Easter 1949.[29]

There were similar patterns in other great houses. At Weston Park, Shropshire, in the 1960s, the Earls of Bradford employed domestic servants from St Helena, one man recalling spending much of his youth barefoot and then, as a teenager, on his first day in England learning to tie a white tie. At Longleat in the 1970s, the Marquess and Marchioness of Bath were looked after by a couple from Portugal (although in his youth there had been forty-three indoor servants); since the late 1950s, the Bromley-Davenports at Capesthorne Hall, Cheshire, have been taken care of by an Italian, Gilda. For fifty-one years, Gilda Mion has been their cook and housekeeper, catering for shooting parties every weekend in the season, with her husband, Luciano, working as a painter and decorator to the estate and eventually in the house, too.[30]

Whilst those born and brought up in houses with large staffs might struggle to manage their own households with a minimum of help, it must have been doubly hard for the generation of staff who had been trained in traditional country-house service and attained senior positions to discover that they had little or none of the support that in their youth they had themselves supplied as junior servants.

Mrs Davidson's observations on the greater workload of post-war service are echoed again over and over. As former butler Stanley Ager pointed out in his memoirs, those who remained in service, or returned to it, had to combine in one person duties that had once been the preserve of many.

Mr Ager was born when Edward VII was on the throne, and his training dated back to the 1920s. He was a butler for more than three decades, retiring in 1975. His book, *The Butler's Guide to Clothes Care, Managing the Table, Running the Home and Other Graces*, published in 1981, includes a short memoir that looks back with warmth on his years of experience of working in beautiful historic houses.[31]

Retirement seemed strange to him: 'At first I didn't feel right being out of uniform and in casual clothes in the morning.' Otherwise, he said, he was content to cease working. 'After all, I have travelled the world, lived in some magnificent houses and been lucky with my employers. But I still miss the staff. They fought amongst themselves and they always caused me far more trouble than the Lord and Lady – yet I miss them most of all.' As this narrative has shown, the community of the staff could be all-important to the enjoyment of being a domestic servant.[32]

Mr Ager began his life in service in 1922, aged fourteen, as the hall boy at Croome Court, Worcestershire, 'the lowest servant of all', in the household of Lord Coventry. 'On my first day it seemed like a house full of servants; there were some forty people of all ages working there. Everyone was friendly except the housekeeper.' As for so many young people in the nineteenth and early twentieth centuries, his choice seemed made for him: 'after my parents died, entering service seemed the best way of supporting myself.'

Like many younger or more junior-ranking servants, learning the ropes, he did most of his work 'in the servants' quarters at the back of the house. I didn't go to the front where the family lived except for the dining room, until I had worked at Croome Court for six months. When I did, the flowers in the reception rooms struck me first of all . . . I was awed by the general opulence – the silver candlesticks and inkstands on the writing desks, the tapestries on the walls and the thick rugs.'[33]

As was usual in the pre-war era, he learnt his trade by waiting on the senior members of staff: 'most young servants moved to a different house after about a year or so to gain promotion and to experience how various houses were run.' Mr. Ager worked in several, including St Michael's Mount in Cornwall, returning there in 1930 to become valet to the 2nd Lord St Levan.[34] 'I travelled all around the world with him. Wherever he wanted to go, he just went. If it was cold when he returned to England, we'd pop off again. I made all the arrangements, bought the tickets and more or less made the world smooth for him and his party.'[35] In 1933 he married and left to become butler to a Mr Dunkels, then to a Colonel Trotter in Berwickshire.

After serving in the army during the Second World War, he returned to work for the colonel, who died shortly afterwards. Mr Ager was then invited to St Michael's Mount once more as butler to the 3rd Lord St Levan, who had succeeded his uncle: 'I said I'd come back for three months, which turned into nearly thirty years.'

Cultural shifts during this period made their impact. In the 1920s, 'when I was a footman, the senior staff stood very much on their dignity, and the rest of the staff were acutely aware of their status within the house. No one could help out anyone else. We didn't help the kitchen people, however busy they were, and we certainly wouldn't help a housemaid.'[36] Two decades later, the pattern was very different. 'After the war most people were unable to afford the same amount of staff. I saw great changes in service as our people's life-styles became less grand. In my youth the butler was always available if the family needed him; otherwise, he merely supervised the staff. He had worked hard all his life, and he wasn't going to continue if he could help it!'[37]

By the 1960s, his role had altered out of all recognition: 'A butler in the old days would never have dreamed of doing as much day-to-day work as I did. He wouldn't have cleaned the silver, laid the table or seen to it that the reception rooms were orderly – those jobs belonged to the first footman. Nor did any of my staff wait on me as they would have done on a butler in the past.'[38] He kept his standards high, and was very proud of the many staff he had trained, some of whom had gone on into royal service. He was careful to retain his classic butler's uniform from the 1930s until his retirement: 'a butler would wear a black evening tailcoat all day long. In the evening he changed from the gray trousers into a pair of black trousers with a fine silk line running down the side.'[39]

Although nannies and au pairs are familiar to us today, they cannot replace the sense of absolute safety produced by the English country-house nursery and the classic British nanny. This was very much the experience of the present Lord Crathorne, whose childhood was spent at Crathorne Hall in Yorkshire in the 1940s and 1950s.[40] He was looked after by Nanny Messenger, who was born in 1891 and came to work for his family in 1939, living at Crathorne Hall until her death in 1976.

During the 1940s and 1950s, she was one of only half a dozen indoor staff. When his parents had first moved into the house, there was also a butler, Mr Jeffreys, a cook, Mrs Davidson, a housekeeper and an assistant cook. 'The whole family had tea in her room every day for thirty-six years. I have tremendously warm memories of her; she was a perfectly wonderful lady who epitomised all the best things about the English nanny. After my mother died in 1969, she really became the core of family life.'[41]

Nursery tea, with Nanny and the children, became such an institution that every guest in the house would be expected. As Lord Crathorne's father was a government minister, over the years this included Harold Macmillan, Alec Douglas-Home, and Ted Heath. Later there were university friends like John Cleese and Tim Brooke-Taylor. 'It was always at four o'clock, and Cook prepared cakes, while Nanny made very delicate strawberry jam sandwiches. She heard all sorts of interesting and personal things at the tea table, but never repeated a word, never gossiped about it.'[42]

When asked whether his nanny was ever a rival to his mother in his affections, he replied:

No, not at all, she would always make it clear that my mother was the most important person in our lives. I remember my mother remarking how, during the war years, Nanny would pack away the clothes we had grown out of, so that they would be there for our children, such was her confidence that the world would go on as before. Actually, Nanny made a lot of our clothes, she was endlessly knitting. I can remember her asking my mother how she liked buttons fixed. She never ever got cross with David and me, but somehow discipline was enforced by the way she treated us; she led by example, I suppose.[43]

The daily routine

began with breakfast in the nursery, which was on the first floor, and part of the servants' wing. There was a nursery, a small scullery, bed-rooms for my brother and me, and one for Nanny beyond that. We had all our meals with Nanny in the nursery, although we might have lunch with our parents in the dining room if there were no other guests. Nanny would read to us, and spend time with us making things out of paper and pipe cleaners.

In the summer we would often walk down to the river with a picnic and play there. If we were playing outside she had a little horn she would blow to summon us back for meals, like the ones game-keepers used at the end of a drive. She had a great love of nature and would explain it all to us, birds, trees and fields. It was also wartime and we couldn't drive anywhere. We were, I think, the focus of her whole life and we couldn't have been closer or happier. It was a very idyllic life. She really created a very idyllic world for us.[44]

After the death of the present Lord Crathorne's father, the huge family home, built for an entirely Edwardian way of life, was turned into a comfortable hotel. Since the 1970s the present Lord Crathorne has lived in a much smaller modern house on the same estate. While nannies are a familiar feature in country houses – as they are still in many thousands of English families today – Miss Messenger belongs to the last era of the career nanny, who would expect to devote her whole working life to one family. It is the end of a long tradition that is centuries old.[45]

The forced retreats and adaptations of country-house service are amply illustrated by the career of another butler, this time from a younger generation. He began service immediately after the war in a house with a full complement of staff that went through several phases of reduction. Micheal Kenneally, butler to the Sykes family at Sledmere for forty years, occupies a special place in Yorkshire country-house legend. He arrived from Ireland in 1952 to become pantry boy to landowner and baronet, Sir Richard Sykes. As one of Sir Richard's sons, Christopher Simon Sykes, recalled, Sledmere 'was still run on an Edwardian scale, with a house staff of at least 10, as well as nannies, governesses and chauffeurs.'[46]

A strict hierarchy was in place, 'at the top of which was the butler, Cassidy (never Mr in those days), and Michael Kenneally at the bottom. He slept in a room in the attics. If a visiting servant came to stay who outranked him, the pantry boy had to move out on to a truckle bed in the corridor.' As Mr Sykes later remarked: 'Imagine anyone putting up with that now.'[47]

Kenneally became footman and then in 1959 butler. According to Mr Sykes, 'He turned buttling into an art form. He dressed the part to perfection, black jacket and pinstripes for formal daywear; a white apron for cleaning the silver; and a black tailcoat for grand dinners. Those under him were drilled in the laying of an impeccable table.'[48] Legendary for his pranks, Mr Kenneally once tried to serve dessert from a bicycle, dressing up as a maid and curtseying to Prince Bernhard of the Netherlands. He was also described as liable to 'over-indulge in butler's perks' – unfinished bottles of wine. Mr Sykes says: 'As children we spent all our time in the kitchen areas, more than in the front part of the house. Michael was like a friendly adult figure and our parents never objected to us spending our time there.'[49]

Inevitably, Mr Kenneally had to contend with the inevitable staff shrinkage, even though the household continued to be run on an 'Edwardian scale' until the death of Sir Richard Sykes in 1978. The house and estate were inherited by his son, Sir Tatton, who employed a smaller staff. Mr Kenneally had to run 'a pared-down household in which he found himself as much janitor as butler'. In addition to his traditional duties, he found, like many modern butlers, that 'he became clock winder, boiler man, electrician, and cellar man and dogkeeper. He could turn his hand to anything.'

Mr Kenneally died in 1999, only fifteen days after retiring. Christopher Simon Sykes, Sir Tatton's brother, observes: 'He was not replaced, partly because it would have been so difficult to replace Michael; it is today a much more mobile profession and the school-trained butler is a rather more mobile figure, unlikely to spend his whole career with one family.'[50]

Mr Kenneally was only one among many who defined life at Sledmere in the 1950s of Christopher Simon Sykes's childhood, described in his book, *The Big House* (2005): 'the person we were all most in awe of in the house was Dorothy, the housekeeper. [She was] short, with pebble-lens spectacles . . . a devout Catholic, with a strong character and a short temper, which meant she was absolutely not to be crossed'. Like all housekeepers from the seventeenth century onwards, 'she knew every inch of the house like the back of her hand and woe betide anyone who moved anything without her permission.'

The centre of her world was the two pantries, tall rooms with tiled floors and huge china sinks, repositories for the brushes and dusters, mops, buckets and cleansers 'with which her team of four or five ladies would arm themselves for their daily battle against dirt and dust.' They started at dawn, so that the house awoke to the sound of the shutters being opened and the smell of fires being lit.[51]

Mr Sykes also recalls the chauffeur and valet Jack Clark, who had worked for his father since the late 1930s and returned to his post after wartime service. Clark 'saw more of Papa than he did of his wife, Lilian, who ran the village post office'. 'Jack', as he was known, was 'the living incarnation of Jeeves', always dressed immaculately in a blue suit, plus his chauffeur's hat. His first duties of the day were as valet, taking Sir Richard his breakfast, running his bath and laying out his clothes.

Mr Sykes remembers Jack saying, 'I always chose his clothes because I knew exactly what he would wear.' He spent the rest of the day in the garage, until the evening when he would lay out his father's dinner jacket, even if there were no guests. When his father went down for drinks, 'he would turn down the bed and lay out his pyjamas. If there were guests he would help in the dining room.' In fact, Mr Sykes says that Jack was so hard-working that he would often be found helping with the washing up in houses where his employer was staying.[52]

Sledmere is now looked after by a team of dailies who come in from the local village. There is still a full-time cook, Mrs Maureen Magee, who has been there for twenty-seven years, beginning in 1982, and has strong memories of working with Michael Kenneally. She took over from a previous cook, 'who worked with me and showed me what was what. She told me lots of short cuts and high-lighted things in the recipe books that were family favourites.'[53] There 'was still a full-time housekeeper and butler, Michael, then', and extra help would be brought in for shooting parties. When the shooting is let now, 'the same family come every year and stay in the house. I cook for them too. This includes a good breakfast, a shoot lunch at the house, of two courses, cheese and celery, and then dinner of three courses, cheese, celery and coffee.'[54]

Mrs Magee says: 'I think sometimes it has been like two gener-ations since I arrived. Sir Tatton had just taken over when I came, and is much more informal than his parents, who changed every night for dinner.' The country-house tradition is maintained, however: 'Food is served at table and guests help themselves, although some things like a first course or fruit fool can look attractive if served in indi-vidual portions. This is not the country-house tradition and the old butler Michael would say: "It's not a café, you know!" The advantage is that guests take only what they like and there is no waste.'[55]

Tea continues to be served in silver teapots by maids dressed in black and white. Mrs Magee loves to see everything prepared for a grand dinner party: 'The housemaids clean the silver; everything comes out on the polished mahogany. The girls take a great pride in the presentation and arrange a display down the middle of the table. It can look absolutely wonderful, with the drapes drawn, and the fire lit.'

Today Mrs Magee shares the cooking of shoot dinners with friend and colleague Hester (a specialist in desserts: 'She's marvellous, I don't know how I would manage without her. She is in her thirties and very energetic'), who also runs the teashop for the visitors to the house. Opening houses to the public often brought new blood into country-house staffs, making them larger than they were in the immediate post-war years.[56]

Although Mrs Magee originally came from a different part of Yorkshire, the family of her husband Ken, whom she met at Sledmere, have a long connection to the Sledmere estate. Ken's father was the farm bailiff, and he himself used to work at the famous Sledmere stud, founded in 1801. Now he works part-time in the gardens. They live today in a lodge to the estate.

In the smaller staffs of the 1950s and 1960s, the stalwarts of country-house life were often a married couple, living in the house and providing devoted care, both to the building and to the family, who because of the demands of their other estates or commitments in London might themselves often be in residence for only a few months of the year.[57] One such couple, Alec and Annie Bagshaw, lived in and looked after Boughton House in Northamptonshire in the 1950s, 1960s and early 1970s, working there for two successive Dukes of Buccleuch and their families. Not only was the panelling in the great hall made by Mr Bagshaw but he also catalogued the armoury and prepared it for display to the visiting public. Their daughter, Mrs Rosalinde Tebbut, offers a fascinating testimony to their lives.

> My father was born in 1909, and started in the estates workshop in 1932. He was a journeyman before coming to Boughton; his grandfather was a carpenter attached to Boughton too. From 1942, my father was in the Royal Navy and when he came out in 1945 he was attached directly to Boughton House, helping to keep the house going.
>
> When I grew up we lived in the village of Warkton. My mother worked at Boughton as a housemaid, because my father was already employed there as a carpenter. About the time I got married in 1956, Mrs Foy, the housekeeper, retired and my mother took over from her. Mrs Foy had been quite a traditional type, and the butler, Mr Batts, used to look after the dining room, the wine cellar, the silver and service. My parents lived in from 1957 and retired in the early 1970s, by which time my father had been working at Boughton for forty-five years.[58]

The Bagshaws were placed in sole charge of Boughton while the duke, his family and other staff travelled between London and their other estates, Bowhill in the Borders and Drumlanrig: 'My mother and father enjoyed their work, and always took their annual holidays when the duke and duchess moved to Scotland. The butler and cook would go with them to their other estates and each house had its own housekeeper.'

Most of the housework was done by daily cleaners, while Mr Bagshaw, although officially the carpenter, effectively became the man of all works and custodian:

> My father also did things like picking up the duke from the station. A lot of the staff at Boughton then would travel down from Scotland to live in while the family were there and then go back again when they left.
>
> They were wonderful employers. When someone wrote a book saying how horrible working as a servant was, my mother was really indignant and said she had been wonderfully treated. Although she couldn't deny the author's own experience, hers was quite different. She had a pleasant time working at Boughton; the work was quite specialised and knowledge came with the years.
>
> It was a proper little community and you had to get on with people. Things changed when the new duke [Walter], the present duke's father, inherited the estate in 1973. They still had big house parties between Easter and August. The new duke's wife, Duchess Jane, used to send notes to my mother detailing what rooms were required for which guest, who was staying and what they needed. The same routine was followed every year. Fruit and vegetables came from the kitchen gardens, and flowers were cut for the rooms. Duke Walter would come for the odd weekend on his own and my mother would cook for him then. The duke, a big forestry man, would come just to look at the tree planting.[59]

Mr Bagshaw became an authority on one aspect of the collection:

> My father created the armoury, for the guns and pistols, when the house opened to the public, and became very knowledgeable. He was even consulted by the Tower of London. He also restored furniture. He was the house carpenter but in a way he was more like a curator, and he used to help hang pictures and tapestries. He helped clean the silver too – it was usually done by him or the butler. After my parents retired they both acted as guides at Boughton.

They really loved that house and I used to tease them that it meant more to them than I did. In truth, we all enjoyed Boughton. Our family could use the pool and tennis courts when the duke's family were away.[60]

In modern times the country house is usually maintained by the daily cleaner, sometimes working in teams of two or three. In many cases they may have long associations with the family or the estate and may even have worked for the same house for twenty or thirty years. One such is Della Robins, the daily at Chavenage in Gloucestershire. When asked about her forty-eight years with the family and the house, she revealed a familiar nexus of relationships.

I came to Chavenage when I was fifteen and a half, and went to the local school. The Lowsley-Williamses were looking for someone to help look after the children, so I was taken on as a nanny's help. When my parents were divorced, my mother became housekeeper to Frank Baker, a widower and the cowman at Chavenage to Major Lowsley-Williams. Frank retired in 1966 and later he and my mother got married. My husband's father was the maintenance man at Chavenage. My father-in-law, Fred Robins, also worked at Chavenage for over fifty years.[61]

When Della arrived in 1961, there had been some post-war scaling down but there was still a traditional household of staff:

When I came there was a cook, Mrs Bianek (who was a Polish refugee), and her husband, and a butler, George Thomas, and someone to do the laundry. Originally there were three gardeners, Mr Bianek, Mr Medcroft and Mr Jay. I had a short overlap with a nanny, and then became the nanny myself. It's just me now! Outside, today, there is Paddy Jackson, who was once the groom and now helps do the lawn, the logs and the outside jobs.

At first I lived with my parents in a cottage on the estate. I was up at half past eight and back home by five-thirty or six o'clock. I married in 1966, and when our first son was born in 1967 I worked different hours. I didn't think about how long I would work at Chavenage, it all just happened. When the cook left she wasn't replaced, and Mrs Lowsley-Williams took over the cooking, but there was always some member of staff about. Thomas the butler died about twenty years ago. I have a great affection for the house; it hasn't changed over the years, despite the numbers of visitors.[62]

[Her original duties were] mostly looking after the children and babysitting but then I took over the cleaning. I especially like cleaning the brass. The hardest thing was polishing the oak boards, but better Hoovers and polishers have made the job a lot easier. When I was first here there were three cleaning ladies but they had only white fluffy mops and had to get down on their knees to apply the polish. It was just a family home then and there were nothing like the number of visitors we have today with weddings, corporate days and coach parties. The floors can get pretty dreadful when you have a wedding party.

[On a typical day] I come in every morning, do the ironing, make the beds, and look after the living area. Then if there has been a wedding or event at the weekend, I move on to the front rooms of the house. On open days I do the flowers in the house and in the chapel, usually with flowers from the garden.

I can still remember the house when it was lived in by Mr Lowsley-Williams's uncle, Colonel John, and his two sisters. One sister, Mrs del Court, used to take us to Sunday school in Tetbury, and always organised a party here at Chavenage for the children on the estate. When Colonel John was still alive, as children we looked upon the house as something special.

My mother worked as a cleaner for the major, Mr Lowsley-Williams's father, at the Manor Farm. Now, after cleaning in the morning I help Joanna [Lowsley-Williams] with the catering, lunches and cream teas, especially when we have coach parties, but mostly serving the public. I enjoy it; you meet such a range of people. There are not so many people working for the estate now as there were in the early 1960s; it's all contracted out. Paddy and I are the only two full-time workers left. When I first got married Barry and I lived in the house where I had grown up, then we were offered the flat in the stables at Chavenage, and later we moved to Avening where my husband came from. Both my children were christened in the church and my daughter had the blessing for her wedding there.[63]

If the cleaner is still central to country-house life, so is the indispensable maintenance man. One of the longest-serving members of staff at Alnwick Castle in Northumberland is Graham Luke, who in 1965, at the age of fifteen, was taken on as an apprentice joiner in the estate works. 'I saw the advertisement in the local paper. I first earned £2 17s 6d, in "olden-day money" as my children call it. I worked forty-four hours a week including Saturday mornings.' He has now been involved with the care of the castle for thirty-five years. 'It's a wonderful building, unique, I love it. It's the Windsor of the North.'[64]

He first reported to 'the clerk of works, known as "Cappy" Hepple – as in flat cap, I think. I remember that I thought he was incredibly old then, but I was only fifteen. He was then probably the age I am now and he retired soon after I joined. After that, Ian August became clerk of works. We still have a maintenance department of joiners, painters and builders, but no plumbers or electricians. We did once but not any more. When I first came the staff was not that big, about ten, but in the 1970s it went up to twenty-five.'

At that time the estate workers were renovating cottages:

The estate had a lot of them; most of north Northumberland belonged to the duke, with lots of little villages. In 1975 we started rewiring the castle, putting in the telephone as well as intruder and fire alarms. By then I was a joiner. I came to work up at the castle and just never left. Officially now I am the 'maintenance liaison officer', which means if there is a problem in the castle, or in any of the family's houses, I have to go and inspect it, and assess whether our own works department can deal with it or not.

To the fifteen-year-old that he was then, the duke and duchess seemed:

very regal, and part of a much more formal life. Everything was run by a housekeeper, Mrs Richardson, who used to frighten the life out of me. She was next to God and what she said went. Oh, she was a demon. Nobody was allowed into the castle without her say-so. Even if you had come to do some work she had asked for, you would be met at the back door and sent along to her sitting room. Then you would have to state what your business was, what exactly you were going to do, and usually why you hadn't done it sooner to boot.

She had a room lined with oak cupboards for the linen. Sometimes you would see the maids queuing up for fresh supplies. The cupboards are all gone now. She had a chaise longue in there and a coal fire. It was the duty of one of the maids to lay and light that fire every morning, and then Mrs Richardson would have her breakfast in front of it.

From my perspective, the butler was the duke's butler, and the housekeeper was the duchess's housekeeper, that's how I remember it. The present duke and duchess don't want the daily interference of a butler in the way that Duke Hugh's butler used to run his bath in the morning and do everything. They naturally want more privacy. Today they have a household controller, but there are still eight daily ladies, just as in Duke Hugh's time.

In the 1960s everyone knew who everyone was. Alnwick estate was more formal and intimidating in some ways but it was more of a family too. Most of the staff employed at that time had some connection with the estate. When I applied for my job, the farmer whom my father worked for knew the under-agent at Alnwick, who gave me a letter of introduction.

Duke Hugh used to hunt four days a week and as a result he knew every farmer and every shepherd. Each day he would go out around noon and look round the farms, perhaps because he wanted a hunt jump put right, and then he would call in at the farm. It drove the cook mad, because lunch was always planned for one o'clock. In the 1960s during Duke Hugh's time the stables were hallowed ground. The stud groom was Fred Lister. I think he and Duke Hugh had grown up together and they were certainly good friends. Sometimes the duke would go to the stables and have a whisky with Fred.[65]

The servants' quarters of the past two centuries are no longer in use nor are they part of the highly enjoyable tourist route. The ornate Gothic Revival kitchen is now a refectory for a visiting American college; the old servants' hall has been turned into a library, although subterranean passages still connect the kitchen to the dining room. The old stables, partly an exhibition site for liveries and carriages, now house the restaurant and shop. Mr Luke's affection for – and knowledge of – the building that has been so long in his care is evident in every room.[66]

There are consistent themes in these stories: of country-house service becoming a life's work, of association with the estate through marriage or family connections. Martin Gee, the current head gardener at Weston Park in Shropshire, has worked there for forty years and his family has had remarkably long connections with Weston.

The first member of my family to work here came in the early nine-teenth century from Norfolk as a ploughman. There is a painting of him by Weaver in the house. He was recommended to the family by Coke of Norfolk as the owner of Holkham Hall was known because the owner wanted someone to work with Suffolk Punch horses. Since then, my family have all worked in agriculture or as gamekeepers and carpenters on this estate.

When my father left school he went into agriculture and eventually came to the gardens here. He served in the army during the war and returned to his old job at Weston in peacetime. I came just after leav-ing school. Weston is my life. Staff numbers went down gradually from the late 1960s because the work wasn't very well paid and they were probably trying to reduce staff numbers as well. It was still a family home, and the cook and the butler both came from St Helena. You could get a British passport if you spent two years in domestic service. We had one very cold winter and none of them had ever seen ice before. Most of the cleaning staff came from the village.

My father used to talk about all the characters here when he first came in the 1940s. (Someone said I was a Weston 'character' now!) There were still thirty gardeners in those days and there were fifteen when I joined in 1969, but now there are just three, with me as head gardener. We do have other help, volunteers and students, as the house and park are now in a trust, the Weston Park Foundation. Today you can do a lot more work on your own with the aid of tech-nology, but then things have changed in the country generally. At one time most of the village children would have begun working on the estate and gradually moved on. Everyone used to know everyone else who lived here, which isn't so true now, although there is still a hard core.[67]

There is a similar pattern of long service at Holkham Hall in Norfolk, one of the best-known country houses still in private family hands and still at the heart of a substantial landed estate. The present Earl of Leicester – who has recently handed over the house to his son, Viscount Coke – first got involved in the management of the estate in the 1960s, before eventually inheriting from his cousin in the 1970s.

He has vivid memories of his first visits to Holkham, which contrasted with his own childhood in South Africa: 'There was Rees, the butler, and Mrs Stubbs, who came in to clean and would sometimes serve meals, when she used to stand behind Lord Leicester's chair, surveying the scene.' He remembers asking his cousin, Tommy Leicester, 'why he did not entertain that much. He said it was because they found it so difficult to get servants and his generation were simply not brought up to make their own beds. Before the First World War, Holkham still had something like fifty indoor servants.'[68]

The territorial nature of service life emerges from a story from his mother's early visits to Holkham in the 1930s: 'The librarian asked the butler: "Am I to understand that crumbs on the library table are the preserve of the butler?" To which the butler replied, "Yes", but with a deft pass of his hand sweeping the crumbs to the floor, he added, "And now they are the preserve of the housekeeper."'

When the Earl of Leicester moved into the house in 1980, there was a small staff:

> The butler-chauffeur was Peter Fielder, who stayed for a time. There was also a houseman who laid fires, and Tommy Leicester's carer, who cooked. One cleaning lady, Carol Cox, is still working for us; we later had a couple who looked after the state rooms. In the 1970s, Fred Jolly, a former policeman, became security man, and a flat was made for him and his wife in the house. He was so able that he quickly took on other jobs until he became the administrator. Then we had Norman Smith, as butler-chauffeur, who was ex-army.
>
> Fred Jolly knew of lists where you could advertise for retiring servicemen. Norman had worked in the officers' mess in his last years in the army, so he knew what was needed. David Palmer, who came later as butler, had also been in the army and was with us until we retired to the house where we live now. There were usually three gardeners and seven or eight gamekeepers.[69]

Still working for the Leicesters today is Maurice Bray, who was born on the estate and started work at Holkham on 1 September 1958 in the estates building department:

There were different types of trades and everyone had a specific job. There was a man to mend the fences, another to mend the gates, someone to repair the cottages and so on, which worked very well. The workshop was on the first floor, with a great big open fire at one end. The oldest man, Mr Frank Stubbs, had his bench close to the fire, while I, being the youngest, had mine at the other end, near the open door and the draughts.[70]

The indoor staff included Mr Upton, 'a permanent electrician, who also looked after the boilers and was always pushing round a barrowful of coke. He replaced all the light bulbs too.'

If the buildings department had work to do in the house, 'we had to report to the butler, Mr Rees, a Scotsman. He was a jovial type, but you would not think of walking about the house without first reporting to him. He retired in the 1970s.' Mrs Stubbs, the mother of one of Mr Bray's colleagues, went in daily to do cleaning and washing.

The buildings department was reduced substantially in the 1960s and Mr Bray later became clerk of works, moving on in 2000 to help run the linseed oil business set up by the estate. He is now still working for the Leicesters, helping them settle into their new home in the grounds. He described working for a great estate as being 'like being part of a family. People would always assist you. We also used things that were to hand, from flint to timber.'[71]

Ian Macnab, the current head forester, joined the estate staff in 1957; his father had worked in the gardens, and his mother had been a laundrymaid. His training was thorough: 'In those days you looked to spend two years in the nursery, growing trees in plantations, raising, weeding, and planting out. After a couple of years you would start to work in the woods.' Those he worked for were 'supportive but ruled with a rod of iron; they wouldn't stand for backchat'.[72]

Both men considered their training in the 1950s to be strict and both felt a keen sense of history, in their own jobs and in those of their colleagues. Maurice Bray remarked: 'I often used to think what a wonderful sight the park was when walking in to work, when all those commuters are shut up in cars or trains.' Ian Macnab adds:

'I used to think the view of the hall from the monument must be a hell of a sight for visitors, but to us, it's just the hall.'

Lord Leicester commissioned an important series of group portraits by Andrew Festing to record the contribution of all those whose service contributed to the maintenance of the house, both for the family and for the visiting public:

> The main catalyst was that in 1993 I had three heads of departments retiring who had been with me since I was first involved in running the estate in 1973. They were Ken Hume, clerk of the works, the administrator and the chief clerk. Whatever I have achieved here is in large part thanks to them, and I was looking for a way of recording this. I also thought that visitors to the house see plenty of my family and ancestors, but not much of the people who look after us and this estate.
>
> Then I thought of the servant portraits at Erddig. After that first one, of the heads of department, with the agent and the farm manager, we had others of the office staff, and the house staff, including the administrator, David Palmer the butler, Carol Cox the cleaner, and the house electrician. We have also had ones done of the woods department, the farms department and the building department, but there are still more to do.[73]

Whilst Holkham retains a working community, the large service areas of the original, eighteenth-century house are used now mostly for purposes other than their original ones, not least because fewer staff are needed, and most of them live in houses on the estate, rather than at Holkham itself.

Through the ages, architects have taken different approaches to the problems of accommodating quantities of domestic staff in traditional country houses. With the modern trend for cleaning and maintenance staff to live elsewhere, much was done in the 1960 and 1970s to create more serviceable family apartments within the main house, with smaller kitchens where the families could cook for themselves, with or without help.[74] A picture of current attitudes emerges from the views of two architects who specialise in building new country houses or adapting older ones to comfortable modern life. They were asked to comment on what staff their clients tend to have and how much this informs the designs of their houses.

For Hugh Petter, a partner of Robert Adam Architects, a firm that has built over one hundred new country houses in the past twenty years, it was 'still quite usual to encounter a housekeeper, a nanny and a personal secretary. The smartest houses might well have a butler, a driver and one or two gardeners, sometimes a groom and a stable lad.' The firm has often been asked to build a new house on an estate where the old house had been pulled down:

> Then we might well be asked to design a new lodge or staff cottage, but these days more staff live out than in. I think people don't want a life with hot and cold running staff, while staff themselves need their own private spaces in which to lead their own private lives. Most of our clients have a housekeeper, whose husband might do odd jobs or gardening.
>
> It is still quite usual to be asked to provide a flat for the house-keeper, either in the main house, or maybe over the garage, so that when the family are away there is someone near by for security reasons. These are likely to be comfortable flats, well proportioned and bigger in scale than historic servants' accommodation. In old country houses the family itself tends to colonise the old servants' quarters, but in smarter houses there will be a nice family kitchen as well as a working catering kitchen for entertaining.

Some features are persistent:

> We are still designing quite large butler's pantries for new houses, which are requested more than you might think and are effectively serveries. Laundries are often asked for, and these days usually sited on the first floor, so that laundry can be processed on the bedroom floor, saving a lot of carrying up and down stairs. There is still quite a strong desire to have a second staircase for staff, so they don't have to go through the main rooms, especially when people are entertaining. We have also had requests for staff sitting rooms, often suitable for chauffeurs while waiting, and for offices for personal secretaries.[75]

Another architect, Ptolemy Dean, currently working on several new country houses, concurs:

> All country house owners are concerned to have somebody living on site for security. Service accommodation has always been an

important part of the architectural expression of a country house, especially when you think of the work of Lutyens. I have recently designed a new house with a powerhouse, garages, and a self-contained staff flat in a new service courtyard. I am often asked to design staff cottages.

One thing is clear: there is no expectation of a string of servants' bedrooms in the attics, while basements are generally used only for wine or services such as electrical plant rooms and laundries. The days of the basement servants' quarters, indeed of the servants' hall, have really vanished for ever.[76]

Domestic staff are still a component in country houses, even if very different from their Edwardian counterparts. That this is still a lively employment market is shown in the advertising pages of *The Lady* magazine as well as the back pages of *Country Life* and its ilk, which still sport numerous adverts for domestic and estate jobs. There are several schools for butlers in existence, including those founded by Ivor Spencer, while gardeners will now often be trained at horticultural college, and cooks at catering colleges. Indeed, it has been argued that there has been something of a revival in domestic staff numbers in more recent years.[77] On 3 June 2007, the *New York Post* even ran an article on the international shortage of butlers in which it was observed that butlers were required by newly wealthy families to help them learn how to enjoy their wealth with the polish associated with the old rich. It was calculated in the *Post* that top butlers were earning $200,000.[78] The *Guardian* had also run an article on the scarcity of trained butlers four days earlier.

Stephanie Rough, director of the established company Greycoat Placements, deals with placing full-time and temporary staff for many country houses. She argues that, as with country houses through the ages, staffing numbers vary hugely and depend on the family and size of property: 'People who entertain only a little might have just a housekeeper and two dailies.' She was asked to imagine the likely staff today of a country house at the centre of a 2,000-acre estate with an owner in his forties working in the City. 'Probably they would have three or four people working in the house: a couple perhaps, a daily and a cook, with extra staff brought in for events, and a head gardener plus one other. Depending on the estate, there might perhaps be an estate manager of some sort. With a married couple, the wife would usually act as housekeeper while the husband might act as butler, or houseman, or do more general duties, such as driving, security and maintenance.'[79]

Is a butler is still something people look for?

A family who entertain a lot might want a butler, but he might be called a butler-houseman or house manager. Today, a butler is not so much about formal entertaining, but managing staff, sorting out the digital camera, iPod, Blackberry and house technology; liaising with contractors; and being the first port of call for bills and administration. This trend is much more on the management side, but there is still a demand for the very traditional 'service' butler. Some people have full-time drivers.

What sort of person would be a typical contemporary housekeeper?

Again, a kind of house manager, running the household, sorting out the laundry and making beds, who could cover for the butler. One could be on duty when the other is off, and vice versa. Housekeepers or house managers tend to have a grounding in some related skill, as a chef or a property manager; there is still some sense of working your way up through the ranks, perhaps having come from working on yachts, in ski chalets or in hotel management.[80]

Where are the many foreign couples drawn from who go into service? 'There are certainly a number of Asians, Filipinos, Eastern Europeans and St Helenians.' She too has found that it is not unusual to come across people, often local, who have worked in the same country house for thirty or forty years: 'In the countryside, bigger estates would certainly be more likely to employ locals. Staff who are treated with respect and valued will stay a long time. Country houses do take a lot of looking after, especially if you have a house party; the laundry alone could take a week to sort out. No two houses are quite the same these days. Managing staff can be quite demanding.'

Is the word servant still used at all? 'No, nobody really uses the word servant any more; people do use the word staff, although not everyone likes it. People still use the words butler and housekeeper, although the word maid is used less and less. There are a number of other phrases used, such as confidential aide or personal aide, although some lines are blurred.'

Modern attitudes can vary enormously. 'One of our housekeepers was being interviewed and asked whether there would be any cleaning involved. Her potential employer said, "no, you're the housekeeper". She asked the same question at another interview and the answer was, "of course, you're the housekeeper", which shows that people have different ideas about these job titles.'[81]

One of Miss Rough's colleagues, Laura Hurrel, who is in her twenties, was recently on the other side of the fence:

> I worked as a housekeeper for several families, travelling between London, country residences and abroad, including the owners of a traditional country estate. Things have certainly changed in terms of job titles and technology. There is less of an accepted structure. When I worked for the owners of a country house, I did so alongside the staff there, organising functions, and meeting and greeting.
>
> Those going into housekeeping now tend to come from a background like nannying, hotels or corporate hospitality, and there are a lot of couples whose children have grown up and left home. It requires a lot of practical skills and what is required can vary widely.

What is it like working in another family's home? 'You do have to be careful not to get too involved in their lives, to know when not to listen and to leave people alone. You have to be aware of sensitivities and be discreet.' It all sounds very familiar.[82]

In recent times, 'conservation cleaning' has taken a higher profile in the work of the National Trust when caring for and presenting country houses to the public, whether they are still occupied by a family or not. It is recognisably work that was once undertaken by the historic hierarchies of housemaids, footmen and housekeepers. According to Helen Lloyd, the head housekeeper for the National Trust, serious research has been done into the traditional housekeeping methods of country-house servants to understand best practice.[83]

'In earlier periods, the expensive furniture of the day was incredibly valuable so it was looked after just as the most expensive technology is cared for today· for instance, furniture was always supplied with case covers. The elaborate process of coaching household servants was for centuries predicated on a process of training, in which they would gradually assume responsibility for more and more precious objects. They really understood how to care for things, as we can see from the extraordinary range of brushes available for every possible purpose.'[84]

The National Trust has evolved a formula for the care of houses, dictated by the size of house, the density of furnishings and the number of visitors: 'It is the activity of people that makes dust, be it a private family or the visitors.' The National Trust's recent *Manual of Housekeeping* gives a detailed description of the preferred staffing levels needed to care for a house and its contents. There would normally be a house manager, with curatorial training or a qualification; a house steward, with direct responsibility for the people doing the physical work, as well as managing the opening up and closing of the house; and an assistant, to provide cover seven days a week.

Then there are the 'conservation assistants': depending on the number of rooms and the density of furniture, anywhere between two and nine, but probably averaging around four. Most houses would also have various assistant cleaners who, although not specially trained, clean the offices and the other visitor facilities.[85] It is all these people who make a critical difference in the care and presentation of beautiful objects and magnificent rooms. Whilst we admire their dedication today, we should also give full credit to those in centuries past whose working lives were spent in preserving and protecting these works of art and fine furnishings.

However, the privately owned and family-occupied country house must concern itself with more than conservation, although it is certainly essential. Chatsworth, in Derbyshire, is no exception to modern trends. Many observers have praised the Dowager Duchess's role in the heroic revival of this great palace, both as an admired visitor attraction and as a family home.[86]

The funeral procession of the late duke on 11 May 2004 was attended by all those who worked in the house, garden, shops, restaurants and on the wider estate, dressed in the uniform of their roles, and was widely reported in the national and local press. It was an iconic image of the private country-house community, still going strong in the twenty-first century although of a kind more typical of the largest traditional estates, on which this book has focused. Having inherited the house and extensive estates in 1950, the 11th Duke had to face 80 per cent death duties, which took many years to discharge, via the sale of land and the house's treasures such as important art-works and rare books. The bill was eventually settled, so that Chatsworth could continue to be occupied by the descendants of its sixteenth-century builder. Today it is home to the 12th Duke and his family.[87]

In the story of its revival, a major factor is the two-way devotion between the Chatsworth staff and the Cavendish family. When I wrote to the duchess, asking about staffing at Chatsworth, she responded to my letter by sharing memories of those who had made it all possible, and inviting me to come to meet some of them. I visit on a crisp winter's day, with sun and mist making that famous Derbyshire valley, with the dreamlike baroque palace at its heart, seem all the more beguiling – and the Devonshires' joint achievement in keeping it together all the more inspiring. For the duchess, who has retired to a house in the beautifully sited estate village of Edensor, one element stands out in the story of those who have worked at Chatsworth. 'Trust is essential. It's got to be done on trust or it might as well not be done at all.'

Chatsworth, which the duchess made her life's work for nearly half a century, is, as with many great houses, a complex organism, 'like a museum and a grand hotel combined, but it has to be a home too, otherwise it is simply a museum'.[88] She introduces me to three of her staff who had each worked for her for forty years or more. As she said: 'They have been the absolute lynchpins of everything, men of such amazing calibre.' These were Henry Coleman, who is still her butler today and was both butler and valet to the late duke since 1968; Alan Shimwell, her chauffeur and loader, also since 1968; and Jim Link, who started working for the estate in January 1950, in the forestry department, and went on to become head gardener.

I start by meeting the family's long-term butler, a legend to the many distinguished guests entertained by the duke and duchess. Henry Coleman began his working life at Chatsworth in March 1963:

> I came as a footman, aged only sixteen, and after five years became butler. I had first started work at Lismore Castle in the forestry nursery, and when the family came to Lismore at Easter for their annual visit I was asked to take the logs around for the fires, with the odd man. The butler told me that there was a footman's place going at Chatsworth and asked whether I was interested. Being the eldest of twelve children, all living at home, I jumped at the chance.

There was a substantial permanent staff in the house at the time, with ten or twelve indoor staff:

> three in the kitchen, two in the pantry, two housekeepers, four daily women, two chauffeurs, a lady's maid, a nurserymaid, a nanny, a butler, two footmen, and another two or three who could be called on when we were busy.
>
> I learnt my job from three butlers: Mr Bryson; John Pollard, who was butler for fifteen years, both here and at Lismore; and Mr Edward Waterstone, the then dowager's butler, who was with her for fifty years. He taught me a lot. There was another who had worked for the duke's grandfather. They were all of the generation before the First World War, all the real McCoy, all very nice, and all getting on in years. They would help out at various parties at Chatsworth. They would tell me how to get on in general, how to look after things, what not to say and what not to do – that was very important.[89]

Alan Shimwell joined the Chatsworth staff in 1952: 'I was eight years on the estate farms and then went into the gardens. My first job at Chatsworth was stooking corn, so that the water ran off and not into the stooks.' He moved into driving almost by chance: 'In 1968, the duchess asked whether I could go to Bolton Abbey with her because the chauffeur was off sick, and then I became her driver. In 1970 I started loading for her on shooting weekends and I went on doing it for thirty-three years. We went all over England, including royal places, such as Sandringham, or to Lord Gage on the south coast. There would be nine or ten guns and often the weather would be terrible; you used to turn blue. I packed up driving five years ago and now look after the poultry, the duchess's own, and do a bit of gardening.'[90]

Jim Link recently retired after fifty years in the gardens. 'When I first came, I looked after the forest nursery, then drove lorries, then went on to the demesne department. Then I helped in the gardens, under Denis Hopkins.' Mr Link had grown up at Chatsworth: 'My father was the head gardener here and I was brought up in a flat in the stable yard. I wanted an outdoor job and forestry sounded good. Father asked the head forester and that was that.'[91]

As was so often the case, he was trained on the job:

I learnt everything about forestry from older people – at that time the people near retirement were looked after and the young got to do all the heavy work. We had a good foreman, Len Newton, and also Billy Bond. As you learnt how to do each thing, you were moved on to the next thing. In the demesne department we looked after roads and drains and trees; these were some of my best years – creating, planting. The old men really knew everything. Technology has changed a lot. I enjoyed my time in the garden, doing work that has a visible result.

The garden staff were probably closer to the house staff than some estate departments are because of the flowers we grew to decorate the house. My uncle Jim used to bring in orchids and flowers from the garden and greenhouses. The kitchen was supplied with vegetables too. Once lupins were wanted for the American ambassador's room. The gardener took them up there, put them in the vases, and great heaps of greenfly fell off on the dressing table. There were greenfly everywhere.[92]

Both Mr Shimwell and Mr Coleman would follow the household from Chatsworth to the other family houses, Bolton Abbey and Lismore Castle, both in Ireland, a pattern that was typical of great households in previous centuries but is much less so now. Mr Shimwell recalls: 'We would go to Bolton Abbey for 12 August for the grouse shooting and stay four weeks.' Mr Coleman adds: 'His Grace would go out for the beginning of the salmon fishing and then Her Grace would arrive in March for the Easter holidays. The cook would come, Mrs Canning, and the housekeeper, Maud Barnes, a house-maid, and Mary Feeney, Her Grace's sewing maid.'

What was it like having to slot into another household? Mr Coleman says: 'You were made to feel welcome. You were part of a family. We used to look forward to going. It was much more fun when we started driving there. It was quite a business, travelling on the train with the staff and the luggage; I used to have to look after twenty-two pieces, which I had to get on and off the train when we changed at Manchester and Liverpool. We'd get on the boat to Dublin, and then it was back on another train to Limerick and then another to Lismore, still with all that luggage.'

There were some compensations: 'When we used to land in Dublin, we would have to wait two hours in a square there to get a can of oil before we could set off for Lismore. The cook, Mrs Canning, loved picnics, so we always used to have to stop en route for one of her picnics; they were good, mind you.'[93]

As in so many great country houses with long-serving staff, there is considerable interconnection between the families of the estate and the house staff. Mr Coleman's wife has also worked for the family; his brother-in-law is the butler and house manager at Lismore Castle; and one of his sons is the silver steward for the public side of Chatsworth. Alan Shimwell is related to two former comptrollers of the house. Mr Shimwell's uncle Walter began as a bell boy in 1908, aged twelve, sitting by the bells to fetch the relevant visiting valet when called, and became the much-admired comptroller in 1921 at the young age of twenty-six and later clerk of works, overseeing the restoration of the house in the 1950s and '60s. Jim Link is the son of a former head gardener who also worked for fifty years in the gardens and is brother-in-law to Mr Shimwell.[94]

How would they all describe working in a great country-house environment to those who have never experienced it? Mr Link, born and raised at Chatsworth, instantly replies: 'It's little community, we were brought up together.' At eighteen he went off to do National Service: 'You do have comradeship in the army, but when you came back, you really appreciated everything at home.

'We were really a family and we looked up to the duke and

duchess. We knew they were always behind us, and if we ever had any trouble you had a big ally there. They would bend over backwards to look after you; and you wanted to give them something in return for all that.' Mr Shimwell adds: 'The duke would always talk about how staff loyalty was very important: no argument.' He valued the fact that his work was recognised: 'When we went down to London, which made a long day, once we were back home, whatever time it was, there would always be a thank you and a goodnight. Always.'

Helen Marchant, the duchess's long-term secretary, agrees with Mr Shimwell: 'It was completely reciprocated. The duke was always trying to improve "the social wage", with the pool, gym and golf course for people who worked on the house and estate; he was always trying to pay the staff back for the loyalty they showed. He was duke for such a long time, and many people started with him in the 1950s and 1960s. You have to remember the challenge of the 80 per cent death duties that they had to face.' Mr Shimwell added: 'We didn't know whether we would have jobs at the end of it all, but the duke gave you confidence that he would pull through.'[95] And they did.

As we come to the end of the first decade of the twenty-first century, the privately owned country house is run more and more by people far removed from pre-war patterns and traditions. Country-house owners today expect to live in greater privacy than their parents and grandparents, but while they may cook and drive themselves, most of them still have to rely on some staff, such as secretaries, nannies, cleaners and especially gardeners, possibly bringing in regular agency staff for bigger social events.[96]

As we have seen, some of the bigger country houses, whilst also drawing on agency staff when necessary, are dependent on permanent teams of staff, calling on the services of their own estate departments where they continue to be maintained. Few, whether security men, drivers, cleaners or cooks, few are likely to live in the actual house, and all operate in a world that is in many ways different from that of their forebears. What is so surprising is that the complex world of domestic service has persisted so vigorously in the middle of the twentieth century and beyond, even if in rapidly changing guise.

The word servant may well have disappeared from everyday discourse, and there may be no obvious pattern of employment of domestic staff today, but country houses require assistance to make them work, just as they did five hundred years ago, even with modern technology to regulate heat, light and alarms from a distant laptop. In the end, one factor has remained the same through the centuries: that whatever the work involved, there must also, crucially, be some degree of human companionship, involving loyalty and trust.

Acknowledgements

In writing on such a subject, any writer will be indebted to the scholarship and publications of others. In this area, the most important and helpful were those by Peter Brears, J.T. Cliffe, Mark Girouard, Adeline Hartcup, Jean Hecht, Pamela Horn, Pamela Sambrook, Giles Waterfield and Merlin Waterson. I would like to acknowledge my profound gratitude and debt to those authors, particularly Pamela Horn and Pamela Sambrook, as well as to all those cited in the notes and bibliography.

I would also like to thank the many scholars, authors, curators, archivists and friends who have helped guide and encourage my researches for this book. I would like to mention especially Clive Aslet, Charles Bain-Smith, Sir David Cannadine, Nicholas Cooper, Warren Davis, Ptolemy Dean, Trevor Dooley, Liz and Martin Drury, Gareth Edwards, Julian Fellowes, Leslie Geddes-Brown, Philippa Glanville, John Goodall, Emily Gowers, David Griffin, Michael Hall, Andrew Hann, John Hardy, Bevis Hillier, Maurice Howard, Tim Knox, Lucinda Lambton, Helen Lloyd, Patricia Macarthy, Edward MacParland, the late Hugh Massingberd, Mary Miers, Tessa Murdoch, William Palin, Jeremy Pearson, John Martin Robinson, Pippa Shirley, Peter Sinclair, Julian Spicer, Sarah Staniforth, Hew Stevenson, Nino Strachey, Sir Keith Thomas, Geoffrey Tyack, Hugo Vickers, Giles Waterfield, Sue Wilson, Lucy Worsley and Sir Peregrine Worsthorne. Edward Town spared me his time to show me round Knole, and Jane Troughton of York University identified and transcribed relevant letters in the Wynn archive. Especial thanks to Lydia Lebus for her invaluable support as a researcher, particularly in contacting the owners and archivists of so many country houses around the British Isles.

Many archivists, curators and librarians at country houses and other collections have been immensely helpful with guidance and direction, tours and access to documents and buildings, including Rosemary Baird at Goodwood House, Sussex; Jean Bray at Sudeley Castle, Gloucestershire; Dai Evans at Petworth House, Sussex; Robin Harcourt-Williams at Hatfield House, Hertfordshire; Kale Harris at Longleat; Christine Hiskey at Holkham Hall, Norfolk; Paul Holden at Llanhydrock, Cornwall; Christopher Hunwick at Alnwick Castle, Northumberland; Charles Lister at Boughton House, Northampton-shire, Anne MacVeigh at the Public Record Office of Northern Ireland; Basil Morgan at Rockingham Castle; Christopher Ridgway at Castle Howard; Sara Rodger at Arundel Castle, Sussex; Jennifer Thorp at Highclere Castle; Collette Warbrick and her colleagues Rachel Boak and Diana Stone at Waddesdon Manor, Buckinghamshire; and Richard Williams, archivist of Mapledurham House, Berkshire. Also to Andre Gailani of the Punch Library, Justin Hobson and Helen Carey at the Country Life Picture Library, and Jonathan Smith, archivist, of Trinity College, Cambridge.

There are also many country-house owners and those have who lived in and worked in country houses, all of whom gave me time for interviews, tours and advice, especially: David Bateman, Sir John Becher, Charles Berkeley, the Hon Mary Birkbeck, Lady Mairi Bury, the Earl and Countess of Carnavon, James Cartland, Henry Coleman, the Hon. Hugh Crossley, the Dowager Duchess of Devonshire, Peter Frost-Pennington, Martin Gee, the Earl of Glasgow, the Knight of Glin, the Hon. Desmond Guinness, Edward Harley, James Hervey-Bathurst, Laura Hurrell, Lord Inglewood, Sir John Leslie, Bt, Sammy Leslie, Jim Link, Auriol, Marchioness of Linlithgow, David and Rhona Lowsley-Williams, Ian MacNab, Maureen Magee, Sir David and Lady Mary Mansell-Lewis, Lord Neidpath, Della Robins, the Earl and Countess of Rosebery, Stephanie Rough, Lord Sackville-West, the Earl and Countess of Sandwich, Alan Shimwell, Sir Reresby and Lady Sitwell, David Stacey, Christopher Simon Sykes, Sir Tatton Sykes, and Rosalinde Tebbut.

I have to thank my colleagues on *Country Life* magazine, not least for giving me the wonderful opportunity to visit so many country houses over the past fourteen years, and to the BBC and the National Trust for the same great privilege. Also all the owners of country houses I have visited, all those who work in them and, indeed, all those who work to maintain and open such houses to an interested public. I am continually humbled by the dedication, devotion and hard work of country-house servants in history, as well as their staffs in modern times, and I hope that this book does some justice to the skills and dedication that I have encountered and perhaps understood only now for the first time.

I am immensely grateful to Clare Alexander, of Aitken Alexander, my literary agent, for all her wisdom and kind encouragement and to Roland Philipps of John Murray Publishers for his faith in the project and his wise editorial insight and helpful guidance, also to Helen Hawksfield of John Murray for all her hard work, kind support and enthusiasm, and to Celia Levett for her masterly copy-edit that helped improve the text so much, and to Sara Marafini for her design work and to Anna Kenny-Ginard for her work on promoting the book, and to all those who make it possible to produce a book in the twenty-first century.

A special thanks to my family, my wife Sophie, my daughters Georgia and Miranda, and our dog Archie, who all support me in everything I do.

For the following permissions to quote from copyright material, I am immensely grateful to:

To the Dowager Duchess of Devonshire for permission to quote from her book *The House: A Portrait of Chatsworth*; Mrs Gill Joyce for permission to quote from the memoirs of her father Stanley Ager, and to Fiona St Aubyn his co-author, and to James St Aubyn of St Michael's Mount; the trustees of the Goodwood Estates for permission to quote from the memoirs of Mrs Jean Hibbert; to Sir Josslyn Gore-Booth, Bt, for permission to quote from the Thomas Kilgallon memoir; to Mr Ian McCorquodale for permission to quote from the *Etiquette Handbook* written by Dame Barbara Cartland, first published in 1952 and re-issued in 2008 by Random House; to the Duke of Northumberland Estates for permission to quote from manuscripts held in Alnwick Castle relating to the 1st Duke and

Duchess's Household Regulations and the Kildare Household Regulations; to the Master and Fellows of Trinity College, Cambridge, for access to, and permission to quote from, the diaries of Hannah Cullwick; to Lord Sackville for permission to quote from the Knole Household Catalogue; to Christopher Simon Sykes for permission to quote from his memoir, *The Big House: The Story of a Country House and its Family*, published by HarperCollins in 2005; to Taylor & Francis for permission to quote from the memoirs of maidservants published in John Burnett's *Useful Toil*; to A.P. Watt and the literary estate of H.G. Wells for permission to quote from H.G. Wells' *Experiments in Autobiography*, published in 1934, and *Tono Bungay*, published in 1909; to Frances Lincoln Ltd for permission to quote from *The English House*, 2007, by Hermann Muthesius, translated by Dennis Sharp.

Attempts to trace the copyright holders of Frederick Gorst, *Of Carriages and Kings*, published in 1956 by W.T. Allen (now a title of Random House), and of Rosina Harrison, *Rose: My Life in Service*, published in 1975 and *Gentleman's Gentleman* edited by Rosina Harrison, by Cassell plc (now a division of Orion Publishing Group), were unsuccessful.

Every effort has been made to trace copyright holders, but if there are any errors or omissions, John Murray (Publishers) will be pleased to insert the appropriate acknowledgement in any subsequent edition.

Notes

Introduction

1. Samuel Johnson, *A Dictionary of the English Language*, London 1755 reprinted in facsimile (Times Books), London 1979.
2. For surveys that include discussions of urban and middle-class households at this time, see Pamela Horn, *Flunkeys and Scullions: Life Below Stairs in Georgian England* (2004), *The Rise and Fall of the Victorian Servant* (1991), and *Life Below Stairs in the 20th Century* (2004).
3. Horn, *Flunkeys*, pp. 16–19, and example dated 27 January 1922 (ten male servants £7 10s and 4 dogs £1 10s) in the Highclere archives, thanks to Lydia Lebus and by kind permission of the Earl of Carnarvon.
4. *Daily Telegraph*, 11 May 2004.
5. *Shorter Oxford Dictionary* (1972) and see Naomi Tadmer, *Family and Friends in Eighteenth-Century England* (2001).
6. Susan Whyman, *Sociability and Power in Late-Stuart England* (2002), p. 60, cites the example of a private coachman, employed by the Verneys in the late-seventeenth-century, who believes it is below him to be a servant, so he leaves to work as a cabman in London.
7. Sarah and Samuel Adams, in *The Complete Servant* (1825), and Arthur Young, *General View of the Agriculture of Hertfordshire* (1804), as quoted on www.hertfordshire-genealogy.co.uk.
8. Andrew Hann, 'Report on the Service Wing of Audley End' (2007); Eric Horne, *What the Butler Winked at* (1923); and report by Fred Scott for Manchester Statistical Society in 1889, see www.manchester2002.uk.com/history/victorian.
9. Merlin Waterson, *The Servants' Hall* (1980).
10. Horn, *Flunkeys*, p. 189.
11. John Burnett, *Useful Toil* (1975), p. 146.
12. Burnett, *Useful Toil*, p. 146.

13. C.M. Woolgar, *The Great Household in Medieval England* (1999), pp. 8–14.

14. Frederick Gorst, *Of Carriages and Kings* (1956), p. 132.

15. Mark Girouard, *Life in the English Country House* (1979), pp. 190–9, and Horn, *Rise and Fall*, p. 25.

16. John Bateman, *The Great Landowners of Great Britain and Ireland* (1971), first published 1876; the Appendix on p. 595 shows that, at that date, there were around 1,688 principal landowners, including peers and owners of large estates. Assuming these great country landowners employed 120 servants each (indoors and out), this could account for only around 84,000 of the total employed in domestic service, with gentry households as well, still less than 250,000.

17. Giles Waterfield (ed.), *Below Stairs* (2004), p. 10, and Burnett, *Useful Toil,* pp. 136–7.

18. 1911 Census, as published January 2009.

19. Fiona Reynolds, conversation with the author, 30 January 2009.

20. Barbara Tuchman's *The Proud Tower* (1966) shows how landowners remained at the centre of the political world until political reforms in 1911, with their town houses at the hub of political life.

21. Robert McCrum, *Wodehouse: A Life* (2004), p. 22.

22. Pierre Caron de Beaumarchais (1732–99), entry in the *Encyclopedia Britannica* (1911), in which we are told how much Napoleon admired his play, *The Marriage of Figaro,* banned by the French king.

23. John Galsworthy, *The Country House* (1907), pp. 1–2.

24. James Sutherland (ed.), *Oxford Book of Literary Anecdotes* (1975), p. 377.

25. D.H. Lawrence, *Lady Chatterley's Lover* (Penguin), London 1960 and also see *Lady Chatterley's Trial* (Penguin), London 2005.

26. Julian Fellowes, interview with the author, 30 January 2009; Mr Fellowes wrote the screenplay for *Gosford Park,* directed by Robert Altman and released in 2001.

27. Julian Fellowes, interview with the author, 30 January 2009.

28. Countess of Rosebery, interview with the author, 10 December 2008.

29. Christine Horton conversation with the author, September 2004.

30. Della Robins, interview with author, 17 December 2008.

31. Stradey Castle and Renishaw Hall were both featured in the BBC2 series *Curious House Guest,* screened in 2006.

32. The Earl of Leicester, interview with the author, 20 December 2008.

33. James Miller, *Hidden Treasure Houses* (2006), pp. 78–99.
34. Earl and Countess of Rosebery, interview with the author, 10 December 2008.
35. Philip Ziegler, *Osbert Sitwell* (1999), p. 11.

Chapter 1: The Visible and Glorious Household

1. Peter Fleming, *Family and Household in Medieval England* (2000), p. 7.
2. Girouard, *Life in the English Country House,* p. 8.
3. Woolgar, pp. 9 and 10.
4. Woolgar, p. 4.
5. Fleming, p. 29.
6. Alison Sim, *Masters and Servants in Tudor England* (2006), pp. 69–79.
7. Girouard, *Life in the English Country House,* p. 71.
8. Woolgar, p. 1.
9. For the surviving titles of the royal household, see http://www.royal.gov.uk/TheRoyalHousehold/OfficialRoyalposts/OfficialRoyalposts.aspx.
10. John Goodall, *English Castle Architecture, 1066–1086,* forthcoming from Yale University Press. I am very grateful to Dr Goodall for the opportunity to read in draft his chapter on the household.
11. Girouard, *Life in the English Country House,* pp. 14–18.
12. *The National Trust Handbook* (2009).
13. Goodall, *English Castle Architecture.*
14. Girouard, *Life in the English Country House,* p. 71.
15. Goodall, *English Castle Architecture.*
16. 'The Household Book of Algernon Percy, 5th Earl of Northumberland', usually known as 'the Northumberland Household Book' (Sections 43–9), as reprinted in *English Historical Documents: 1485–1558,* 1996, pp. 905–9, edited by C.H. Williams (hereafter cited as Northumberland Household Book (1511/12)): for a web site version, see Victoria.tc.ca/~tgodwin/duncanweb/documents/Northumberland.html. I was very privileged to see the original in the Duke of Northumberland's estates archives at Alnwick Castle; there is also an eighteenth-century edition, edited by Thomas Percy.
17. Goodall, *English Castle Architecture,* and Woolgar, p. 50.
18. Norman Davis (ed.), *The Paston Letters* (1983), p. 111.

19. *Paston Letters*, p. 76.
20. *Paston Letters*, p. 76.
21. *Paston Letters*, pp. 54–5.
22. P.W. Fleming, 'Household servants of the Yorkist and early Tudor gentry', in *Early Tudor England* (1989), p. 31.
23. Colin Richmond, 'Paston family', in *Oxford Dictionary of National Biography* (2004–9).
24. Shakespeare, *Hamlet*, Act IV, scene v.
25. Mark Girouard, 'Sir John Thynne (1512/13–1580)', *Oxford Dictionary of National Biography* (2004–9).
26. John Russell, 'The Book of Nurture', (afterwards cited as Russell) as published in Edith Rickert and D.F. Naylor, *Babee's Book: Medieval Manners for the Young: Done into Modern English from Dr Furnivall's Texts*; see also 'Book of Courtesy', pp. 79–121. (1908), pp. 26–38.
27. Kenneth Vickers, *Humphry Duke of Gloucester: A Biography* (1907), and G.-L. Harris, 'Humphry, Duke of Gloucester (1391–1447)' in *Oxford Dictionary of National Biography* (2004–9).
28. Peter Brears, *The Boke of Keruynge* (2003), pp. 2–3, and Molly Harrison and D.H. Royston, *How They Lived*, Vol. II, p. 166–7.
29. Woolgar, pp. 34–5.
30. Peter Fleming, *Family and Household in Medieval England* (2002).
31. Dorothy Stuart, *English Abigail* (1946), p. 2.
32. Douglas Gray, 'John Russell', in *Oxford Dictionary of National Biography* (2004–9).
33. Russell, p. 27; Stanley Ager and Fiona St Aubyn, *The Butler's Guide to Clothes Care, Managing the Table, Running the Home & Other Graces* (1980), p. 11, has retired butler Mr Ager's memories, looking back to the 1920s when he recalled: 'A cook was usually very bad-tempered; if she wasn't struggling against a clock, she was struggling against an oven.' I am grateful to Mrs Gill Joyce for permission to quote from her father's memoir.
34. Russell, p. 76.
35. Brears, p. 2.
36. Russell, p. 56.
37. Russell, p. 52.
38. Russell, p. 50.
39. Woolgar, p. 136.
40. Russell, p. 51.
41. Russell, p. 51.

42. Russell, p. 52.
43. Russell, p. 52.
44. Russell, p. 52.
45. Woolgar, pp. 22–3.
46. Russell, pp. 54–5.
47. Russell, pp. 55–6.
48. Russell, p. 62.
49. Russell, pp. 58–9.
50. Sim, p. 99, and Woolgar, p. 159.
51. Russell, p. 62.
52. Russell, p. 58.
53. Russell, pp. 63–6.
54. Russell, p. 63.
55. Russell, p. 64.
56. Russell, p. 65.
57. Russell, p. 66.
58. Russell, p. 68.
59. Russell, pp. 69–70.
60. Girouard, *Life in the English Country House*, pp. 14–16.
61. Girouard, *Life in the English Country House*, p. 20.
62. Woolgar, p. 15.
63. Phyllis Cunnington, *Costume of Household Servants* (1974), pp. 15–30.
64. Sim, pp. 72–4.
65. Woolgar, p. 25.
66. C.L. Kingsford, *Stonor Letter Papers* (1996), p. 21.
67. Northumberland Household Book (1511), in (ed.) Williams, (1966), pp. 1088–9.
68. 'Northumberland Household Book 1511', in (ed.) Williams, (1966), pp. 905–9. The date is now usually given as 1511/12.
69. Goodall, *English Castle Architecture*.
70. J. Scarisbrick, *The Reformation and The English People* (1984).
71. *Shorter Oxford Dictionary* (1972), p. 835: 'Of unknown etymology'; the original sense seems to be 'Boy, male child'.
72. 'Northumberland Household Book (1511)' in (ed.) Williams, (1966), p. 906.
73. Peter Ackroyd, *The Life of Thomas More* (1999), p. 255.
74. 'Northumberland Household Book (1511)' in (ed.) Williams, (1966), p. 1089.

75. For early brewing, see Peter Sambrook, *Country House Brewing: 1500–1900* (1996).

76. Kate Mertes, *The English Noble Household, 1250–1600* (1988), pp. 1–17 and 103–36.

77. Woolgar, p. 39.

78. Woolgar, pp. 32–3.

79. Luttrell Psalter (ff. 207v–208), see Janet Backhouse, *The Luttrell Psalter* (1989).

80. P.W. Fleming, 'Household Servants of the Yorkist and Early Tudor Gentry' in *Early Tudor England* (1989), p. 29.

81. Sim, p. 69.

82. Woolgar, p. 38.

83. Girouard, *Life in the English Country House*, p. 16; and Molly Harrison (ed.), *How They Lived*, Vol. II, p. 167.

84. Douglas Gray, 'Geoffrey Chaucer (1340–1400)', *Oxford Dictionary of National Biography* (2004–9).

85. Ackroyd, *Life of Thomas More*, p. 29.

86. Mark Thornton Burnett, *Masters and Servants in English Renaissance Drama and Culture* (1997), p. 177.

87. Rosemary O'Day, 'Roger Ascham (1514/15–1568)', *New Oxford Dictionary of National Biography* (2004–9).

88. Goodall, *English Castle Architecture*.

89. Sim, p. 84.

90. Woolgar, pp. 87–9.

91. George Cavendish, *The Life and Death of Cardinal Wolsey*, first published by early English Text Society (No. 243), Oxford University Press, London 1959, edited by R.S. Sylvester, and accessible on the University of Toronto website 'Renaissance English Texts' Web Development Group, University of Toronto Library, 1997, general editor: Lan Lancashire; see (afterwards cited as Cavendish), http://www.library.utoronto.ca/utel/ret/cavendish/cavendish.html.

92. Cavendish, pp. 1–23.

93. Cavendish, p. 68.

94. Susan Groom et al., *The Taste of Fire* (2007).

95. Sim, pp. 81–2.

96. Maurice Howard, *The Early Tudor Country House: Architecture and Politics 1490–1550* (1987), pp. 72–8.

97. Sim, p. 82.

98. Sim, p. 82.

99. John Russell, 'Book of Courtesy', in Edith Rickert and D.J. Naylor, *Babee's Book: Medieval Manners for the Young* (1908), pp. 79–121.

100. Woolgar, pp. 61–3.

101. Howard, p. 73.

102. Information on Westenhanger from the architect Charles Bain-Smith.

103. Howard, p. 72.

104. Woolgar, p. 73.

105. George Edelen (ed.), *The Description of England by William Harrison* (1968), p. 201.

106. Alice Friedman, *House and Household in Elizabethan England: Wollaton Hall and the Willoughby Family* (1988), pp. 41–5 (afterwards Friedman).

107. Friedman, p. 44–5.

108. Friedman, pp. 44–5.

109. Friedman, Appendix A, 'The Willoughby Household Orders of 1572', pp. 185–6.

110. Friedman, p. 185.

111. Friedman, p. 186.

112. Friedman, p. 186.

113. Friedman, p. 186.

114. I.M., *A Health to the Gentlemanly Profession of Serving-Men* (1598) (Shakespeare Association Facsimile 1931), afterwards cited as *A Health*.

115. *A Health*, fol. B2 verso.

116. *A Health*, fol. B3 recto.

117. *A Health*, fol. B3 recto.

118. *A Health*, fol. C3 recto.

119. *A Health*, fol. C3 recto.

120. *A Health*, fol. D1 verso.

121. Nicholas Cooper, *Houses of the Gentry 1480–1680* (1999), p. 271.

Chapter 2: The Beginning of the Back Stairs and the Servants' Hall

1. Cooper, pp. 268–72.

2. Philippa Glanville, and Hilary Young, *Elegant Eating* (2002), pp. 48–50.

3. J.T. Cliffe, *The World of the Country House in Seventeenth-Century England* (1999), p. 96 (afterwards cited as Cliffe).

4. Girouard, *Life in the English Country House*, p. 138.
5. Lucy Worsley, *Cavalier: A Tale of Chivalry, Passion and Great Houses* (2007), p. 241.
6. Cliffe, p. 198.
7. Cooper, pp. 270–1.
8. *The Gentlewomans Companion* (1675), pp. 5–9.
9. John Considine, 'Hannah Wolley (1622?–1647?)', *Oxford Dictionary of National Biography* (2004–9), and Gilly Lehmann, *The British Housewife* (2003), pp. 48–9.
10. Diane Purkiss, *The People's Civil War* (2007), pp. 347–50; Lehmann, pp. 48–9.
11. Vicary Gibbs (ed.), *The Complete Peerage* (1932), Vol. III p. 600.
12. Nikolaus Pevnser and James Bettley (eds), *Buildings of England: Essex* (2006), p. 552.
13. Gibbs, p. 600.
14. Robert May, *The Accomplisht Cook* (1684).
15. *Cook's Guide* (1664), as quoted in Matthew Hamlyn, *The Recipes of Hannah Wooley* (1988), p. 12.
16. *Cook's Guide* (1664), as quoted in Matthew Hamlyn, *The Recipes of Hannah Wooley* (1988), p. 12.
17. Gilly Lehmann, *The British Housewife* (2003), pp. 48–9; and see Women Writers Resource Project at the Lewis H. Beck Center, Emory University, 1998.
18. *The Gentlewomans Companion* (1675), pp. 11–13.
19. *Queen-Like Closet* (1670), pp. 378–9.
20. *The Gentlewomans Companion* (1675), p. 204.
21. *The Gentlewomans Companion* (1675), pp. 5–9.
22. At Knole, by kind permission of Lord Sackville; also in David Clifford (ed.), *The Diaries of Lady Anne Clifford* (2003), pp. 274–5.
23. John Aubrey, *Brief Lives* (1982), p. 225.
24. Clifford, p. 101.
25. Robert Sackville-West, *Knole* (1994), p. 12.
26. Lita-Rose Betcherman, *Court Lady and Country Wife* (2005), p. 127.
27. The Knole Catalogue is quoted with permission of Lord Sackville.
28. Miles Hadfield, *A History of British Gardening* (1985).
29. Jennifer Potter, *Strange Blooms: The Curious Lives and Adventures of the John Tradescants* (2006), pp. 9 and 63–4.
30. Potter, *Strange Blooms*, p. 64

31. Christina Hole, *English Home-Life 1500 to 1800* (1947), p. 37.

32. Clifford, p. 274.

33. Clifford, p. 32.

34. Clifford, p. 33.

35. Clifford, p. 80.

36. Clifford, pp. 98–9.

37. Sara-Jayne Steen (ed.), *The Letters of Lady Arbella Stuart* (1994), p. 234.

38. Dorothea Townshend, *The Life and Letters of the Great Earl of Cork* (1904), pp. 125–30; the household list is on p. 302; bequests to servants are listed on pp. 499–502 (afterwards cited as Townshend).

39. Townshend, p. 126.

40. Toby Barnard, 'Robert Boyle, First Earl of Cork (1566–1643); *Oxford Dictionary of National Biography* (2004–9).

41. Townshend, p. 300.

42. Townshend, pp. 499–502.

43. Townshend, pp. 1288–9.

44. Cliffe, pp. 105–6.

45. Cliffe, pp. 96–7.

46. Cliffe, pp. 105–106.

47. Adam Eyre, *Diary*, quoted in Christina Hole, *English Home-Life* (1974), p. 18.

48. William Gouge, *An Exposition of the Domesticall Duties* (1622), pp. 499–500.

49. Cliffe, p. 97.

50. Daniel Parsons (ed.), *The Diary of Sir Henry Slingsby* (1836) (afterwards cited as *Slingsby*), pp. 5–6 and pp. 26–7.

51. *Slingsby*, p. 23.

52. Cynthia Herrup, *A House in Gross Disorder* (1999), pp. 16–24 and pp. 40–3.

53. Herrup, p. 19.

54. Herrup, p. 19.

55. Herrup, p. 19.

56. John Morrill, *Revolt in the Provinces: The People of England and the Tragedies of War* (1999), pp. 57–68 and 164.

57. Audrey Sidebotham, *Brampton Bryan: Church and Castle* (1990), pp. 17–19.

58. Thomas Taylor-Lewis (ed.), *Letters of the Lady Brilliana Harley* (1854), pp. xix–xx.

59. Sir Harry Verney, *The Verneys of Claydon* (1968), pp. 33 and 40 (afterwards Verney).
60. Charles Carlton, *Going to the Wars* (1992), p. 51.
61. Verney, p. 33 and p. 40.
62. Daniel Defoe, *Memoirs of a Cavalier* (1908), p. 173.
63. John Aubrey, *Brief Lives* (1982), p. 154.
64. Verney, pp. 46–7.
65. Miriam Slater, *Family Life in the Seventeenth Century* (1984), pp. 112–13.
66. Slater, p. 113.
67. Verney, p. 47.
68. Slater, p. 72.
69. Verney, p. 51.
70. Verney, p. 82.
71. Verney, p. 85.
72. Susan Whyman, *Sociability and Power in Late-Stuart England* (1999), p. 26 (afterwards Whyman).
73. Whyman, p. 35.
74. Verney, p. 171.
75. Whyman, p. 117.
76. Whyman, p. 22.
77. Dorothy Stuart, *The English Abigail* (1946), pp. 61–81.
78. Whyman, p. 60.
79. Gladys Scott Thomson, *Life in a noble household 1641–1700* (1965), pp. 85–91 (afterwards Scott Thomson).
80. Scott Thomson, pp. 118 and 328–30.
81. Scott Thomson, p. 119.
82. Scott Thomson, pp. 120–1.
83. Scott Thomson, pp. 142–3 and p. 151.
84. Scott Thomson, pp. 124–5.
85. Scott Thomson, p. 125.
86. Cliffe, p. 101.
87. Cliffe, p. 101.
88. D.R. Hainsworth, *Stewards, Lords and People: The Estate Steward and his World in Later Stuart England* (1992), p. 47.
89. Cliffe, p. 105.
90. Giles Waterfield et al. (eds), *Below Stairs* (2004), p. 143 (afterwards Waterfield).

91. Sim, pp. 36–8.

92. See M. Sherlock, *The Story of the Jamaican People* (1998) and Bonham C. Richardson, *The Caribbean in the Wider World 1492–1992* (1992).

93. Claire Tomalin, *Samuel Pepys: The Unequalled Self* (2002), p. 410, n. 27.

94. Whyman, p. 7.

95. Andrew Browning (ed.), *Memoirs of Sir John Reresby* (2nd edn, 1991), p. 108 (afterwards Browning).

96. Browning, p. 108.

97. Browning, p. 109.

98. For more on the current debate on authorship, see Women Writers Resource Project at the Lewis H. Beck Center at Emory University, Atlanta; see http://chaucer.library.emory.edu/wwrp.

99. *The Gentlewomans Companion* (2nd edn, 1675), pp. 204–17; also see *The Compleat Servant Maid* (1685).

100. *The Gentlewomans Companion*, p. 205.

101. *The Gentlewomans Companion*, p. 121.

102. *The Gentlewomans Companion*, p. 206.

103. *The Gentlewomans Companion*, pp. 207–8.

104. *The Gentlewomans Companion*, pp. 212–13.

105. *The Gentlewomans Companion*, p. 213.

106. *The Gentlewomans Companion*, p. 214.

107. *The Gentlewomans Companion*, pp. 214–15.

108. *The Gentlewomans Companion*, pp. 215–16.

109. *The Gentlewomans Companion*, p. 216.

110. *The Gentlewomans Companion*, pp. 215–16.

111. *The Gentlewomans Companion*, pp. 108–10.

112. *The Gentlewomans Companion*, p. 110

113. Worsley, p. 240.

114. Worsley, p. 236.

115. Cliffe, p. 97.

116. Tom Jaine, 'Mary Evelyn's Oeconomis to a Married Friend' (1677), *Petits Propos Calinaries*, Vol. 73, July 2003, pp. 59–73 (afterwards Jaine), which includes a full version of the text from a manuscript at the Harry Ransom Humanities Research Center, Texas; the review is published on dialspace.dial.pipex.com.

117. Jaine, p. 65.

118. Jaine, p. 66.

119. Jaine, p. 71.
120. Jaine, p. 71.
121. Jaine, p. 72.
122. Jaine, p. 72.
123. Girouard, *Life in the English Country House* p. 138, and Colin Plate, *The Great Rebuildings of Tudor and Stuart England* (1994), pp. 157–8, p. 103.
124. Christopher Morris (ed.), *The Illustrated Journeys of Celia Fiennes* (1982), p. 47.
125. Cliffe, pp. 103–4.
126. Cliffe, p. 104.
127. Cliffe, p. 104.
128. John Evelyn, *Diary* (1956), pp. 639–40.
129. Cooper, p. 272.
130. Cooper, p. 272.
131. Cooper, pp. 287–9.
132. Cooper, p. 289.
133. Mary Yakushi, and others (ed.), *The Treasure Houses of Britain* (1985), p. 147.
134. Cliffe, p. 104.

Chapter 3: The Household in the Age of Conspicuous Consumption

1. See especially Mark Girouard, *Life in the English Country House* (1978), pp. 181–244; Christopher Christie, *The British Country House in the Eighteenth Century* (2000), pp. 98–128; and Pamela Horn, *Flunkeys and Scullions: Life Below Stairs in Georgian England* (2004); Jean Hecht, *The Domestic Servant Class in Eighteenth Century England* (1956).
2. Phyllis Cunnington, *The Costume of Household Servants*, p. 49.
3. Hartcup, p. 17.
4. John Macdonald, *Memoirs of an Eighteenth-Century Footman* (1985), edited by Peter Quennell (original published 1790), afterwards cited as Macdonald.
5. Macdonald, p. xv.
6. Macdonald, p. ix.
7. Macdonald, p. 145.

8. Gillian Pugh, *London's Forgotten Children* (2007).

9. Macdonald, p. 11.

10. Macdonald, p. 20.

11. Macdonald, p. 24.

12. Macdonald, pp. 26–7.

13. Information from James Knox and Mrs Dalrymple-Hamilton.

14. Macdonald, p. 27.

15. Macdonald, p. 31.

16. Macdonald, p. 33.

17. Macdonald, p. 38.

18. Macdonald, pp. 38–9.

19. Macdonald, p. 50.

20. Macdonald, p. 52.

21. Horn, *Flunkeys*, pp. 155–8.

22. Jonathan Swift, *Directions to Servants* (2003), first printed 1745, pp. 3–5.

23. Swift, p. viii.

24. *Spectator*, vol. II, Monday, 11 June 1711, p. 40.

25. Ralph Dutton, *The English Country House* (1935), p. 63.

26. Hecht, p. 57.

27. Horn, *Flunkeys*, pp. 16–19.

28. Horn, *Flunkeys*, p. 19; and E.S. Turner, *What the Butler Saw* (1962), pp. 289–90.

29. Horn, *Rise and Fall*, p. 6.

30. Horn, *Flunkeys*, p. 38; and Girouard, *Life in the English Country House*, pp. 139–140.

31. D. Mortlock, *Aristocratic Splendour* (2007), p. 193.

32. Christie, p. 117.

33. Hecht, pp. 40–1.

34. Christie, p. 117.

35. Hecht, pp. 40–1.

36. Horn, *Flunkeys*, pp. 17–19.

37. Hecht, pp. 42–3.

38. Christie, p. 117; and Duke of Norfolk estates, Arundel Castle, MS A93, wages lists for 1779 and 1781.

39. Hecht, pp. 42–3.

40. Horn, *Flunkeys*, pp. 147–8.

41. Mortlock, p. 197.

42. Turner, pp. 154–5.
43. Horn, *Flunkeys*, pp. 147–8.
44. Samuel and Sarah Adams, *The Complete Servant* (1825), p. 7.
45. Horn, *Flunkeys*, p. 153.
46. Hecht, p. 45.
47. Hecht, p. 46.
48. Hecht, p. 47.
49. Christie, p. 118.
50. Horn, *Flunkeys*, p. 153.
51. Pamela Sambrook, *Keeping Their Place* (2007), pp. 55–7 (afterwards Sambrook).
52. Hecht, p. 50.
53. Hecht, p. 50.
54. Christie, p. 136.
55. Hecht, p. 50.
56. T.F.T. Baker (ed.), *Victoria County History of the County of Middlesex*, vol. V (1976), p. 120.
57. 'General Instructions' of the 1730s, copy on display at Boughton House, outside the armoury; and information from the Duke of Buccleuch.
58. Waterfield, pp. 45–6.
59. Horn, *Flunkeys*, pp. 214–15.
60. Gilly Lehmann, *The British Housewife* (2003), p. 139 (afterwards Lehmann).
61. Mary-Anne Garry, 'Upstairs and Downstairs', in the *Holkham Newsletter* (2007), p. 5.
62. Hannah Glasse, *The Art of Cookery Made Plain and Easy* (1747).
63. Lehmann, p. 75.
64. Horn, *Flunkeys*, p. 136.
65. Lehmann, p. 76.
66. Lehmann, p. 75.
67. Hannah Glasse, *The Servants Directory, Improved, or, House-keepers Companion* (1762), pp. 1–8.
68. Glasse, pp. 1–8.
69. Glasse, *Servants*, pp. 11–14.
70. Duke of Northumberland Estates, DNP MSS, 121 (93), p. 118.
71. Glasse, *Servants'*, p. 45.
72. Horn, *Flunkeys*, p. 150.

73. Tessa Murdoch (ed.), *Noble Households* (2006), p. 282.

74. Christina Hardyment, *Behind the Scenes: Domestic Arrangements in Historic Houses* (1997), p. 200.

75. Sambrook, pp. 129–30, 144, and 162–3.

76. Hardyment, p. 90.

77. Christie, p. 114.

78. Glasse, *Servants*, p. 42.

79. Letter from Michael Blount III to his father Michael Blount II, 20 October, 1787, from the Blount family papers, at Mapledurhan House, Berkshire, with thanks to Dr R.G. Williams, archivist.

80. Horn, *Flunkeys*, p. 147.

81. Christie, p. 114.

82. Christie, pp. 114–15.

83. Lehmann, p. 302.

84. Gordon Lyndall, *Vindication: A Life of Mary Wollstonecraft* (2005), p. 93.

85. Christie, p. 116.

86. Turner, p. 63.

87. G.F. Berkeley, *My Life and Recollections* (1865), pp. 30–1.

88. Horn, *Flunkeys*, p. 242.

89. Turner, p. 64.

90. Horn, *Flunkeys*, p. 155.

91. Christie, p. 188.

92. Horn, *Flunkeys*, p. 175.

93. Horn, *Flunkeys*, pp. 176–7.

94. Waterfield et al. (eds), p. 155.

95. Mortlock, p. 203.

96. Horn, *Flunkeys*, p. 176.

97. Horn, *Flunkeys*, pp. 164–73.

98. E.I. Carlyle (revised by Anne Pimlott-Baker), 'William Speechly (1723–1819)', *Oxford Dictionary of National Biography* (2004–9).

99. George Clutton, 'The Gardeners of the eighth Lord Petre', *Essex Naturalist*, vol. 32 (1967–71), pp. 201–210 (afterwards Clutton).

100. Clutton, pp. 201–210.

101. Hecht, p. 49.

102. John Abercrombie, *Abercrombie's Practical gardener*, 2nd edn (1817). I am very grateful to Brent Elliot of the RHS library for pointing out this story.

103. John Phibbs, 'Lancelot Brown (baptised 1716–d. 1783)', *Oxford Dictionary of National Biography* (2004–9); and see Dorothy Stroud, *Capability Brown* (1950).

104. Hecht, p. 50.

105. Horn, *Flunkeys*, p. 179.

106. Horn, *Flunkeys*, pp. 179–80.

107. Horn, *Flunkeys*, p. 181.

108. Horn, *Flunkeys*, p. 182.

109. Horn, *Flunkeys*, p. 184.

110. Merlin Waterson, *The Servants' Hall: A Domestic History of A Country House (1990)*, p. 141.

Chapter 4: Behind the Green Baize Door

1. L.G. Mitchell (ed.), *The Purefoy Letters* (1973), pp. 137–9, (afterwards *Purefoy*).

2. *Purefoy*, pp. 137–9.

3. Wynn papers, from Nostell Priory, now in the West Yorkshire Archives Service, Wakefield (WYW), 1352, A1.5A.4; my thanks to Jane Troughton for her transcription of these letters between Jane, Countess of Dundonald and Sabine, Lady Wynn.

4. Asa Briggs, *How They Lived*, vol. III (1969), p. 142.

5. Wynn papers, WYW 1352, A1.5A.4; my thanks to Jane Troughton.

6. Pamela Sambrook, *Keeping their Place*, p. 35.

7. Horn, *Flunkeys*, pp. 87–90.

8. Horn, *Flunkeys*, p. 89; Kenneth Little, *Negroes in Britain*, 2nd edn (1972), p. 195 (afterwards Little).

9. Horn, *Flunkeys*, p. 90.

10. Richard Hewlings, 'Who was Burlington's Black Servant', *Country Life* (2004), vol. 198, pp. 64–5; and Little, p. 189.

11. Horn, *Flunkeys*, p. 83.

12. Little, p. 196.

13. Information from Lydia Lebus; the headstone and the verse are still extant.

14. Horn, *Flunkeys*, p. 82, Little, p. 189, and Christie, pp. 120–1.

15. Little, pp. 221–2.

16. Horn, *Flunkeys*, pp. 84–5.

17. Horn, *Flunkeys*, pp. 84 5.
18. Little, p. 192; this is the number of people of African extraction in London in the 1790s.
19. Christie, p. 120.
20. Horn *Flunkeys*, pp. 95–7.
21. Information from Lord Sackville; Robert Sackville-West, *Knole* (1994), p. 34.
22. *The Spectator* (1711), no. 88, Monday, 11 June, pp. 36–8.
23. Jonathan Swift, *Directions to Servants* (1745, republished by Hesperus Press, 2005), (afterwards Swift).
24. Swift, p. 3.
25. Swift, p. 5.
26. Swift, pp. 5–6.
27. *Irish Wit and Humour: Anecdote and Biography of Swift, Curran, O'Leary and O'Connell* (1872), pp. 24–30.
28. Swift, p. vii.
29. *Purefoy*, p. 142.
30. *Purefoy*, p. 144.
31. *Purefoy*, p. 147.
32. Hertfordshire County Archives, ref MS DE/P/F 193, letter of Lord Cowper to his wife, date 5 June 1720, f. 78 with especial thanks to Lucy Worsley for drawing my attention to this letter and sharing her transcript.
33. Brian Dolan, *Ladies of the Grand Tour* (2001), p. 138.
34. Dolan, pp. 138–9.
35. Stella Tillyard, *Aristocrats* (1994), pp. 217–9 gives a full account of the Kildares' household; and Patricia McCarthy in *Irish Architectural and Decorative Studies*, vol. IV, 2003, pp. 120–139 (afterwards McCarthy); the original manuscript is in the Duke of Northumberland Estates, the relevant material in fols 15–23.
36. Notes made by the late John Cornforth.
37. Tillyard, pp. 217–19.
38. McCarthy, pp. 120–5.
39. McCarthy, pp. 120–5.
40. Tillyard, pp. 218–9.
41. McCarthy, pp. 218–9.
42. Arthur Young, *A Tour of Ireland*, first published 1780 (1925), p. 200.
43. McCarthy, pp. 120–5.

44. Tillyard, p. 218.
45. Archives of the Duke of Northumberland Estates at Alnwick Castle, DNP MS 164 and 121, with thanks to archivist Chris Hunwick for his generous assistance in guiding me to this important material.
46. Alnwick Castle, DNP MS 164(e), p. 30.
47. Alnwick Castle, DNP MS 164(e), p. 44.
48. Alnwick Castle, DNP MS 164(e), p. 44.
49. Alnwick Castle, DNP MS 164(d), p. 1.
50. Alnwick Castle, DNP MS 164(d), p. 2.
51. Alnwick Castle, DNP MS 164(d), p. 4.
52. Alnwick Castle, DNP MS 164(d), pp. 23–5.
53. Alnwick Castle, DNP MS 121(92), p. 43.
54. Alnwick Castle, DNP MS 121(63), p. 239.
55. Alnwick Castle, DNP MS 121(63), p. 231.
56. Mortlock, p. 206.
57. Jonas Hanway, *Eight Letters to His Grace the Duke of — on the custom of Vails-Giving in England* (1760), pp. 1–9.
58. Turner, pp. 51–3.
59. Michael Blount II to his son, 1 February 1761, Blount MSS, of Mapledurham House, Berkshire, with especial thanks to archivist Dr R.G. Williams for generously allowing me access to his extensive transcripts.
60. Hainsworth, p. 15.
61. Christie, p. 179; Adrian Tinniswood, *The Polite Tourist: Four Centuries of Country House Visiting* (1998).
62. Isaac Ware, *A Complete Body of Architecture* (1756–7), reprinted 1971, Book III.
63. Ware, Book III, p. 406.
64. Ware, Book III, p. 411.
65. Ware, Book III, p. 412.
66. Ware, Book III, p. 413.
67. Information from Mr Rodney Melville.
68. Girouard, *Life in the Country House*, p. 219; Hardyment, p. 43.
69. Christine Hiskey, 'Downstairs – the Servants and their Life', in Leo Schmidt (ed.), *Holkham* (2006), pp. 181–5 (afterwards Hiskey).
70. Hiskey, p. 181.
71. Hiskey, p. 185.
72. Hiskey, p. 181.

73. Hiskey, p. 185.
74. Hiskey pp. 181–6.
75. Tessa Murdoch (ed.), *Noble Households: Eighteenth-Century Inventories of Great English Houses: A Tribute to John Cornforth* (2006), pp. 56–7.
76. Murdoch, p. 57.
77. Murdoch, p. 255.
78. Murdoch, pp. 58 and 255.
79. Murdoch, pp. 280–1.

Chapter 5: The Apogee

1. *Servant's Practical Guide* (1880), quoted in Horne, *Rise and Fall*, p. 17.
2. Nathaniel Parker Willis, *Pencillings by the Way* (1844), pp. 444–5.
3. Booker T. Washington, *Up from Slavery* (1901), p. 286.
4. F.M.L. Thompson, *English Landed Society in the Nineteenth Century* (1964), pp. 122–4 and 186–97.
5. Jessica Gerard, *Country House Life: Family and Servants 1815–1914* (1994) pp. 190–91 (afterwards Gerard).
6. H.G. Wells, *An Experiment in Autobiography* (1934), p. 110.
7. Sambrook, *Keeping Their Place*, pp. 201–4.
8. Wells, *Experiment in Autobiography*, p. 110.
9. Wells, *Experiment in Autobiography*, p. 110.
10. Eric Horne, *What the Butler Winked at* (1923), p. 65.
11. Wells, *Experiment in Autobiography*, pp. 136–8.
12. H.G. Wells, *Tono-Bungay* (first published 1909) (1964) Pan edition, p. 14.
13. Wells, *Tono-Bungay*, p. 18.
14. Sambrook, *Keeping Their Place*, p. 203.
15. Sambrook, *Keeping Their Place*, p. 204.
16. Samuel and Sarah Adams, *The Complete Servant* (1825) (afterwards cited as Adams); see also the modern reprint by Southover Press, 1989, edited by Anne Haly with an introduction by Pamela Horn.
17. Isabella Beeton, *The Book of Household Management* (1861) (afterwards Beeton), reprinted in facsimile in 1985; it also can be seen at www.mrsbeeton.com.
18. Adams, p. ii.
19. Adams, p. iii.

20. Wilton Household Regulations, typescript, p. 1, 2053 Wiltshire and Swindon Record Office; my thanks to John Martin Robinson for drawing my attention to the Wilton papers.
21. Wilton Household Regulations, typescript, p. 1.
22. Hartcup, p. 128.
23. Hartcup, p. 128.
24. Christopher Simon Sykes, *Country House Camera* (1980), pp. 56–61.
25. Hartcup, pp. 132–5.
26. *Petworth Guidebook*; and conversation with the curator, Dai Evans.
27. Adams, p. 7.
28. Adams, p. 7 and M.K. Ashley, *Joseph Ashley of Tysoe 1859–1919: a study of village life* (1961), pp. 146–7.
29. Adams, p. 52.
30. Pamela Horn, *The Rise and Fall of the Victorian Servant* (1995), p. 62.
31. Horn, *Rise and Fall*, p. 65.
32. Elizabeth Mavor, 'Lady Eleanor Butler (1739–1829) and Sarah Ponsonby (1755–1831)', in *Oxford Dictionary of Biography* (2004–9).
33. Information from Lydia Lebus.
34. Horn, *Rise and Fall*, pp. 50–2; Waterson, *The Servants' Hall* (1990), pp. 81–2.
35. Duchess of Devonshire, *The House: A Portrait of Chatsworth* (1982), p. 172.
36. Horn, *Rise and Fall*, p. 63.
37. Hardyment, p. 50.
38. Horn, *Rise and Fall*, p. 64.
39. Waterfield, p. 18.
40. Information from Christopher Ridgway, curator of Castle Howard.
41. Hartcup, p. 45.
42. Adams, p. 51.
43. Beeton, para 55.
44. Beeton, paras 55–62.
45. Hartcup, pp. 57–8.
46. Jonathan Gathorne-Hardy, *The Rise and Fall of the British Nanny* (1972), pp. 68–9 (afterwards Gathorne-Hardy).
47. Adams, p. 254.
48. Beeton, para 2397.
49. Gathorne-Hardy, p. 17.
50. Gathorne-Hardy, p. 303.

51. Horn, *Rise and Fall*, p. 79.
52. Gathorne-Hardy, p. 26.
53. Hartcup, p. 111.
54. Thanks to Lydia Lebus for identifying this.
55. Maria Edgeworth, letter of 1 January 1820, published in Augustus Hare (ed.), *Life and Letters of Maria Edgeworth* (1894).
56. Hartcup, p. 111.
57. Adams, pp. 272–3.
58. Elizabeth Smith, *Memoirs of a Highland Lady* (1911), pp. 172–4.
59. Kathryn Hughes, *The Victorian Governess* (1983), p. 91; Alice Renton, *Tyrant or Victim: A History of the British Governess* (1991), pp. 74–5.
60. Hughes, *Victorian Governess*, p. 59.
61. G. Berkeley, *My Life and Recollections* (1865), pp. 99–101.
62. Adams, p. 194.
63. Beeton, para 84.
64. Horn, *Rise and Fall*, p. 71.
65. Beeton, para 85.
66. Adams, pp. 233–4.
67. Andrew Hann, 'The Service Wing at Audley End House' report (2007), p. 13 with thanks to Dr Hann and his English Heritage colleagues for sharing their research so readily; this research informs the current presentation of the servants' areas at Audley End.
68. Hartcup, p. 58.
69. Horn, *Rise and Fall*, p. 67; Hartcup, p. 50.
70. Adams, pp. 236–7.
71. Beeton, paras 2243–63.
72. Horn, *Rise and Fall*, p. 68.
73. Hartcup, pp. 33–4.
74. Horn, p. 167.
75. Adams, pp. 276–7.
76. Adams, p. 235; Hartcup, p. 57.
77. Adams, p. 277.
78. Adams, p. 280; Hardyment, pp. 62–7.
79. Adams, p. 281.
80. Hartcup, p. 57.
81. Hartcup, p. 83.
82. Gerard, p. 245; Turner, p. 263.
83. Countess of Fingall, *Seventy Years Young* (1937), p. 208.

84. William Lanceley, *From Hall-Boy to House-Steward* (1925), p. 16 (afterwards Lanceley).

85. Adams, p. 294.

86. Dorothy Howell-Thomas, *Goodwood: Letters from Below Stairs* (1976), p. 7, with many thanks to Rosemary Baird of Goodwood House for drawing my attention to this.

87. Beeton, para 2373.

88. Beeton, paras 2374–87.

89. Beeton, para 2387

90. Beeton, paras 2387.

91. Hann, p. 40.

92. Beeton, para 2357 ff.

93. Adams, p. 295.

94. Beeton, paras 2364–8.

95. Adams, p. 336.

96. Horn, *Rise and Fall*, p. 90.

97. Adams, p. 338.

98. Beeton, para 2155.

99. This is also evident from earlier periods, as in D.R. Hainsworth, *Stewards, Lords and People* (1992).

100. Caroline Wood, 'Music-Making in a Yorkshire Country House', in *Nineteenth Century British Music Studies'*, ed. Zon Bennet (1999), p. 222, thanks to Jane Troughton for drawing my attention to this.

101. Hartcup, p. 26.

102. Horn, *Rise and Fall*, p. 91.

103. Lanceley, p. 41.

104. Adams, pp. 339–40.

105. Beeton, para 2164.

106. Adams, pp. 340–1.

107. Glanville (ed.), *Elegant Eating*, pp. 50–1 and Beeton, para 2188.

108. Wilton Household Regulations, typescript, p. 13.

109. Information from Sara Rodger, the archivist at Arundel Castle.

110. Hartcup, pp. 45–6.

111. Pamela Sambrook, *The Country House Servant* (2002), p. 93.

112. Hartcup, *Below Stairs*, p. 46.

113. See Hatfield Household Regulations, reproduced in Hartcup, p. 97.

114. Adams, pp. 361–2.

115. Adams, p. 363.

116. Turner, p. 167.
117. Turner, pp. 167–9.
118. Turner, p. 168.
119. Horn, *Rise and Fall*, pp. 100–1.
120. Adams, pp. 368–9.
121. Gerard, p. 203. The modern-day value of wages was calculated using the 'Measuring Worth' site at 'Economic History', Ethnet.ac.uk, of the University of Illinois at Chicago www.measuringworth.com.
122. Adams, p. 369.
123. Hartcup, p. 52.
124. Waterfield, pp. 74–5.
125. Advice from the Duke of Buccleuch; and Waterfield, pp. 74–5.
126. Duke of Devonshire, *A Handbook of Chatsworth and Hardwick* (1845), p. 150.
127. Adams, pp. 372–3.
128. Turner, p. 175.
129. Adams, p. 373.
130. Turner, p. 176; Pamela Sambrook, *A Country House at Work* (2003), p. 59.
131. Sambrook, *A Country House at Work*, p. 99.
132. Adams, p. 376.
133. Adams, p. 376.
134. Adams, p. 380.
135. Adams, pp. 382–3.
136. Adams, p. 383.
137. Adams, p. 383.
138. Hartcup, p. 37.
139. Hartcup, p. 37.
140. Beeton, paras 2189–95.
141. E.M. Butler (ed.), *A Regency Visitor: The English Tour of Prince Pückler-Muskau Described in his Letters 1826–1828* (1957), p. 155.
142. Adams, pp. 409–10.
143. John Kenworthy-Brown, 'Joseph Paxton (1803–1865)', in *Oxford Dictionary of National Biography* (2004–9) and Kate Colquhon, *A Thing in Disguise: the Visionary Life of Joseph Paxton* (2004).
144. Devonshire, *The House*, p. 210.
145. Gerard, p. 198.
146. Hartcup, p. 115.

147. Horn, *Rise and Fall*, p. 105.
148. Gerard, p. 208.
149. Fingall, p. 159.
150. Beeton, para 2153.
151. Beeton, para 2154.
152. Beeton, para 2154.
153. Beeton, para 2154.
154. Beeton, para 1.
155. Beeton, para 17.
156. Horn, *Rise and Fall*, pp. 123–4.
157. Gerard, p. 164.
158. Gerard, p. 233.
159. Gerard, p. 155.
160. Gerard, pp. 234–5.

Chapter 6: Moving Up or Moving On

1. Gerard, p. 253.
2. Hardyment, pp. 92–4.
3. Horn, *Flunkeys*, p. 243.
4. Gerard, p. 252.
5. 'The families of Annesley Park', extract from a private family history, sent to me by Celia Hanbury, a descendant.
6. Catherine Osborne (ed.), *Memorials of Lady Osborne* (1870), vol. 1, pp. 5–8.
7. Osborne, p. 5.
8. Osborne, p. 8.
9. Osborne, p. 7.
10. Osborne, pp. 7–8.
11. Elizabeth Smith, *Memoirs of a Highland Lady* (1911), pp. 170–3.
12. Smith, *Memoirs*, p. 171.
13. Smith, *Memoirs*, pp. 173 and 377.
14. I am much indebted to the excellent edition edited by Liz Stanley, *The Diaries of Hannah Cullwick* (1984), afterwards Cullwick; the original manuscript of the diaries is in the library of Trinity College, Cambridge; my thanks to the Master and Fellows, and to the archivist Jonathan Smith, for allowing me to inspect these originals.

15. Trinity MSS, Munby Collection 8814, 'Hannah's Places', pp. 4–5, Cullwick, pp. 38–41.
16. Cullwick, p. 293.
17. Trinity MSS Munby Collection 8814, 'Hannah's Places', pp. 4–5.
18. Trinity MSS Munby Collection 8814, 'Hannah's Places', Cullwick, pp. 6–8.
19. Cullwick, p. 38.
20. Cullwick, pp. 38–9.
21. Cullwick, p. 40.
22. Cullwick, p. 40.
23. Trinity MSS, Munby Collection 8814, 'Hannah's Places', Cullwick, pp. 19–20.
24. Cullwick, p. 41.
25. Cullwick, p. 41.
26. Cullwick, p. 85.
27. Cullwick, p. 107.
28. Lanceley, p. 14.
29. Lanceley, p. 14.
30. Lanceley, p. 23.
31. Lanceley, p. 23.
32. Gerard, p. 210.
33. Gerard, p. 208.
34. Gerard, pp. 208 and 218.
35. Information from James Cartland of Carnfield Hall, Derbyshire.
36. Anon., 'The Summer Excursion', in *Transactions of the Thoroton Society*, vol. III (1899).
37. Horn, *Rise and Fall*, p. 186.
38. Kilgallon memoirs, typescript version (afterwards Kilgallon), now in the Gore-Booth papers in the Public Record Office of Northern Ireland, with thanks for Dr Anne MacVeigh of PRONI, for her assistance for getting me access to them, quoted here with kind permission of Sir Joscelyn Gore-Booth, Bt. Kilgallon's memoirs were used as a source for the chapter on Lissadell in Mark Bence-Jones, *Life in the Irish Country House* (1996), otherwise unpublished.
39. Anne Marreco, *The Rebel Countess* (1967).
40. Mona Hearn, *Below Stairs* (1993).
41. Kilgallon, p. 1.
42. Kilgallon, p. 4.

43. Kilgallon, p. 5
44. Kilgallon, p. 8.
45. Kilgallon, pp. 20–1.
46. Kilgallon, p. 21.
47. Kilgallon, pp. 22–3.
48. Kilgallon, p. 23.
49. Kilgallon, p. 19.
50. Kilgallon, p. 23.
51. Kilgallon, p. 23.
52. Kilgallon, p. 24.
53. Kilgallon, p. 25.
54. Kilgallon, p. 26.
55. Kilgallon, p. 26.
56. Eric Horne, *What the Butler Winked at* (1923), p. 62 (afterwards Horne).
57. Horne, p. 78.
58. Horne, p. 63.
59. Horne, p. 64.
60. Horne, p. 64.
61. Horne, p. 64.
62. Horne, pp. 65–6.
63. Horne, p. 66
64. Horne, pp. 66–7.
65. Horne, pp. 68–9.
66. Horne, p. 84.
67. Horne, p. 71.
68. Horne, p. 71.
69. Horne, pp. 77–9.
70. Horne, p. 83.
71. Horne, p. 85.
72. Horne, p. 93.
73. Horne, p. 94.
74. Horne, p. 95.
75. Horne, pp. 96–7.
76. Horne, pp. 98–9.
77. Horne, p. 127.
78. Horn, *Rise and Fall*, p. 50.

79. Information from Basil Morgan, the Rockingham Castle archivist, extracted in a pamphlet, 'Diary of a Victorian Lady', pp. 1–2.
80. Information from Basil Morgan, the Rockingham Castle archivist, extracted in the pamphlet 'Diary of a Victorian Lady', p. 2.
81. Sambrook, *Keeping their Place*, pp. 6–7.
82. Sambrook, *Keeping their Place*, p. 5.
83. Sambrook, *Keeping their Place*, pp. 10–11.
84. Sambrook, *Keeping their Place*, p. 29.
85. Horn, *Rise and Fall*, p. 53.
86. Horn, *Rise and Fall*, p. 54.
87. Carnavon papers, Highclere Castle, Box 3, no. 6, HMC 174, 6/7 May 1873, quoted by kind permission of the Earl and Countess of Carnavon and thanks to Lydia Lebus for researching this material.
88. Carnavon papers, Box 3, no. 6, HMC 174, 6/7 May 1873.
89. Carnavon papers, Box 3, no. 6, HMC 174, 6/7 May 1873.
90. Horn, *Rise and Fall*, p. 51.
91. Horn, *Rise and Fall*, p. 52.
92. MSS at Arundel Castle, dated June 1860, courtesy of the Arundel Castle trustees, and of David Clifton.
93. Information from Mrs Sara Rodger, archivist at Arundel Castle.
94. Hartcup, pp. 96–8.
95. James Miller, *Hidden Treasure Houses* (2006), pp. 80–95.
96. Copies of these early plans of the house are exhibited at Dalmeny.
97. Duke of Devonshire, *Handbook of Chatsworth and Hardwick* (1845), pp. 148–9.
98. Devonshire, *Handbook*, p. 149.
99. Devonshire, *Handbook*, pp. 149–50.
100. Turner, p. 169.
101. Turner, p. 169.
102. Hardyment, pp. 43–5.
103. Francis Goodwin, *Rural Architecture* (1835), pp. 3–4 and plates.
104. Goodwin, p. 3.
105. Goodwin, p. 4.
106. William White, 'Humewood, Co. Wicklow', in *Proceedings of the Royal Institute of British Architects* (session 1868–9), 1869, pp. 77–78, and plates (afterwards cited as White).
107. White, pp. 77–80.

108. White, p. 80.
109. White, p. 85.
110. The plans for Humewood are in the Irish Architectural Archive in Dublin; I am grateful to the IAA's director for drawing my attention to them.
111. Hardyment, p. 18.
112. Hardyment, p. 19.
113. Roger Kerr, *The Gentleman's House* (1864), p. 64 (afterwards Kerr).
114. Kerr, pp. 66–8.
115. Kerr, pp. 66–8.
116. Kerr, p. 198.
117. Kerr, pp. 199–200.
118. Kerr, p. 199.
119. Kerr, pp. 199–200.
120. Kerr, p. 203.
121. Kerr, p. 202.
122. Jill Franklin, *The Gentleman's Country House and its Plan* (1981), p. 91 (afterwards Franklin); Kerr, p. 294 (afterwards Kerr).
123. Kerr, p. 202.
124. Franklin, p. 92.
125. Franklin, p. 93.
126. Kerr, p. 221.
127. Franklin, p. 95; Kerr, p. 224.
128. Sambrook, *A Country House at Work*, p. 103.
129. Kerr, p. 224.
130. Hardyment, pp. 50–61.
131. Kerr, pp. 228–9.
132. Kerr, p. 231.
133. Hardyment, pp. 64–7.
134. Franklin, p. 95.
135. Franklin, p. 95.
136. Franklin, p. 101.
137. Shared bedrooms were the norm for under servants; see the illustration of the dormitory at Mamhead.
138. Michael Trinick, *Lanhydrock*, revised edition (1992), pp. 14–18.
139. Trinick, p. 22.
140. Trinick, pp. 22–30.
141. Hardyment, p. 25.

142. Mark Girouard, *The Victorian Country House* (1979), p. 27.
143. Earl and Countess of Aberdeen, *We Twa: Reminiscences of Lord and Lady Aberdeen*, vol. 2 (1929), pp. 1–10 (afterwards Aberdeen).
144. Aberdeen, p. 2.
145. Aberdeen, p. 2.
146. Aberdeen, p. 5.
147. Aberdeen, p. 7.
148. Aberdeen, p. 10.
149. H.G. Wells, *Tono-Bungay* (1964), pp. 12–13.

Chapter 7: In Retreat from a Golden Age

1. Pamela Horn, *Life Below Stairs in the Twentieth Century* (2003), p. 12.
2. Horn, *Rise and Fall*, p. 171; Gerard, *Country House Life*, pp. 282–3.
3. Horn, *Rise and Fall*, p. 185.
4. Horn, *Life Below Stairs*, p. 11.
5. Horn, *Life Below Stairs*, p. 10.
6. Frederick Gorst, *Carriages and Kings* (1956), pp. 126–7 (afterwards Gorst).
7. Gorst, p. 136.
8. Gorst, p. 137.
9. Gorst, p. 136.
10. Gorst, pp. 128–9.
11. Gorst, p. 149.
12. Gorst, p. 151.
13. Gorst, pp. 132–3.
14. Gorst, p. 133.
15. Gorst, p. 133.
16. Gorst, p. 133.
17. Gorst, pp. 132–3.
18. Gorst, p. 134.
19. Gorst, p. 134.
20. Gorst, p. 141.
21. Gorst, pp. 159–60.
22. Gorst, p. 13.
23. Gorst, p. 130.
24. Story told by the Dowager Duchess of Devonshire in an interview with the author, 9 January 2009.

25. Rosina Harrison (ed.), *Gentlemen's Gentlemen* (1978), pp. 26–7.
26. Catherine Bailey, *Black Diamonds* (2007), pp. 6–7.
27. Michael Hall, *Waddesdon Manor: The Heritage of a Rothschild House* (2002), pp. 204–10 (afterwards Hall).
28. Hall, pp. 194–210.
29. Hall, pp. 224–5.
30. Hall, pp. 230–1.
31. Interview with Mr Gautier, conducted by the National Trust in June 1992, typescript in the Waddesdon Collection.
32. Letter in the Waddeson Collection, dated 20 November 1917.
33. Notes from his grandson, John Macleod.
34. Notes from John Macleod.
35. Horn, *Life Below Stairs*, pp. 117–18.
36. Tom Turner, *Memoirs of a Gamekeeper* (1954), pp. 17–32 and 51–61.
37. Jonathan Ruffer, *The Big Shots* (1978), p. 57.
38. Merlin Waterson (ed.), *The Country House Remembered: Recollections of Life Between the Wars* (1985), p. 88.
39. Merlin Waterson (ed.), *The Country House Remembered*, p. 88.
40. Herman Muthesius, *The English House* (1904–5), edited and translated by Dennis Sharp, republished by Frances Lincoln in 2007, vol. II, pp. 61–2 (afterwards Muthesius).
41. Muthesius, II, p. 62.
42. Muthesius, II, p. 63.
43. Muthesius, II, p. 74.
44. Muthesius, II, p. 73.
45. Clive Aslet, *The Last Country Houses* (1982), p. 99 (afterwards Aslet).
46. Seen on a visit to Waddesdon Manor.
47. National Trust guidebook, *Castle Drogo* (1995), pp. 20–3.
48. Hardyment, p. 44.
49. Aslet, pp. 105–6.
50. Lady Diana Cooper, *The Rainbow Comes and Goes*, first published 1954 (1982), pp. 34–5.
51. Cooper, *The Rainbow Comes and Goes*, p. 35.
52. Harrison (ed.), *Gentlemen's Gentlemen*, p. 33.
53. Devonshire, *The House*, p. 58.
54. Fingall, pp. 115–16.
55. Horn, *Life Below Stairs*, p. 23.
56. Horn, *Life Below Stairs*, p. 23.

57. Horn, *Life Below Stairs*, pp. 23–4.
58. Letter from John Whittley, kept at Sudeley Castle; my thanks to Lydia Lebus and Jean Bray, the archivist at Sudeley.
59. Horn, *Life Below Stairs*, p. 25.
60. From the diary of James Stevenson of Braidwood, Lanarkshire, 6 November 1915, with thanks to Hew Stevenson for identifying these passages, and James Stevenson-Hamilton for permission to use them.
61. 2 June 1917, from the diary of Colonel James Stevenson.
62. 6 March 1924, from the diary of Colonel James Stevenson.
63. Aslet, p. 99.
64. Horn, *Life Below Stairs*, p. 36.
65. Lanceley, p. 155.
66. Lanceley, pp. 155–6.
67. Lanceley, pp. 157–9.
68. Horne, p. 9.
69. Horne, p. 13.
70. Horne, p. 109.
71. Horne, p. 263.
72. Horn, *Life Below Stairs*, p. 25.
73. Horn, *Life Below Stairs*, p. 25.
74. Horn, *Life Below Stairs*, p. 42.
75. Horn, *Life Below Stairs*, p. 36.
76. Frank Dawes, *Not in Front of the Servants* (1973), p. 147.
77. Gorden Grimmett in Harrison (ed.), *Gentlemen's Gentlemen*, p. 26.
78. Harrison (ed.), *Gentlemen's Gentlemen*, pp. 33–5.
79. Harrison (ed.), *Gentlemen's Gentlemen*, pp. 17–18.
80. Charles Smith, *Fifty years with Mounbatten* (1980), pp. 17–19.
81. Charles Smith, p. 18.
82. Charles Smith, p. 19.
83. Devonshire, *The House*, pp. 55–7.
84. Devonshire, *The House*, pp. 55–7.
85. Rosina Harrison, *Rose: My Life in Service* (1975), pp. 110–11.
86. Harrison, *My Life*, pp. 128–9.
87. Mrs Davidson, typescript of 1971 interview with James Dugdale, now Lord Crathorne; quoted with kind permission.
88. Mrs Davidson (1971).
89. Mrs Davidson (1971).

90. Waterson (ed.), *The Country House Remembered*, p. 195.
91. Memoirs of Mrs Jean Hibbert (afterwards Hibbert), typescript courtesy of the Trustees of the Goodwood Collection, p. 67.
92. Hibbert, p. 68.
93. Hibbert, p. 69.
94. Hibbert, p. 69.
95. Hibbert, p. 71.
96. Hibbert, p. 71.
97. Hibbert, pp. 71–2.
98. Hibbert, p. 81.
99. John Burnett, *Useful Toil* (1975), pp. 220–1 (afterwards Burnett).
100. Burnett, p. 223.
101. Burnett, p. 224.
102. Burnett, p. 224.
103. Burnett, pp. 225–6.
104. Burnett, pp. 225–6.
105. Burnett, pp. 238–41.
106. Harrison, *My Life*, pp. 32–4.
107. Harrison, *My Life*, p. 53.
108. Harrison, *My Life*, p. 84.
109. Harrison, *My Life*, p. 84.
110. Harrison, *My Life*, p. 87.
111. Philip Ziegler, *Osbert Sitwell* (1998), p. 12.
112. Osbert Sitwell, *Cruel Month* (1977), p. 92 (afterwards Sitwell).
113. Sitwell, p. 92.
114. Robert McCrum, *Wodehouse: A Life* (2004), p. 22.
115. P.G. Wodehouse, *Money in the Bank* (1942).
116. Lavinia Smiley, *A Nice Clean Plate* (1981), pp. 6–12 and 32, and 70–72.
117. Smiley, p. 12.
118. Waterson (ed.), *Country House Remembered*, p. 205.
119. Sir John Leslie, Bt, interview with the author, May 2008, and Mark Bence-Jones, *Life in the Irish Country House* (1996), pp. 69–71.
120. The Hon. Mrs Mary Birkbeck, interview with the author, December 2008, and letter to the author, January 2009.
121. Sir Peregrine Worsthorne, *Tricks of Memory* (1993), p. 41.
122. Worsthorne, p. 35.

Chapter 8: Staying On: A Changing World

1. John Cornforth, *Country Houses of England, 1948–1998* (1998), pp. 31–2.
2. Caroline Seebohm, *The Country House: A Wartime History 1939–45* (1989), p. 39 (afterwards Seebohm).
3. Observation by Julian Fellowes in an interview with the author, 30 January 2009.
4. From 'Notes on the Life of Harvey Lane' transcript by David Stacey of Leigh Manor, Shropshire.
5. From 'Notes on the Life of Harvey Lane'.
6. Christopher Simon Sykes, *The Big House* (2005), pp. 346–56.
7. *Stately Service: Then and Now* (2007), pp. 11–15, and 'Notes on the Life of Harvey Lane'.
8. *Stately Service: Then and Now* (2007), pp. 11–15.
9. Seebohm, p. 39.
10. John Martin Robinson, *The Country House at War* (1989).
11. Margaret Powell, *Below Stairs* (1984), p. 153.
12. Ernest Gowers, *Houses of Outstanding Historic or Architectural Interest* (1950), section ii, paragraph 10.
13. Gowers, *Houses of Outstanding Historic Interest* (1950), section ii, paragraph 12.
14. Interview with Mrs Davidson in 1971, typescript, by kind permission of Lord Crathorne.
15. Interview with Mrs Davidson (1971).
16. Harrison, *My Life*, pp. 178–9.
17. Harrison, *My Life*, p. 203.
18. Harrison, *My Life*, p. 203.
19. Lesley Lewis, *Private Life of a Country House* (1982), p. 134.
20. Horn, *Life Below Stairs*, p. 235.
21. Information from Lady Mairi Bury of Mount Stewart, interview with the author, 5 September 2005.
22. Sir John Leslie, interview with the author, May 2008.
23. Barbara Cartland, *Etiquette Handbook* (2008), first published 1962, pp. 61–3 (afterwards Cartland).
24. Cartland, p. 147.
25. Cartland, p. 63.
26. Cartland, p. 63.
27. Cartland, p. 64.

28. Information on the West Indies from John Hardy, recalling his father's staff in the 1950s at Radbrooke Hall, Cheshire.
29. Devonshire, *The House*, pp. 74–5 and 87.
30. Information about staff from St Helena from Martin Gee of Weston Park and Martin Drury; Horn, *Life Below Stairs*, pp. 263–73; and information about Mrs Mion at Capesthorne Hall from an interview with Lydia Lebus.
31. Stanley Ager and Fiona St Aubyn, *The Butler's Guide* (1980), p. 9 (afterwards Ager). By kind permission of his daughter, Mrs Gill Joyce, and his co-author, Fiona St Aubyn.
32. Ager, p. 8.
33. Ager, p. 8.
34. Ager, p. 10.
35. Ager, p. 13.
36. Ager, p. 13.
37. Ager, p. 19.
38. Ager, p. 19.
39. Ager, p. 13.
40. Lord Crathorne, interview with author, 14 December 2008.
41. Lord Crathorne, interview.
42. Lord Crathorne, interview.
43. Lord Crathorne, interview.
44. Lord Crathorne, interview.
45. Gathorne-Hardy, pp. 30–70.
46. Obituary of Michael Kenneally, *Daily Telegraph*, 30 October 1999, by Christopher Simon Sykes, and Christopher Simon Sykes, interview with the author, 19 January 2009.
47. Christopher Simon Sykes, interview.
48. *Daily Telegraph* Obituary, 30 October 1999.
49. Christopher Simon Sykes, *The Big House: The Story of a Country House and its Family* (2005), p. 351; and interview.
50. Christopher Simon Sykes, interview.
51. Sykes, *The Big House*, p. 351, and interview.
52. Mrs Maureen Magee, interview with the author, 16 December 2008.
54. Maureen Magee, interview.
55. Maureen Magee, interview.
56. Maureen Magee, interview.

57. Examples given in VisitBritain's *Stately Service: Then and Now*, pp. 12–15.
58. Mrs Rosalinde Tebbut, interview with the author, 1 December 2008.
59. Rosalinde Tebbut, interview.
60. Rosalinde Tebbut, interview.
61. Mrs Della Robins, interview with the author, 17 December 2008.
62. Della Robins, interview.
63. Della Robins, interview.
64. Graham Luke, interview with the author, 17 July 2008.
65. Graham Luke, interview.
66. Graham Luke, interview.
67. Martin Gee, interview with the author, 11 November 2008.
68. The Earl of Leicester, interview with the author, 27 November 2008.
69. Earl of Leicester, interview.
70. Maurice Bray, interview with the author, 27 November 2008.
71. Maurice Bray, interview.
72. Ian Macnab, interview with the author, 27 November 2008.
73. Waterfield, p. 194.
74. For example at Dalmeny, discussed in the introduction.
75. Hugh Petter, of Robert Adam Architects, interview with the author, 14 January 2009.
76. Ptolemy Dean of Ptolemy Dean Architects Ltd, interview with the author, 12 January 2009.
77. John Aidan Byrne, 'Calling for Jeeves', *New York Post*, 3 June 2007; see nypost.com.
78. Kathryn Hughes. 'Downstairs Upstairs', *The Guardian*, 31 May 2007.
79. Stephanie Rough, of Greycoat Placements Agency, interview with the author, 11 December 2008
80. Stephanie Rough, interview.
81. Stephanie Rough, interview.
82. Laura Hurrel, of Greycoat Placements Agency, interview with the author, 11 December 2008.
83. *The National Trust Manual of Housekeeping: The Care of Collections in Houses Open to the Public* (2005), especially Madeline Abey-Koch, 'History of Housekeeping', pp. 21–31, and Helen Lloyd, of the National Trust, interview with the author, 30 January 2009.
84. Helen Lloyd, interview.
85. *National Trust Manual of Housekeeping*, pp. 21–31.

86. Cornforth, p. 291.
87. Devonshire, *The House*, pp. 76–77.
88. The Dowager Duchess of Devonshire, interview with the author, 9 January 2009.
89. Henry Coleman, interview with the author, 9 January 2009.
90. Alan Shimwell, interview with the author, 9 January 2009.
91. Jim Link, interview with the author, 9 January 2009.
92. Jim Link, interview.
93. Helen Marchant, interview with the author, 9 January 2009.
94. Devonshire, *The House*, pp. 52–54, and interviews.
95. Devonshire, *The House*, pp. 76–77, and interviews.
96. Julian Fellowes, interview with the author, 30 January 2009.

Bibliography and Sources

GENERAL

Burnett, John, *Useful Toil: Autobiographies of Working People from the 1820s to the 1920s* (Allen Lane), London, 1975

Burnett, John, *Destiny Obscure: Autobiographies of Childhood, Education and Family from the 1820s to the 1920s* (Penguin), London, 1982

Dutton, Ralph, *The English Country House* (Batsford), London, 1935

Gilbert, Christopher, *Back-Stairs Furniture from Country Houses, Temple Newsam* (Leeds City Council), Leeds, 1977

Girouard, Mark, *Life in the English Country House* (Yale University Press), New Haven and London, 1979

Glanville, Philippa and Young, Hilary, *Elegant Eating* (Victoria and Albert Museum Publications), London, 2002

Groom, Suzanne et al., *The Taste of the Fire* (Historic Royal Palaces), Hampton Court, 2007

Hardyment, Christina, *Behind the Scenes: Domestic Arrangements in Historic Houses* (National Trust), London, 1997

Hartcup, Adeline, *Below Stairs in the Great Country Houses* (Sidgwick & Jackson), London, 1980

Hayward, Edward, *Upstairs and Downstairs: Life in an English Country House* (Pitkin Guides), Andover, 1998

Hearn, Mona, *Below Stairs: Domestic Service Remembered in Dublin and Beyond 1880–1922* (Lilliput Press), Dublin, 1993

Hibbert, Christopher, *The English: A Social History 1066–1945* (Guild Publishing), Brighton, 1987

Hole, Christina, *English Home-Life 1500–1800* (B.T. Batsford), London, 1947

Larsen, Ruth (ed.), *Maids and Mistresses: Celebrating 300 years of Women and the Yorkshire Country House* (YCHIP), York, 2004

Matthew, Colin, and Harrison, Brian (eds), *Oxford Dictionary of National*

UP AND DOWN STAIRS

Biography (Oxford University Press), Oxford, 2004–9, and www.odnb.com

National Trust, *National Trust Handbook* (National Trust), Swindon, 2009

Richardson, Bonham C., *The Caribbean in the Wide World 1492–1992* (Cambridge University Press), Cambridge, 1992

Sambrook, Pamela, *The Country House Servant* (Alan Sutton Publishing), Stroud, 2002

Sambrook, Pamela, *A Country House at Work* (National Trust), London, 2003

Sambrook, Pamela, *Keeping Their Place: Domestic Service in the Country House* (Alan Sutton Publishing), Stroud, 2007

Sambrook, Pamela and Brears, Peter, *The Country House Kitchen 1650–1900* (Alan Sutton Publishing), Stroud, 1997

Stuart, Dorothy, *The English Abigail* (Macmillan), London, 1946

Tinniswood, Adrian, *The Polite Tourist: Four Centuries of Country House Visiting* (National Trust), London, 1998

Turner, E.S., *What the Butler Saw* (Michael Joseph), London, 1962

VisitBritain, *Stately Service: Then and Now* (Visitbritain Publishing in association with the Historic Houses Association), London, 2007

Waterfield, Giles et al. (eds), *Below Stairs: 400 years of Servants' Portraits* (National Portrait Gallery), London, 2004

Waterfield, Merlin, *The Servants' Hall: The Domestic History of a Country House* (National Trust), London, 2nd Edn, 1990

Weiner, Martin, *English Culture and the Decline of the Industrial Spirit 1850–1980* (Penguin), London, 1992

FROM THE MEDIEVAL TO THE TUDOR PERIOD

Ackroyd, Peter, *The Life of Thomas More* (Vintage), London, 1999

Airs, Malcolm, *The Tudor and Jacobean Country House: A Building History* (Alan Sutton), Stroud, 1995

Anon (I.M.)., *A Health to the Gentlemanly Profession of Serving-men 1598* (Shakespeare Association Facsimile), Oxford University Press, London, 1931

Backhouse, Janet, *The Luttrell Psalter* (British Library), London, 1989

Brears, Peter, *Cooking and Dining in Medieval England* (Prospect Books), Totnes, 2008

Brears, Peter (ed.), *The Boke of Keruynge* (Southover Press), Lewes, 2003

Cavendish, George, *The Life and Death of Cardinal Wolsey* (ed. R. Sylvester), (Oxford University Press), London, 1959

Davis, Norman, *The Paston Letters* (Oxford University Press), Oxford, 1983

Edelen, George (ed.), *The Description of England by William Harrison*, The Folger Shakespeare Library (Cornell University Press), Ithaca, New York, 1968

Fleming, Peter, *Family and Household in Medieval England* (Palgrave Macmillan), London, 2000

Fleming, Peter, 'Household Servants of the tourist and early Tudor gentry', in Williams, Daniel (ed.), *Early Tudor England: Proceedings of the Harlaxton Symposium*, Woodbridge, 1989, pp. 19–36

Friedman, Alice, *House and Household in Elizabethan England: Wollaton Hall and the Willoughby Family* (University of Chicago Press), Chicago, 1988

Goodall, John, *English Castle Architecture 1066–1650* (Yale University Press), New Haven and London, 2009

Harrison, Molly and Royston, O.M. (eds), *How They Lived*, Vol. II (Basil Blackwell), Oxford, 1963

Howard, Maurice, *The Early Tudor Country House: Architecture and Politics 1490–1550* (George Philip), London, 1987

Mertes, Kate, *The English Noble Household, 1250–1600* (Basil Blackwell), Oxford, 1998

Rickert, Edith and Naylor, L.J. (trans.), *Babee's Book: Medieval Manners for the Young: Done into Modern English from Dr. Furnivall's Texts* (Chatto and Windus), London, 1908

Sim, Alison, *Masters and Servants in Tudor England* (Sutton Publishing), Stroud, 2006

Thornton-Burnett, Mark, *Masters and Servants in English Renaissance Drama and Culture* (Macmillan), London, 1997

Williams, C.H., (ed.), *English Historical Documents 1458–1558* (Eyre and Spottiswoode), London 1967.

Woolgar, C.M., *The Great Household in Medieval England* (Yale University Press), New Haven and London, 1999

THE SEVENTEENTH CENTURY

Aubrey, John, *Brief Lives* (Penguin), London, 1982

Batho, G.R. (ed.), *The Household Papers of Henry Percy Ninth Earl of Northumberland (1564–1632)*, Camden third series, vol. XCIII (Royal Historical Society), London, 1962

Broad, John, *Transforming English Rural Society: The Verneys and the Claydons 1600–1820* (Cambridge University Press), Cambridge, 2004

Browning, Andrew (ed.), *Memoirs of Sir John Reresby* (Royal Historical Society), London, 1991

Carlton, Charles, *Going to the Wars: The Experience of the English Civil Wars 1638–1651* (Routledge), London and New York, 1992

Cliffe, J.T., *The World of the Country House in Seventeenth-Century England* (Yale University Press), New Haven and London, 1999

Clifford, D.J.H. (ed.), *The Diaries of Lady Anne Clifford* (Sutton Publishing), London, 1990

Cooper, Nicholas, *Houses of the Gentry 1480–1680* (Yale University Press), New Haven and London, 1999

Defoe, Daniel, *Memoirs of a Cavalier* (Cambridge University Press), Cambridge, 1908

Evelyn, John, *The Diary of John Evelyn* (Oxford University Press), London, 1959

Fiennes, Celia, *The Illustrated Journeys of Celia Fiennes 1685–c1712*, edited by Christopher Morris (Macdonald & Co.), London and Sydney, 1982

Hainsworth, D.R., *Stewards, Lords and People: The Estate Steward and his World in Later Stuart England* (Cambridge University Press), Cambridge, 1992

Hamlyn, Matthew, *The Recipes of Hannah Woolley: English Cookery of the Seventeenth Century* (Heinemann), London, 1988

Herrup, Cynthia, *A House in Gross Disorder: Sex, Law and the 2nd Earl of Castlehaven* (Oxford University Press), Oxford, 1999

Jaine, Tom, 'Mary Evelyn's "Oeconomics to a Married Friend, 1677"' in *Petits Propos Culinaires*, Vol. 73, July 2003, as published on dialspace.dial.pipex.com

Kelsall, Malcolm, *Great Good Place: The Country House and English Literature* (Columbia University Press), New York, 1994

Morrill, John, *Revolt in the Provinces: The English People and the Tragedies of War 1634–1648*, revised edn (Longman), London and New York, 1999

Parsons, Daniel (ed.), *The Diary of Sir Henry Slingsby* (Longman), London, 1836

Platt, Colin, *The Great Rebuildings of Tudor and Stuart England: Revolutions in Architectural Taste* (Routledge), London, 1994

Potter, Jennifer, *Strange Blooms: The Curious Lives and Adventures of the John Tradescants* (Atlantic), London, 2006

Purkiss, Diane, *The English Civil War: A People's History* (Harper Perennial), London, 2007

Royle, Trevor, *Civil War: The Wars of the Three Kingdoms 1638–1660* (Abacus), London, 2004

Scott-Thomson, Gladys, *Life in a Noble Household 1641–1700* (Jonathan Cape), London, 1965

Sidebotham, Andrew, *Brampton Bryan: Church and Castle*, Brampton Bryan, 1990

Slater, Miriam, *Family Life in the Seventeenth Century: The Verneys of Claydon House* (Routledge & Kegan Paul), London, 1984

Steen, Sara-Jane (ed.), *The Letters of Lady Arbella Stuart* (Oxford University Press), Oxford, 1994

Steer, Francis (ed.), 'Easton Lodge Inventory, 1637', in *Essex Review*, Colchester, Vol. LXI, January 1952

Taylor-Lewis, Thomas (ed.), *Letters of the Lady Brilliana Harley* (Camden Society), London, 1854

Tomalin, Claire, *Samuel Pepys: The Unequalled Self* (Penguin), London, 2002

Verney, Sir Harry, *The Verneys of Claydon: A Seventeenth-Century English Family* (Robert Maxwell), London, 1968

Wall, Wendy, *Staging Domesticity: Household Work and Identity in Early Modern Drama* (Cambridge University Press), Cambridge, 1992

Whyman, Susan, *Sociability and Power in Late-Stuart England: The Cultural Worlds of the Verneys 1660–1720* (Oxford University Press), Oxford, 1999

Woolley, Hannah, *The Gentlewomans Companion* (Maxwell), London, 1675

Worsley, Lucy, *Cavalier: A Tale of Chivalry, Passion and Great Houses* (Faber), London, 2007

THE EIGHTEENTH CENTURY

Baird, Rosemary, *Goodwood: Art and Architecture, Sport and Family* (Frances Lincoln), London, 2007

Briggs, Asa (ed.), 'How They Lived', Vol. III (Basil Blackwell), Oxford, 1969

Christie, Christopher, *The British Country House in the Eighteenth Century* (Manchester University Press), Manchester, 2000

Clutton, George (Sir), 'The Gardeners of the Eighth Lord Petre', *Essex Naturalist*, Vol.32 (1967–71), pp. 201–210.

Collins-Baker, C.H., *Life and Circumstances of James Brydges, First Duke of Chandos* (Clarendon Press), Oxford, 1949

Dolan, Brian, *Ladies of the Grand Tour* (Flamingo), London, 2002

Glasse, Hannah, *The Servants Directory, Improved, or, House-Keepers Companion* (J. Potts), Dublin, 2nd edn, 1762

Gordon, Lyndall, *Vindication: A Life of Mary Wollstonecraft* (Virago), London, 2006

Hanway, Jonas, *Eight Letters to His Grace the Duke of — on the custom of Vails-Giving in England*, London, 1760

Hecht, Jean, *The Domestic Servant Class in Eighteenth Century England* (Routledge & Kegan Paul), London, 1956

Hill, Bridget, *English Domestic Servants in the 18th Century* (Oxford University Press), Oxford, 1996

Horn, Pamela, *Flunkeys and Scullions: Life Below Stairs in Georgian England* (Sutton Publishing), Stroud, 2004

King, Reyahr (et al), *Ignatius Sancho: An African Man of Letters* (National Portrait Gallery), London, 1997

Lehmann, Gilly, *The British Housewife: Cookery Books, Cooking and Society in Eighteenth-Century Britain* (Prospect Books), Totnes, 2003

Little, Kenneth, *Negroes in Britain: A Study of Racial Relations in English Society* (Routledge & Kegan Paul), London, 1947

Macarthey, Patricia, 'Vails and Travails: how Lord Kildare kept his household in order', in *Irish Architectural and Decorative Studies*, Vol. IV (2003), pp. 120–39.

Macdonald, John, *Memoirs of an Eighteenth-Century Footman* (Century Publishing), London, 1985

Mitchell, L.G. (ed.), *The Purefoy Letters* (Sidgwick & Jackson), London, 1973

Mortlock, D.P., *Aristocratic Splendour: Money and the World of Thomas Coke Earl of Leicester* (The History Press), Stroud, 2007

Murdoch, Tessa (ed.), *Noble Households: Eighteeenth-Century Inventories of Great English Houses* (John Adamson), Cambridge, 2006

Schmidt, Leo (ed.), *Holkham* (Prestel), London, 2006

Stone, Lawrence, *The Family, Sex and Marriage 1500–1800* (Harper & Row), London and New York, 1977

Stone, Lawrence, *The Road to Divorce: England 1530–1987* (Oxford University Press), Oxford, 1992

Swift, Jonathan, *Directions to Servants*, 1745, as published in Hesperus Classics series (Hesperus Press), London, 2003

Tillyard, Stella, *Aristocrats: Caroline, Emily, Louisa and Sarah Lennox 1740–1832* (Chatto & Windus), London, 1994

Ware, Isaac, *A Complete Body of Architecture*, London, 1768 (reprint by Gregg Publishing, New York, 1971)

Wilson, Richard and Mackley, Alan, *Creating Paradise: The Building of the English Country House 1660–1880* (Hambledon and London), London and New York, 2000

THE NINETEENTH CENTURY

Aberdeen, Earl and Countess of, *'We Twa': Reminiscences of Lord and Lady Aberdeen* (Collins), 12 Vols, London, 1929

Adams, Samuel and Sarah, *The Complete Servant* (Knight and Lacey), London, 1825; there is a modern reprint (Southern Press), Lewes, 1989, edited by Ann Haly and with an introduction by Pamela Horn

Ashby, M.K., *Joseph Ashby of Tysoe 1859–1919: A Study of Village Life* (1961)

Atkinson, Diane, *Love and Dirt: The Mariage of Arthur Munby and Hannah Cullwick* (Macmillan), London, 2003

Bateman, John, *The Great Landowners of Great Britain and Ireland* (Harrison), London, 1883; there is a 1971 reprint by Leicester University Press

Beeton, Isabella, *The Book of Household Management* (S.O. Beeton), London, 1861 and reprinted in facsimile by Chancellor Press, London, 1985

Berkeley, the Hon. Grantley, *My Life and Recollections* (Hurst & Blackett), London, 1865

Bence-Jones, Mark, *Life in the Irish Country House* (Constable), London, 1996

Brandon, Ruth, *Other People's Daughters: The Life and Times of the Governess* (Weidenfeld & Nicolson), London, 2008

Butler, E.M. (ed.), *A Regency Visitor: The English Tour of Prince Pückler-Muskau Described in his Letters 1826–1828* (Collins), London, 1957

Colquhon, Kate, *A Thing in Disguise: The Visionary Life of Joseph Paxton* (Fourth Estate), London, 2004

Cresswell, William, *Diary of a Victorian Gardener* (English Heritage), Swindon, 2006

Devonshire, Duke of, *Handbook to Chatsworth and Hardwick* (privately printed), 1845

Drury, Elizabeth, *Victorian Household Hints* (Marks & Spencer), London, 1981

Franklin, Jill, *The Gentleman's Country House and its Plan 1835–1914* (Kegan & Paul), London, 1981

Gathorne-Hardy, Jonathan, *The Rise and Fall of the British Nanny* (Hodder & Stoughton), London, 1972

Gerard, Jessica, *Country House Life: Family and Servants 1815–1914* (Blackwell), Oxford, 1994

Girouard, Mark, *The Victorian Country House* (Yale University Press), London and New York, 1979

Goodwin, Francis, *Rural Architecture* (John Weale), London, 1835

Hann, Andrew, 'The Service Wing at Audley End House' (English Heritage: Properties Historians' Report), 2007

Hare, Augustus, *Life and Letter of Maria Edgworth* (Edward Arnold), London, 1894

Horn, Pamela, *The Rise and Fall of the Victorian Servant* (Sutton Publishing), Stroud, 1995

Horne, Eric, *What the Butler Winked at* (T. Werner Laurie Ltd), London, 1923

Huggett, Frank, *Life Below Stairs: Domestic Servants in England from Victorian Times* (John Murray), London, 1977

Hughes, Kathryn, *The Victorian Governess* (Hambledon Press), London, 1993

Kerr, Robert, *The Gentleman's House*, 1864 (reprinted in facsimile Johnson Reprint Corporation, New York, 1972)

Lanceley, William, *From Hall-Boy to House-Steward* (Edward Arnold), London, 1925

Osborne, Lady, *Memorials of Lady Osborne*, 1870, 2 vols (Hodges, Foster & Co.), Dublin, 1870

Renton, Alice, *Tyrant or Victim? A History of the British Governess* (Weidenfeld & Nicolson), London, 1991

Smith, Elizabeth, *Memoirs of a Highland Lady*, edited by Lady Strachey (John Murray), 2nd Edn, London, 1911

Stanley, Liz, *The Diaries of Hannah Cullwick, Victorian Maidservant* (Ruttgers University Press), Piscataway, NJ, 1984

Sykes, Christophes Simon, *Country House Camera* (Book Club Associates/ Weidenfeld and Nicolson), London, 1980

Thompson, F.M.L., *English Landed Society in the Nineteenth Century* (Routledge & Kegan Paul), London, 1963

Washington, B.T., *Up From Slavery: An Autobiography* (Doubleday), New York, 1901

Wells, H.G., *Tono-Bungay*, first published 1909, republished 1964 (Pan Books), London, 1964

Wells, H.G., *Experiments in Autobiography* (Victor Gollancz), London, 1934

THE EARLY TWENTIETH CENTURY

Anon., *How to be Happy Though Married* (T. Fisher Unwin), London, c.1900

Aslet, Clive, *The Last Country Houses* (Yale University Press), London and New Haven, 1982

Bailey, Catharine, *Black Diamonds* (Penguin), London, 2008

Cooper, Lady Diana, *The Rainbow Comes and Goes*, 1958 (republished Century, London, 1984)

Dawes, Frank, *Not in Front of the Servants: Domestic Service 1850–1939* (Wayland), London, 1973

Egremont, Lord, *Wyndham and Children First* (Macmillan), London, 1968

Fingall, Countess of, *Seventy Years Young, as Told to Pamela Hinkson* (Collins), London, 1937

Gorst, Frederick, *Carriages and Kings* (W.H. Allen), London, 1956

Hall, Michael, *Waddesdon Manor: The Heritage of a Rothschild House* (Harry N. Abrams), New York, 2002

Harrison, Rosina (ed.), *Gentlemen's Gentlemen* (Sphere Books), London, 1978

Harrison, Rosina, Rose: *My Life in Service* (Cassell), London, 1975

Laurie, Kedrun (ed.), *Cricketer Preferred: Estate Workers at Lyme Park 1898–1946* (Lyme Park Joint Committee), Lyme, 1979

Lees-Milne, James, *Ancestral Voices* (Chatto & Windus), London, 1975

Lewis, Lesley, *The Private Life of a Country House 1912–39* (David & Charles), Newton Abbot, 1980

McCrum, Robert, *Wodehouse: A Life* (Viking Penguin), London, 2004

Powell, Margaret, *Below Stairs* (Peter Davies), London, 1968

Robinson, John Martin, *The Country House at War* (Bodley Head), London, 1989

Ruffer, Jonathan, *The Big Shots: Edwardian Shooting Parties* (Quiller Press), London, 1977

Sackville-West, Vita, *The Edwardians*, 1930 (republished Virago), London, 1983

Seebohm, Caroline, *The Country House: A Wartime History 1939–45* (Weidenfeld & Nicolson), London, 1989

Sitwell, Osbert, *Left Hand! Right Hand!* (Macmillan), 3 vols, London, 1948

Smiley, Lavinia, *A Nice Clean Plate: Recollections 1919–1931* (Michael Russell), Wilby, 1981

Smith, Charles, *Fifty Years with Mountbatten: A Personal Memoir by his Valet and Butler* (Sidgwick & Jackson), London, 1980

Turner, Tom, *Memoirs of a Gamekeeper* (Bles), London, 1954

Waterson, Merlin (ed.), *The Country House Remembered: Recollections of Life Between the Wars* (Routledge & Kegan Paul), London, 1985

Wodehouse, P.G., *Money in the Bank* (Doubleday Doran), New York, 1942

Worsthorne, Peregrine, *Tricks of Memory: An Autobiography* (Weidenfeld & Nicolson), London, 1993

Ziegler, Philip, *Osbert Sitwell* (Random House), London, 1999

THE LATE TWENTIETH CENTURY

Ager, Stanley and St Aubyn, Fiona, *The Butler's Guide to Clothes Care, Managing the Table, Running the Home and Other Graces* (Simon & Schuster), London and New York, 1980

Beard, Madeliene, *English Landed Society in the Twentieth Century* (Routledge), London, 1989

Cartland, Barbara, *Etiquette Handbook: A Guide to Good Behaviour from the Boudoir to the Boardroom*, 1962 (reprinted Random House, London, 2008)

Cornforth, John, *The Country Houses of England, 1948–1998* (Constable), London, 1998

Devonshire, the Duchess of, *The House: A Portrait of Chatsworth* (Macmillan/ Book Club Associates), London, 1982

Devonshire, the Duchess of, *Counting My Chickens and Other Home Thoughts* (Long Barn), Ebrington, 2001

Horn, Pamela, *Life Below Stairs in the Twentieth Century* (Sutton Publishing), Stroud, 2003

Inch, Arthur and Hirst, Arlene, *Dinner is Served: An English Butler's Guide to the Art of the Table* (Running Press), London, 2003

McCrum, Robert, *Wodehouse: A Life* (Penguin), London, 2004

Martin, Brian P., *Tales of Old Gamekeepers* (David & Charles), Newton Abbot, 1989

Musgrave, Toby, *The Head Gardeners* (Aurum Press), London, 2007

National Trust, *The National Trust Manual of Housekeeping: The Care of Collections in Historic Houses Open to the Public* (Butterworth and Heinemann), London, 2005

Nichols, Beverley, *Down the Kitchen Sink* (W.H. Allen), London, 1974

Powell, Margaret, *Below Stairs* (Pan Books), London, 1970

Powers, Alan, *The Twentieth Century House in Britain* (Aurum Press), London, 2004

Robinson, John Martin, *The Latest Country Houses* (Bodley Head), London, 1983

Sebald, W.G., *The Rings of Saturn* (Vintage), London, 2002

Sykes, Christopher Simon, *The Big House: The Story of a Country House and its Family* (Harper Perennial), London, 2005

Tyack, Geoffrey, *Cliveden and the Astor Household Between the Wars*, pamphlet, 1982

Worsthorne, Peregrine, *Tricks of Memory* (Weidenfeld and Nicolson), London, 1993

Illustration Acknowledgements

Index

Crathorne, Lord, 251, 252, 270, 276–7
Crathorne Hall (Yorkshire), 251, 252, 269, 276
Crawford, Earl of, 95–6
Creevey, Thomas, 148, 162
Crewe, Lord, 163
Cromwell, Oliver, 79
Croome Court (Worcestershire), 274
Cross, Thomas, 64–5
Crystal Palace, 176
Culloden, Battle of (1746), 93
Cullwick, Ellen, 189
Cullwick, Hannah, 185–9
Curzon (nurse), 75
Curzon, Lord, 154–5
Curzon, Sir Nathaniel, 113

Dalmeny House (Edinburgh), 13, 208
Damant, Samuel, 152
Daniel, Samuel, 63
Danvers, Sir John, 84
David, Monsieur (chef), 228
Davidson, Mrs (cook), 251–2, 269–70, 276
Davidson, Albert, 252
Davis (nanny), 258
Dean, Ptolemy, 291–2
death duties see taxation and economics
Defoe, Daniel: Moll Flanders, 9; Memoir of a Cavalier, 71–2; The Compleat English Gentleman, 110
Delaney, Mrs (gentlewoman), 106
Denton, Dr, 74
Derby, Earl of, 18, 43, 248
Devereux, Miss (lady's maid), 163
Devonshire, Dukes of, 3, 176–7, 208, 249, 295–6; Handbook of Chatsworth and Hardwick, 151, 172, 208–9

Devonshire, Georgiana, Duchess of, 110, 208
Dick, Wentworth Hume, 211–12
Dickens, Charles: Bleak House, 203
Diehans (servant), 126
Digby, Sir Kenelm, 55
Dissolution of the Monasteries (1535), 36
Ditton Park (Buckinghamshire), 66
domestic service: numbers employed, 6–7, 17–18, 98, 116, 224, 246; see also individually named houses
Dorman Newman (publishers), 56
Dormer, Lord, 55
Dorothy (housekeeper), 279
Douglas-Home, Alec, 276
Doune Castle (Scotland), 184
Drewe, Julius, 240
Drumlanrig Castle (Scotland), 172, 257, 281
du Maurier, Daphne: Rebecca, 10
Dundonald, Jane, Countess of, 118
Durham Castle, 20
Dutton, William, 66

Earle, Sir Richard, 67
East Barsham Manor (Norfolk), 208
East India Company, 123
Easter Rising (1916), 192
Easton Lodge (Essex), 54
Eaton Hall (Cheshire), 6, 177, 237
Eddow, John, 66
Edensor (Chatsworth estate village), 296
Edgehill, Battle of (1642), 71
education, 26, 36, 40–1, 57, 80–1, 92, 119, 156–7, 181, 189, 194, 220–1, 224; see also training of servants
Edward II, King: 1318 Ordinance, 17
Edward III, King, 39, 46